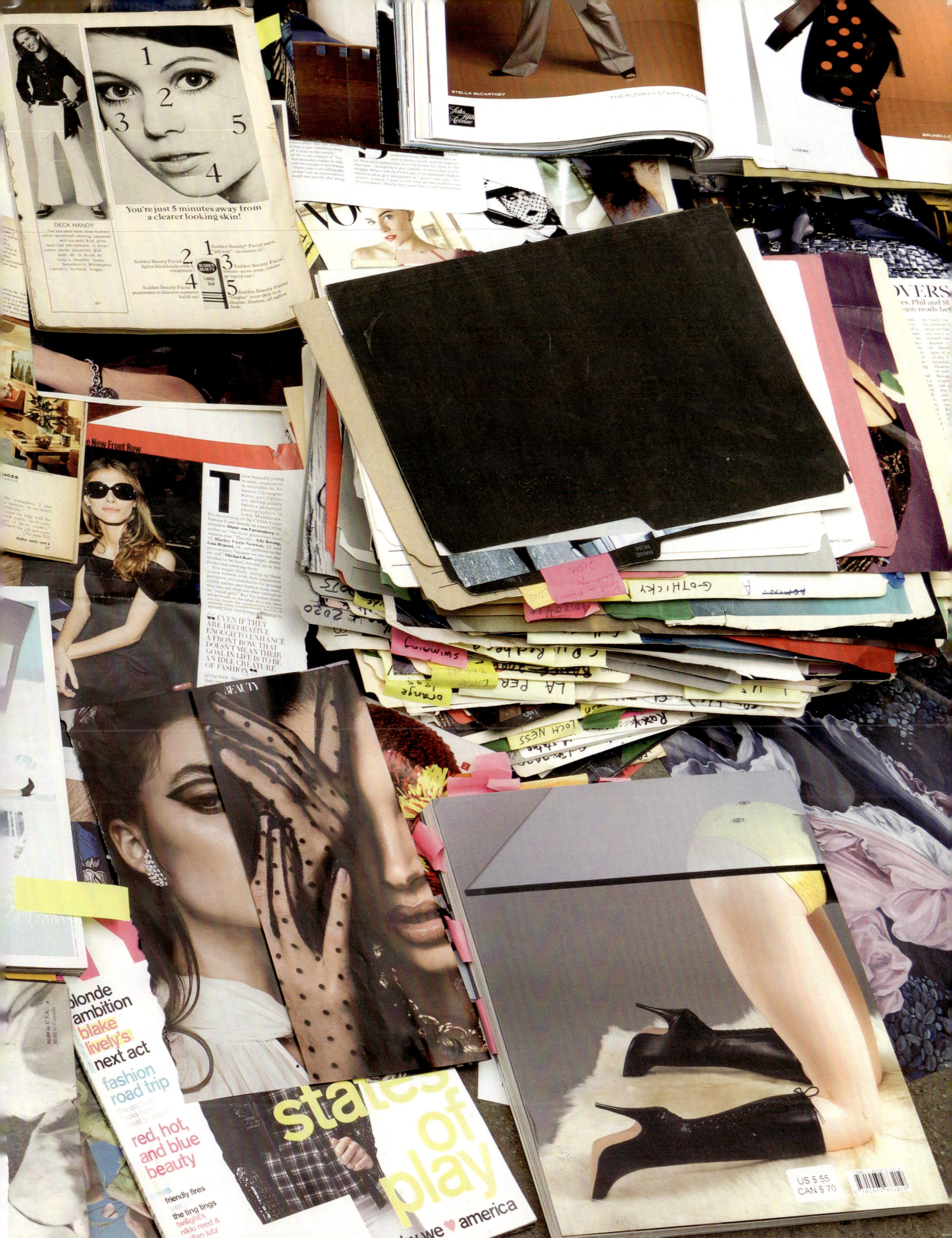
1
2
3
4
5
You're just 5 minutes away from a clearer looking skin!
DECK HANDY
STELLA McCARTNEY
EVEN IF THEY ARE DECORATIVE ENOUGH TO ENHANCE A FRONT ROW, THAT DOESN'T MEAN THEIR GOAL IN LIFE IS TO BE AN IDLE CREATURE OF FASHION
BEAUTY
GOTHICKY
LOCH NESS
blonde ambition
blake lively's next act
fashion road trip
red, hot, and blue beauty
friendly fires
the ting tings
states of play
we ♥ america
US $ 55
CAN $ 70

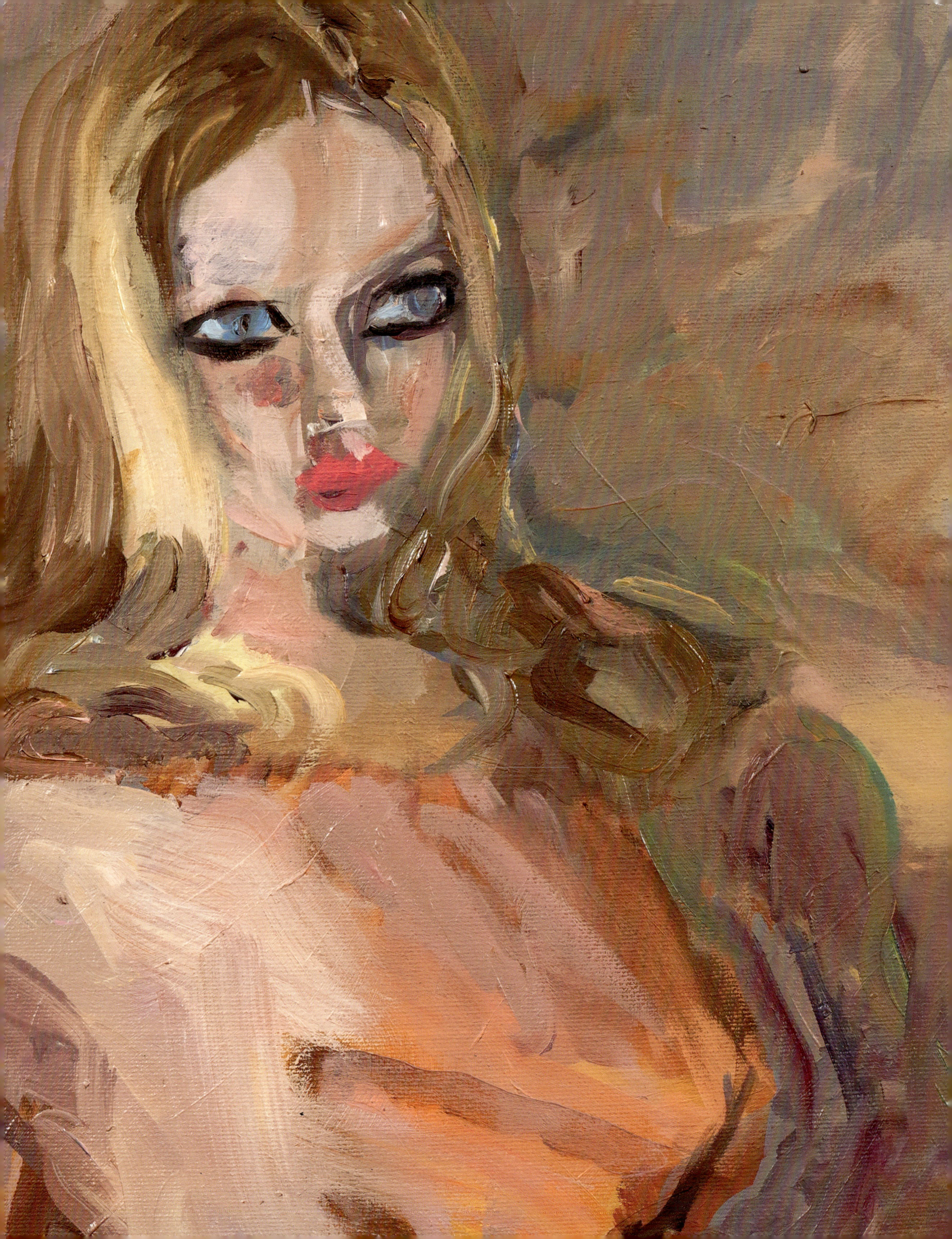

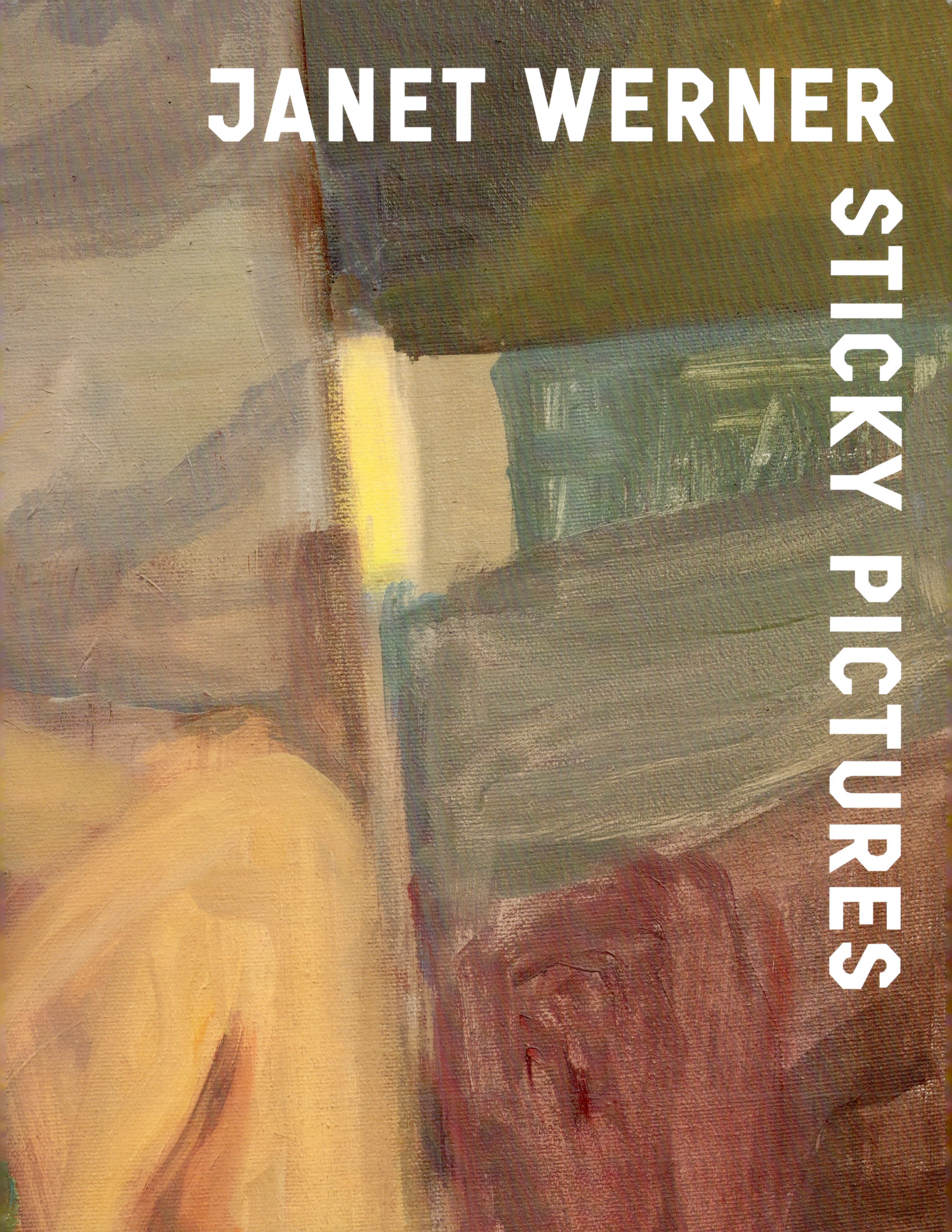
JANET WERNER
STICKY PICTURES

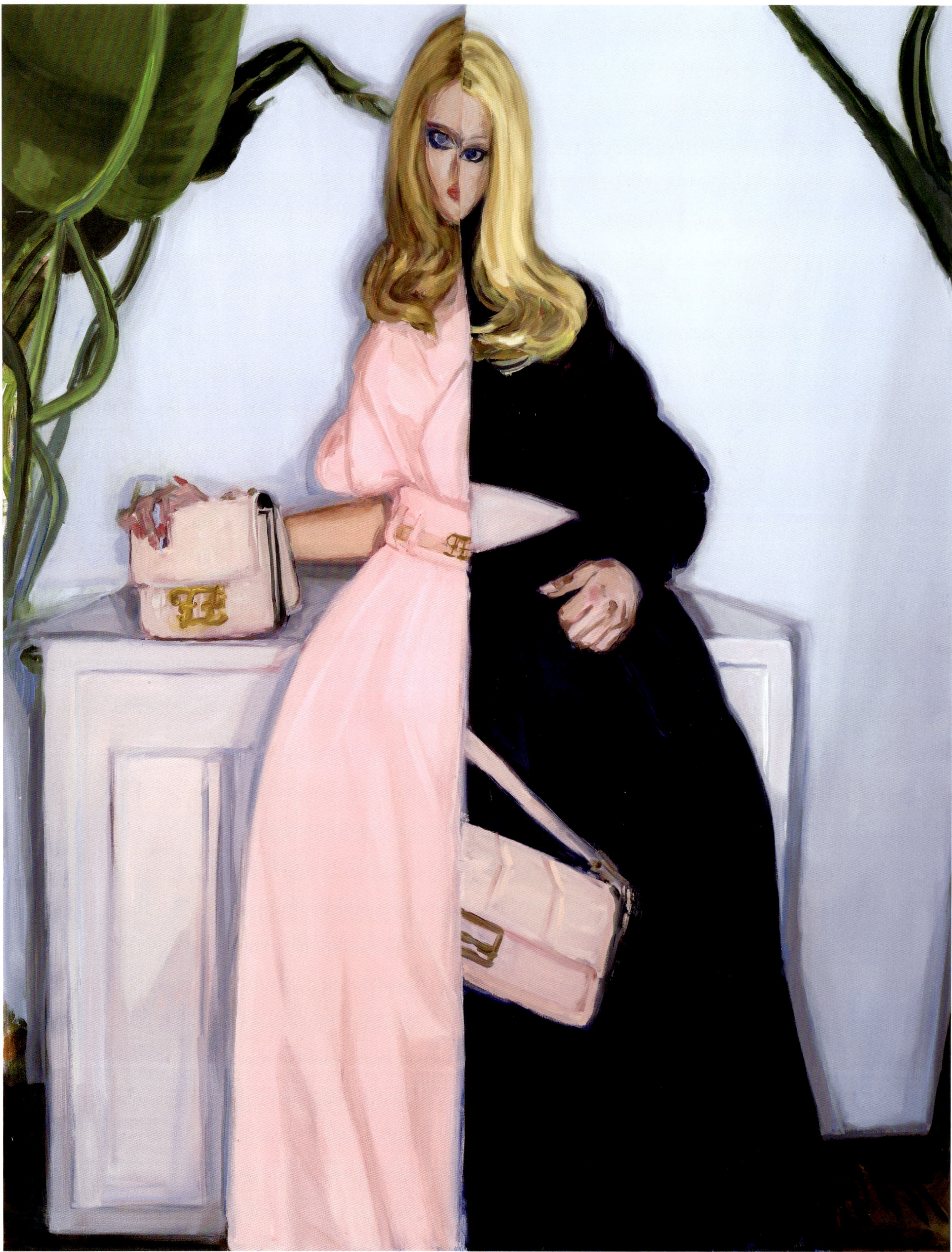

Introduction: Janet Werner's Working Girls

LISA BALDISSERA

When a Young-Girl giggles, she's working.[1]

Since the beginning, the act of "staring" has guided the work of Montreal-based painter Janet Werner. It is a mesmerization that goes both ways: Figures stare out while we, her audience, stare in, equally transfixed. The spell of Werner's complex paintings is to be found not only within the seduction that painting alone offers, but in the artist's embrace of art history itself. Werner's "sticky pictures" stick because they index not only the picture-making machine of popular culture and fashion, but they remind us of their relation to the long lineage of painting—that is, the richness of the painted world within art history. Composition and space, light, architecture, gesture, chromatic temperature and order, and, finally, the history of figuration within painting itself are her enticements.

Janet Werner's paintings have captured the imagination in Canadian and international exhibitions for more than thirty years. Since her graduation from Yale University in 1987 and her first major shows in the early 1990s, she has developed a lexicon of images that interrogate the construction of pictures and, within them, the formulation of the figure. In her work, painting is a nexus for queries of the subject of artifice, the construction of gender, and the pure *jouissance* of sentience itself.

The publication *Sticky Pictures* includes paintings created over the past eight years organized in a series of four thematic chapters: "Sticky Pictures," "Gallery," "Misfits," and "There There." Within each series, figures, objects, and spaces elaborate and energize—with wicked intelligence, humor, and empathy—the neat tasks that late capitalism has framed as signifiers of the good life. Spaces are sometimes even emptied altogether, and instead light fills and animates them, illuminating subtle cues. Figures, when present, are cropped, folded, and restructured by the painter's analytical eye. Painting itself is revealed as a model of construction, sensation, thinking, pleasure, and seduction.

In Werner's pictures, "girls" of all ages—that is, of all chronological ages and of all time periods—linger mostly in "youth." As Werner states, "Even though we ourselves retain all of our ages, we are moving through time—yet we still have these identifications with our earlier selves."[2] The painter's use of architectural shape and decorative patterning found in textiles, stylish interiors, and objects reveals the ways in which bodies, objects, and sites are ultimately held—and constructed within—culture. Werner offers us instead an orientation: It is polar, a place for action rather than a site of emptiness.

The guilelessness of Werner's gaze approximates our own. When we are properly ensconced in Werner's will—our gaze being directed through and around her painted fields—she then goes one step further and removes the figure altogether. We are left to stare into empty rooms or through curtains at tables where traces of former occupants remain. Even within those empty spaces, we still sense a missing figure, as a trace or a scent—never entirely absent. It is as though someone has just left the room.

Neapolitan, 2020
76 × 60 in. / 193 × 152 cm

The French collective Tiqqun articulates a philosophical and conceptual framework for the self that it calls the "Young-Girl," a term that refers to a figure that is neither necessarily young nor female but instead exists as a site of both production and desire within contemporary capitalism. In Tiqqun's manifesto-like text *Preliminary Materials for a Theory of the Young-Girl*, originally published in France in 1999 by the journal *Tiqqun*, the "Young-Girl" is a figure that emerges as a concept—a set of conditions rather than a singular subjectivity. In their work, as in Werner's, the figure exists within a dialectic or in the structure of the *mise en abyme*. Influenced by Italian philosopher Giorgio Agamben and his concept of "bare life,"[3] Tiqqun created their "Young-Girl" as a project that does not refer to a specific author but is indicative of a *point of origin*.

This point of origin centers around the appearance of things—a performing subject within capitalism, located at its empty center. Further articulating this figure, Tiqqun suggests, "The Young-Girl requires not only that you protect her, she also wants the power to educate you. The eternal return of the same styles in fashion is enough to convince: The Young-Girl does not play with appearances. It is appearances that play with her."[4]

Yet while Tiqqun's Young-Girl is a figure that functions as an ironic or empty cipher, Werner objects: "I do not buy into this; I'm an old fashioned existentialist at heart—the negotiating and wrestling with these belief systems takes place through the paint, the process, the manipulation—all the actions that you do to the images . . . there is a performer or performance in there that opposes the idea of the empty centre."[5] Werner prefers action rather than merely its possibility. For Werner, the practice of painting is both an affirmation and a form of resistance.

From Werner's affirming point of origin, the figure of the Young-Girl emerges as a collage of conditions, "a polar figure, orienting, rather than dominating, outcomes."[6] In this way, there is an overall-ness to her gaze: It is not focused on one particular figure. Functioning beyond the psychological, Tiqqun's construction suggests that the primary experience of figuration in contemporary life is as human capital.[7] While in Tiqqun's text vulnerability may be understood as operational and strategic—a self-instrumentalizing form of resistance—in Werner's works, the figures appear even more vulnerable because of the painterly operations that the artist performs; from source to final work, Werner finds a persistent humanism. As she states, "No matter what I do to these figures, I feel there is a 'person.'"[8]

For Werner, the original figures, which are drawn from fashion magazines, popular culture, sculpture, and painting, are "like ciphers—that is the reason to use them: because they are not already invested with specific personalities."[9] Werner submits these found figures to a relentless reconfiguration: In effect, she performs a "program of actions," from cutting to reshaping to radically altering them by removing elements and features, reinventing them by destroying them. Could this be called a little violent? Not exactly. As in any relation, it's complicated: "I have to like them by the end; if I don't then I'm not finished."[10] Her final paintings are an aggregate of many source materials and points of reference. The "she" that Werner finds in these sources is the cherished object of consumer society—a "she" that is elevated while being without agency. According to Tiqqun, this is a figure that is never autonomous. These "girls" seduce while existing only in relation to the gaze; they represent libidinal freedom while being completely constrained by the conditions that produce them since "...seduction is the new opium of the masses. It is liberty for a world without liberty, joy for a world without joy."[11]

Yet Werner's project is an efficient and pleasurable reordering of this world order, and it is achieved through her painterly mastery—splicing, reassembling, and reorienting the hierarchies within these found images. Absurdist and formalist moments—from laugh out loud remixes to painterly licks that nod to 17th-century Dutch realism (just look at Werner's many light-filled homages to the color gray), her work provides a rigorous examination of image-making's operations

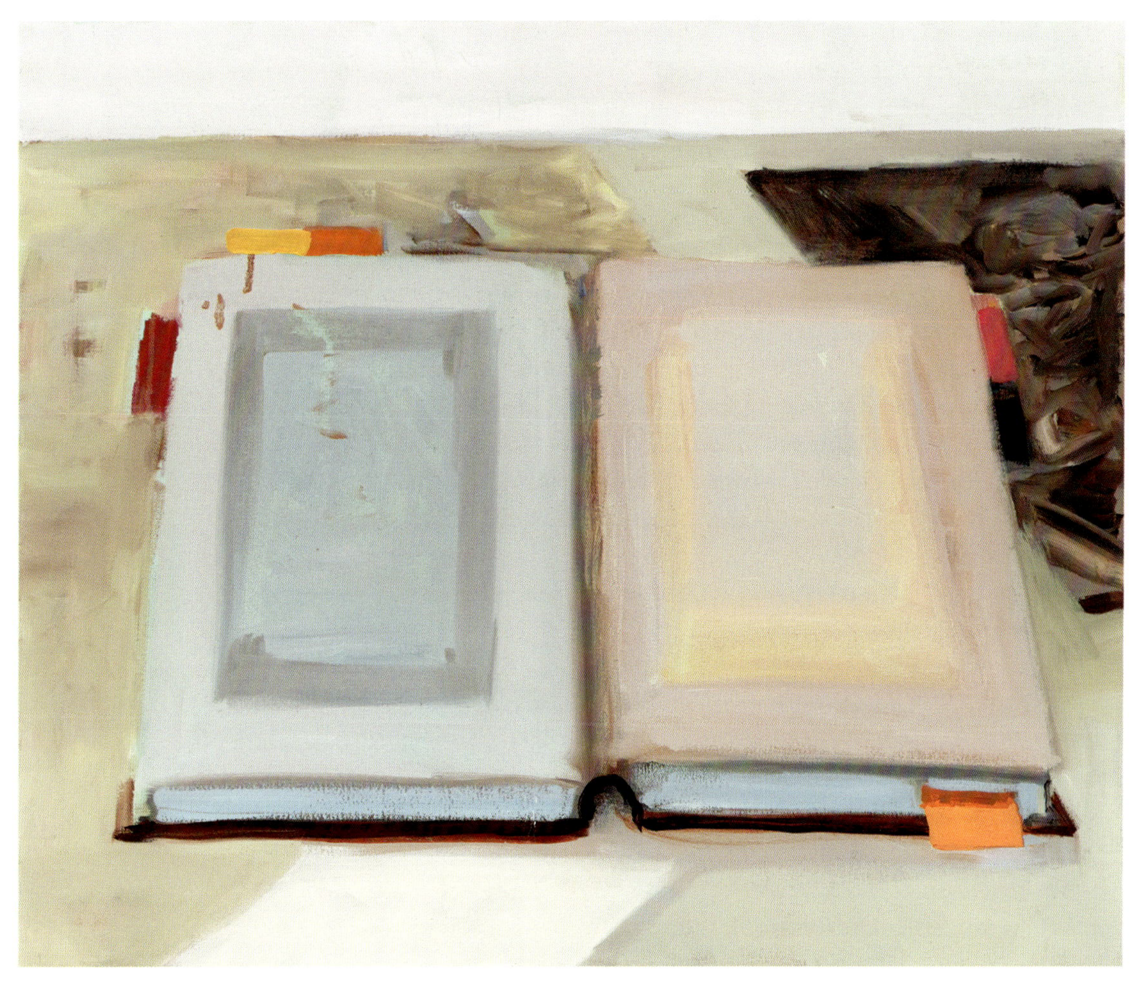

Book 2, 2021
20 × 24 in. / 51 × 61 cm

and the pleasures of the visual. As Werner notes, "We can't help being seduced; in the natural world, there is seduction and beauty—colour, shape, form—it is a reflex to being in the world."[12]

Werner's work interrogates the history of painting and its revelations over the centuries on ideas of power and appearances—after all, the primary subjects until the 19th century were most often the wealthy and powerful, and many were women—to explore the self as an abstraction in the 21st century. Werner's figures reveal subjects under surveillance, whether it is within the ever-evolving and proliferating digital world or within the reverberations of imagination and desire produced within fashion, film, and other forms of popular culture. Neither autonomous nor expressive nor focused primarily on the psychological, Werner's paintings suggest a subject that is in flux and through which one senses instead an *orientation*. These paintings show sites where transactions—but more importantly, transformations—take place. While Tiqqun's "girls" are primfarily distinguished by their appearance as "conduits and victims of contemporary capitalism's pervasive violence,"[13] Werner's go right to the site of the origin of Tiqqun's critique and suggest there is more to be found there: "It is mysterious to me why I use this material; when we look at images we are projecting ourselves in there somewhere. I have faith in that curiosity."[14]

Beauty and trouble coexist in Werner's paintings; Werner suggests by these processes that she may be the one doing the violence, not contemporary capitalism, since she instead argues with it, and it is here we may think of that violence as an argument with the image: "I do not want these figures to be seen simply as victims of contemporary capitalism; they are instead ideas; it is important that they are posing questions, asking questions and opening up the narrative."

While the artist acknowledges that perhaps she cannot escape references to capitalism's seductions and impositions, she notes: "I don't know a thing about fashion—or even how to get dressed!"[15]

Rejecting autobiographical self-expression and instead opting for a new kind of action painting, Werner shows us how the aggregate figure relates to form by referencing deep art historical time, demonstrating how such constructions have evolved from pre-modernity to the present.

Sticky Pictures celebrates Werner's painterly operations in both their unsettling and seductive beauty, revealing the conditions of perception and the act of looking as passageways to understanding the intensity of the world at hand.

Werner's unique combination of abstraction, fictional portraiture, and the rich history of painting are explored in *Sticky Pictures* through an interview with American curator and critic Melissa E. Feldman as well as essays by Montreal-based artist and film scholar Ara Osterweil and curator and art historian François LeTourneux. The book addresses almost a decade of work by this prolific and uncompromising painter who sutures the art historical with the contemporary in a lush, demanding, and ultimately reorientating œuvre that challenges the very act of making pictures—and through this, the work of painting itself.

In a compelling alliterative reconfiguration, the Hebrew word *Tikkun* means "to amend or to fix." In her paintings, Werner posits an enlivening richness that remains, reforms, and asserts itself over the centuries of staring, enraptured, at the world that surrounds us—a testament that we ourselves confirm in the pleasure and rapture of her work. Where Tiqqun is disaffected, Werner instead offers painting and embodiment as forms of enchantment—by remembering what occupying a body is, what it has been, and what it can be—that, despite their constraints, convey exuberance and articulate great attachments and pleasures.

ENDNOTES

1 Tiqqun, *Preliminary Materials for a Theory of the Young-Girl* (Los Angeles: Semiotext(e) Invention Series, 2012), 63.

2 From a conversation with the artist, February 7, 2022.

3 Agamben defines "bare life" as the sheer biological fact of life, prior to and beyond the way that life is lived.

4 Tiqqun, *Young-Girl*, 35.

5 Conversation with artist.

6 Tiqqun, *Young-Girl*, 15.

7 For further discussion, see Michel Feher's essay, "Self-Appreciation; or, The Aspirations of Human Capital" in *Public Culture* (2009) 21 (1): 21–41.

8 Conversation with artist.

9 Conversation with artist.

10 Conversation with artist.

11 Tiqqun, Young-Girl, 97.

12 Conversation with artist.

13 Mira Mattar, "Introduction," in *You Must Make Your Death Public: A Collection of Texts and Media on the Work of Chris Kraus* (London/Berlin: Mute Publishing: 2015), 15.

14 Conversation with artist.

15 Conversation with artist.

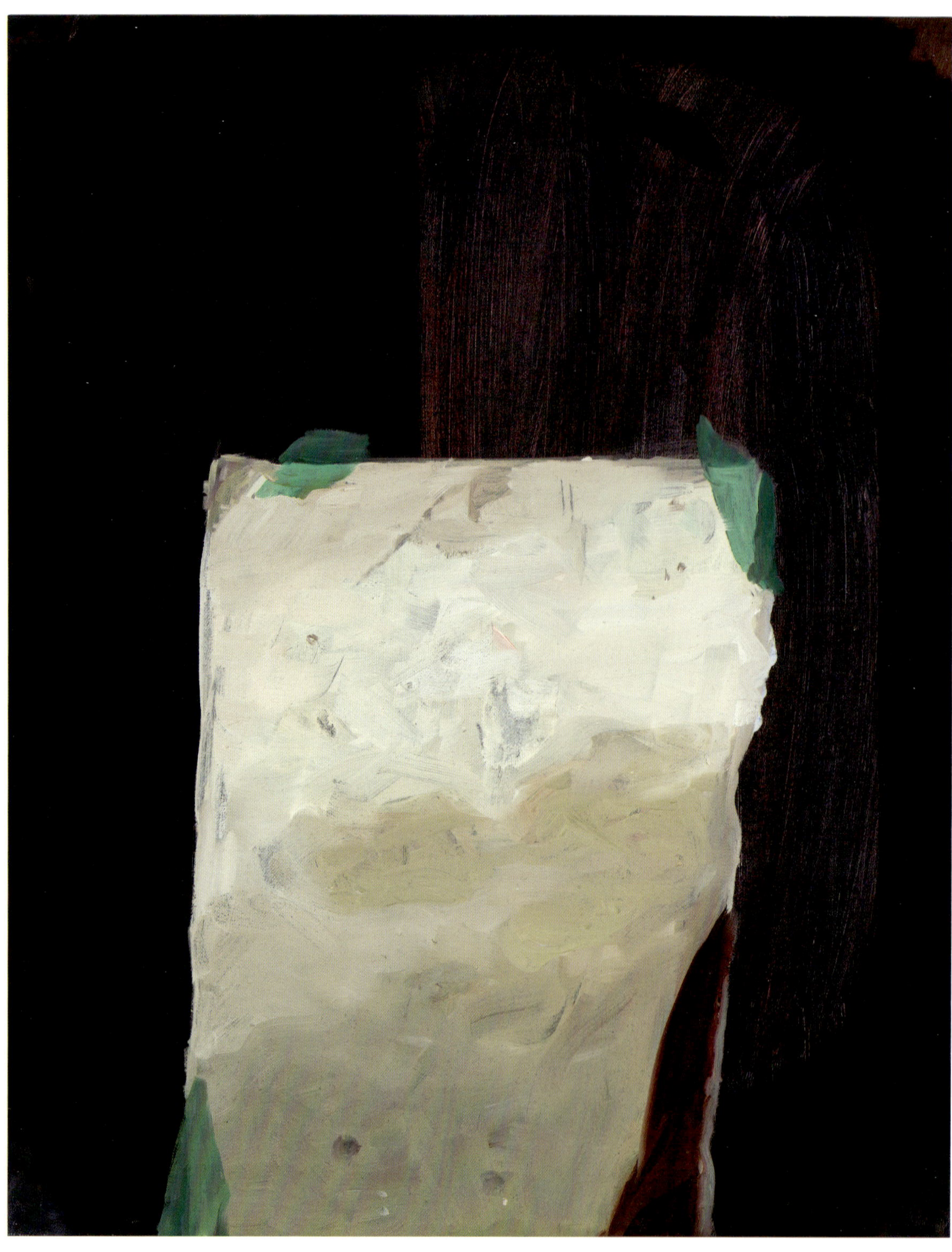

Janet Werner: Object Relations

ARA OSTERWEIL

It is no wonder that Janet Werner is often taken for a portrait painter: Her paintings are populated by women festooned in haute couture. They are painted so masterfully that it is easy to mistake these gorgeously attired objects for actual subjects. Yet as her paintings over the last half decade suggest, the female figure may be nothing more than an ontological problem to hang a dress on.

Ranging in appearance from the gorgeous to the grotesque, the female figure recurs obsessively in Werner's work. However, as the papery creases, pleats, and tears rendered in her paintings propose, Werner does not really paint women but *images* of women appropriated from the pages of fashion magazines and the annals of art history. The difference turns out to be crucial. Not only does the artist avoid the intimacy of painting subjects from life, she deliberately emphasizes the artificiality and two-dimensionality of the magazine muses she pilfers. Subjecting these already flattened subjects to further fragmentation and distortion, Werner enhances their conceptual pliability. Incapable of answering the eternal questions of *who am I?* and *why am I here?*, these figures nonetheless constitute the various shapes these inquiries assume.

By extracting images from the endless piles of *Vogue* magazines scattered on her studio floor, Werner ensures that she never runs out of subjects to paint. Yet the ready-made quality of these airbrushed models creates as many problems as their facile method of appropriation attempts to resolve: How might the artist take something mass-produced and banal—like the capitalist fantasy of the female body as a well-heeled machine—and transform it into something compelling enough to devote a life to working through? Werner's ingenuity in answering this question motivates the rich transformations that her work has undergone over the last decade.

By treating bodies as objects in space that can be stretched, folded, and split without corporeal consequence, Werner's paintings activate the chasm between subjectivity and objecthood. Despite the psychological valence they inspire in the viewer, her recent paintings have shifted away from portraiture toward the still life. Mining the tension between the ruse of being and the collage of the picture plane, Werner divides and redistributes her models' bodies in spatial arrangements fractured by multiple frames. These uncanny juxtapositions allow us to see elegantly turned parts of the body—a leg, an arm, half of a face—not as the fetish objects they were intended to be but as elusive traces of ultimately unknowable subjects. Although she approaches her images from a critical point of view, Werner does not offer any generic critique of female objectification but rather an engagement with the existential terror of being and the nearly equivalent angst of painting. As if holding up a dark mirror to society's fascination with pretty pictures, Werner exposes the void beneath the panoply of exquisite surfaces that disguise and distract us.

ABSTRACT

Take, for instance, a small canvas in which an irregularly edged gray shard appears tacked up with green painter's tape on a black background. Compared to the dazzling array of figures in her larger canvases, *Abstract* (2018; page 12) is a minor work, yet something about its banal shape beguiles. Is it a broken piece of mirror clouded by age or a matte sheaf torn hastily from the glossies? Like Ad Reinhardt, Werner experiments here with the optical crisis catalyzed by painting black on black.

Abstract, 2018
20 × 16 in. / 51 × 41 cm

The nearly indistinguishable layers of darkness gradually reveal their secrets, like a body reluctantly giving up the ghost. Only upon closer inspection does the viewer notice a lozenge-shaped black portal floating in the dark ground behind the pearlized shard. Of course, neither ground is really black, the portal leads nowhere, and the mirrored fragment reflects nothing. (It is bizarrely even less translucent than the green tape that affixes it.) By the time we notice the burgundy sliver haunting the bottom right corner of the frame, Werner has made us so aware of the metaphysical unseen that we wouldn't dare mistake such a mysterious transmission for anything so banal as the edge of a blouse. Surfaces deceive in Werner's work: Her images do not mirror the world as much as they refract what poet Wallace Stevens described as the "nothing that is not there and the nothing that is."[1] Unassuming as it is, this diminutive abstraction teaches us something essential about Werner's work: The figures that populate them are not three-dimensional, corporeal subjects so much as fanciful prostheses wrangled from the void.

CURTAIN

It is a small but profound step from the torn gray shard in *Abstract* to the papery image of a woman with a torn forehead in *Curtain* (2016). As in *Abstract*, the inspiration for *Curtain* has also been ripped from a magazine roughly enough to leave a ragged edge. However, as *Curtain*'s subject is a woman rather than a mere color swatch, one is far more startled by its depiction of gendered violence. However, what strikes here is not the *fact* of such violence—femicide is ubiquitous, after all—but the painting's curious lack of affect. Although the tear parts her frontal lobe, the woman in the picture doesn't seem to worry about her wound. Gazing indifferently beyond the edge of the cropped image, she bears her lobotomy with grace and equanimity. Her blank expression affords us nothing more than what writer Maggie Nelson describes as the "dimly painful . . . sensation of space where it had once been dense and full."[2] Is it possible that despite the ontological distinctions between page and person, a tear in one is no more significant than a tear in the other? Werner's flat equation of the two reminds us that all her appropriated sources are two-dimensional objects shorn of feeling and emptied of viscera. However, there is far more going on here than an ironic appreciation of the thingness of people and the personality of things.

That excess has a name: formalism. The image may startle because of its anesthetized nod to trauma, but it dazzles because of what it does *as a painting*. Like Whistler's *Harmony in Pink and Grey* (*Portrait of Lady Meux*, 1881), *Curtain* is a visual study of the subtle interactions of color. Beneath the image of the torn woman, another image pulsates with pink and gray swirls like one of the crepuscular skies in Whistler's *Nocturnes*. Although I was initially bewitched by the scandal of the woman's wound, upon closer inspection, I became captivated by this *other* painting within the frame, far more subtle—and feeling—than the ostensible drama that surrounds it.

Disguised by the spectacle of damsels in distress, this dialectic between formalist experimentation and conceptual daring is held in exquisite tension in Werner's work. Although there are notably intimate exceptions in both her and Whistler's œuvres—his haunting portrait of his mother comes to mind, as does her burlesque of two agonized *Sisters*—their interest is in painting first and portraiture second. It is for this reason that I often find myself as drawn to Werner's understated still lives—of lonely plants, bouquets, or cluttered tabletops—as I am to her more ostentatious paintings of women. On the rare occasions when the artist relieves herself of the burden of female representation, Werner allows herself the freedom to paint without becoming entangled in the fraught dynamics of personhood. In the breathtaking *Scar Curtain* (2019), for instance, an image of diaphanous drapery leaks light from a window (see page 96). The curtain in question—a sheer, flesh-colored array of undulating verticals—partially obfuscates a field of unruly blue brushstrokes.

CLOCKWISE FROM LEFT

James McNeill Whistler, *Harmony in Pink and Grey: Portrait of Lady Meux*, 1881–82, oil on canvas / huile sur toile, 76.3 × 36.6 in. / 194 × 93 cm. Henry Clay Frick Bequest / Legs de Henry Clay Frick. Photo © The Frick Collection / La collection Frick

Sisters, 2013
22 × 20 in. / 56 × 51 cm

Curtain, 2016
72 × 60 in. / 183 × 152 cm

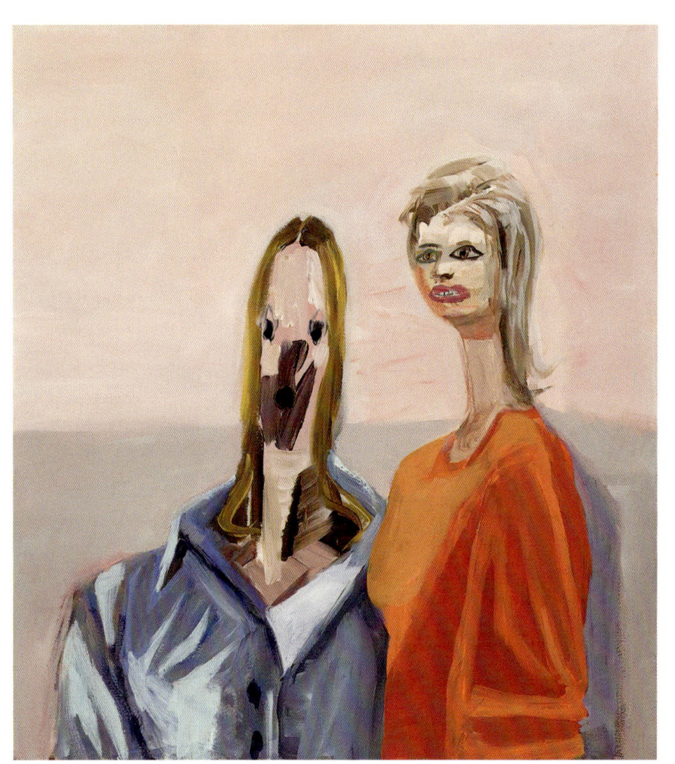

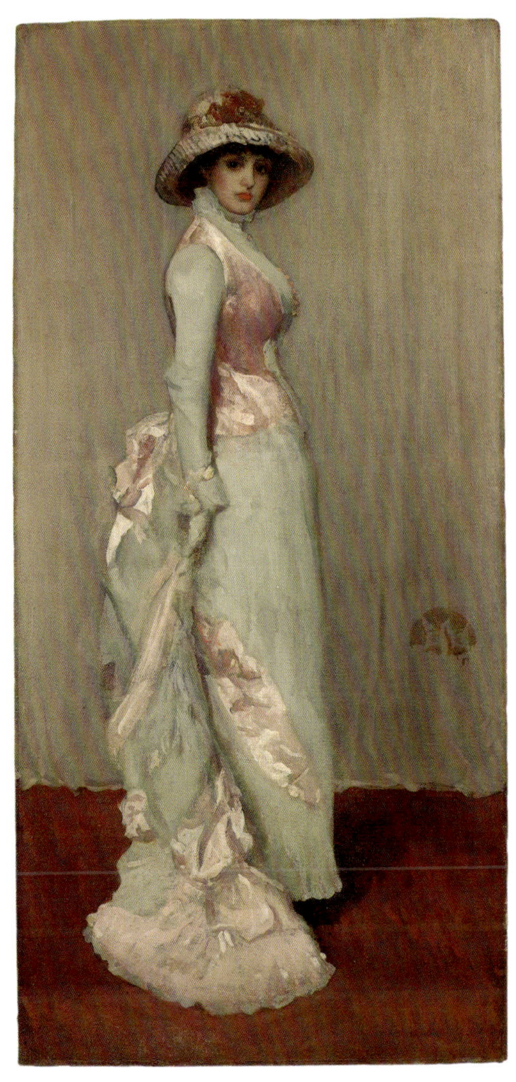

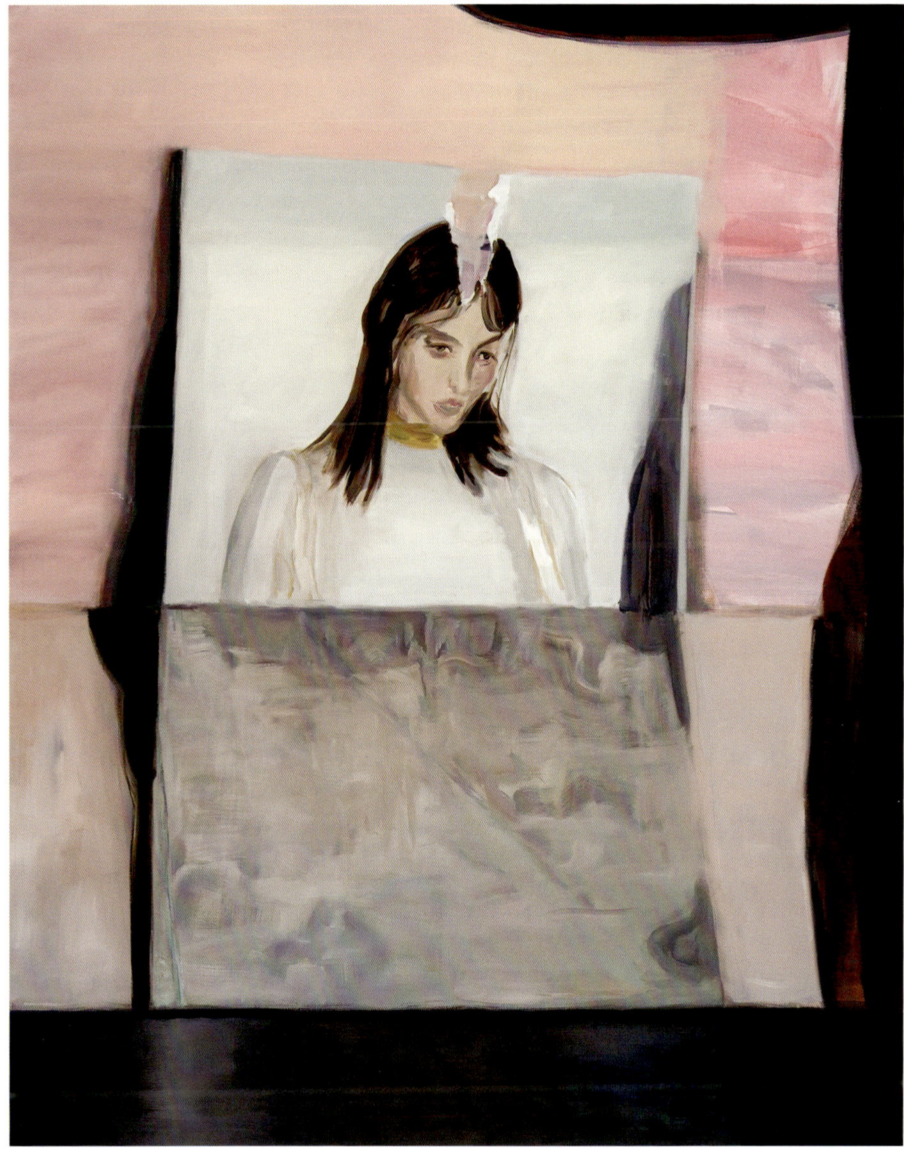

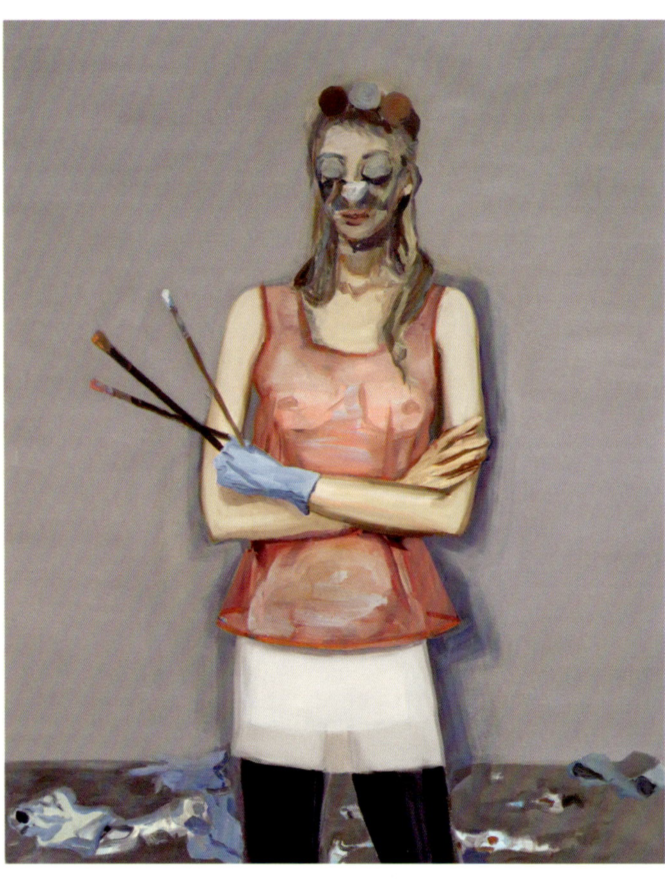

Hovering on the threshold of abstraction, these ostensible branches pine, like us, to be anything than what they are. No wonder curtains abound in Werner's work, along with veils, masks, and other metaphorical defenses against the disclosure of interiority.

EARLIER FIGURES

Werner's earlier paintings (circa 2009–2014) were known for situating oversized female subjects against neutral backgrounds in ways that emphasized the psychological confrontation between subject and viewer. Working with images that fetishize slender white models, Werner created space for the expression of "ugly feelings" within the seductive images of mainstream paradigms of femininity.[3] Yet, even in these images, the painter was always searching for more than a pretty face. By her own admission, Werner's eye is attuned to the plight of well-adorned "clowns" whose unsustainable poses and expressions reveal the ridiculousness of the situations they are compelled to uphold. By exaggerating the grotesqueness of bodies already deformed by the glossies, Werner crystallizes their awkward glamor into emotional states of isolation, vulnerability, and self-doubt. In this way, all her paintings might be read as self-portraits of the artist grappling with the perils of exposure. This is nowhere more evident than in *Dreamer* (2012): Captured in a moment of hesitation, one of the artist's many doppelgängers clutches three loaded paintbrushes in a studio strewn with debris. Although her visage is camouflaged by paint splotches, her breasts are exposed through transparent voile. The figure is both the painter and the unwitting subject of the scene. In a culture in which many opt to meet the constant threat of surveillance with the compulsion toward self-exposure, even the behind-the-scenes act of creation has been dragged into view.

Much of the richness of Werner's painterly vocabulary stems from her attempts to mediate this conundrum. Faces obscured by masks beguile in *Bear* (2010) and *Smearcase* (2011), while others hide behind strips of bark (*Birchman* [2010]), windswept hair (*Walker* [2013; page 153]), or sumptuous arrangements of flowers (*Pet* [2014; page 147]). In other paintings, the subjects of her portraits awkwardly navigate the collapse of surface and depth as their visages crumble like

ABOVE

Dreamer, 2012
67 × 55 in. / 170 × 140 cm

OPPOSITE, CLOCKWISE FROM TOP LEFT

Birchman, 2010
20 × 16 in. / 51 × 41 cm

Smearcase, 2011
60 × 48 in. /
152 × 122 cm

Bear, 2010
88 × 66 in. / 224 × 168 cm

Kinder, 2012
55 × 45 in. / 140 × 114 cm

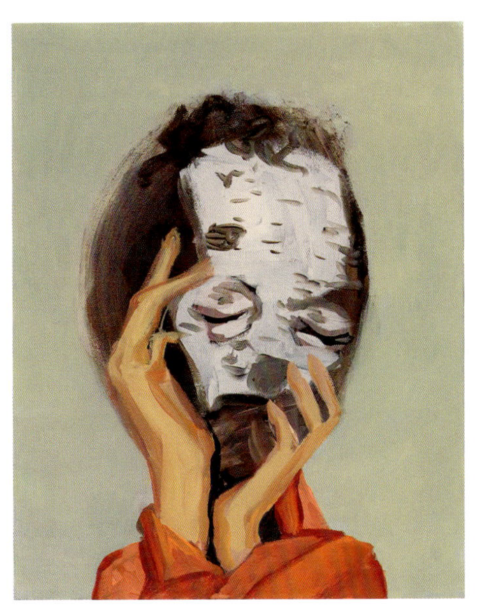

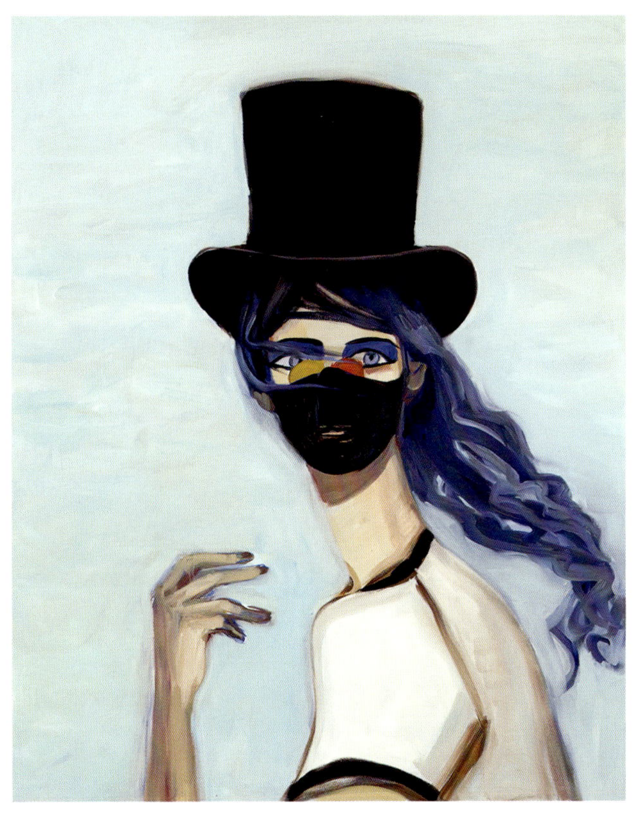

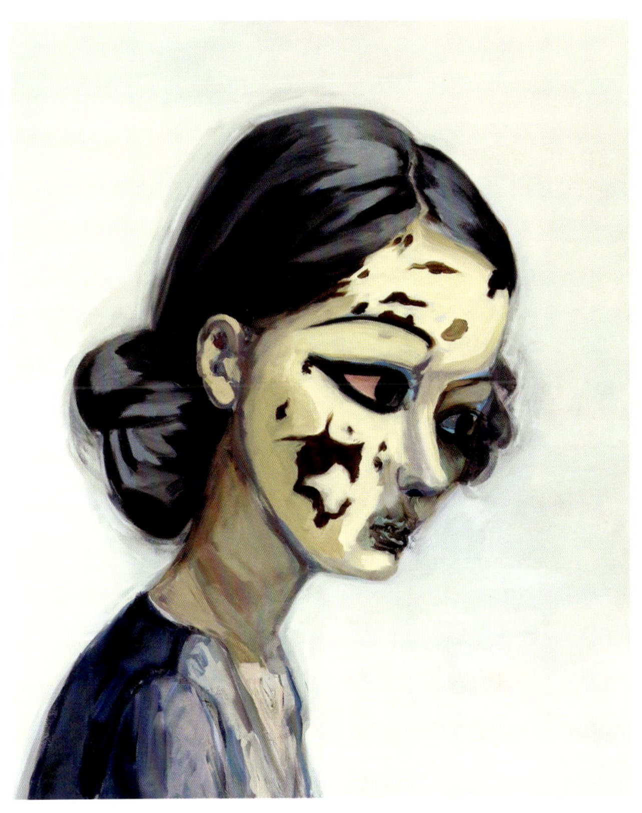

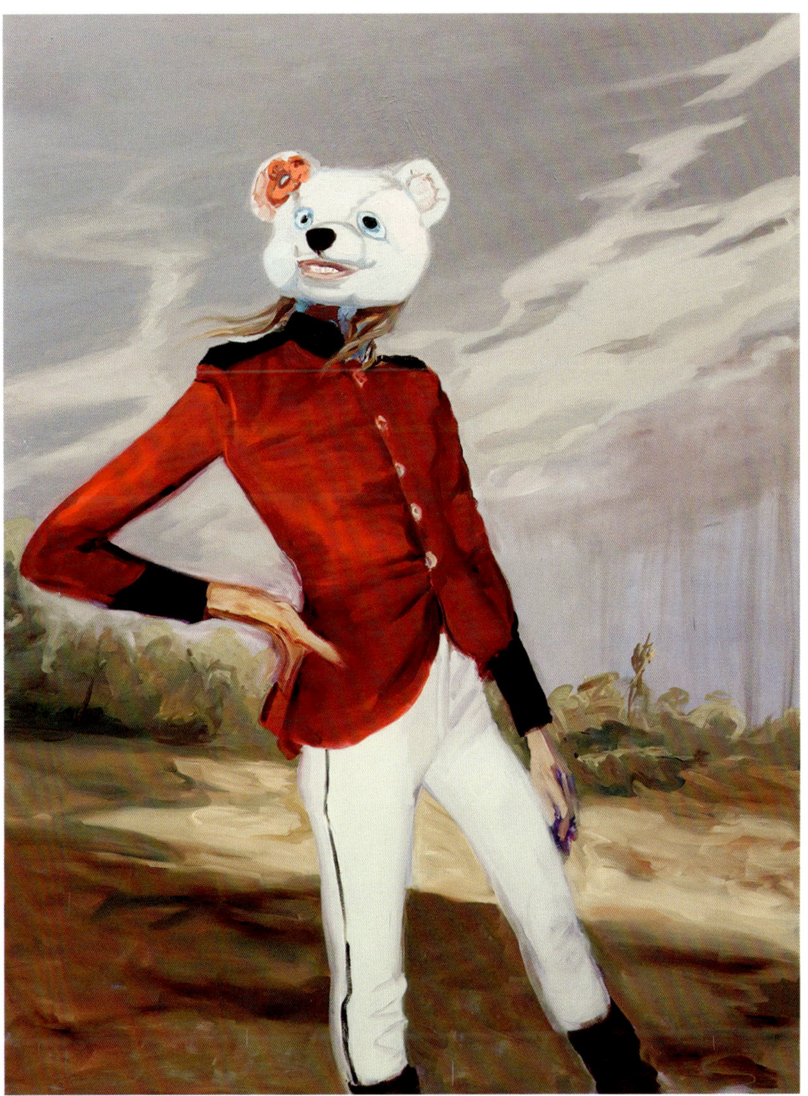

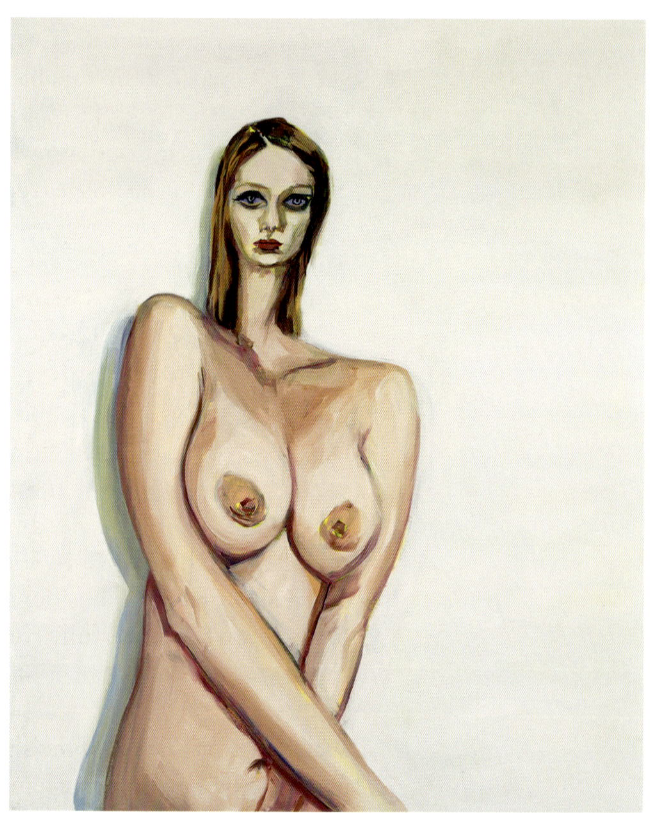

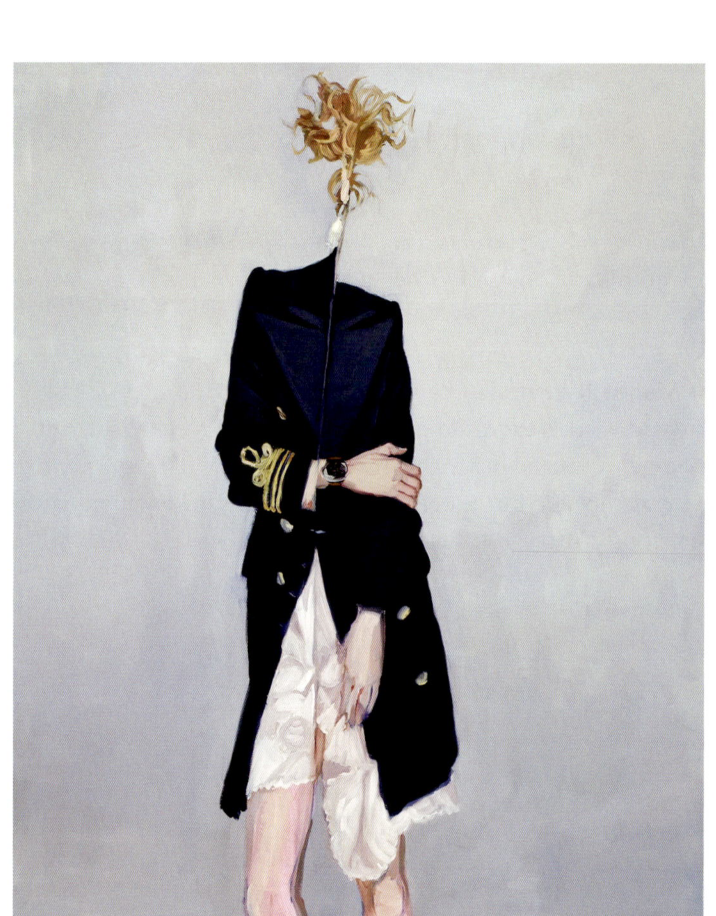

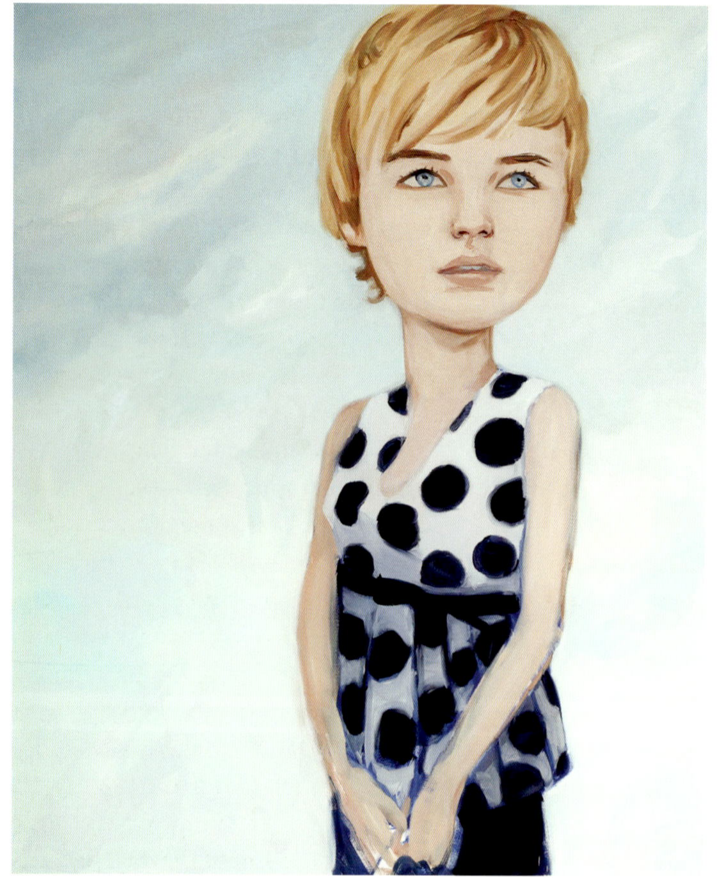

decaying edifices (see *Kinder* [2012]). Yet perhaps most ingeniously, Werner discovered that the very idea of a curtain, capable of concealment and compression, could be applied to complicate the form of the body: In *Folding Woman* (2009), the first of the painter's ongoing series of plicated figures, a vixen dressed in a white nightie and a gilded military jacket sacrifices her face to a cruelly placed crease in the image from which she presumably sprang. The fold deprives her of the facial markers of individual subjectivity while posing plication as a metaphor for interiority itself. Yet while the pleat is a violent act of erasure, Werner also imagines it as a daring feat of self-fashioning. Just because we don't consent to our negation doesn't mean we can't wear it well.

Werner has long relied upon collage to create uncanny juxtapositions in her work. Initially, her impulse was to disguise the seams to harmonize, let's say, an oversized doll's face from one magazine with the tiny, slender body of another (see *Ohio* [2009]). The inverse also proved revelatory, as in *Sheila* (2011), a goon girl with a shrunken head who demurely shields her crotch from the viewer's gaze even as her enormous nude breasts "stare" blankly at the viewer. In the last few years, however, the painter's approach to collage has changed dramatically. Instead of hiding the seams between her images, Werner highlights the spatial and corporeal fissures of these cut-up and reassembled compositions. As her recent work reveals, the mimetic fantasy of plenitude that Werner can so masterfully conjure is even more powerful when it reveals its seams.

STICKY PICTURES

Werner's 2017 *Sticky Pictures* show at Montreal's Parisian Laundry gallery (now Bradley Ertaskiran) proved to be a breakthrough in this regard. In this exquisite suite of paintings of atelier walls and tabletops plastered with images, Werner illuminated her highly mediated process of image poaching. By deprivileging the figure, these images allowed the viewer a more enigmatic engagement with the surrounding space while simultaneously affording a glimpse of the artist's solitary labor. They also explore the relationship between space and surface in ways that defy the traditional relationship between figure and ground.

In a collection of paintings that either marginalized or completely elided the figure, Werner explored the tensions between the world of three-dimensional objects and her two-dimensional source material. These "empty atelier" still lives were nonetheless populated with images tacked to walls, scattered on tables, spilling out of manila folders, and otherwise petitioning to be brought to life. Punctuated by cropped faces and other fragmented body parts, Werner's still lives thus remain haunted by the psychological dimensions of portraiture.

In *Sorcerer* (2016; page 77), a pair of breasts lies discarded on a table, like a cast off bra. Nearby, a golden mirror reflects nothing while a blooming cactus looks perfect enough to be plastic. What is real here and what is a falsie? With Werner's typical sirens minimized or left completely out of the frame, the viewer is allowed an opportunity to reckon with the sorcery of the artist's brush. Lonely as some of these tableaux are—*Sorcerer* is a melancholy, Hopperesque symphony of bluish-grays—they are also profoundly relational in their staging of the intimacy between the artist and her paper-thin muses. In *Hover (the distance between here and there)*, for example, an exquisitely poised hand extends from an impossibly sinuous arm as if to snatch an image from a table scattered with detritus (page 57). Searching for an elusive image the way one yearns for another's body, the artist clutches at meaning with an intensity usually reserved for lovers. As evidenced by portentous visions of a hand thrusting from beyond the frame here and in *Touch hold (still life)* (2019; page 20), this relation is as tactile as it is optical. Yet while Werner proves that she can transform any *objet trouvé* into a captivating image, the chasm between what is and what might be nonetheless persists. At the end of the day, the artist must confront the solitude and limitations of the self, even in a

CLOCKWISE FROM LEFT

Folding Woman, 2009
66 × 53 in. / 168 × 135 cm

Sheila, 2011
54 × 45 in. / 137 × 114 cm

Ohio, 2009
66 × 55 in. / 168 × 140 cm

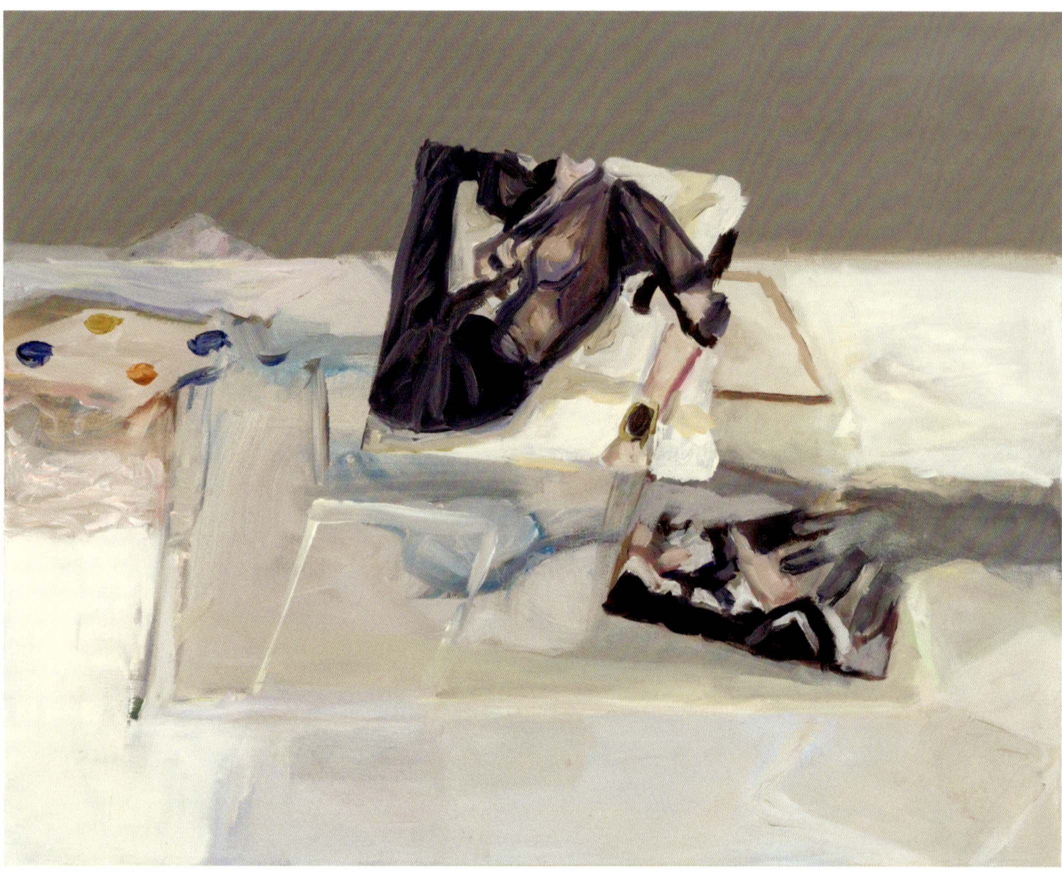

studio overflowing with airbrushed imagoes. Even the long, limber arm of desire that extends over *Hover* cannot span this lack.

As the title of *Touch hold (still life)* attests, Werner's images of emptied rooms are hardly inanimate or lacking in frisson. What I find most striking in this recent strain of her practice is the way in which inanimate objects, or at least non-human ones, interact with her conspicuously artificial figures to theatricalize what psychoanalysts like Melanie Klein and D.W. Winnicott theorized as the psychodynamics of "object relations." As if personifying experiences of neglect, dependence, and longing, the banal objects in Werner's *mise en abymes* command psychological space. Klein famously theorized the breast as the primary "part object" that comes to stand in for the mother. It is no wonder that breasts abound in Werner's work, as well as in Western visual culture more generally, but Werner's recent paintings abound with other objects freighted with the conflict between attachment and self-sufficiency.

Take, for instance, the understated *Plant* (2016; page 65), which situates a potted, spotted begonia in the foreground of a nearly empty room. Of course, this being a still life by Janet Werner, there's a woman lurking somewhere: Way back on the far wall is a taped-up image of a gray-haired woman, hung askance and sliced down her middle. Yet this bisected woman is merely the backdrop to the perfectly self-sufficient begonia unfurling its tendrils without any self-consciousness about what it might lack. Unlike the rest of us, the plant is content to simply grow.

Yielding far more personality than the faceless *Folded Woman*, Werner's begonia hovers in the non-human space between subjecthood and objecthood. So too does the indisputably inanimate *Blue Table* (2019; page 53), a painting of—what else?—a cobalt studio desk leaning against a wall patterned in an ethereal moiré of pale brushstrokes. An image of a wild-maned model dressed in turquoise is tacked above it, but she can hardly compete with the majesty of the table itself. By foregrounding this minimalist structure, Werner reminds us that behind every act of creation is not an emptiness asking to be filled but a world of things indifferent to our efforts. However, while she is not afraid to confront the blankness of the world head-on, Werner's painterly approach is

Touch Hold (still life), 2019
24 × 28 in. / 61 × 71 cm

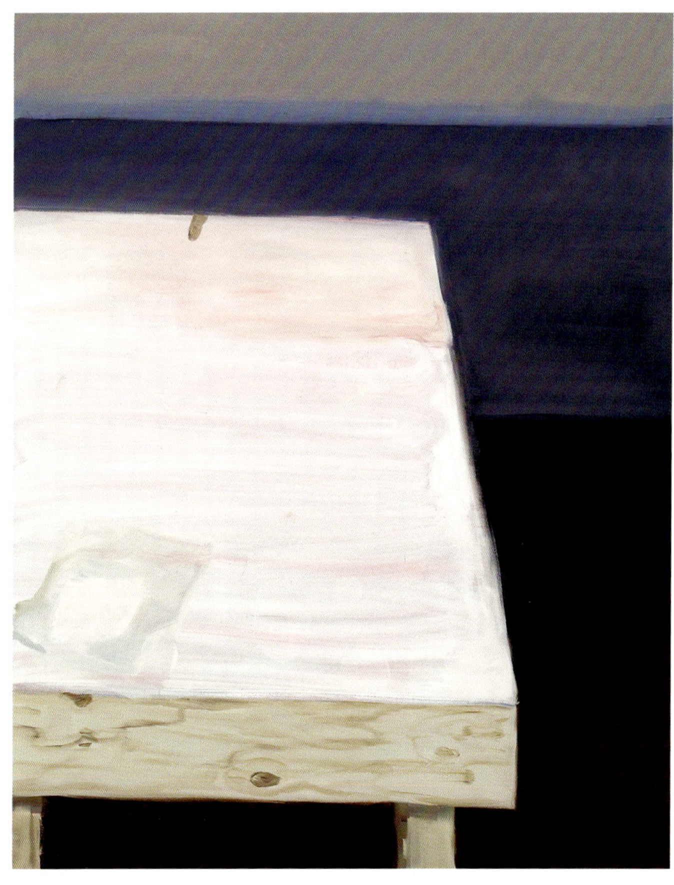

hardly as indifferent as the objects she figures. Rather than staging a mere chromatic comparison between the cobalt table and the turquoise woman, *Blue Table* animates the former's indifference by inverting the conventional hierarchy between subjects and objects: Werner imbues the table with a sense of portraiture while transforming the woman into a still life. Yet the "subject" of the painting is neither the table nor the woman but the totality of the scene as well as its off-scene space. By activating the relation between the table, the torn image of the woman, and the unseen artist, Werner locates the painter's subjectivity in the act of looking. For it is through the act of looking—potentially as much of a tactile as an optical gesture—that the world comes to matter, regardless of whether anyone returns our gaze.

Werner propels this insight to its extreme in one particularly fearless canvas of a parted theatrical curtain rendered in viscous layers of oil. As if beckoning the viewer to enter a void, *Someone, something, no one* (2017; page 75) poetically articulates the stages of disappointment that we experience as our expectations for reciprocity collapse. The curtain, a silky black affair fringed with pale aqua, opens upon an undistinguished gray field. Though parted drapes conventionally promise an imminent spectacle, Werner's ground refuses all inklings of depth or futurity. The labial folds of the curtain itself are all the drama we need—or at least are going to get. Recognizing the world not as a stage poised for dramatic action but as an antechamber emptied of players, Werner's painting shatters the illusion that anyone, or anything, is coming to fill our lack. Yet by vacating the Someone or the Something that usually constitutes the focus of representational painting, Werner reveals the immanence of the interval between the now and the nothing that follows. Though our own desires are suffused with anticipation for what comes next, the imperfect present may be as good as it gets. In this way, Werner's appreciation of the bewitching surfaces of even the most banal objects—like these curtains or the bubble-gum pink plywood table in *Float (pink trace)* (2016)—posits a bold claim for aesthetic and spiritual sufficiency. For only when we give up our expectation that Someone might pass through the curtain and provide Something we desperately crave can we begin to accept that the world is already enchanted enough for anyone who bothers to notice.

Float (pink trace), 2016
60 × 48 in. / 152 × 122 cm

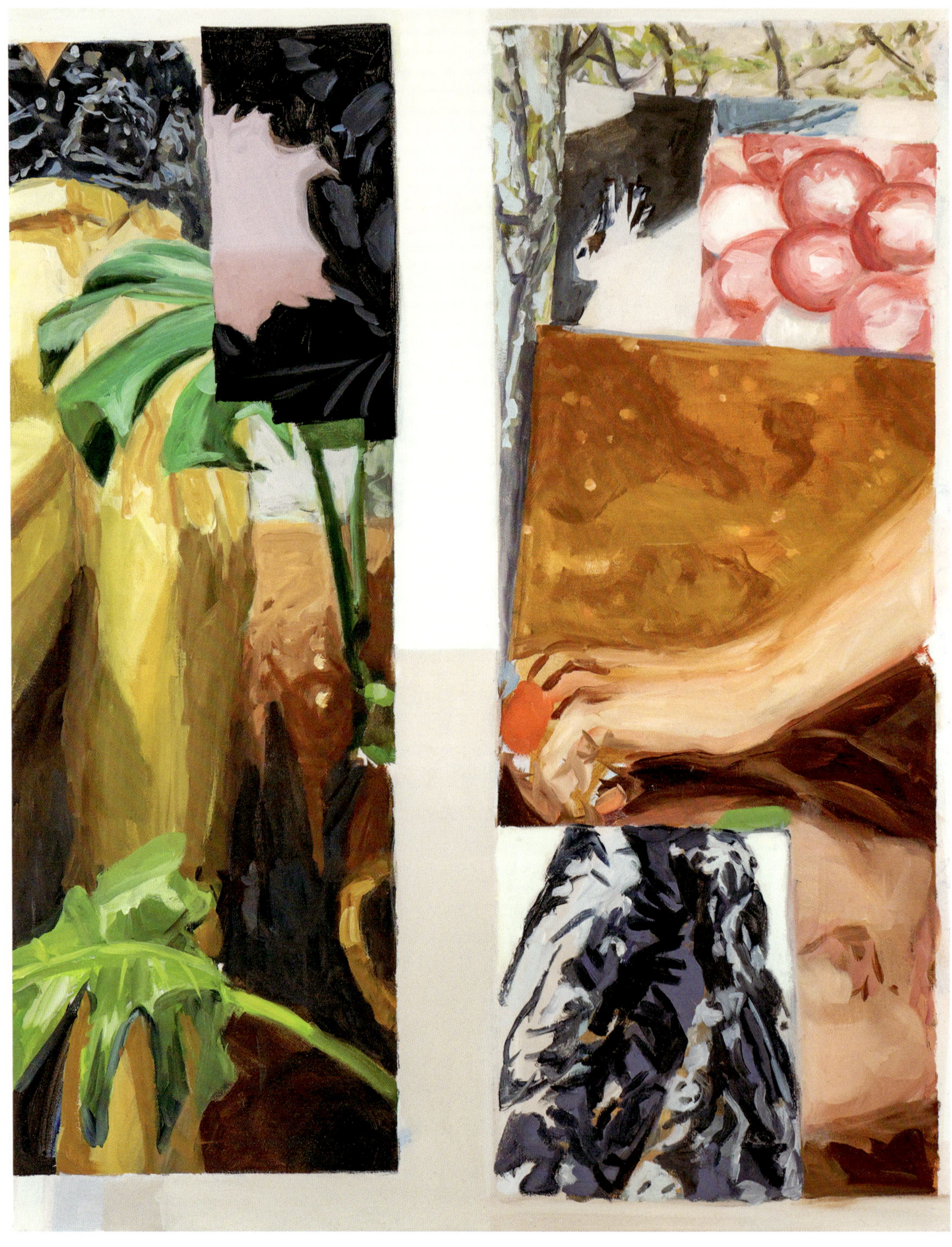

AFTER STICKY PICTURES

Since her revelatory *Sticky Pictures* show, Werner has developed an increasingly sophisticated practice of collage in which she composes her figures from fragments of conspicuously distinct photographic sources. While Werner occasionally still creates a yearning *nature morte*, for the most part, figures have again seized center stage. Since reemerging from her deserted rooms, her women have become monsters of hybridity that refuse the mimetic capacity of figuration. In *Beast* (2019; page 167), for instance, the painter taunts the viewer to guess which of the three foliage-encrusted women depicted might be the "real" one, only to throw up a menacing, leaf-fringed shadow that corresponds to none of them. While shadows connote a world of three-dimensional objects capable of casting volumes of light, the palimpsest of cut-up images reminds us that all painterly substance is illusion, including these women.

Yet there remains a lexicon of patterns, textures, questions, body parts, and partial answers that Werner turns to in her endless invention of new challenges to complicate the picture plane. Some, like the aptly named *Lexicon* (2021), present an inventory of painterly objects and effects—a bejeweled hand, a creased overcoat, the cleaved leaves of a monstera plant—reminding the viewer of some of the things that painters like to paint. Others, like the mysteriously named *Rabbit* (2020; pages 216–7), return more explicitly to the existential quandaries with which Werner's portraiture has always been concerned. Surrounded on two sides by a border of cheerful polka dots, this close-up of a gamine head sliced off at the neck *and* brow is simultaneously an unwitting image of violence *and* an invitation to consider what new perspectives the wreckage of subjectivity might afford. Werner, who was apparently surprised that some viewers mistook this bold cut-up for an image of decapitation, maintains an unusually cool head when confronting the shattered surfaces of selfhood. Gazing out at the viewer with a knowing blue eye, as two lengths of leg (or are they fragments of forearm?) lay scattered where her brain ought to be, the head seems to ponder the mysteries of having become a still life. Returning the haunting gaze of this apparition, I am astonished at how Werner reimagines all our psychic wounds as new apertures through which to see the world.

—

ENDNOTES

1 Wallace Stevens, "The Snow Man," *Poetry* magazine, 1921, https://www.poetryfoundation.org/poems/45235/the-snow-man-56d224a6d4e90.

2 Maggie Nelson, *Jane: A Murder* (New York: Soft Skull Press, 2016), 17.

3 This phrase is borrowed from critic and scholar Sianne Ngai, *Ugly Feelings* (Cambridge, MA: Harvard University Press, 2007).

Lexicon, 2021
33 × 26 in. / 84 × 66 cm

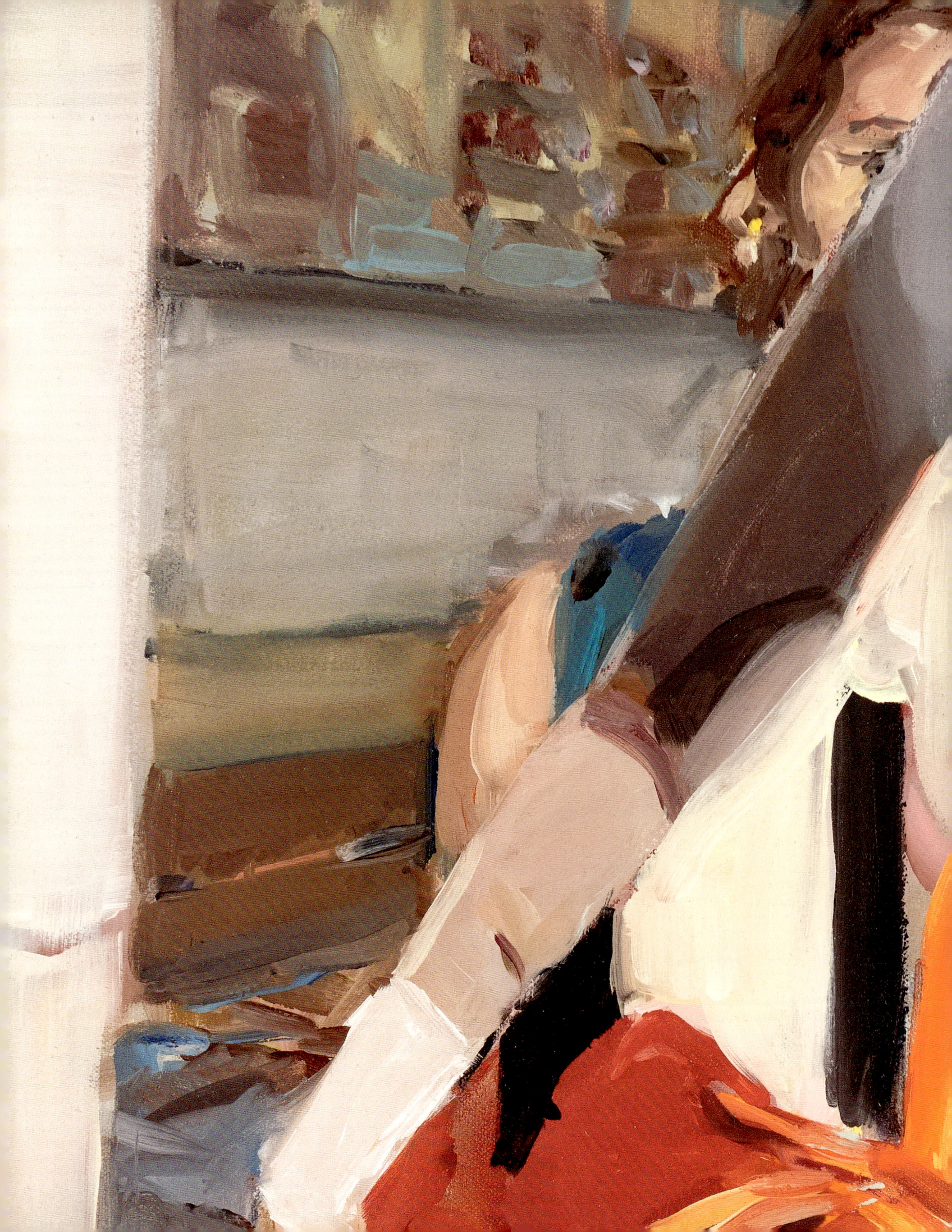

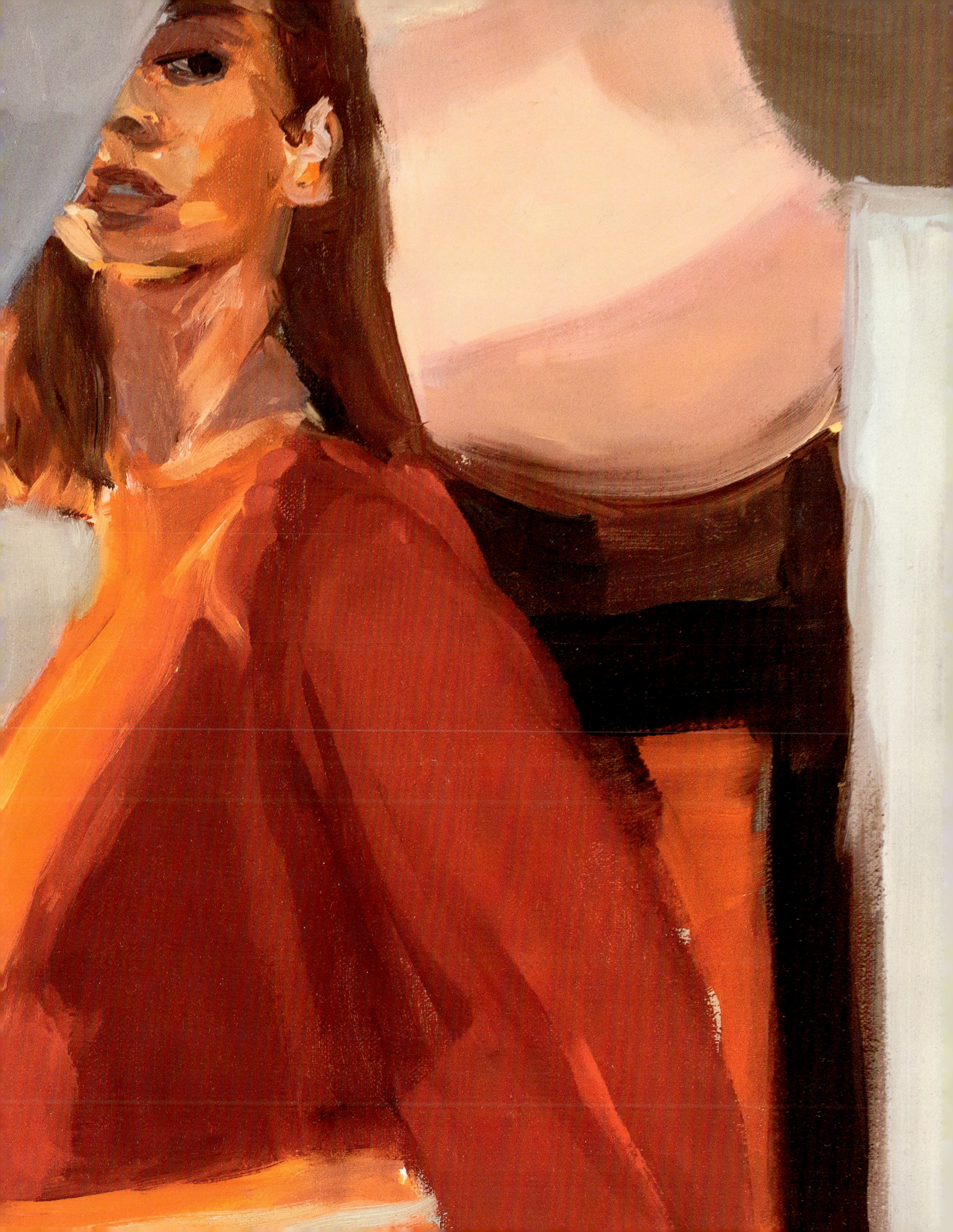

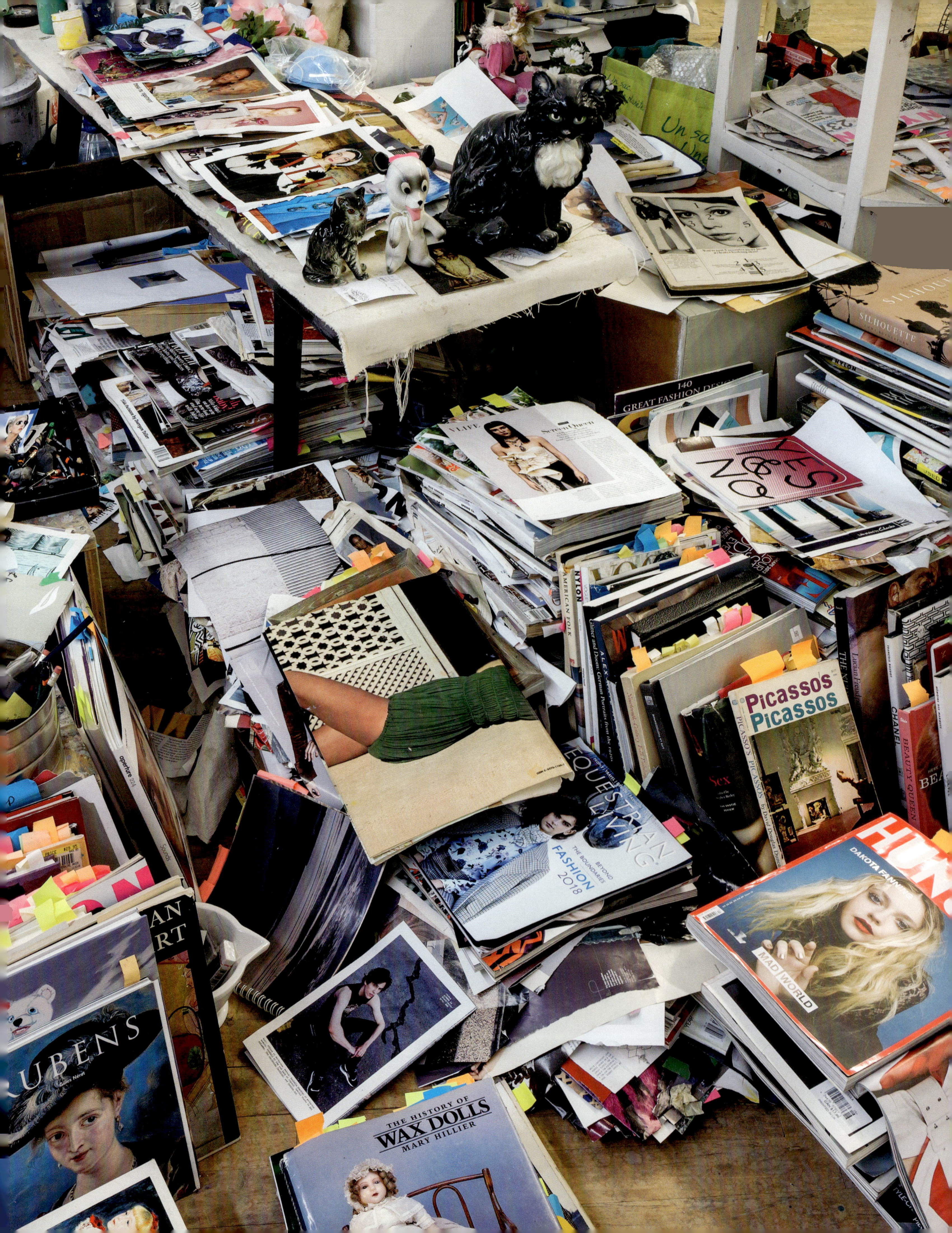

SILHOUETTE
YES NO
Picassos Picassos
EQUESTRIAN LIVING
BEYOND THE BOUNDARIES
FASHION 2018
DAKOTA FANNING
MAD WORLD
RUBENS
THE HISTORY OF WAX DOLLS
MARY HILLIER
BEAUTY QUEEN
CHANEL

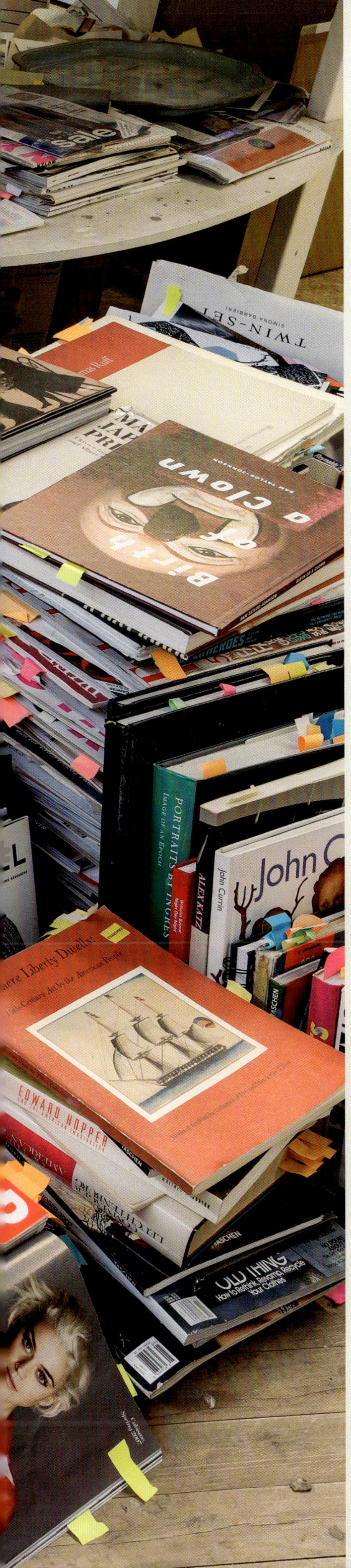

Pictures of You: A conversation with Janet Werner on the shifting grounds of feminism, fashion, and portraiture

MELISSA E. FELDMAN

Janet Werner and I met by chance in the spring of 2019 in Vancouver. I was living in Seattle at the time and was there on one of my frequent art trips. I stopped by Griffin Art Projects, where I had guest curated a show a few years earlier. During my visit, the director, Lisa Baldissera, asked if I would like to meet their artist in residence, Janet Werner. I didn't know the name, but moments later, Werner was standing before me, and her lush, odd, figurative paintings, I discovered, were entirely familiar. Meeting Janet was like looking in the mirror—or at my sister. Our similar looks and age instantly amused us both and led to an easy rapport. Short on time, we agreed to continue our conversation at the Musée d'art contemporain de Montréal (MAC), where a major museum show of her work opened that fall.

Why did I find the work familiar? Because we both came of age in SoHo, New York, in the early 1990s, when acerbic figurative painting was gaining momentum and—along with its unlikely counterpart, third-wave feminist art—taking aim at the politics of representation. This pedigree was visible in her portraits, wherein the Kate Mosses and Linda Evangelistas of the time find a psyche and a soul. It was also evident in the way Werner could make paint do anything: gorgeous, scumbled little passages of gestural abstraction; heart-breakingly spare, cryptic monochromes reminiscent of Luc Tuymans (channeling Munch); flagrant surrealism; dreamy pastoral backdrops reminiscent of a Goya canvas; renderings that swung from deliberately maladroit to the hazy elegance of Bonnard.

Werner falls into a category recently being mined of relevant artists who, whether due to location, social networks, or race/ethnicity, landed outside the tight spotlight of the mainstream art world. For women artists older than Werner, gender would have been an impediment, too. These are artists who remained in the background even though they participated in and contributed to noted artistic shifts and trends.

In this case, the fanfare centered around New York–area painters such as Elizabeth Peyton, Karen Kilimnik, and Werner's fellow Yale classmates John Currin and Lisa Yuskavage. Meanwhile, Werner left the United States for a teaching job in Saskatchewan and eventually settled down in Montreal. While the portraits have

Janet Werner's studio, Montreal, 2019

had a dialogue with her American peers, more recent work seems to be spinning out of that orbit. In 2016 Werner struck new ground with a series of spare, monochrome interiors. The only figures occupying these emptied-out spaces are those found in the odd picture leaning against the wall or in the torn pages of fashion magazines. These occupy lone tabletops cropped in the manner of a Cezanne still life along with art materials, sticky-note-tabbed books, and potted plants. Appearing as actual scenes from the artist's studio, the spaces are in fact entirely invented.

Invention is further amplified in the artist's latest work featuring backdrops resembling de Kooning-esque wallpaper (*Loop*, page 95) or a moody street scene patch-worked with appropriated elements (*Strasse*, page 169). Instead of a Frankenstein-ed whole, the new works make space for different worlds to coexist and set Werner's pictures on a course toward abstraction.

MELISSA E. FELDMAN I know that the show at the MAC focused on work from the last ten years, but could you talk more broadly about your long interest in portraiture?

JANET WERNER The portraits started out as invented figures from imagination without any photographic references. They had a different character. They were frontal and quite flat. I would say they were also more androgynous

MF Would I recognize the work as yours? Sometimes earlier work can look very different.

JW You'd probably recognize it, but it did look very different because it wasn't done under the influence of photography. Those portraits actually came out of an investigation of abstraction. When I was in grad school at Yale a lot of people in the program were working abstractly, including John Currin.

MF Why abstraction? Was there an instructor there who influenced you all, or was that just the trend at the time?

JW No, not really. For me, then and now, if the work's interesting it's because of its formal abstract qualities.

MF Well, yes, that's what I've noticed, that the work is very formalist, but what surprises me is how little that's been addressed in the writing about your work, which tends to focus on the pictorial and your process of messing with fashion images.

JW That's true. It hasn't been addressed.

MF Well, it's become unavoidable given the newer work.

JW The new direction happened at a moment when I wanted to take a break from the portraits. It had been twenty years, and even though I've explored many different approaches to it, it was a bit of a straightjacket that I had to keep finding my way out of, coming at it from different angles. And then for some reason around 2016, I don't know exactly why, I just wanted more. The space has always been important in the portraits, even though it's just a single figure against a ground. I wanted to play with more elements, a bit of architecture, and to pull back and to see what else could come in. The painting of the table with the three pictures on it, *Still Life with Witch* [2019; page 55], was one that inspired me. I liked what was happening on the miniature scale. Something was happening with the paint that was different there also... It was more open.

MF You mean less tightly painted?

JW Yes, less photographic. When you're working on such a small scale, you can't make it photographic. I've been wrestling with the photograph all along because I don't like what it signifies and I don't like how it makes forms.

MF I know your photographs come from fashion magazines. Are they vintage magazines, contemporary, a mixture? Because some of the fashions look dated or historic.

JW The photos I use are almost all from contemporary fashion magazines, but fashion today plays with a mix of historical styles—elements from the 19th or early 20th centuries or from the 60s and 70s can appear alongside the most current fashions. There's a freedom to cross boundaries and time periods, to replay. It's very eclectic so you might be picking up on that.

MF The only invented parts are the interiors and the tabletop still lifes? Everything else is appropriated from magazines?

JW There are also art historical references occasionally, for example *Table with Picasso* [page 60], *After Picabia* [page 84], *Cinnamon (after Gainsborough)* [page 87], and *CDF* [page 42], which references Caspar David Friedrich. Allen Jones has also been an important reference recently.

MF So with the *Sticky Pictures* [2016–2018] series, for example, you have wrestled the photograph down to size. How have

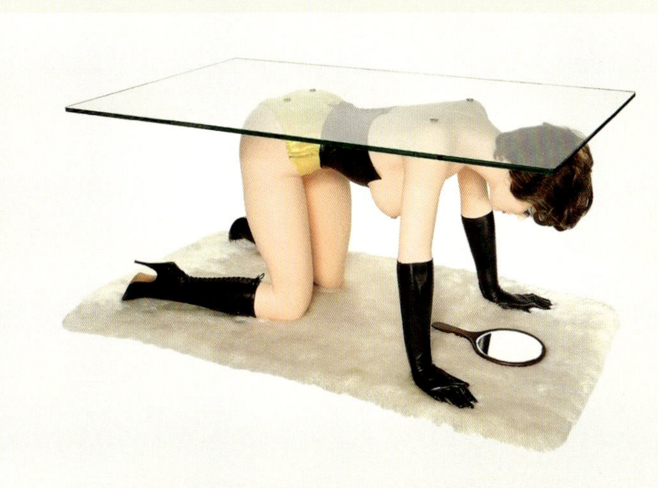

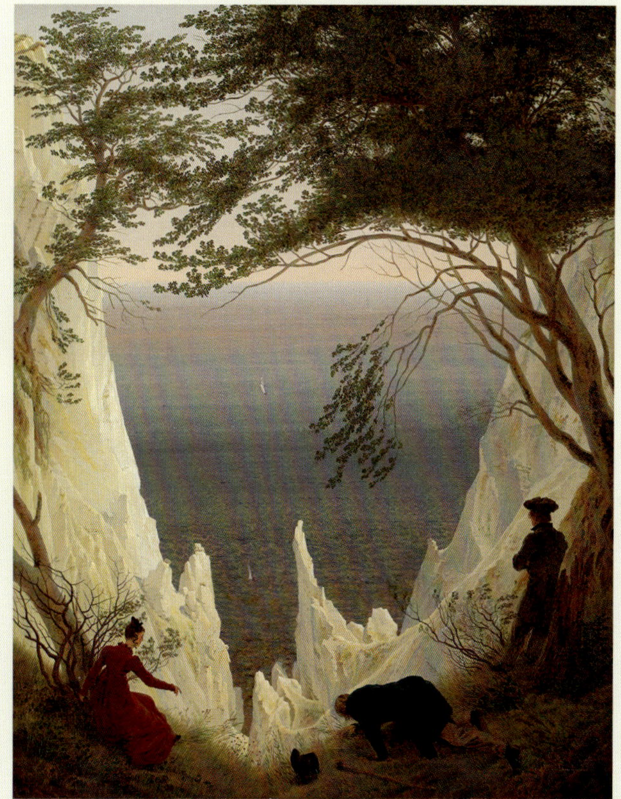

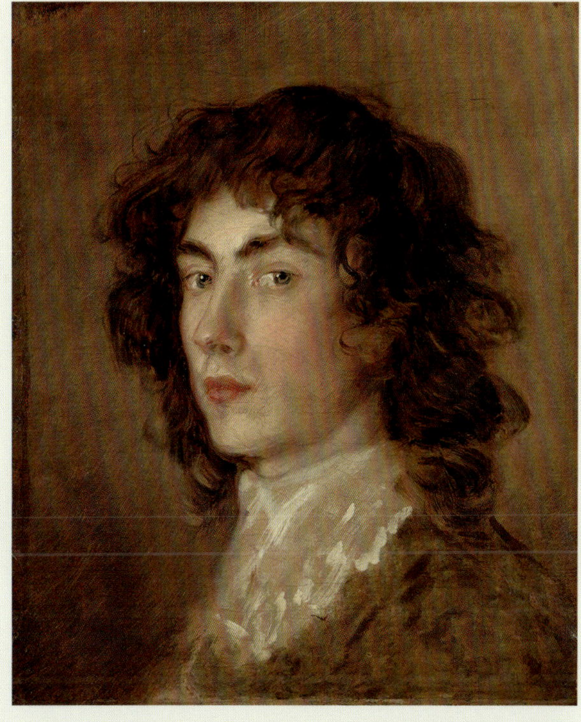

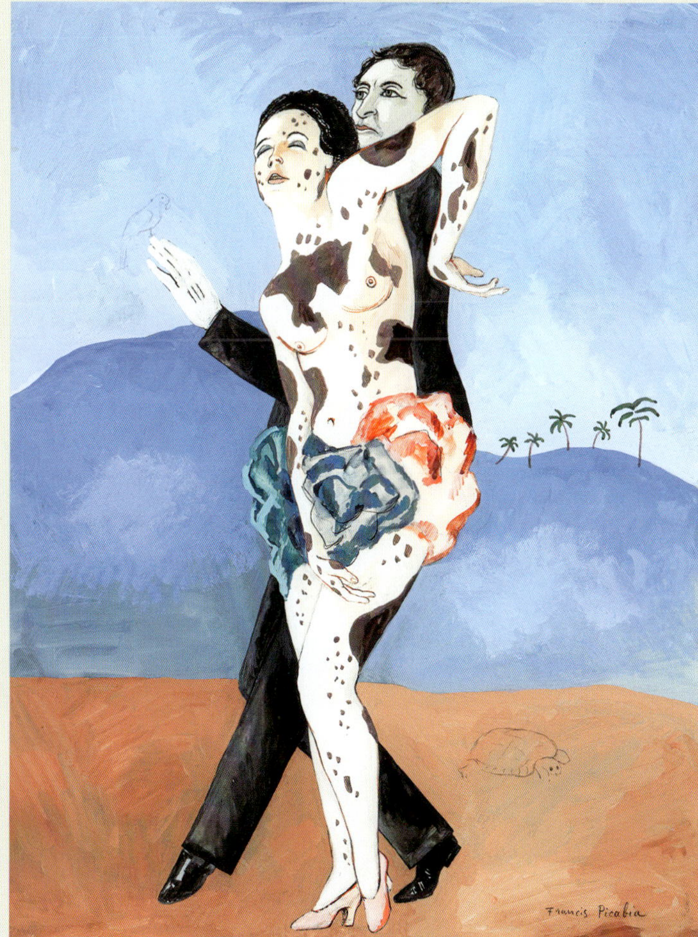

CLOCKWISE FROM TOP LEFT

Allen Jones, *Table*, 1969, mixed media / techniques mixtes, 24 × 51 × 30 in. / 61 × 130 × 76 cm

Caspar David Friedrich, *Chalk Cliffs on Rügen*, 1818, oil on canvas / huile sur toile, 35.6 × 27.9 in. / 91 × 71 cm

Francis Picabia, *Bird and Turtle*, ca./v. 1927, gouache, watercolor, graphite, and Conté crayon on paper / gouache, aquarelle, graphite et crayon Conté sur papier, 25.6 × 19.8 in. / 65 × 50 cm

Thomas Gainsborough, *Gainsborough Dupont*, ca./v. 1770–5, oil on canvas / huile sur toile, 17.9 × 14.8 in. / 46 × 38 cm

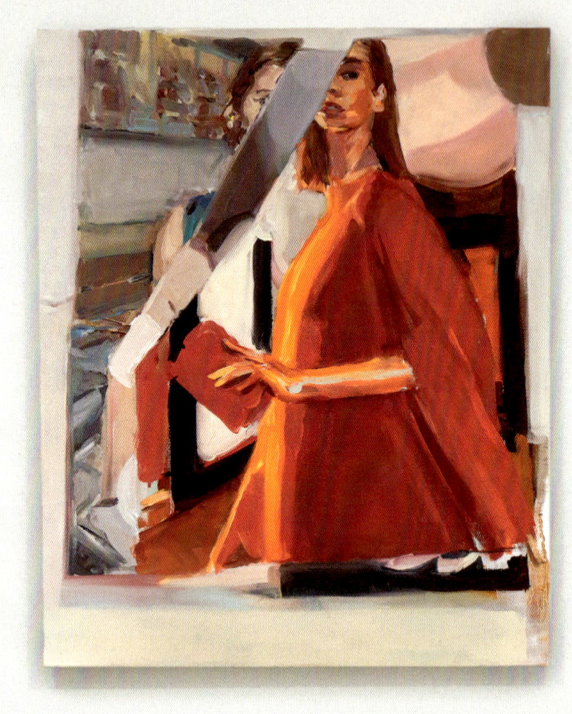

these negative feelings about photography manifested in your portraits?

JW I often have to destroy a portrait when it gets too photographic. I get angry and start undoing it—removing or altering features, messing with the paint—in the process of which something else comes through. The closet expressionist in me comes out, and I'm generally much more satisfied with the result. The paint has to move. But with the interiors, it's the space itself that is the invented part, where I'm messing with the paint.

MF You are referring to a painting like *Green Room* [2018].

JW Yes. *Hover* [2019; page 57] is another example. The space is invented, but the images are borrowed.

MF I'm also curious as to how your work—with its cutting and pasting and distorting of images—might relate to or have been affected by the shifts in art practices with the rise of digital culture over the past couple of decades.

JW The earlier portraits were deliberately minimal and plain, unadorned. I thought of them as existential and psychological in nature. But once I began using fashion sources and collage they shifted somewhat to reflect the larger culture. I'm very conscious now of the proliferation of images and the constant consumption of them that we've become swept up in. I still think of the portraits as being about subjectivity though, and they are meant to recuperate an idea of interiority, the idea of an inner world that is somehow made visible through the representation of the body. I believe this complexity removes them from the objectified treatments found in images of women in the media.

MF What about your portraits in which the subject's face has been obliterated by paint or a mask or folded out of the picture, and the strong element of theatricality that goes with those images? Maybe I'm not understanding what you mean by "interiority," but how do you square the shocking appearance with conveying a sense of inner life?

JW Well, I identify the sense of violence or shock, the obliteration or folding, with metaphors about interior life, life history, trauma, or some sort of narrative action that has taken place or is taking place. The expansion and contraction of body parts, masking, or obliteration of features invite a narrative reading.

MF I think of us as having come of age during third-wave feminism in the early 1990s—Beverly Semmes, Janine Antoni, the rediscovery of the first-generation feminist artists like Hannah Wilke. It colored my worldview and my curatorial work—I showed people like Semmes and Karen Kilimnik in the early 1990s, when I was curator at ICA in Philadelphia. But, you know, even Kilimnik's more media-minded work of the 90s was not motivated by feminism. There's a lot of social critique going on there, but I don't think you could just put it in that box of feminism.

JW Mmm, hmm. Who wants to be in that box? I mean, I'm a feminist, but the work is not programmatic. People sometimes think that because I paint mostly women I'm trying to make a specific statement about women's relationship to the body. I'm not, but the work emerges from a female subjectivity. Looking at images from media and popular culture, it's the images of women that interest me most. It's partly because that's what's out there, it's more available, and it's partly because I'm a woman. I can relate. There's a huge emotional, multidimensional range to those images, as opposed to the images we see of men in the culture, though that's changing. There's an iconic aspect to the images that interests me, you know, the Hollywood-type images.

MF Yeah.

JW There's also something to do with my mother. I don't know why, but, you know, she's my icon of femininity.

MF In what sense? Was she glamorous?

JW Yeah, she was. She was glamorous. I feel when I see these images in culture and media and fashion, there's something there that I recognize. We all do, right? It's built for us to identify with. It really lends itself to both being borrowed from and critiqued.

MF Yes, borrowed from and critiqued. I also see an element of pleasure. How women and those who female-identify express themselves through fashion. Playing with identity through different looks is fun.

JW Yeah. Thanks for bringing that up, because I'm losing sight of that lately. I mean, truly, for me, it's always about fun on some level. I don't play in real life; I play in the studio.

Installation: Bradley Ertaskiran, Montreal, 2021

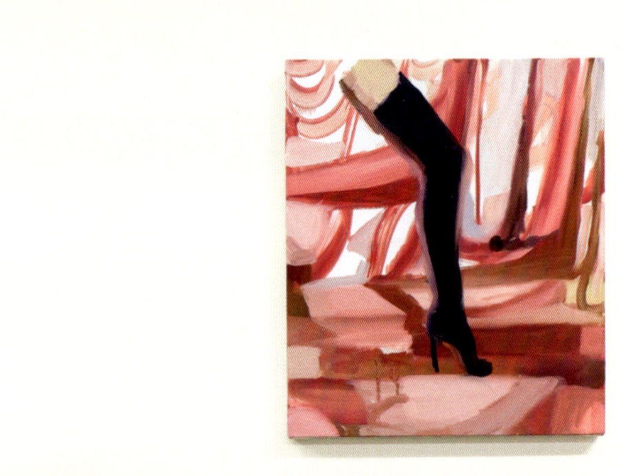

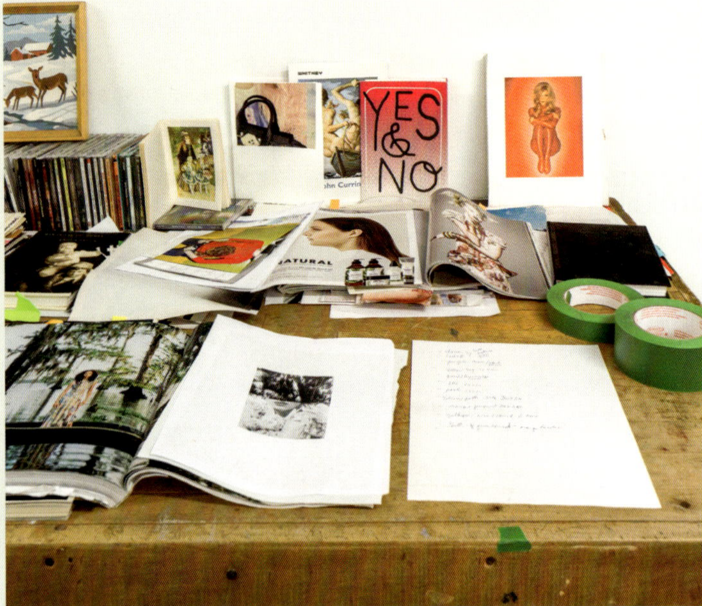

Janet Werner's studio, Montreal, 2022

MF I wanted to ask you about that word "subjectivity." It comes up a lot in the writing about your work. Also "embodiment." What do we mean by subjectivity? One's sense of oneself, right?

JW Yeah, what's true for you, your particular point of view. It's who you are.

MF Or who I think I am.

JW Exactly. But in making the portraits, the fun game is that you can be a lot of other people, not just who you think you are.

MF That's like Cindy Sherman, but with her it doesn't seem to be about self-exploration but rather the representation of women. What about in your work? Do you identify with the identities that you portray?

JW Yeah. Even the ones that are sadomasochistic. Someone recently asked me about violence and sadomasochism in my work. I was quiet for a while, but I do think about violence in a way with the act of painting—you can cover over and destroy—and also what I'm doing by folding and interweaving different body parts. For example, in *Hass* [2017; page 61], I blinded the figure; she can't see. I folded the image so it's just her mouth and this black mask, and it gives me some kind of perverse pleasure to do that, obviously.

MF But you are not necessarily implying that this is what the patriarchy and society and the media have done to her.

JW No, because you could see that as a disempowering, but you can also see that as an empowering thing—that a woman can fold herself up and she can reopen herself.

MF She can hide...

JW ... And explode. That shock that happens when you experience an exquisite corpse. It's a sort of undeniable awakening.

MF Let's talk about the new paintings, which mark a pretty significant shift in your work, I think. The experience they offer the viewer is very different from that of previous work, the portraits in particular. Paintings such as *Miami* [page 202], *Strasse* [page 169], and *Julia* [page 203] have these dueling realities, yet compositionally the parts seem integrated, whole.

JW It does feel like new terrain. After exploring the portrait for so many years I wanted to think of the image in a different way, not just figure/ground, but combining two or more different spaces to make a more complex whole. It complicates the narrative. I'm happy you say it seems integrated because I keep wondering how the splitting of the image operates. In the portraits I used a collage process to alter the figure, but the seams of the collage were hidden so the sense of the figure as a whole was obvious. Now the figure is often split, the seams are visible, and you can see where the image breaks. It's more abstract, but the figure is still a crucial anchor.

MF But has its role changed? I don't see the figures as personae so much anymore. You seem to be treating the images—these very loaded tropes such as *Vogue* fashion, impressionist landscape, and 19th-century portraiture—like so many shapes, colors, and fields of brushwork. There's this constant tension between illusory space and the picture plane, figuration, and abstraction.

JW Yes, it's not so much about the specific characters now. The figures are cropped, sometimes you don't see the face at all, so it's more about what else is happening in the image, the surface/depth tension you mention. The figure is caught in between; there are glitches where the figure disappears, a twist, a misalignment, and the unity that's there is because of the color, shapes, and textures. It's formal, but it's also still narrative. The title of my last show, *There There*, was a reference to the idea that there are two spaces, two or more things going on. It's not a single story but simultaneous narratives or worlds that somehow cohere.

MF So what's driving the juxtaposition of images is also their narrative relationship? For example, *Strasse* [2021; page 169] looks one part 1980s *Vogue* and two parts 1880s French Impressionism. The blue-gray background with its tipped-up angle reminds me of one of Gustave Caillebotte's scenes of Paris in the rain. What's behind their coexistence? How did the woman in the orange halter-top jumpsuit vignetted in the upper left wind up in what looks like the gutter?

JW Good question. The impulse to bring these disparate things together is the driving force at the moment. Maybe narrative is the wrong word because it's more a sense of the absurd I'm drawn to, the image as a conundrum that poses a question. I like this not knowing where you are. There were formal reasons why I chose the bright orange jumpsuit in relation to the gray landscape. It was a color decision. There's a recession into space, something leading you back, and also a block—the figure on the left—prevents you from going back. There's another pair of feet underneath also, but they are slightly out of scale and misaligned. I like the idea of having to jump from one space to the other; something unexpected happens in that gap.

MF In terms of your process, how do the different pieces come together? And how do you go about selecting those pieces in the first place? There is so much source material in those magazines for you to sift through.

JW It's a challenge! I spend hours making collage sketches—going through magazines, flipping pages, folding images in half, juxtaposing them with other images. I'm hoping for an accident, something that will resonate in ways I couldn't anticipate, a chance encounter that will surprise me. It's a strange process. There's a lot of waiting, looking and waiting for an image to float to the surface, to become the starting point for a painting. Sometimes I find a color motive or, lately, a spatial motive. Almost always there's a connection to the figure, to the expression, gaze, or gesture. The clothing is important too, and, of course, in fashion magazines it gets quite elaborate. The clothing creates character and at the same time presents a range of abstract shapes, color, and pattern to play with. The material is endless, and it's very difficult to settle on a starting point. But you know the minute you start painting, everything changes, because the painting has to obey its own logic and it's a very different logic than the photograph.

MF So landing a composition is the most fraught and time-consuming part, and it's smooth sailing once you start painting.

JW Ha, ha, that's very funny. No, no, there's no smooth sailing once you start painting! That's the true test, the performance part. The materiality and scale of painting are different, the process of translating the image into paint, the layering and editing process that happens as the painting is developed. You can't know in advance if it's going to work; things can go wrong at any moment. Then you have to deviate, improvise, or start over.

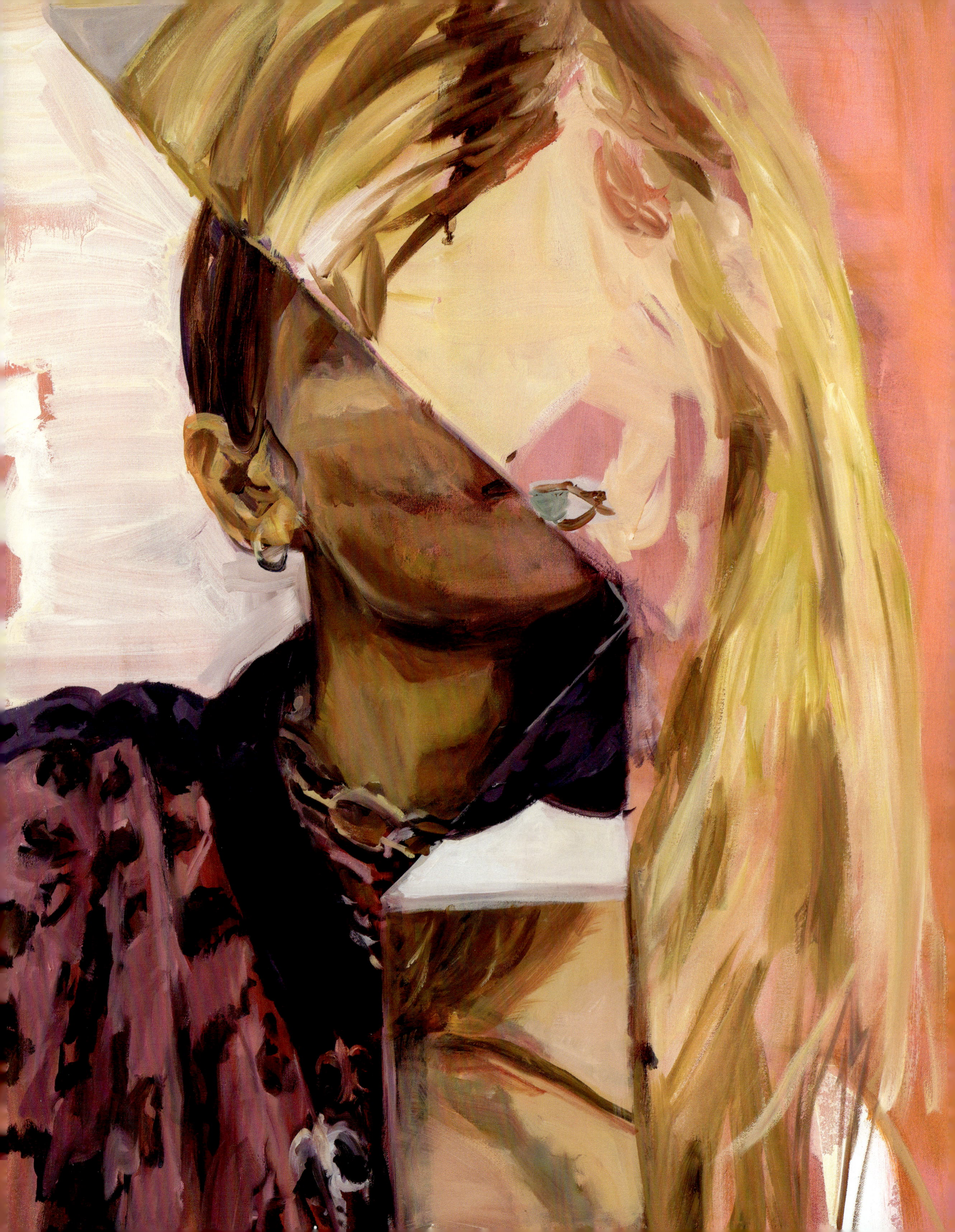

Membra Disjecta: Notes on Janet Werner's Recent Work

FRANÇOIS LETOURNEUX

I.

Since the late 1980s, Janet Werner has been developing her own, distinct brand of fictional portrait, moving progressively (and almost programmatically) from abstract forms and ideograms to stylized, blocky figures, often on quite a small scale and presented in the form of installations. These early figures were soon succeeded by larger, more colorful portraits, executed in an almost photographic style. Since the year 2000, Werner has been undisguisedly employing found fashion photos (mostly of female models) that she routinely manipulates, playing a kind of solo version of *cadavre exquis*. The figures' different parts might be folded, cropped, or rearranged before being further transformed by various pictorial interventions (including iconographical additions, distortions of bodies and objects, and painterly effects).

The composite characters resulting from this process have often been seen as addressing social issues of gender and representation. The figures' prettiness, their sometimes anxious expressions, and the operations of distortion and destruction to which their images are subjected do indeed suggest a kind of ideological conditioning that cultivates and exploits psychological vulnerability. Since Werner began her practice, the number of images of human figures to which our gaze is exposed has multiplied exponentially under the effect of the digital paradigm, and this horde of media characters (real and fictional) has become the main focus of our attention, far ahead of sex, food, drugs, or sports.[1] The plasticity of Werner's characters conjures a feeling of heightened unreality in which our self-image includes diverse degrees of identification with countless archetypes. It is possible to discern in the artist's paintings the echo of the quasi-hallucinatory effects that the manipulation and multiplication of images have engendered in the human psyche over the past several decades: A gulf has opened up between our personal experience of the body and the infinite variation of its "dematerialized" images.

As often noted, Werner's characters are also full of humor and make-believe, playing their own game of seduction and subterfuge. Even an unadorned face may, it is well known, turn into a "mask" merely through a change of expression. And what is makeup, if not layers of paint applied to the body, almost exclusively to the face, whose signs it aims to alter (accentuating or attenuating certain features, adding others)? In our own era, the made-up face is transformed even further under the impact of countless digital filters. The face in painting (a fortiori Werner's composite "fake" portraits, assembled from modified images) is therefore a kind of multilayered mask whose expression may too easily read as "real," although it is the product of a complex politics of representation (whose components are both strategic and involuntary). Lastly, since these paintings generally portray almost complete figures, it is worth recalling that the "mask" (acted or real) sits in the same kind of relationship to the face as the face itself to the rest of the body: It perches there in a relation that, as Hans Belting has explained, unites nature and culture.[2] This casts an obvious shadow on any faith in painting's ability to capture clear delineations between nudity, or psychological authenticity, and social artifice. From the layers of makeup to the skin, the surface of a face to the light-sensitive film, the photograph of a model to the pictorial support, via the artist's own body, these are the contact zones where the fascination of the gaze—even a kind of craving—flourishes.[3]

Crush 2, 2021
33 × 26 in. / 84 × 66 cm

Can allusions to masks and makeup help us establish a typology of "roles" that would shed light on Werner's gallery of characters? Some of them certainly appear to possess caricatural, even quasi-allegorical qualities. But they also display a kind of essential singularity resulting from their reinvention in paint (while the source figures almost always look like "types" in the original shots). Seen together (the inevitable effect of a monographic exhibition or book), these *dramatis personae* appear to also be engaged in a dialogue on the plural nature of subjectivity. From this perspective, Werner's production could be read as a Bakhtinian polyphonic construction, a vast, diffracted self-portrait.[4] The "individual," it seems to suggest, is always multiple. In this sense, Werner's scenographic approach to inner experience constitutes an interesting alternative to the media discourse on identity, which currently tends to offer a limited and rather rigid spectrum of affiliations.

The plural approach to subjectivity just described can be linked to the extensive work on intertextuality that began appearing in the late 1960s and that had considerable impact on the Western art scene of the 20th century's last two decades. Janet Werner belongs to a generation of artists that includes George Condo, Luc Tuymans, Karen Kilimnik, Lisa Yuskavage, and John Currin and that, following the late 1990s' critical reassessment of figurative painting, would bring new impetus to the portrait genre.[5] In contrast to neo-conceptual approaches like that of Gerhard Richter, several of these artists revived the early avant-gardes' use of pictorial pastiche and mass media imagery, exploiting kitsch, mash-up, and parody against the backdrop of a postmodernism that was taking a broad interest in consumer culture and complex identity issues.[6] This return of the medium to the forefront of contemporary art heralded its popularity among younger creators today.

II.

Over the past decade, references to humor and the carnivalesque have receded somewhat from Werner's work, and she has adopted a more "measured" approach that displays a certain affiliation with Manet and the definition of modernity offered by Baudelaire in his famous essay on Constantin Guys.[7] As we look at Werner's paintings, several key subjects mentioned in the poet's article come to mind—the quintessentially "modern" phenomena, according to Baudelaire, not depicted in paintings found at the Salon or in the Louvre at the time: the life of women, makeup, fashion, and the figure of the dandy. We are also reminded of the poet's remarks on the technique of the modern painter, especially the all-important "speed of execution."[8] Impossible, too, not to reflect on the aesthetic of the fragment that infuses Baudelaire's work in general (and that of his famous interpreter, Walter Benjamin, who was so fascinated by the figures of the *flâneur* and the ragpicker), and which is also found in Manet, whose painting includes endless examples of iconographic or material "cuts," indissociable from his use of quotation.[9]

It is interesting to note that Manet, long hailed as one of the founding figures of modernism (in the Greenbergian sense of the term, which prioritized the flatness of the pictorial surface), has gradually become affiliated with a form of "anti-modernist" modernity owing to the importance he assigned to the tradition of painting, scenographic artifice, accessories and costumes, and stylistic pastiche as parodic "second-hand," which are all elements that find an echo in Werner's recent work.[10]

There is also the question of the photographic model, often exploited by Manet in his paintings to the point that even the handling of his figures notoriously retained evidence of this origin ("It was as though he had painted not Victorine Meurent but her photo, not her image but its reproduction").[11] And, finally, there is the more particular (and decisive) matter of the *alla prima* treatment—for want of a better term (it must in any case be distinguished from any type of

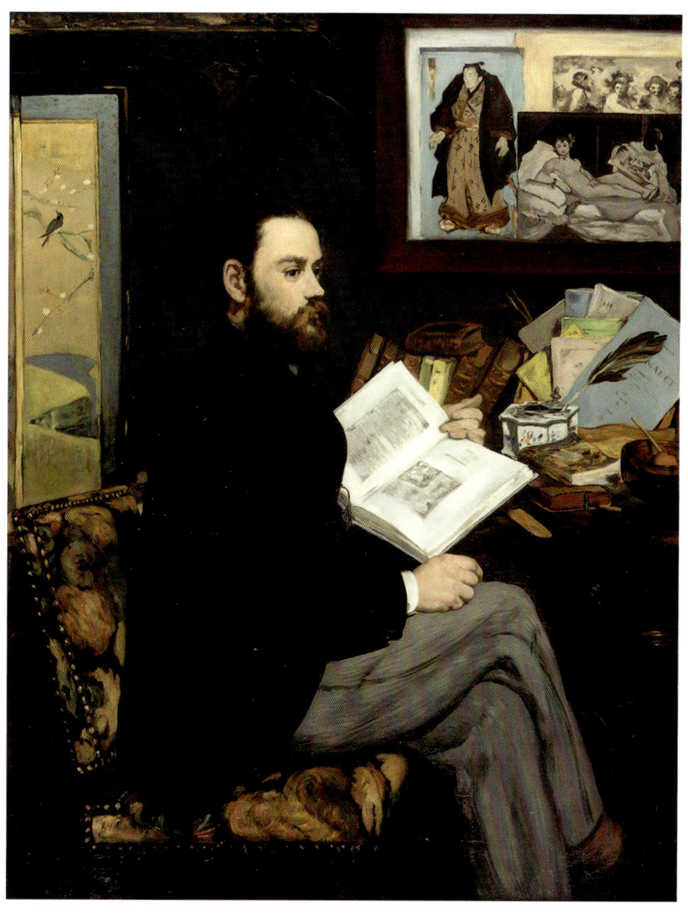

proto-expressionism)—of the photographic source. Manet had been one of the first to adopt this approach, followed, much later, by Picabia (whose nudes based on postcards were rehabilitated around 2000) and many other artists working in the late 20th century, such as Luc Tuymans. What these painters have in common is a way of explicitly emphasizing the reuse of a photograph while handling the source with a certain autographic "partiality." This is the very antithesis of photorealism and Gerhard Richter's analytically deconstructive approach (which represents a kind of late 20th-century pictorial orthodoxy).

The form this version of photomechanical reuse most commonly takes is undoubtedly the *mise en abyme* of the reproduction, placed in the painting "parallel to" the picture plane (a subversion of the pictorial trompe l'œil tradition). This motif could already be observed in the background of Manet's *Zola*, and it reappeared periodically over the following century, sometimes even as the central feature of the image—in some of Malcolm Morley's paintings from the early 1970s, for instance (his role is probably underrated in this lineage). A similar strategy is also at work in the paintings Werner has produced since 2015. The source photographs are portrayed parallel to the picture plane but also in perspective, appearing pinned to a wall, lying on a work table, or in the studio among the artist's paintings. Subsequent to this "contextual" turn, the site of production often becomes the subject of the paintings, which sometimes lack figures altogether. In these cases, there remains nothing but indexical or metonymic traces of their presence, which underscores the materiality and constructed nature of the pictorial apparatus.

This concomitance of a *mise en abyme* of the photographic source and its autographic, pictorial representation is one of the central issues in Werner's recent work, regarding which the digression on Baudelairian modernity might offer yet another interpretative possibility. For what can be the significance of an approach such as this, given that it essentially harks back to a tradition that predates the age of photomechanical reproduction, when the conditions of production in portraiture were entirely different?

Edouard Manet, *Emile Zola*, 1868, oil on canvas / huile sur toile, 57.7 × 45 in. / 147 × 114 cm. Musée d'Orsay, Paris. Photo © RMN-Grand Palais / Art Resource, NY; Adrien Didierjean

Prior to the 19th century, the key signs of a portrait (visual, psychological, ideological) had generally to be captured live, in person, through a series of sensory strategies and informational compressions, streaming swiftly and fluidly between *matière* and body (a kind of "transfer miracle," interestingly summed up in the words addressed by Picasso to one of his models before a sitting: "Are you ready for the extraction?").[12] Several features of pictorial, autographic style in pre-photography portraiture derive in part from this economy of means (painting as a kind of embodied "shorthand," selecting, synthesizing and abbreviating visual information in a way that photography does not).[13]

Clearly, in this context, the preference ultimately goes to the figural and the symbolic rather than the entire visual field, which, with its "riot of details," can even become a source of embarrassment to the artist. "A multitude of trivialities are magnified," writes Baudelaire, "a multitude of little things become usurpers of attention. The more the artist pays impartial attention to detail, the greater does anarchy become."[14]

Aside from this defense of visual discrimination, what is remarkable is the degree to which Baudelaire emphasizes the role of the body in his description of the artist: observing the world in real time, memorizing elements, refiguring then physically executing the work—the crucial moment when the artist's body meets the materiality of the medium.[15]

In light of Baudelaire's insistence on embodiment and the medium's materiality, it would be possible to reformulate the question posed earlier even more precisely and ask "What does it mean exactly to make paintings today, in the style adopted by Werner, based on fashion photographs—a very specific type of imagery that could be described as generally designed to de-individualize and dis-embody bodies to the highest degree?"

Although in fashion the body is assumed to be mainly used as a support for a garment or accessory, the exact opposite could in fact also be argued, that the clothes and accessories are relatively unimportant and merely serve themselves as supports for the staging of a particular ideology of the body (its bio-instrumentalization, even a more or less avowed celebration of its death).[16] After a lengthy (neo-)modernist digression (and in an age of heightened technical nihilism), a number of painters seem to have gradually rediscovered an important medial notion that was already discernible in Manet's era: namely, that the advent of photography ultimately had the effect of "revealing" the autographic (corporeal) nature of painting. From the late 19th century on, it became increasingly evident that a painting is not (or not only) an image (frequently an image of the body), but first and foremost the material trace of an embodied act of language.

Janet Werner's practice "ascends" the flux of the dematerialized images of fashion. But while her paintings reflect an evident fascination for this world, they also "reinject" the empty forms of the mediatized body with kinetic intelligence and a singularity of language (if somewhat parodic). The photographed models that serve as the artist's source, "flatbedded" and slightly disjointed, may well also act as projection screens, pure material supports.[17] In any case, the *mise en abyme* that combines and distorts in the same space fragments of real models (folded, displaced, and reassembled) and fuses them with fictional synthetic characters precludes any delusion of transparency, rather emphasizing the constructed nature of the scenes (echoing, here again, Manet's use of photomontage and the aesthetics of condensation as well as the pastiche, collage, and *mise en abyme* evident in the work of his best-known emulators, Picasso and Picabia[18]).

In fact, this construction process itself could be said to constitute the principal subject of Werner's recent practice. It could even be maintained that the paintings act as a kind of interface between bodies, around the dual issue of language and spectacle. In this sense, rather than a simple comment on the fate of bodies in the age of their interchangeability (their artificial manufacture), Werner's work can be read as a praxis or even (if we accept the diffracted self-portrait hypothesis) a reflection on autographic pictorial style conceived as an agent of plasticity and self-fashioning (a "technology of the self").[19] This type of "technology" should not be seen as a form of "folding into oneself" but, on the contrary, as an understanding of the self *through* the Other that defines painting as a reflexive "*abîme*" of affects that have been seized and rewoven.[20]

After half a century of neoliberalism, the process of self-stylization is generally understood not from the perspective of an ontological dimension of language but rather as a simple shaping of the body as image, a dissolution of the self in the same spectacular mimetic flux that reduces the organism solely to quantitative performance.[21] From the viewpoint of private experience, this new doxa seems now to quite easily accept that, as far as the issue of "reality" is concerned, an extraordinary inversion is destined to take place between concrete life ("meat life") and digital life. Werner's work has always been a site of mediation between inner experience and the collective and mediatized transformations of the body, but it is only in the last few years that this mediation has fully revealed itself as a more explicit and crucial reflection on what is at stake in the history of painting as a language and the medium's lengthy and fraught negotiation with the expanded history of "images."

—

ENDNOTES

1 Paul Bloom, "First Person Plural," *The Atlantic*, November 2008, https://www.theatlantic.com/magazine/archive/2008/11/first-person-plural/307055/.

2 "The *mask upon the face* and the *face on the body* do not ultimately stand in contradiction to each other. On the contrary, they have the same relationship that unites nature and culture." Hans Belting, *Face and Mask: A Double History* (Princeton and Oxford: Princeton University Press, 2017), 18. On the face-body relation, see also Gilles Deleuze and Félix Guattari, "Année Zéro – Visagéité," chap. 7 in *Mille plateaux* (Paris: Les Éditions de Minuit, 1980).

3 Of interest here are the recent reflections of the German critic Isabelle Graw, who suggests that the seductive power of the "highly successful" medium of painting resides in a vitalist fantasy involving an *imprint* in paint (index) of the artist's body (transforming the painting itself into a "quasi person"). Isabelle Graw, *The Love of Painting: Genealogy of a Success Medium* (Berlin and New York: Sternberg Press, 2018).

4 The Russian literary theorist Mikhaïl Bakhtin characterizes the novels of Dostoevsky as a dynamic ensemble where there unfolds "not a multitude of characters and fates in a single objective world, illuminated by a single authorial consciousness; rather a plurality of consciousnesses, with equal rights and each with its own world, combine but are not merged in the unity of the event." Each of these consciousnesses, writes Bakhtin, "is not impelled toward a well-rounded, finalized, systemically monologic whole. It lives a tense life on the borders of someone else's thought, someone else's consciousness." Mikhaïl M. Bakhtin, *Problems of Dostoevsky's Poetics*, ed. and trans. Caryl Emerson (Minneapolis: University of Minnesota Press, 1984), 6, 32. See also Tzvetan Todorov, "Anthropologie philosophique," in Mikhaïl Bakhtine, *Le principe dialogique, suivi de Ecrits du Cercle de Bakhtine* (Paris: Seuil, 1981).

5 Werner actually studied alongside the last two while in the MFA program at Yale University (1985–1987).

6 See, as characteristic examples of this approach, the exhibition *John Currin, Elizabeth Peyton, Luc Tuymans: Projects 60*, curated by Laura Hoptman and presented at MoMA, New York, in 1997, and especially *Dear Painter, Paint me… Painting the Figure Since Late Picabia*, organized by Sabine Folie, Alison M. Gingeras, and Blazenka Perica and presented at the Centre Georges-Pompidou, Paris, the Kunsthalle Wien, Vienna, and the Schirn Kunsthalle, Frankfurt, in 2002 and 2003.

7 Charles Baudelaire, *The Painter of Modern Life*, trans. P. E. Charvet (London: Penguin Books, 2010). This essay features Baudelaire's famous definition of modernity: "Modernity is the transient, the fleeting, the contingent; it is one half of art, the other being the eternal and the immovable" (p. 18). Earlier in the text, the poet explains that this definition is based on a "rational and *historical* theory of beauty, in contrast to the theory of a unique and absolute beauty … Beauty is made up, on the one hand, of an element that is eternal and invariable, though to determine how much of it there is is extremely difficult, and, on the other of a relative circumstantial element,

which we may like to call, successively or at one and the same time, contemporaneity, fashion, morality, passion. Without this second element, which is like the amusing, teasing, appetite-whetting coating of the divine cake, the first element would be indigestible, tasteless, unadapted and inappropriate to human nature. I challenge anyone to find any sample whatsoever of beauty that does not contain these two elements" (p. 8; italics added). For a discussion of the apparent divergences between Manet and Baudelaire, see J. A. Hiddleston, "Baudelaire, Manet, and Modernity," *The Modern Language Review 87*, no. 3 (July 1992), 567–575.

8 "For sketches of manners, for the portrayal of bourgeois life and the fashion scene, the quickest and the cheapest technical means will evidently be the best. The more beauty the artist puts into it, the more valuable will the work be; but there is in the trivial things of life, in the daily changing of external things, a speed of movement that imposes upon the artist an equal speed of execution." Baudelaire, *Painter*, 9.

9 Walter Benjamin, "Paris, the Capital of the Nineteenth Century," in *The Arcades Project*, trans. Howard Eiland and Kevin McLaughlin (Cambridge, Mass. and London: Harvard University Press, 1999). On the question of the fragment in modernity and its role in Manet's work, see Linda Nochlin, *The Body in Pieces: The Fragment as a Metaphor of Modernity* (London: Thames & Hudson, 1994). See also *David Frisby, Fragments of Modernity: Theories of Modernity in the Work of Simmel, Kracauer and Benjamin* (Cambridge: Polity Press, 1985).

10 Manet is described as the "first of the anti-modernists" in Éric Alliez, ed., with Jean-Clet Martin, "Sur la voie nouvelle du contemporain. Le plan Manet," chap. 3 in *L'œil-cerveau. Nouvelles histoires de la peinture modern* (Paris: Vrin, 2007), 184. On the subject of parody, see Yve-Alain Bois, "Picasso the Trickster," in *Picasso Harlequin 1917–1937*, (Milan: Skira, 2008), exhibition catalog. See also Gérard Genette, *Palimpsestes. La littérature au second degré*, sections 2–4 (Paris: Seuil, 1982); Dragan Kujundzic, "Tynianov and Bakhtin: Parody as a Malfunctioning Gramophone of History," in *The Returns of History: Russian Nietzscheans After Modernity* (Albany: SUNY, "The Margins of Literature" collection, 1997), 37–48.

11 Jean Clay, "Onguents, fards, pollens," in *Bonjour Monsieur Manet*, eds. Catherine David, Isabelle Monod-Fontaine, and Frédérique Mirotchnikoff (Paris: Centre Georges Pompidou, 1983), exhibition catalog, 6.

12 David Elliott, "Janet Werner: Paint Person," *Canadian Art* (summer 2002), 48. Pat Gilmour, "Piero Crommelynck," *Print Quarterly* 18, no. 2, 2001, 164–190.

13 Baudelaire, *Painter*, 21.

14 Baudelaire, *Painter*, 22–23.

15 Constantin Guys is described as directing "his steady gaze on a sheet of paper, exactly the same gaze as he directed just now at the things about him, brandishing his pencil, his pen, his brush, splashing water from the glass up to the ceiling, wiping his pen on his shirt, hurried, vigorous, active, as though he was afraid the images might escape him, quarrelsome though alone" (Baudelaire, *Painter*, 17). Further on, the poet describes the ideal connection between visual memory and an execution that is "as unconscious, as *flowing*, as the process of digesting is for the brain of a healthy man after dinner" (Baudelaire, *Painter*, 23).

16 In 1824 the Italian poet Giacomo Leopardi wrote a fine poem that took the form of an allegorical dialogue between Fashion and Death, a kind of mutual declaration of love in which the two protagonists call themselves "sisters" and swear to work in greater harmony in the future (Giacomo Leopardi, *Operette morali*, "Dialog della moda et della morte," Bari, 1928). In his "Exposé of 1935," Walter Benjamin follows a quote from this poem with the following remark: "Fashion stands in opposition to the organic. It couples the living body to the inorganic world. To the living, it defends the rights of the corpse. The fetishism that succumbs to the sex appeal of the inorganic is its vital nerve. The cult of the commodity presses such fetishism into its service." Benjamin, 8.

17 The notion of the "flatbed" picture plane was introduced by the American art historian Leo Steinberg in an article published in *Artforum* in 1972. The expression, borrowed from the world of printing, describes the "picture plane of the 1960s," typified in the work of Robert Rauschenberg, which "makes its symbolic allusion to hard surfaces such as tabletops, studio floors, charts, bulletin boards—any receptor surface on which objects are scattered, on which data is entered, on which information may be received, printed, impressed—whether coherently or in confusion. The pictures of the last fifteen to twenty years insist on a radically new orientation, in which the painted surface is no longer the analogue of a visual experience of nature but of operational processes." Leo Steinberg, "Other Criteria: The Flatbed Picture Plane," in *Other Criteria: Confrontations with Twentieth-Century Art* (New York: Oxford University Press, 1972).

18 On the many aspects of the aesthetics of abbreviation in Manet's work, see Alliez, 2007, and also Jonathan Crary, "1879: Unbinding Vision," chap. 2 in *Suspensions of Perception: Attention, Spectacle, and Modern Culture* (Cambridge and London: MIT Press, 1999).

19 On the notion of plasticity, see Catherine Malabou, ed., *Plasticité* (Paris: Léo Scheer, 2000). On the notion of technologies of the self, see Michel Foucault, "Technologies of the Self," in *Technologies of the Self: A Seminar with Michel Foucault*, eds. Luther Martin, Huck Gutman, Patrick H. Hutton (Amherst: University of Massachusetts Press, 1988). For more on these topics, see also Laurent Jenny, "Du style comme pratique," *Littérature* 118 (2000).

20 "Thus the lover of universal life moves into the crowd as though into an enormous reservoir of electricity. He, the lover of life, may also be compared to a mirror as vast as this crowd; to a kaleidoscope endowed with consciousness, which with every one of its movements presents a pattern of life, in all its multiplicity, and the flowing grace of all the elements that go to compose life. It is an *ego* athirst for the *non-ego*, and reflecting it at every moment in energies more vivid than life itself, always inconstant and fleeting." Baudelaire, *Painter*, 14.

21 On Foucault and early neoliberalism, see especially Mitchell Dean and Daniel Zamora, *Le dernier homme et la fin de la révolution. Foucault après Mai 68* (Montréal: Lux Éditeur, 2019).

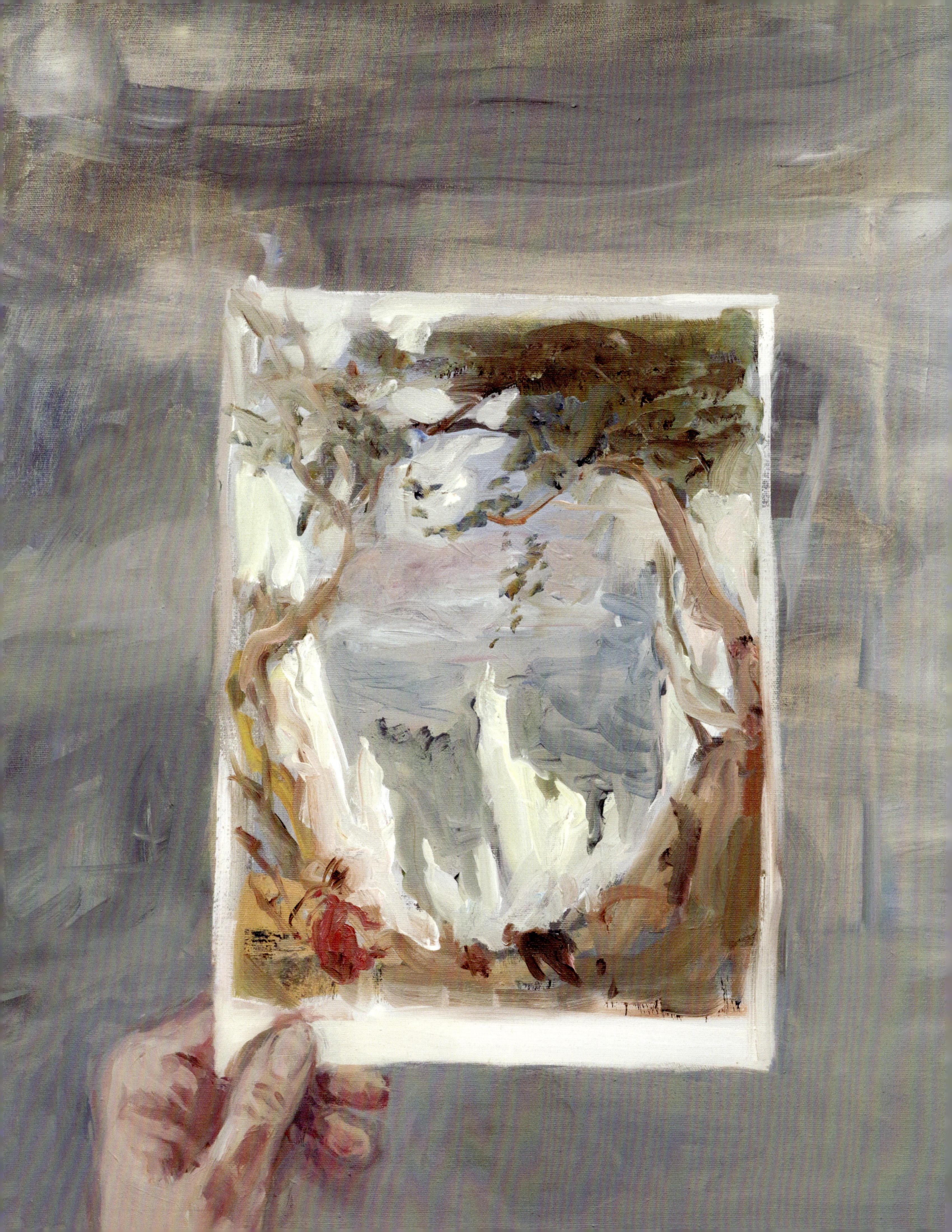

Membra Disjecta:
Notes sur le travail récent de Janet Werner

FRANÇOIS LETOURNEUX

I.

Depuis la fin des années 1980, Janet Werner a développé un genre unique de portrait fictif, passant tout d'abord (et de façon quasi programmatique) de formes abstraites et d'idéogrammes à des figures un peu brutes et stylisées, de dimensions souvent modestes, disposées en installations. À ces premières figures succédèrent rapidement des portraits plus colorés de taille croissante, dans un style qui empruntait à la photographie. Depuis l'an 2000, Werner utilise explicitement des clichés de mode trouvés (principalement de modèles féminins), qu'elle manipule fréquemment selon la technique du cadavre exquis. Des parties des figures s'y trouvent pliées, découpées, réarrangées puis de nouveau transformées par diverses opérations picturales (ajouts iconographiques, déformation des corps et des objets, jeux de matières, etc.).

Les personnages composites qui résultent de ce processus ont souvent été abordés du point de vue de questions de genre et de représentation. Leur joliesse, leur expression parfois inquiète, ainsi que les processus de distorsion ou de destruction auxquels leur image peut être soumise, évoquent en effet un conditionnement idéologique qui exploite et cultive la vulnérabilité psychologique. Depuis que Werner a commencé sa carrière, le nombre d'images de figures humaines auxquelles notre regard est soumis a explosé sous l'effet du paradigme numérique ; et cette foule médiatique de personnages (réels ou fictifs) est devenue l'objet privilégié de notre attention, bien avant la sexualité, la nourriture, la drogue ou le sport[1]. La plasticité des personnages de Werner nous parle d'un sentiment d'irréalité accrue, où l'image que nous nous faisons de nous-mêmes inclut divers degrés d'identification à ces innombrables archétypes. On peut lire dans les tableaux de l'artiste l'écho des effets quasi hallucinatoires que la manipulation et la multiplication des images ont générés dans la psyché au cours des dernières décennies : un gouffre s'y creuse entre l'expérience personnelle du corps et l'infinie variation de ses images « dématérialisées ».

Comme on l'a souvent noté, les personnages de Werner évoquent aussi les mondes de l'humour et de l'imaginaire, jouant eux-mêmes de séduction et de faux-semblants. Le visage nu, avant même d'être paré, peut notoirement se constituer en « masque » sous l'effet d'une modification de l'expression. Et qu'est-ce que le maquillage, si ce n'est une suite de films de peinture appliqués au corps, principalement au visage, pour en modifier les signes (accentuant ou obscurcissant certains éléments, en introduisant d'autres) ? À notre époque, finalement, le visage maquillé se transforme encore davantage sous l'action d'innombrables filtres numériques. Le visage en peinture, a fortiori le « faux portrait » composite wernérien, réalisé à partir d'images modifiées, est donc une sorte de masque à couches multiples dont on peut trop facilement tenter de lire l'expression « réelle », alors qu'il s'inscrit dans une politique de représentation complexe (dont les éléments sont aussi stratégiques qu'involontaires). Finalement, comme ces tableaux dépeignent habituellement des figures quasi complètes, rappelons que le masque, acté ou réel, entretient le même type de rapport avec le visage que le visage lui-même avec l'ensemble du corps : il s'y pose dans une relation qui, souligne Hans Belting, unifie la nature et la culture[2]. Ainsi s'efface évidemment l'espoir de voir captée en peinture toute distinction certaine entre une quelconque nudité ou authenticité psychologique et l'effet des artifices sociaux.

CDF, 2020
24 × 20 in. / 61 × 51 cm

Des couches de maquillage à la peau, de la surface d'un visage à la pellicule photosensible, du modèle au support pictural, via le propre corps de l'artiste : autant de zones-contact où se noue la fascination du regard – voire même un effet de convoitise[3].

De telles allusions au masque et au maquillage doivent-elles nous mettre sur la piste d'une typologie de « rôles » qui éclairerait cette galerie de personnages ? Certes, plusieurs d'entre eux paraissent posséder des qualités caricaturales, voire allégoriques. Mais ils possèdent aussi une sorte de singularité irréductible, qui résulte de leur réinvention en peinture (alors qu'ils apparaissent presque systématiquement comme des « types » dans les clichés d'origine). Vus ensemble (effet qu'une exposition ou un livre monographique produisent inévitablement), ces *dramatis personae* paraissent aussi engager un dialogue sur la nature plurielle de la subjectivité. À cet égard, l'œuvre de Werner pourrait bien être lu comme une construction polyphonique bakhtinienne[4], un vaste autoportrait diffracté. L'« individu », semble-t-il dire, est toujours multiple. Ainsi, l'approche scénographique de l'expérience intérieure proposée par Werner offre une alternative intéressante au discours médiatique sur l'identité, qui tend actuellement à proposer un spectre restreint et plutôt rigide de positions d'appartenance.

L'abord pluriel de la subjectivité dont il vient d'être question s'attache aux importants travaux sur l'intertextualité qui sont apparus vers la fin des années 1960 et ont considérablement marqué la scène artistique des deux dernières décennies du XXe siècle. Janet Werner fait en effet partie d'une génération d'artistes comme George Condo, Luc Tuymans, Karen Kilimnik, Lisa Yuskavage ou John Currin[5], qui donnèrent une nouvelle impulsion à la forme du portrait, dans la foulée du réexamen critique de la peinture figurative, à la fin des années 1990. Contrairement à l'approche néo-conceptuelle d'un Gerhard Richter, celle de plusieurs de ces artistes reprenait l'emploi, par les premières avant-gardes, du pastiche pictural et d'images de médias de masse[6], recourant au kitsch, à la technique du *mash-up* et à la parodie, dans le contexte d'un postmodernisme qui investissait plus généralement la culture de consommation et la question complexe de l'identité. Ce retour du médium sur l'avant-scène de l'art contemporain annonçait déjà sa forte popularité auprès de la jeune génération d'aujourd'hui.

II.

Au cours de la dernière décennie, les références à l'humour et au carnavalesque se sont estompées dans la production de Werner au profit d'une approche plus « mesurée », qui rappelle quelque peu l'héritage de Manet et la définition de la modernité proposée par Baudelaire dans son célèbre article sur Constantin Guys[7]. En regardant les tableaux de Werner, plusieurs sujets clefs de cet article nous reviennent à l'esprit, ces phénomènes « modernes » par excellence, selon Baudelaire, que l'on ne retrouvait pas dépeints dans les œuvres du Salon ou du Louvre : le monde des femmes de l'époque, du maquillage et de la mode, ou encore la figure du dandy. On repense aussi aux commentaires du poète sur la technique du peintre moderne, notamment sur sa nécessaire « vélocité d'exécution[8] ». Impossible également de ne pas songer à l'esthétique du fragment que l'on retrouve plus généralement chez Baudelaire (ainsi que dans le travail de son célèbre interprète, Walter Benjamin, particulièrement attentif aux figures du flâneur et du chiffonnier), mais aussi chez Manet[9], dont l'œuvre est marqué d'innombrables découpes iconographiques ou matérielles, indissociables de son usage de la citation.

Rappelons d'ailleurs à ce sujet qu'après avoir bien longtemps été salué comme figure fondatrice du modernisme pictural (dans l'acception greenbergienne de ce terme, qui mettait l'accent sur la planéité du tableau), la pratique de Manet s'est progressivement vue rattacher à un mouvement de modernité « antimoderniste », en raison de l'importance accordée par l'artiste à la tradition

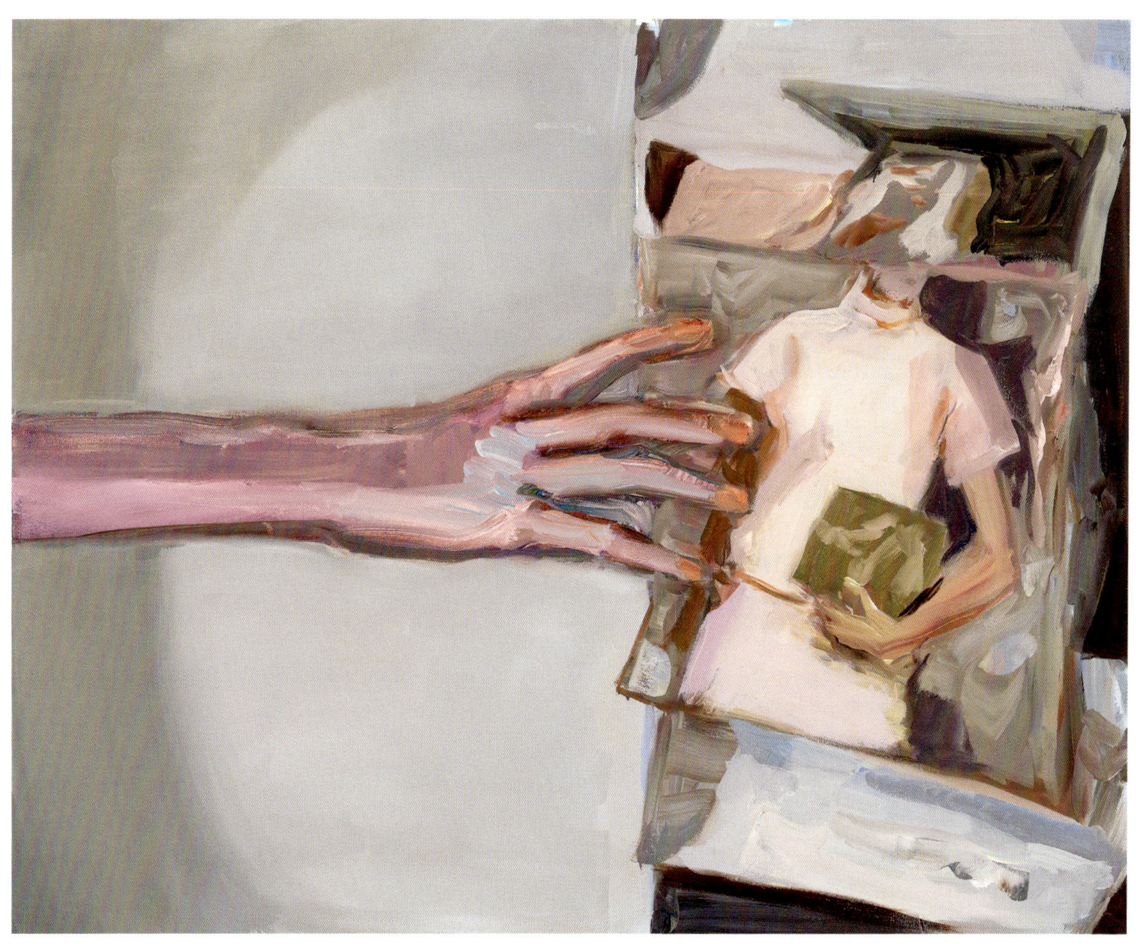

Reach, 2019
22 × 28 in. / 56 × 71 cm

picturale, à l'artifice scénographique, aux accessoires et aux costumes, et au pastiche stylistique compris comme « seconde main » parodique[10]. Tous ces aspects font aussi retour dans l'œuvre récent de Werner.

Il y a aussi, bien entendu, la question du modèle photographique, fréquemment utilisé par Manet dans sa peinture, au point que le traitement pictural des figures en garde notoirement la trace (« Il aurait peint en quelque sorte non Victorine Meurent mais sa photo, non son image mais sa reproduction[11] »). Et pour finir, la question plus spécifique (et décisive encore) du traitement pictural de la source photographique, de type *alla prima* (faute d'un meilleur terme ; du moins faut-il le distinguer d'un quelconque proto-expressionnisme). Manet avait été l'un des premiers à adopter cette approche, après qui il faut évidemment mentionner, beaucoup plus tardivement, Picabia (dont les nus réalisés à partir de cartes postales sont réhabilités au tournant des années 2000), et bien d'autres encore à la fin du XXe siècle, comme Luc Tuymans. Ces peintres ont en commun de souligner explicitement le remploi photographique, tout en traitant la source avec une certaine « partialité » autographique. Une telle approche se situe aux antipodes du photoréalisme ou de la déconstruction analytique d'un Gerhard Richter (qui représente en quelque sorte l'orthodoxie picturale de la seconde moitié du XXe siècle).

La forme la plus commune que prend cette désignation du remploi photomécanique est évidemment la mise en abyme de la reproduction, disposée « parallèlement » au plan orthogonal du tableau (un détournement de la tradition du trompe-l'œil pictural). On observe déjà ce motif à l'arrière-plan du *Zola* de Manet (voir page 37). Il réapparaît périodiquement au siècle suivant, parfois même en tant qu'objet principal de la représentation, comme dans certains tableaux de Malcolm Morley du début des années 1970 (probablement trop peu estimés du point de vue de cette histoire). Une stratégie semblable intervient dans les tableaux de Werner depuis 2015. Les photographies sources y sont dépeintes parallèlement au plan du tableau, mais aussi en perspective. Elles apparaissent épinglées au mur, sur une table de travail ou parmi les tableaux réalisés par l'artiste dans l'espace de l'atelier. Suite à ce tournant « contextuel », où le site de production devient souvent le sujet de la représentation, les œuvres font parfois même l'économie de figures. N'apparaissent plus alors que des traces indicielles ou métonymiques de leur présence, qui font ressortir la matérialité et la dimension construite du dispositif pictural.

Cette concomitance de la mise en abyme de la source photographique et de son traitement pictural autographique est un enjeu central de la production récente de Werner, vis-à-vis duquel le détour par la modernité baudelairienne offre peut-être une autre piste de lecture. Quel sens, en effet, ce traitement peut-il bien avoir, considérant qu'il renoue finalement avec une tradition qui précède l'ère de la reproduction photomécanique, dans laquelle les conditions de production du portrait étaient tout autres ?

Jusqu'au XIXe siècle en effet, les signes clefs du portrait (visuels, psychologiques, idéologiques) devaient le plus souvent être captés sur le vif (en coprésence), par une série de stratégies sensorielles et de compression de l'information, donnant lieu à des échanges fluides et rapides entre la matière et les corps (un apparent « transfert miracle[12] » qu'illustrent assez bien les paroles adressées un jour par Picasso à l'un de ses modèles, avant la séance de pose : « Êtes-vous prêts pour l'extraction ?[13] »). Plusieurs aspects du style pictural autographique, avant l'avènement de la photographie, découlent pour partie de cette économie de moyens (la peinture comme notation ou *shorthand* incorporé : discriminant, « synthétisant et abrégeant[14] » les informations visuelles, ce que la photographie ne fait pas).

Évidemment, dans un tel contexte, la préférence va, pour finir, au figural et au symbolique plutôt qu'à la totalité du champ visuel, qui peut même devenir pour l'artiste une source d'embarras, avec son « émeute de détails » : « Toute trivialité, écrit Baudelaire, devient énorme ; mainte petitesse, usurpatrice. Plus l'artiste se penche avec impartialité vers le détail, plus l'anarchie augmente[15]. » Outre cette valorisation de la discrimination visuelle, il est remarquable que Baudelaire insiste autant sur le rôle du corps, lorsqu'il décrit le processus d'observation du monde en temps réel, le travail de mémorisation, puis de re-figuration et, finalement, l'exécution elle-même, ce moment de rencontre crucial entre le corps de l'artiste et la matérialité du médium[16].

À partir de cette insistance sur le corps et la matérialité du médium, nous pourrions reformuler la question précédente de façon plus précise encore, et demander : que signifie exactement le fait de peindre aujourd'hui, dans le style emprunté par Werner, d'après la photographie de mode, qui est un type très particulier de cliché dont on peut dire qu'il est le plus souvent conçu pour désindividuer et désincarner au maximum les corps ?

En effet, bien que, dans la mode, le corps soit habituellement employé comme simple support pour le vêtement ou l'accessoire, une idée contraire pourrait tout aussi bien être avancée, à savoir que les vêtements et les accessoires y importent finalement assez peu, qu'ils ne sont eux-mêmes que des supports pour la mise en scène d'une idéologie particulière du corps (une bio-instrumentalisation, si ce n'est d'une célébration plus ou moins occulte de sa mort[17]). Après la longue parenthèse (néo-) moderniste (et à une époque de nihilisme technique avancé), de nombreux peintres semblent avoir progressivement redécouvert une importante notion médiale qui commençait déjà à devenir perceptible à l'époque de Manet, à savoir que l'apparition de la photographie avait finalement joué le rôle de « révélateur » de la nature autographique (corporelle) de la peinture. Il devient en effet plus clair à partir de la fin du XIXe siècle qu'un tableau n'est pas (ou pas seulement) une image (typiquement, une image de corps), mais d'abord et avant tout la trace matérielle d'un acte de langage incorporé.

Le projet de Janet Werner « remonte » le flux des images dématérialisées de la mode. Certes, on y lit une certaine fascination pour ce monde, mais ses tableaux « réinjectent » aussi dans les formes vides du corps médiatisé une intelligence kinésique et une singularité de langage (fût-elle relativement parodique). Sans doute les modèles photographiés qui servent de source à l'artiste, mis à plat et légèrement écartelés[18], demeurent-ils aussi des écrans de projection, de purs supports matériels. Quoi qu'il en soit, la mise en abyme qui entremêle et dénature dans un même espace les fragments de modèles réels (pliés, retournés et collés), et les intègre à des personnages synthétiques fictifs, récuse tout fantasme de transparence, soulignant au contraire la nature construite de ces scènes (échos, ici encore, du photomontage et de l'esthétique du raccord chez Manet[19], puis des travaux sur le pastiche, le collage et la mise en abyme chez ses plus célèbres épigones, Picasso et Picabia).

C'est d'ailleurs ce chantier même qui devient, pourrait-on dire, le sujet propre de la pratique récente de Werner. On pourrait même dire que les tableaux y deviennent une sorte d'*interface* entre les corps, autour du double enjeu du langage et du spectacle. À cet égard, davantage qu'un simple commentaire sur le destin des corps à l'ère de leur interchangeabilité (c'est-à-dire de leur fabrication artificielle), le travail de Werner peut être lu comme une praxis, voire même, suivant l'hypothèse de l'autoportrait diffracté, comme une réflexion sur le style pictural autographique en tant qu'agent de plasticité et technique de soi *(self-fashioning)*[20]. Une telle « technique » ne parle pas d'un quelconque repli sur soi, mais bien au contraire d'une compréhension de soi à travers l'Autre[21], qui définit la peinture comme « abîme » réflexif d'affects, saisis et re-tramés.

Au terme d'un demi-siècle de néolibéralisme[22], le processus d'auto-stylisation est plus souvent compris non pas du point de vue de la dimension ontologique du langage, mais bien comme simple entraînement du corps-image, comme fonte de soi dans le flux mimétique spectaculaire, qui réduit aussi l'organisme à la stricte performance quantitative. Du point de vue de l'intimité, cette nouvelle doxa semble même admettre désormais sans trop de difficulté qu'en ce qui concerne la notion de « réalité », une interversion extraordinaire est vouée à s'accomplir entre la vie concrète (la « vie de viande ») et la vie numérique. Si l'œuvre de Werner a toujours été le lieu d'une médiation entre l'expérience intérieure et les transformations collectives et médiatiques du corps, ce n'est qu'au cours des dernières années que cette médiation s'est pleinement révélée comme réflexion plus explicite et cruciale sur les enjeux historiques du langage pictural, et sur sa longue et difficile négociation avec le devenir plus large de « l'image ».

—

NOTES EN FIN DE TEXTE

1 Paul Bloom, « First Person Plural », *The Atlantic*, 2008, https://www.theatlantic.com/magazine/archive/2008/11/first-person-plural/307055/.

2 « The *mask upon the face* and the *face on the body* do not ultimately stand in contradiction to each other. On the contrary, they have the same relationship that unites nature and culture. » Hans Belting, *Face and Mask. A Double History*, Princeton et Oxford, Princeton University Press, 2017, p. 18. Sur l'articulation visage-corps, voir aussi Gilles Deleuze et Félix Guattari, « Année Zéro - Visagéité », chap. 7 dans *Mille plateaux*, Paris, Les Éditions de Minuit, 1980.

3 Fait qu'éclairent de façon intéressante les réflexions récentes de la critique allemande Isabelle Graw, selon qui l'effet de séduction particulier de la peinture, ce « médium à succès », relèverait essentiellement d'un fantasme vitaliste, lié à l'*empreinte* [*index*] laissée par l'artiste dans le tableau (faisant de ce dernier une « quasi-personne »). Isabelle Graw, *The Love of Painting. Genealogy of a Success Medium*, Berlin et New York, Sternberg Press, 2018.

4 Le théoricien de la littérature russe Mikhaïl Bakhtine a proposé de voir dans le roman dostoïevskien un ensemble dynamique où n'intervient pas une « pluralité de caractères et de destins se développant au sein

d'un monde unique, monde objectif éclairé par l'unique conscience de l'auteur, mais véritablement [une] multiplicité de consciences pleinement qualifiées, possédant chacune leur monde et se combinant [...] dans l'unité d'un événement tout en restant non confondues ». Chacune de ces consciences « ne vise pas, écrit Bakhtine, à former un tout poli et achevé qui serait système et monologue. Elle mène une existence tendue aux frontières de la pensée de l'autre, de la conscience de l'autre. » Mikhaïl M. Bakhtine, *Problèmes de la poétique de Dostoïevski*, Lausanne, L'Âge d'Homme, 1970, p. 10 et 42. Voir aussi Tzvetan Todorov, « Anthropologie philosophique », *Mikhaïl Bakhtine le principe dialogique*, suivi de *Écrits du Cercle de Bakhtine*, Paris, Seuil, 1981.

5 Werner côtoya d'ailleurs ces deux derniers artistes alors qu'elle était inscrite au programme de maîtrise en arts visuels de l'Université Yale (1985-1987).

6 Voir comme exemples caractéristiques de cette mouvance l'exposition *John Currin, Elizabeth Peyton, Luc Tuymans. Projects 60*, commissariée par Laura Hoptman et présentée au MoMA (New York) en 1997, et surtout *Dear Painter, Paint me... Painting the Figure Since Late Picabia*, organisée par Sabine Folie, Alison M. Gingeras et Blazenka Perica, présentée au Centre Georges-Pompidou (Paris), à la Kunsthalle Wien (Vienne) et à la Schirn Kunsthalle (Francfort) en 2002 et 2003.

7 Charles Baudelaire, « Le peintre de la vie moderne », *Critique d'art*, suivi de *Critique musicale*, Paris, Gallimard, coll. « Folio », 1992. Dans cet article, Baudelaire produit sa définition bien connue de la modernité : « La modernité, c'est le transitoire, le fugitif, le contingent, la moitié de l'art, dont l'autre moitié est l'éternel et l'immuable », p. 355. Plus tôt dans le texte, le poète précise que cette définition s'ancre dans « une théorie rationnelle et *historique* du beau, en opposition avec la théorie du beau unique et absolu » [nous soulignons] : « Le beau est fait d'un élément éternel, invariable, dont la quantité est excessivement difficile à déterminer, et d'un élément relatif, circonstanciel, qui sera, si l'on veut, tour à tour ou tout ensemble, l'époque, la mode, la morale, la passion. Sans ce second élément, qui est comme l'enveloppe amusante, titillante, apéritive, du divin gâteau, le premier élément serait indigestible, inappréciable, non adapté et non approprié à la nature humaine. Je défie qu'on découvre un échantillon quelconque de beauté qui ne contienne pas ces deux éléments », p. 345. Pour une discussion des divergences apparentes entre Manet et Baudelaire, voir J. A. Hiddleston, « Baudelaire, Manet, and Modernity », *The Modern Language Review*, vol. 87, n° 3 (juillet 1992), p. 567-575.

8 « Pour le croquis de mœurs, la représentation de la vie bourgeoise et les spectacles de la mode, le moyen le plus expéditif et le moins coûteux est évidemment le meilleur. Plus l'artiste y mettra de beauté, plus l'œuvre sera précieuse ; mais il y a dans la vie triviale, dans la métamorphose journalière des choses extérieures, un mouvement rapide qui commande à l'artiste une égale vélocité d'exécution. » Baudelaire, *loc. cit.*, p. 346.

9 Walter Benjamin, *Paris, Capitale du XIXe siècle. Le livre des passages*, Paris, Les Éditions du Cerf, 2009. Sur la question du fragment dans la modernité et sur son rôle chez Manet, voir Linda Nochlin, *The Body in Pieces. The Fragment as a Metaphor of Modernity*, Londres, Thames & Hudson, 1994. Voir aussi David Frisby, *Fragments of Modernity: Theories of Modernity in the Work of Simmel, Kracauer and Benjamin*, Cambridge, Polity Press, 1985.

10 Manet est qualifié de « premier des antimodernistes » dans Éric Alliez (avec la collaboration de Jean-Clet Martin), « Sur la voie nouvelle du contemporain : le plan Manet », chap. 3 dans *L'œil-cerveau. Nouvelles histoires de la peinture moderne*, Paris, Vrin, 2007, p. 184. Sur la question de la parodie, voir Yve-Alain Bois, « Picasso the trickster », *Picasso Harlequin 1917-1937*, catalogue d'exposition, Complesso del Vittoriano, Rome (11 octobre 2008-8 février 2009), Milan, Skira, 2009. Voir aussi Gérard Genette, *Palimpsestes. La littérature au second degré*, Paris, Seuil, 1982, sections II-IV ; et Dragan Kujundzic, « Tynianov and Bakhtin: Parody as a Malfunctioning Gramophone of History », *The Returns of History: Russian Nietzscheans After Modernity*, Albany, SUNY, coll. « The Margins of Literature », 1997, p. 37-48.

11 Jean Clay, « Onguents, fards, pollens », *Bonjour Monsieur Manet*, catalogue d'exposition, dir. Catherine David, Isabelle Monod-Fontaine, Frédérique Mirotchnikoff, Paris, Centre Georges Pompidou, 1983, p. 6.

12 David Elliott, « Janet Werner: Paint Person », *Canadian Art*, été 2002, p. 48.

13 Pat Gilmour, « Piero Crommelynck », *Print Quarterly*, vol. 18, n° 2, p. 164-190.

14 Baudelaire, *loc. cit.*, p. 346.

15 Baudelaire, *loc. cit.*, p. 358-359.

16 Constantin Guys est décrit comme « dardant sur une feuille de papier le même regard qu'il attachait tout à l'heure sur les choses, s'escrimant avec son crayon, sa plume, son pinceau, faisant jaillir l'eau du verre au plafond, essuyant sa plume sur sa chemise, pressé, violent, actif, comme s'il craignait que les images ne lui échappent, querelleur quoique seul, et se bousculant lui-même », p. 353. Plus loin, le poète décrit l'articulation

idéale de la mémoire visuelle et de l'exécution comme « aussi inconsciente, aussi *coulante* que l'est la digestion pour le cerveau de l'homme bien portant qui a dîné », p. 359.

17 En 1824, le poète italien Giacomo Leopardi écrit un beau poème prenant la forme d'un dialogue allégorique entre la Mode et la Mort, qui est une sorte de déclaration d'amour mutuelle, les deux figures se disant « sœurs » et se promettant de mieux travailler ensemble à l'avenir (Giacomo Leopardi, *Operette morali*, « Dialog della moda et della morte », Bari, 1928). Dans son « Exposé de 1935 », Walter Benjamin fait suivre une citation de ce poème du commentaire suivant : « La mode est en conflit avec l'organique. Elle accouple le monde vivant au monde inorganique. Vis-à-vis du vivant elle défend les droits du cadavre. Le fétichisme qui succombe au sex-appeal de l'inorganique est le nerf vital de la mode. Le culte de la marchandise le prend à son service. » *Op. cit.* note 9, p. 40.

18 L'expression « mis à plat » fait référence à l'esthétique du *flatbed* décrite par l'historien de l'art américain Leo Steinberg dans un article publié dans la revue *Artforum* en 1972. L'expression, venue du monde de l'imprimerie, décrit « le plan pictural des années 1960 », caractéristique de l'œuvre de Robert Rauschenberg, qui « fait allusion symbolique à des surfaces dures telles que dessus de tables, planchers d'ateliers, graphiques, tableaux d'affichage – toute surface réceptive sur laquelle des objets sont éparpillés, des données inscrites, de l'information reçue, imprimée, publiée – de façon cohérente ou pêle-mêle. Les images des dernières quinze ou vingt années insistent sur une orientation radicalement neuve, dans laquelle la surface peinte n'est plus analogue à une expérience visuelle de la nature, mais à un processus opératoire » [notre traduction]. Leo Steinberg, « Other Criteria: The Flatbed Picture Plane », *Other Criteria: Confrontations with Twentieth-Century Art*, New York, Oxford University Press, 1972.

19 Sur les multiples enjeux de l'esthétique du raccord chez Manet, voir Alliez, *loc. cit.*, ainsi que Jonathan Crary, « 1879: Unbinding Vision », chap. 2 dans *Suspensions of Perception. Attention, Spectacle, and Modern Culture*, Cambridge et Londres, MIT Press, 1999.

20 Sur la notion de plasticité, voir Catherine Malabou (dir.), *Plasticité*, Paris, Léo Scheer, 2000. Sur la notion de technique de soi, voir Michel Foucault, « Technologies of the Self », *Technologies of the Self. A Seminar with Michel Foucault*, Luther Martin, Huck Gutman, Patrick H. Hutton, Amherst, University of Massachusetts Press, 1988. Voir également sur ces questions Laurent Jenny, « Du style comme pratique », *Littérature*, n° 118, 2000.

21 « Ainsi l'amoureux de la vie universelle entre dans la foule comme dans un immense réservoir d'électricité. On peut aussi le comparer, lui, à un miroir aussi immense que cette foule ; à un kaléidoscope doué de conscience, qui, à chacun de ses mouvements, représente la vie multiple et la grâce mouvante de tous les éléments de la vie. C'est un *moi* insatiable du *non-moi*, qui, à chaque instant, le rend et l'exprime en images plus vivantes que la vie elle-même, toujours instable et fugitive. » Baudelaire, *loc. cit.*, p. 352.

22 Sur Foucault et le néo-libéralisme naissant, voir notamment Mitchell Dean et Daniel Zamora, *Le dernier homme et la fin de la révolution. Foucault après Mai 68*, Montréal, Lux Éditeur, 2019.

STICKY PICTURES

BLUE TABLE 2019

76 × 60 in. / 193 × 152 cm

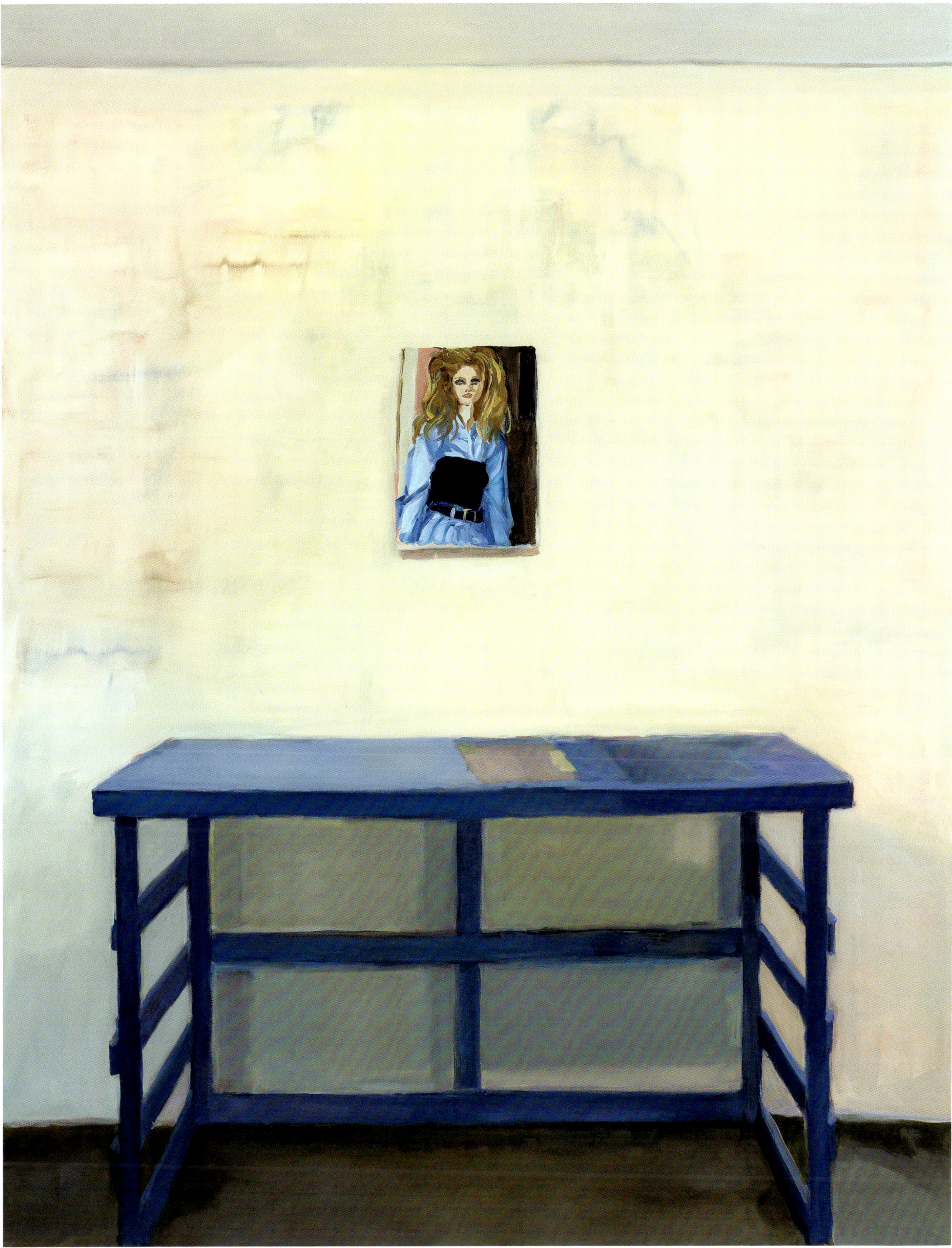

STILL LIFE WITH WITCH 2019

76 × 60 in. / 193 × 152 cm

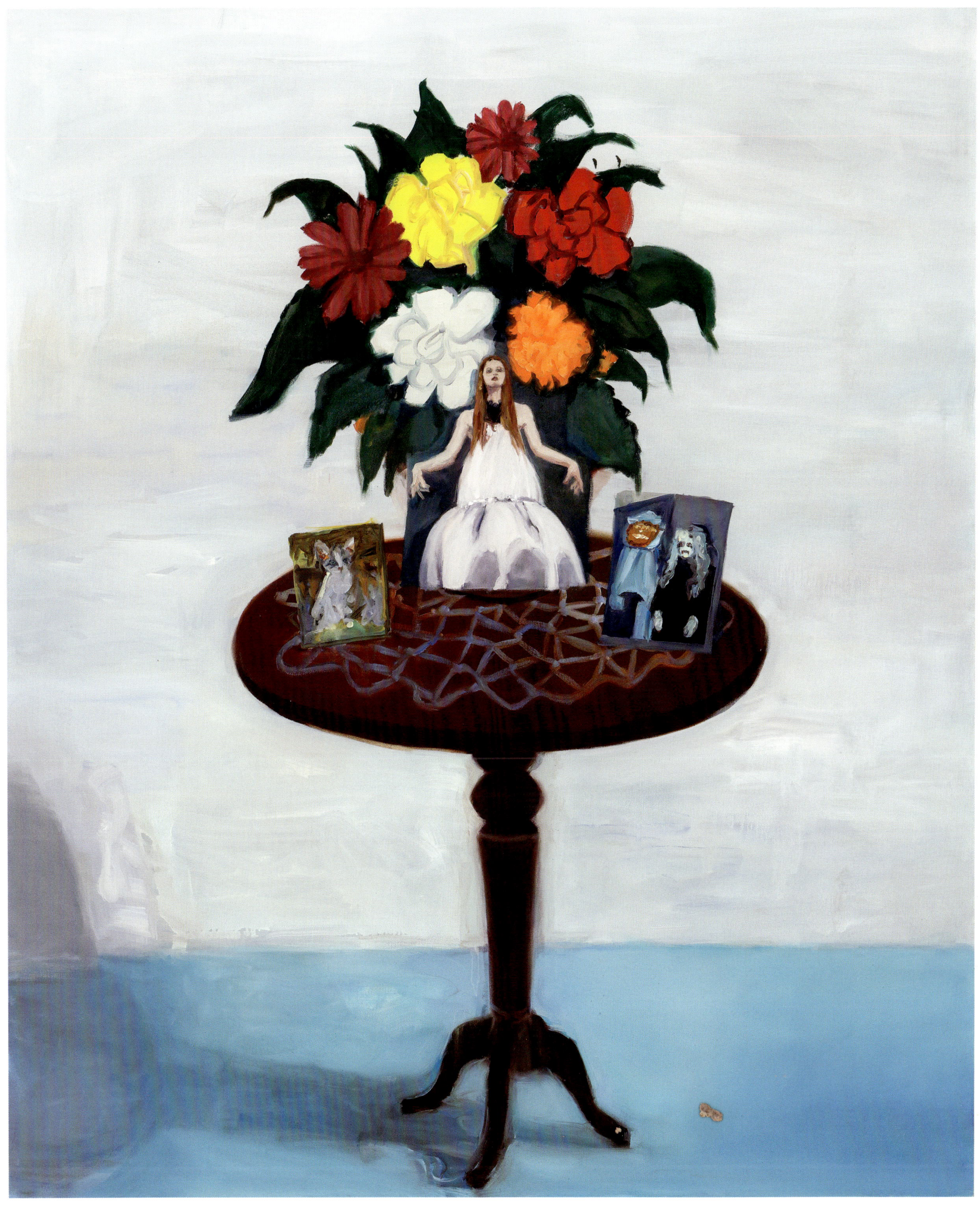

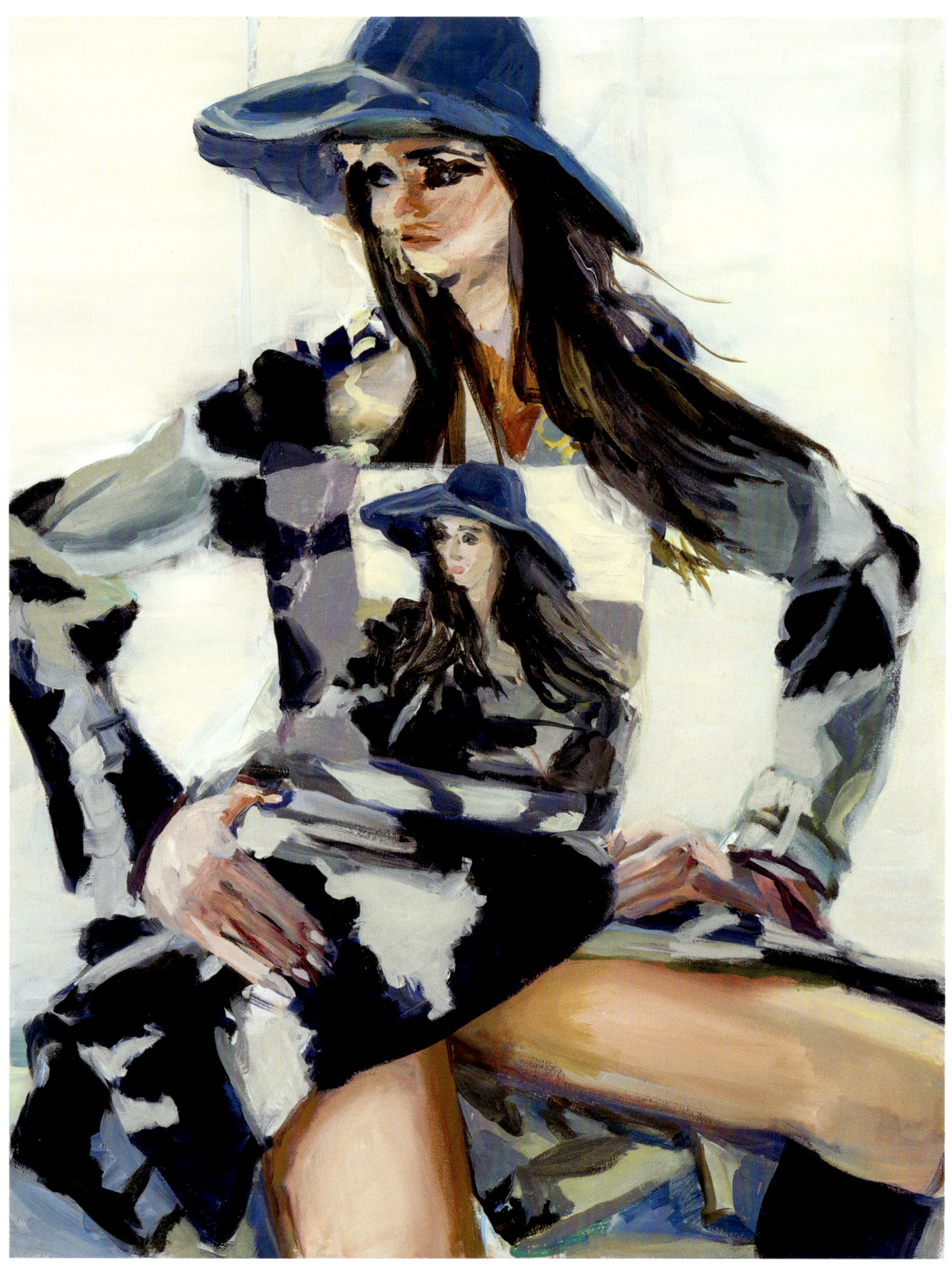

ABOVE

DOUBLE (BLUE HAT) 2019

31 × 24 in. / 79 × 61 cm

OPPOSITE

HOVER (THE DISTANCE BETWEEN HERE AND THERE) 2017

74 × 60 in. / 188 × 152 cm

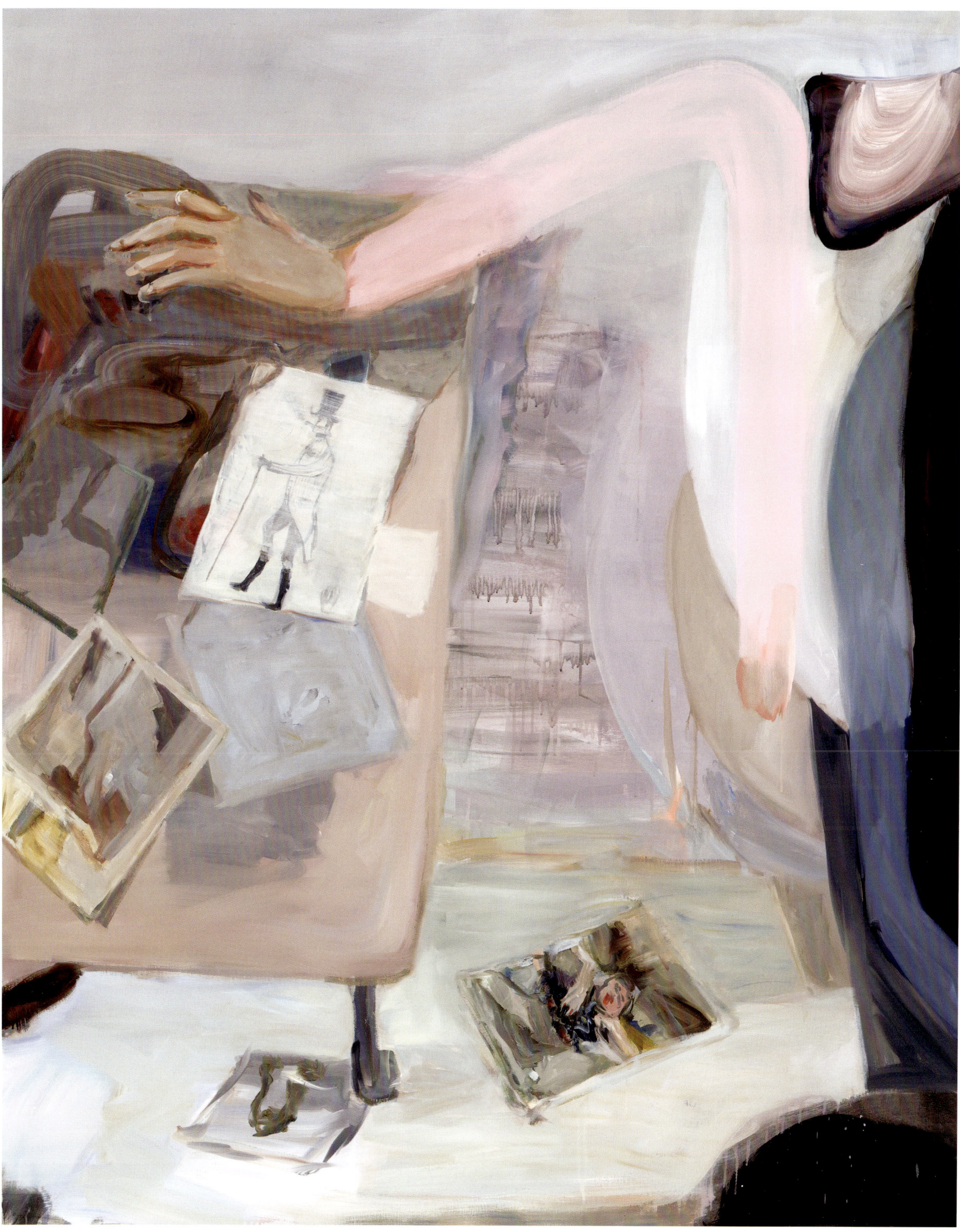

VO MARS 2017

67 × 84 in. / 170 × 213 cm

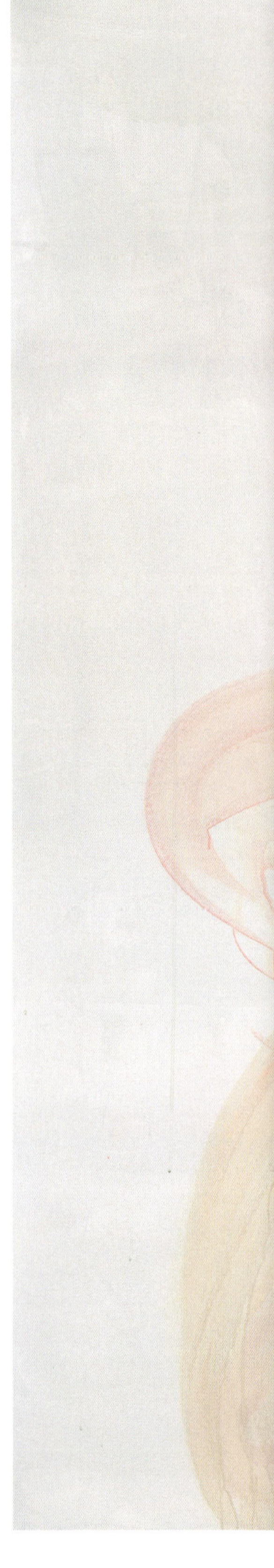

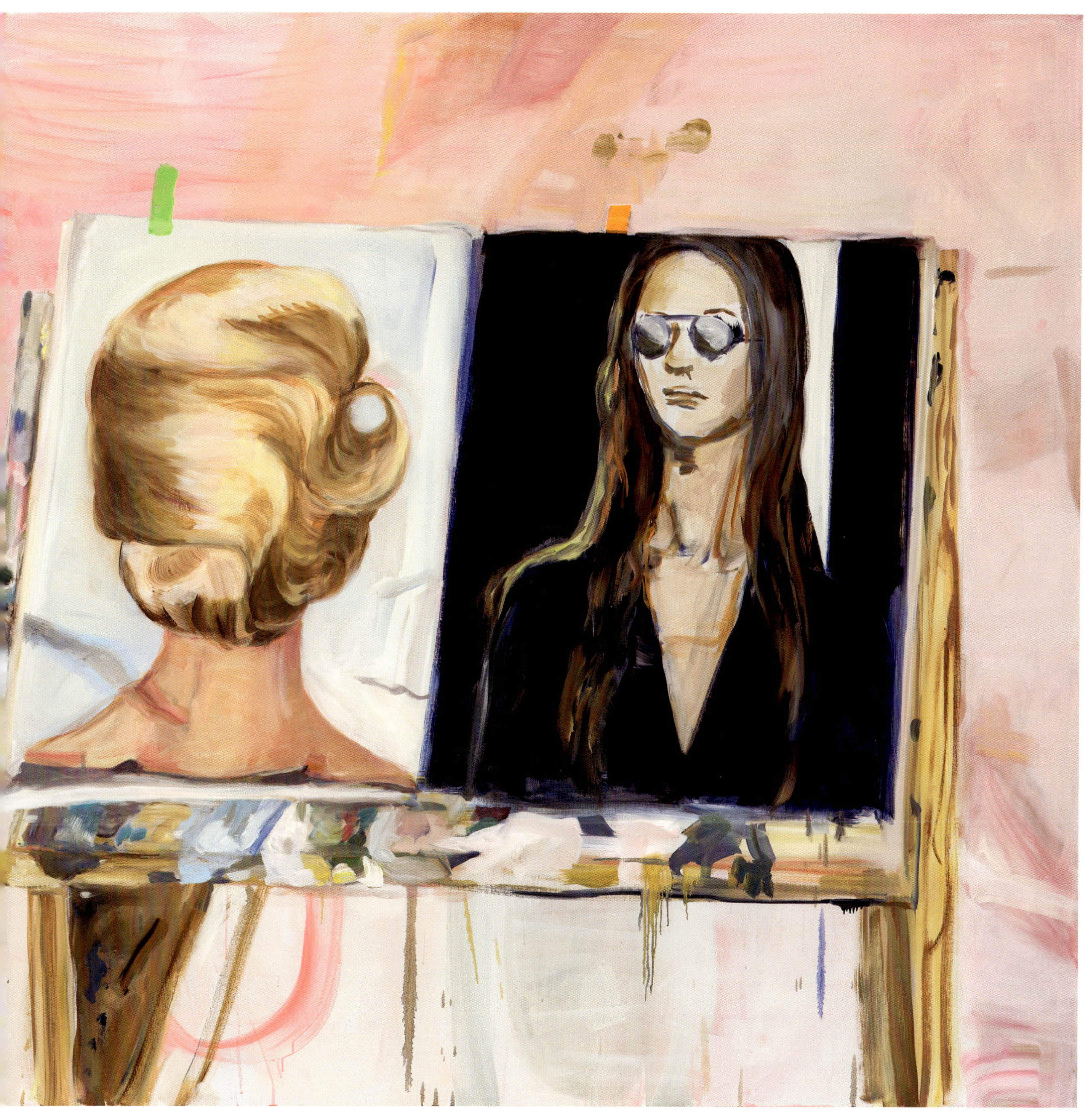

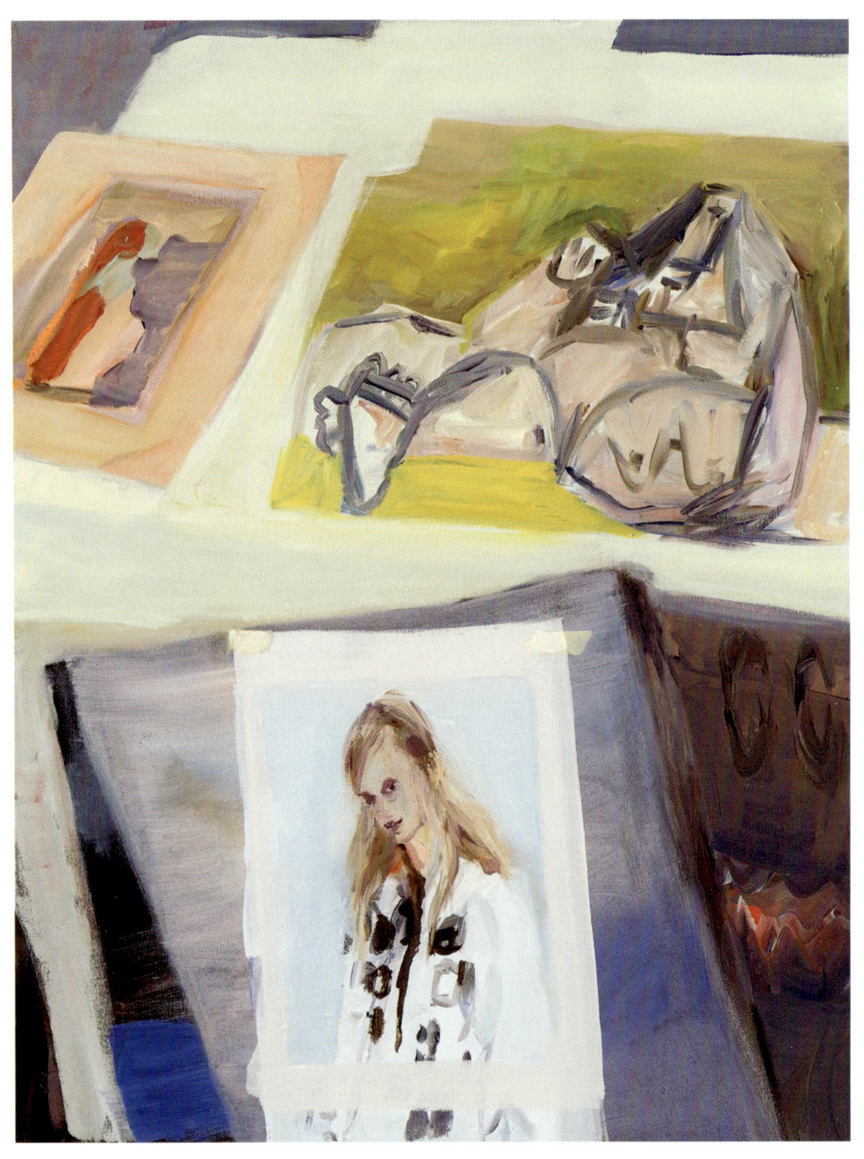

ABOVE

TABLE WITH PICASSO 2018

31 × 24 in. / 79 × 61 cm

OPPOSITE

HASS 2017

60 × 48 in. / 152 × 122 cm

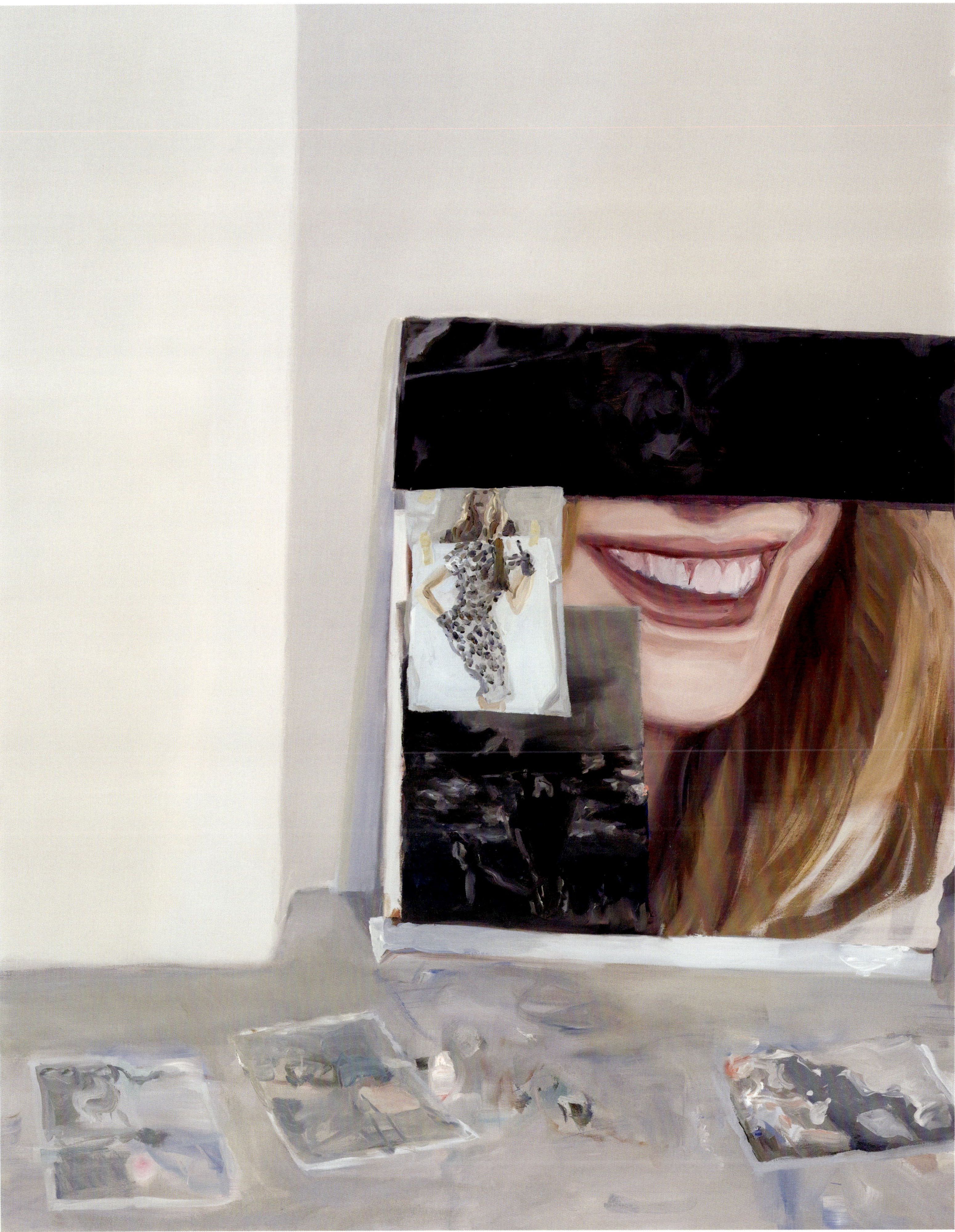

GREEN ROOM AJ 2018

48 × 60 in. / 122 × 152 cm

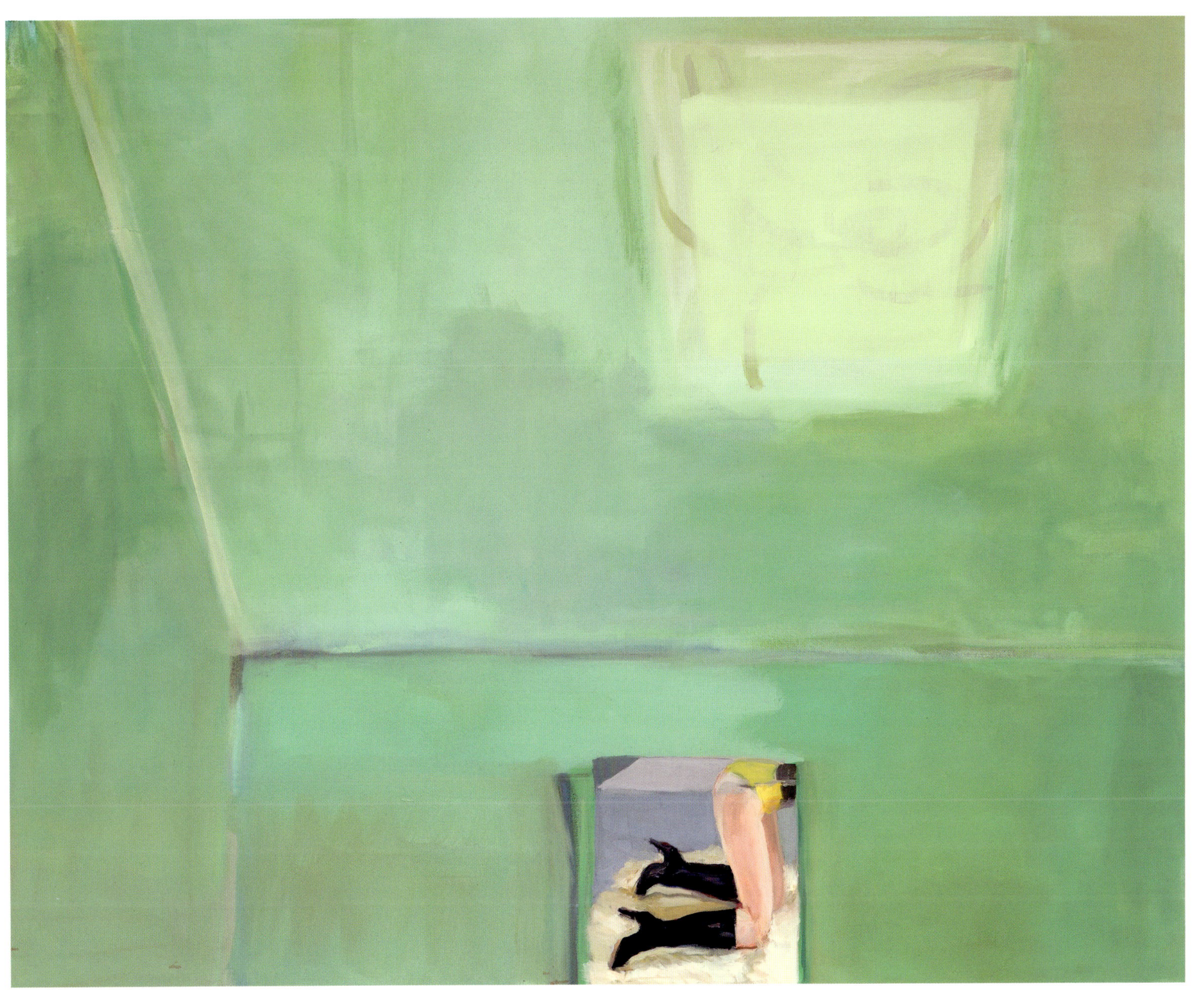

UNTITLED (PLANT) 2016

72 × 60 in. / 183 × 152 cm

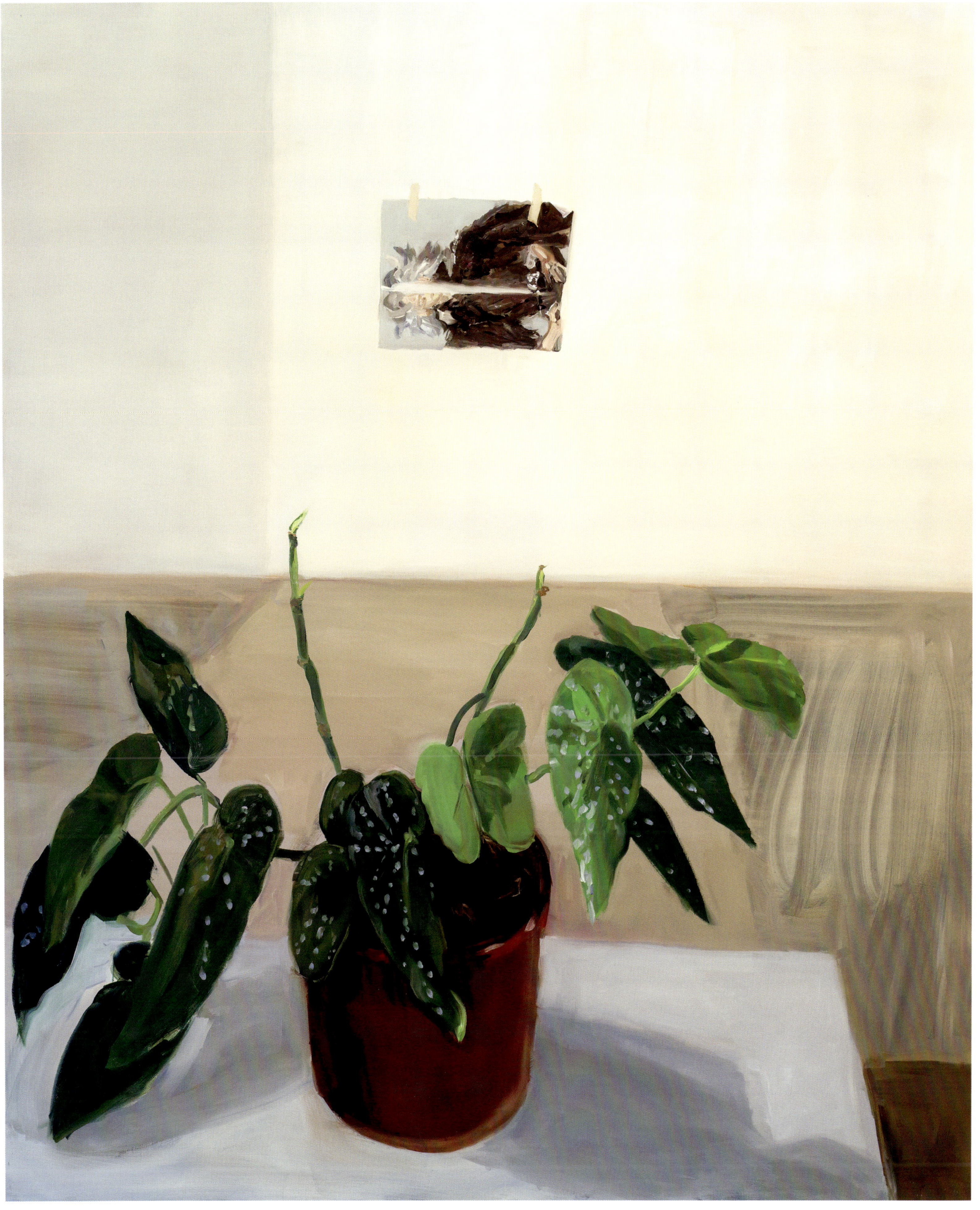

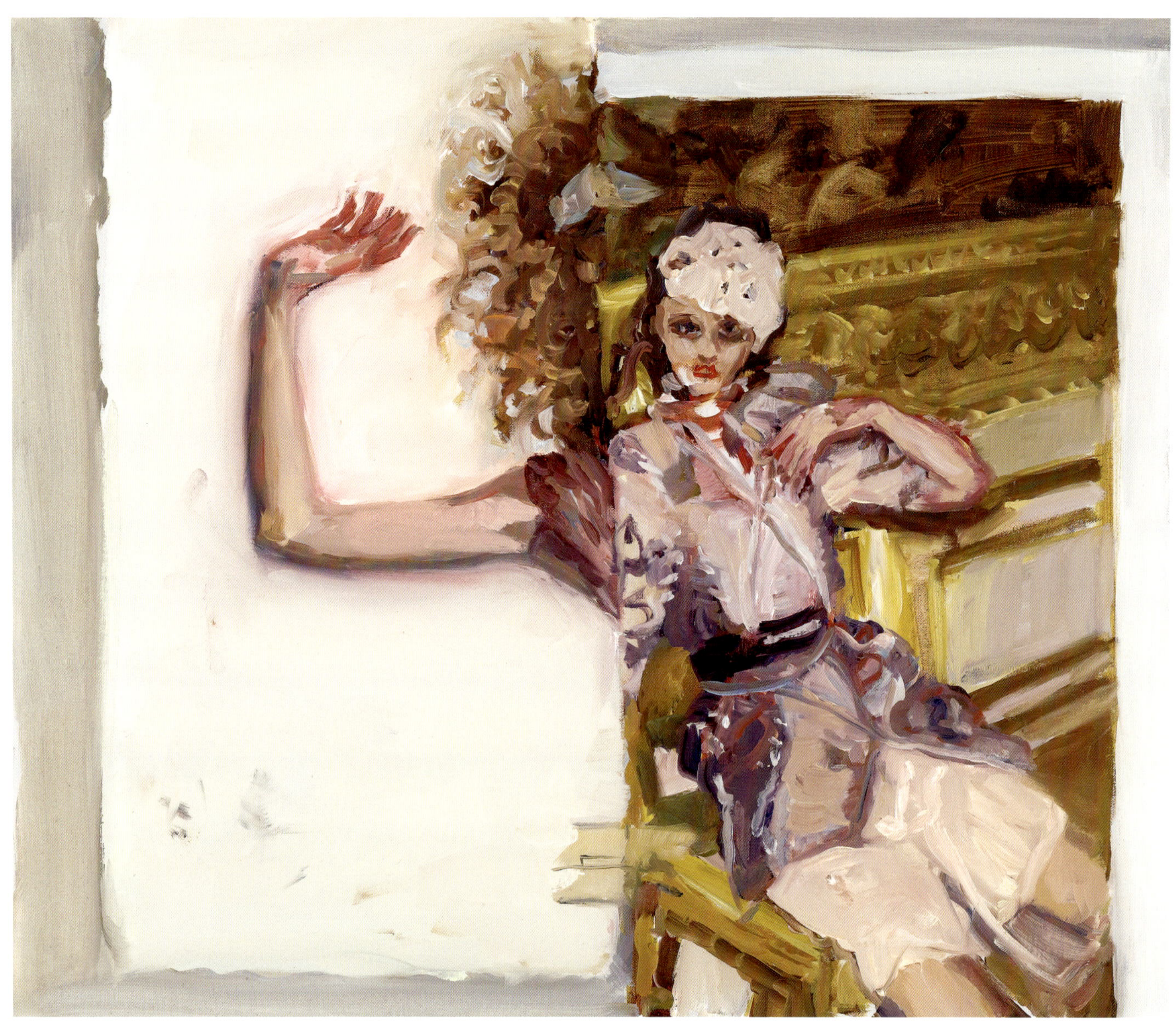

ABOVE

HALF HALF 2016

20 × 24 in. / 51 × 61 cm

OPPOSITE

LEANING IN 2016

60 × 48 in. / 152 × 122 cm

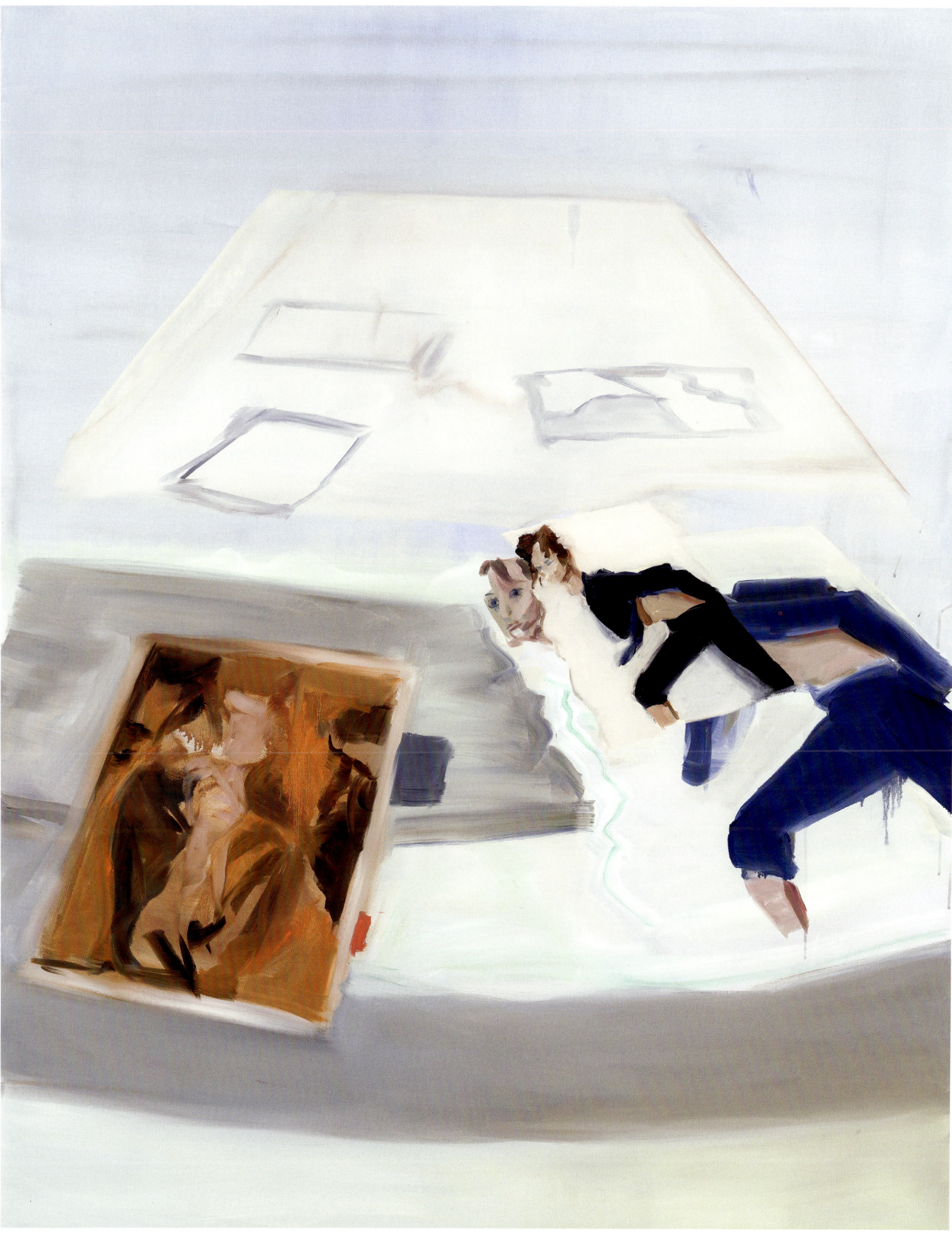

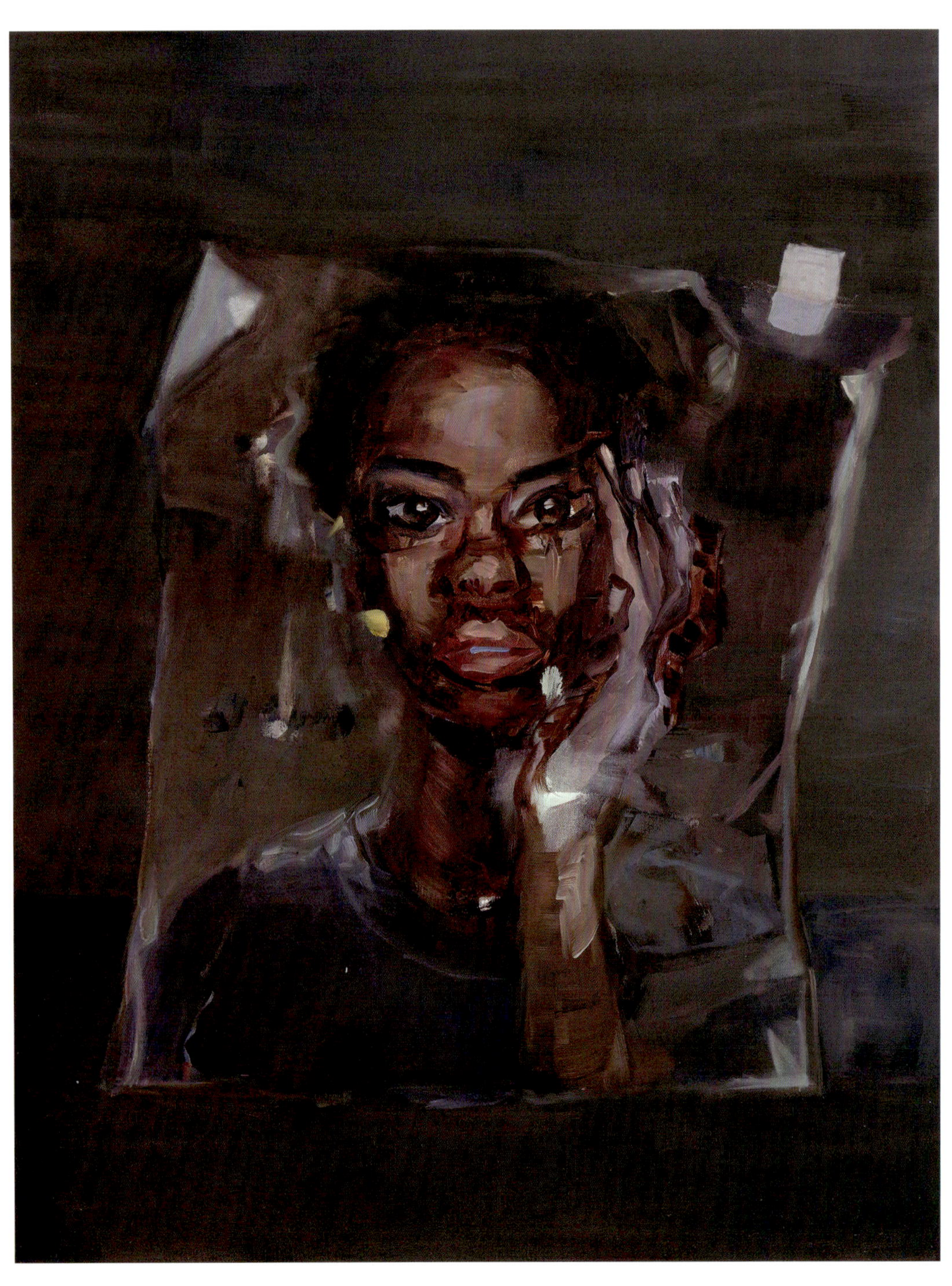

UNTITLED (DI) 2018

31 × 24 in. / 79 × 61 cm

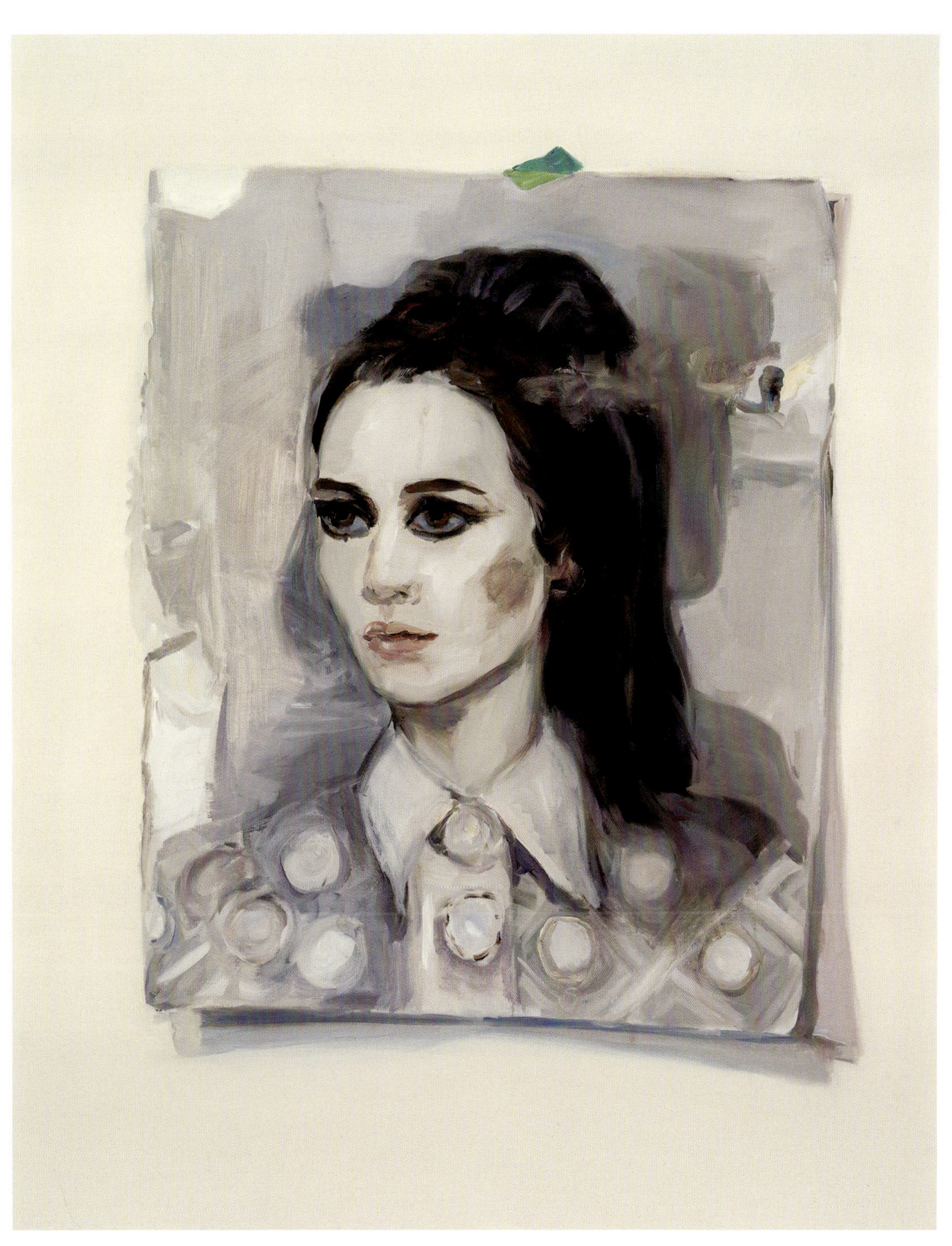

HARPER VALLEY 2017

40 × 32 in. / 102 × 81 cm

STUDIO (MIRO) 2017

60 × 72 in. / 152 × 183 cm

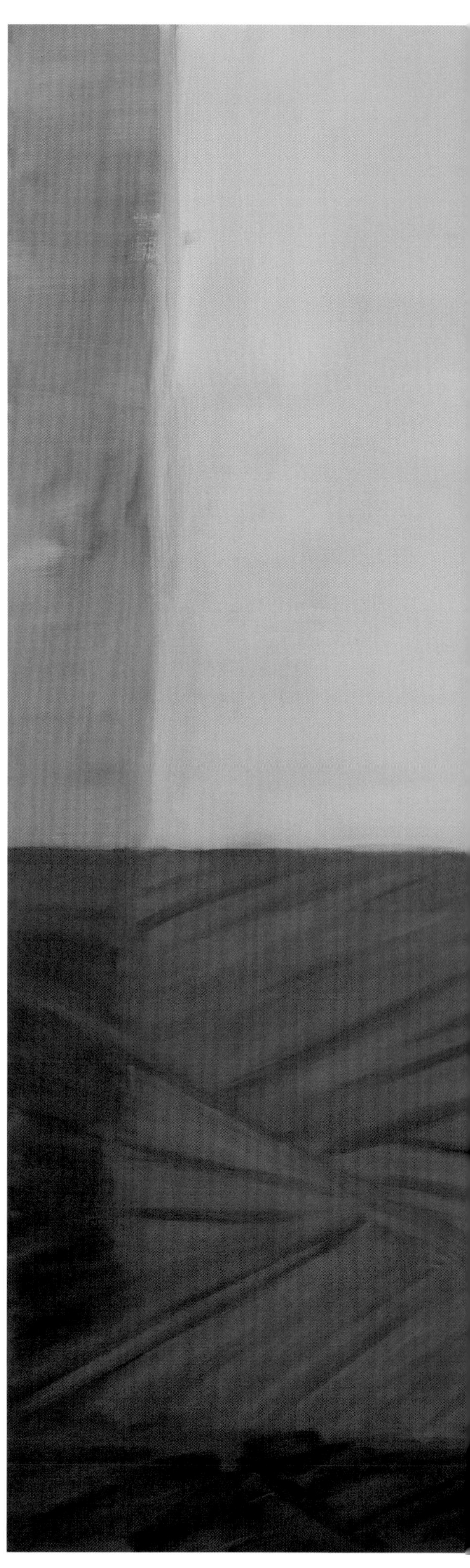

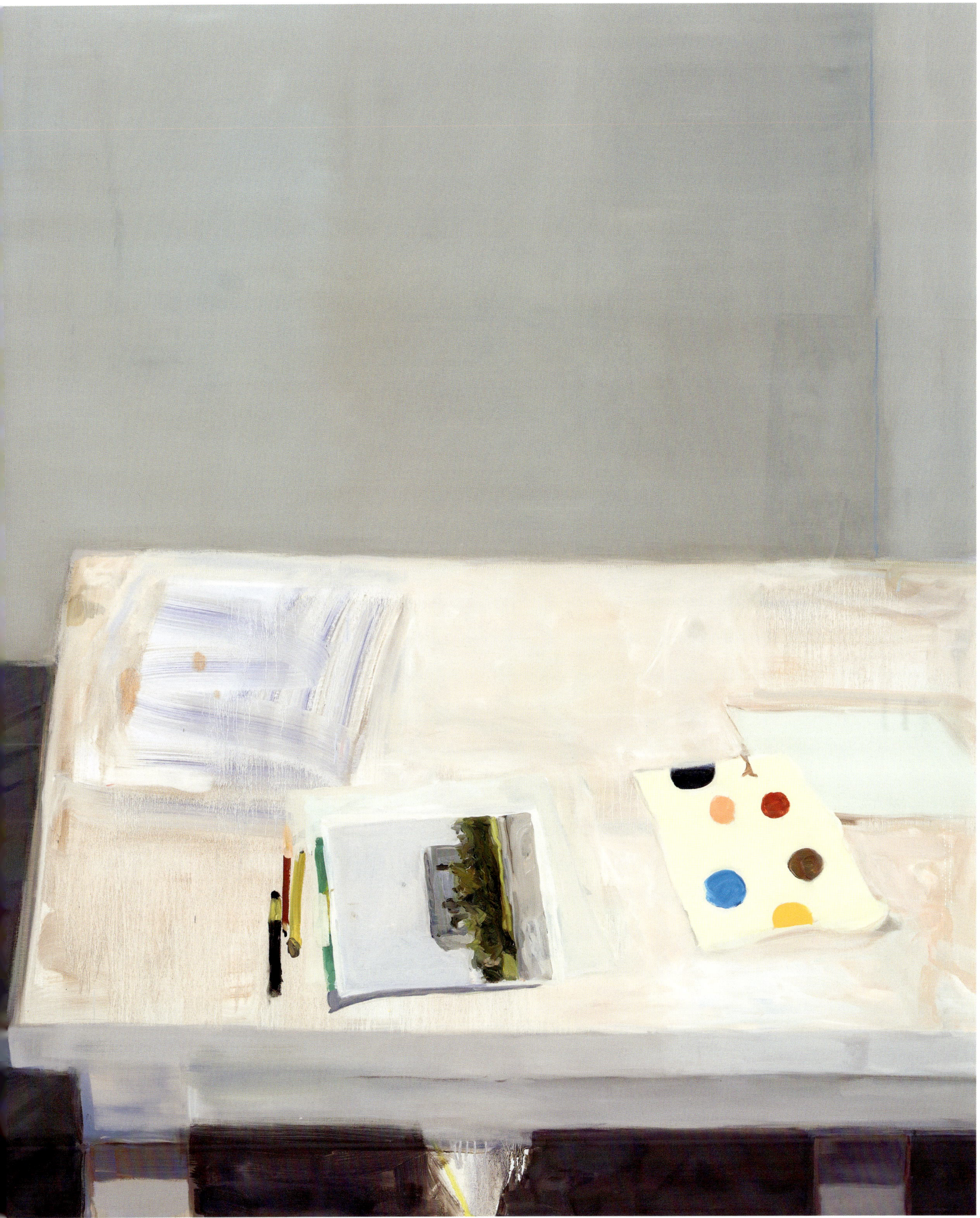

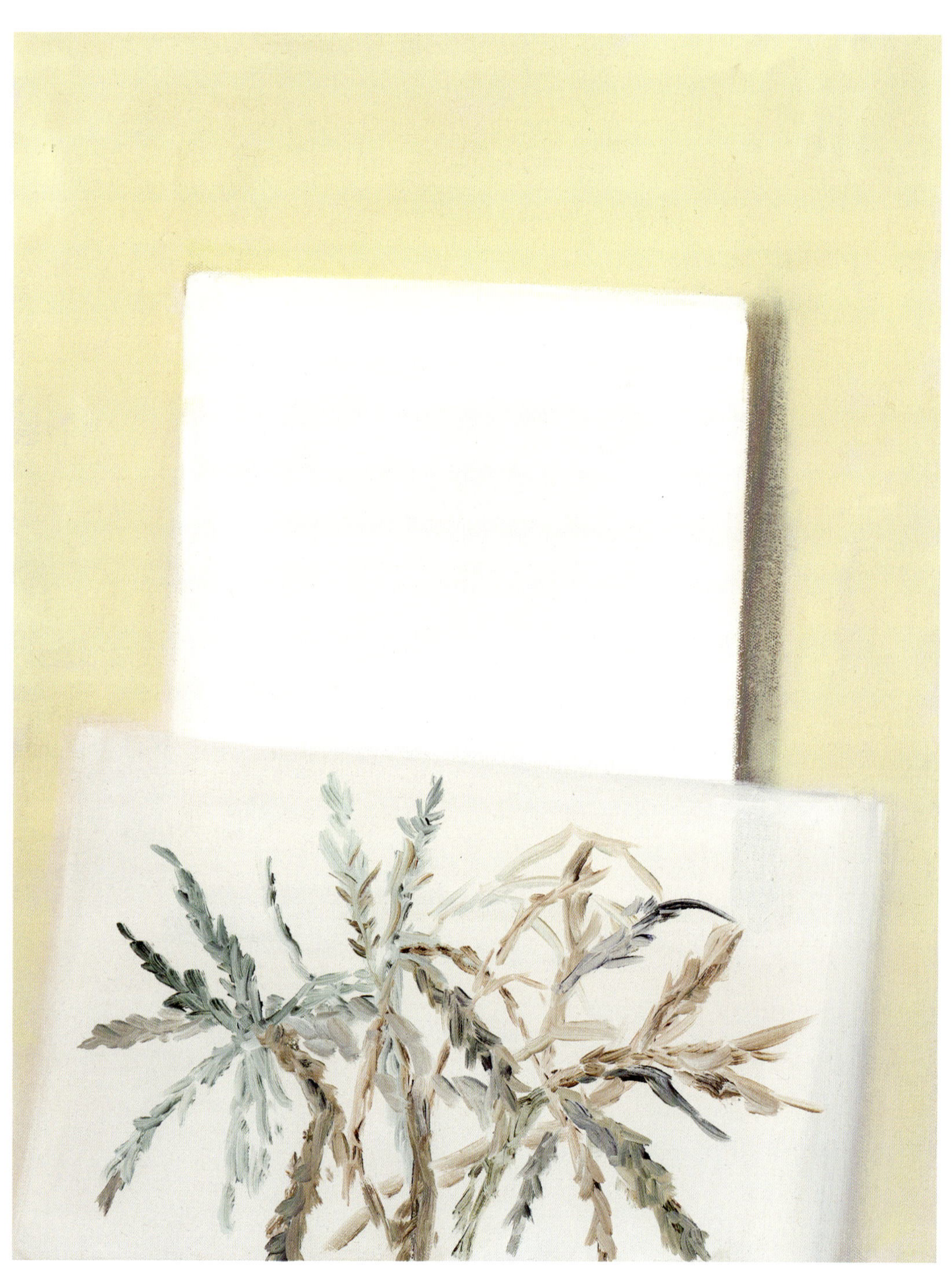

SLIP 2017

20 × 16 in. / 51 × 41 cm

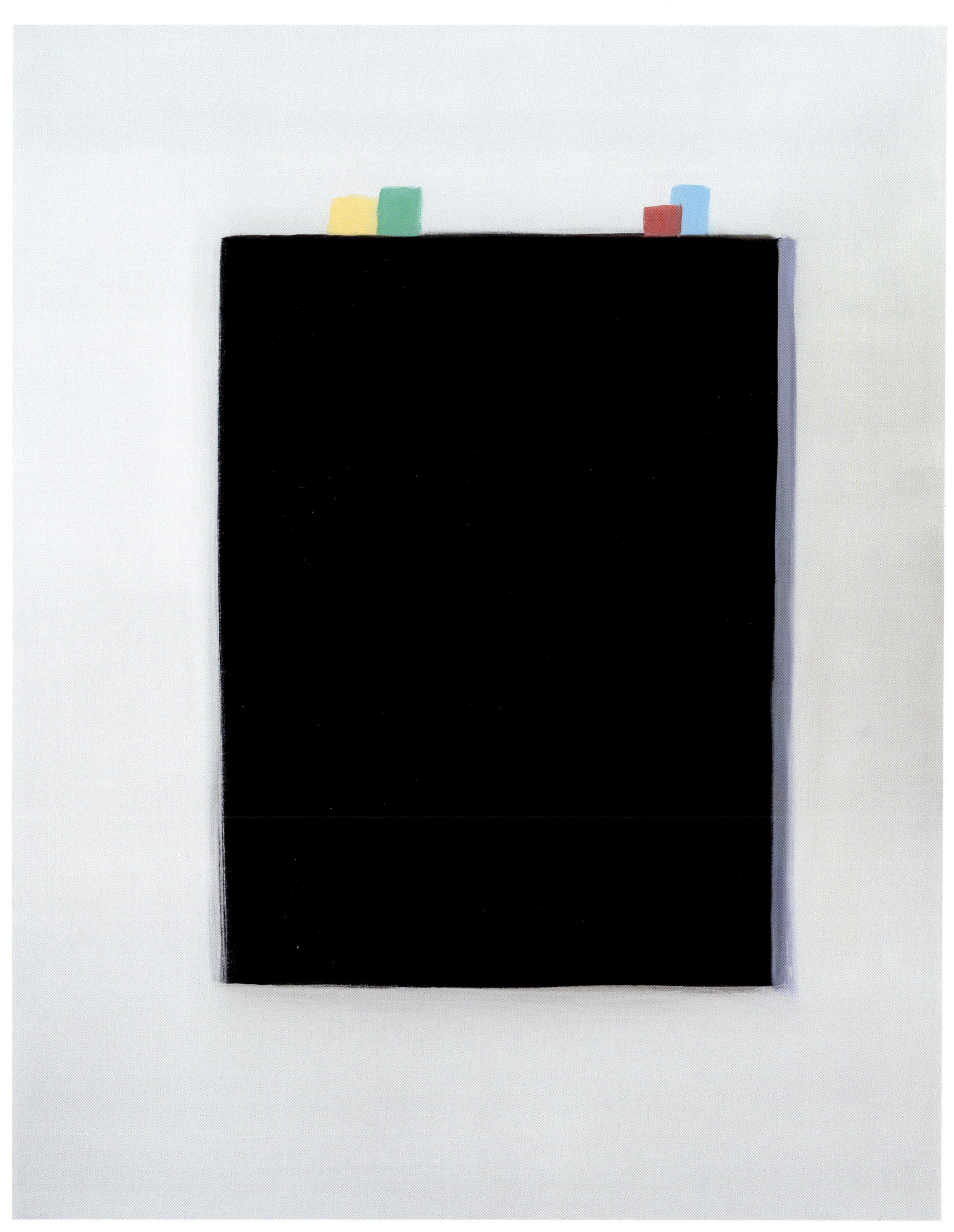

BLACK BOOK 2017

40 × 32 in. / 102 × 81 cm

SOMEONE, SOMETHING, NO ONE 2017

67 × 60 in. / 170 × 152 cm

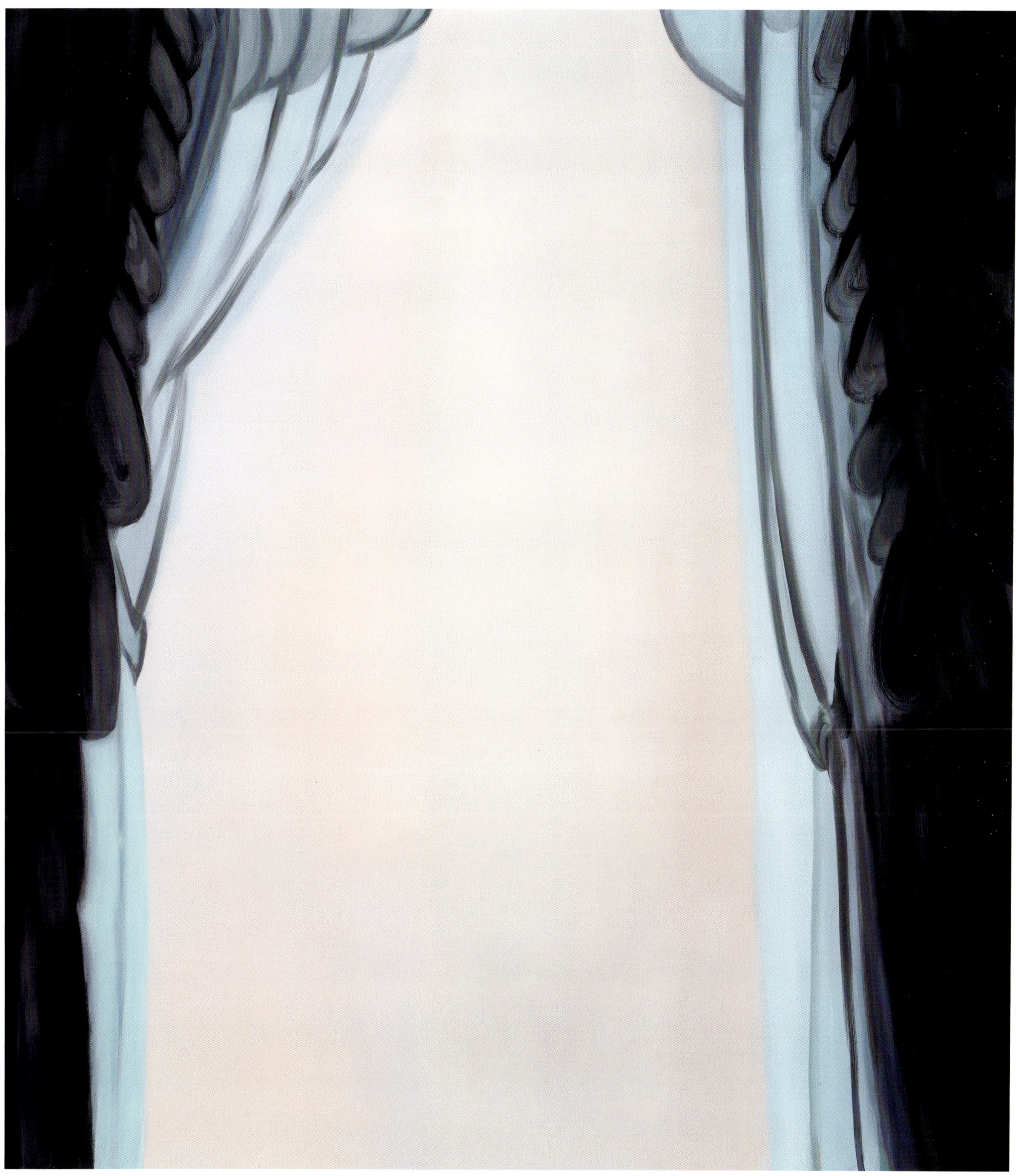

SORCERER 2016

75 × 60 in. / 191 × 152 cm

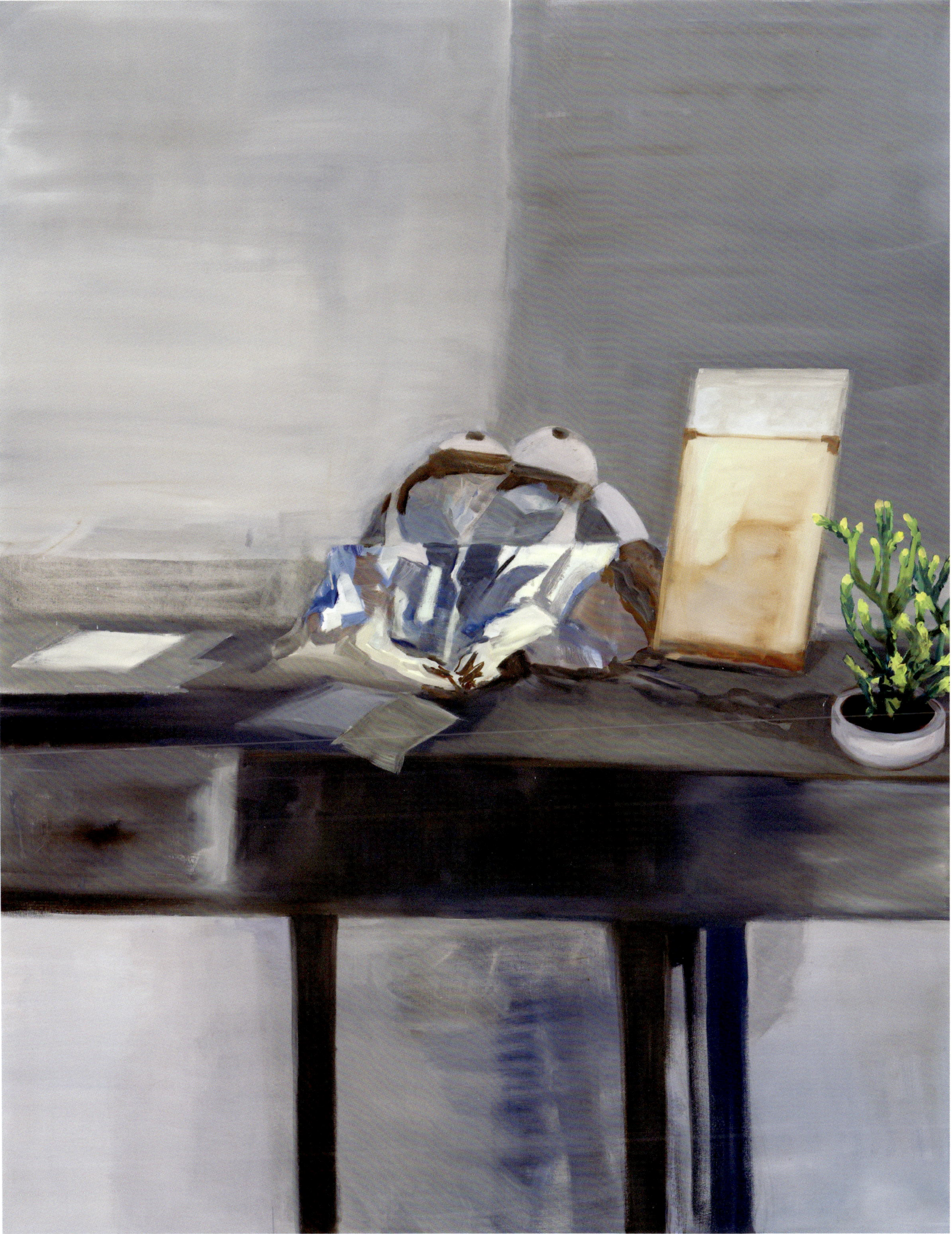

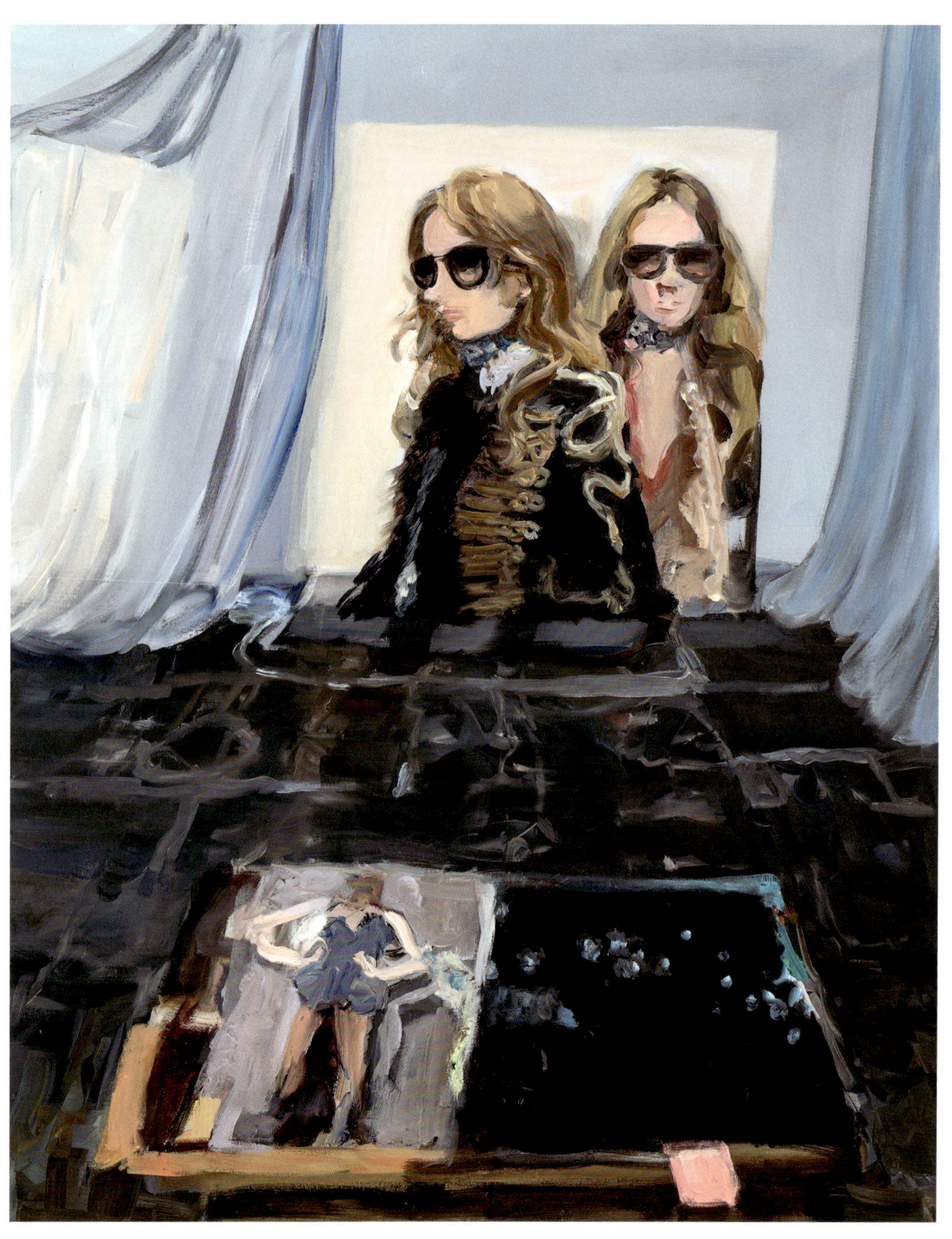

THEATRE (THE DOUBLE) 2017

40 × 32 in. / 102 × 81 cm

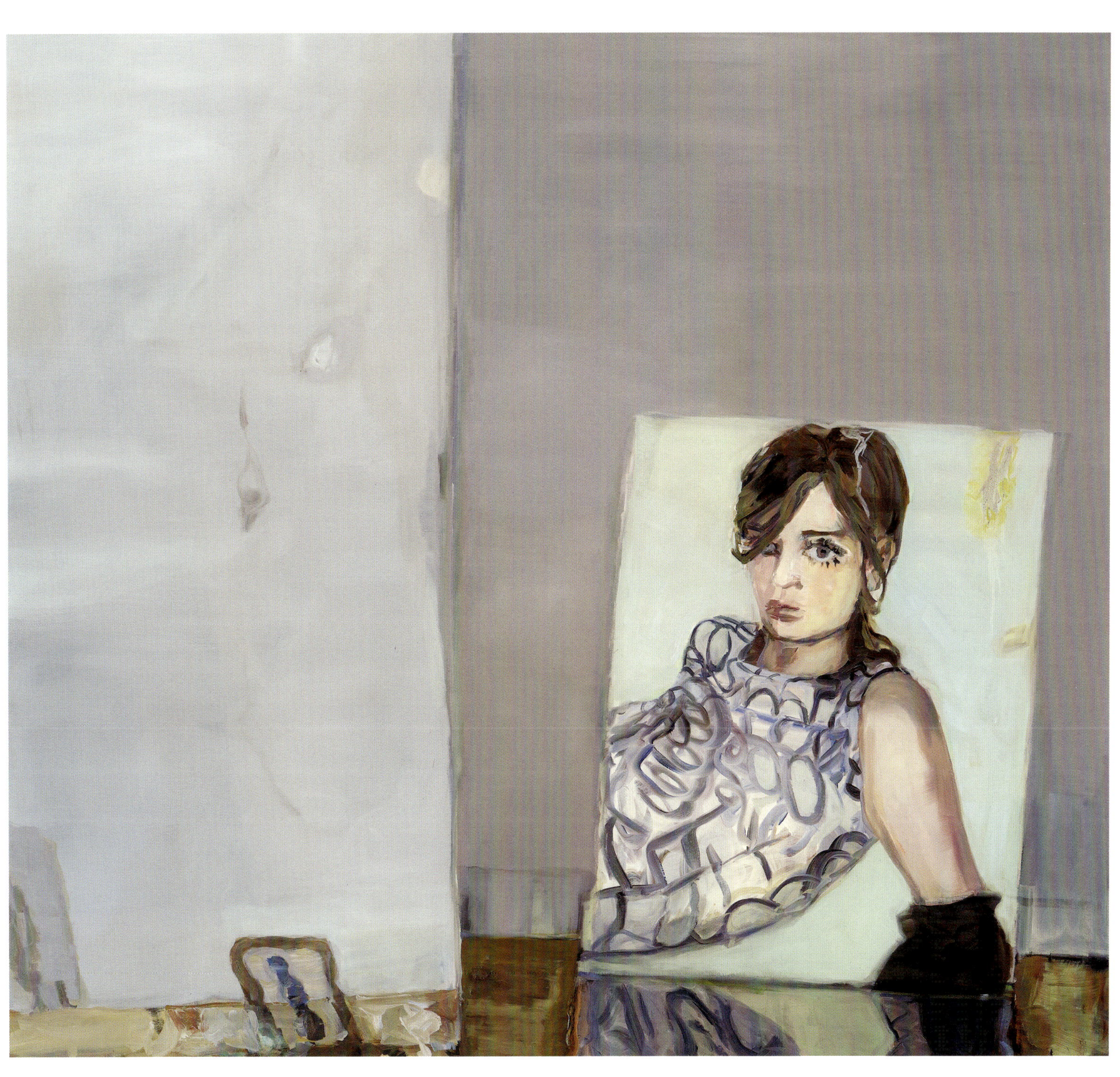

RECLINER (DEATH IN VENICE) 2018

60 × 67 in. / 152 × 170 cm

GALLERY 2017

88 × 67 in. / 224 × 170 cm

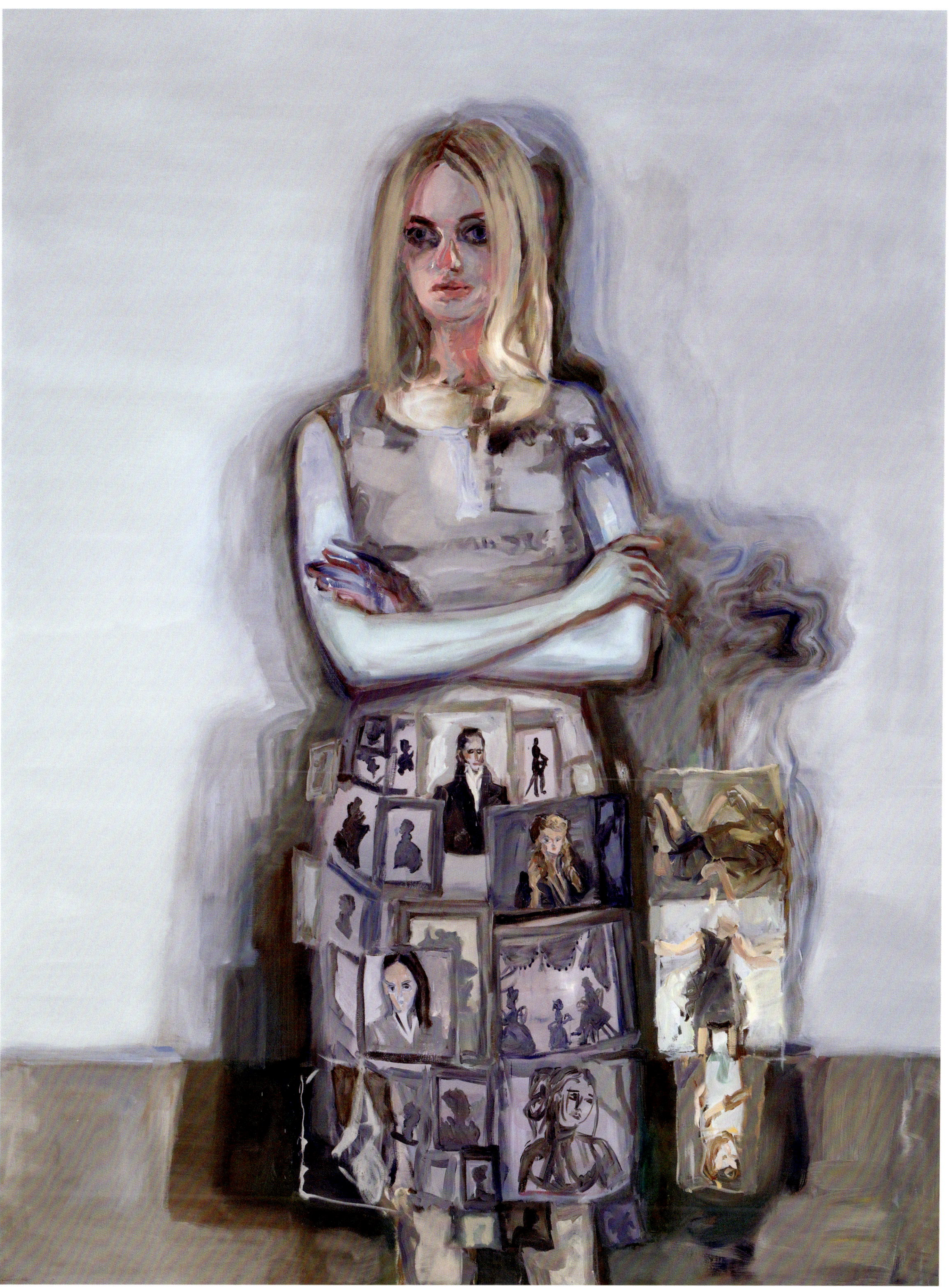

WHAT TIME IS IT, MR. WOLF? 2017

84 × 67 in. / 213 × 170 cm

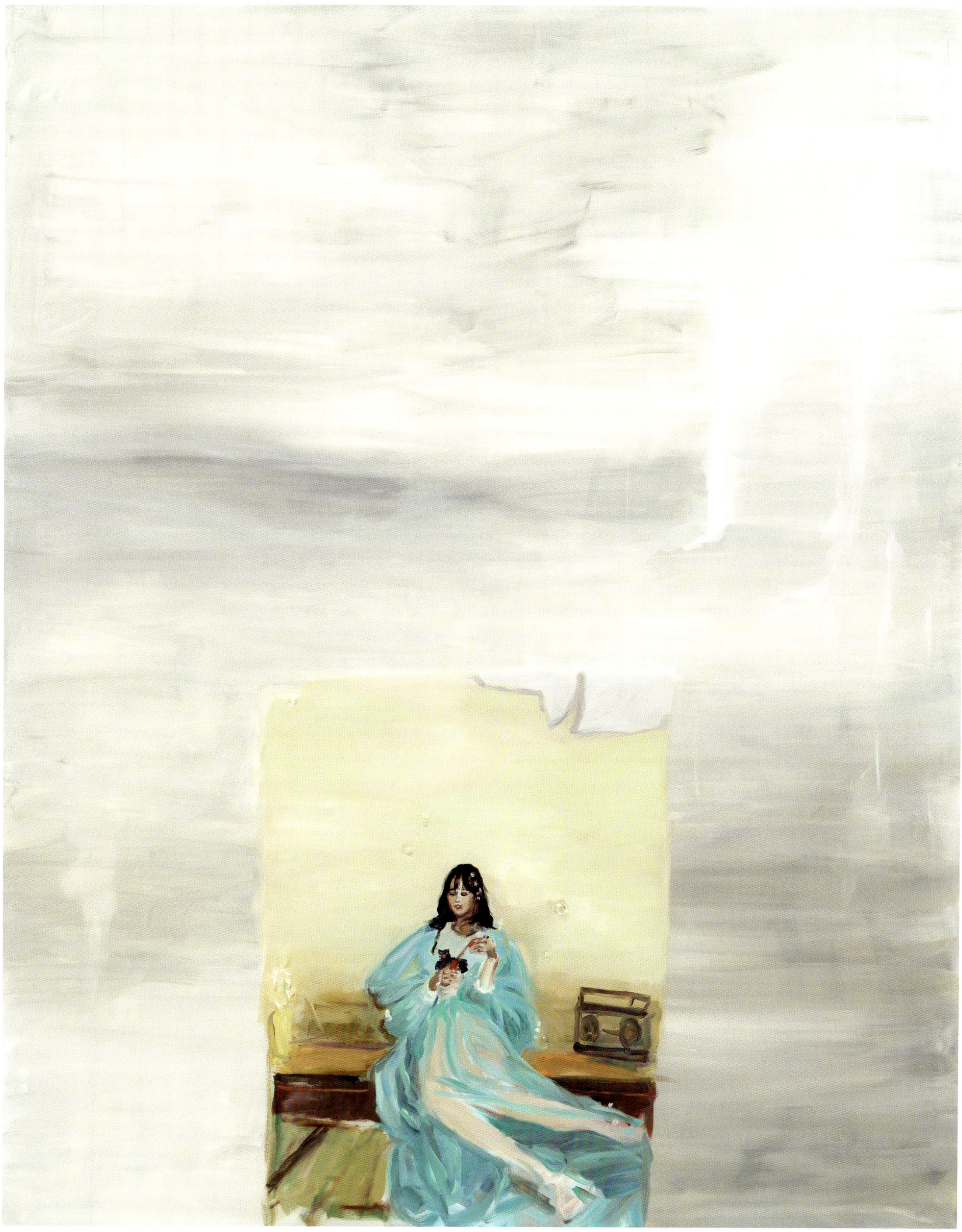

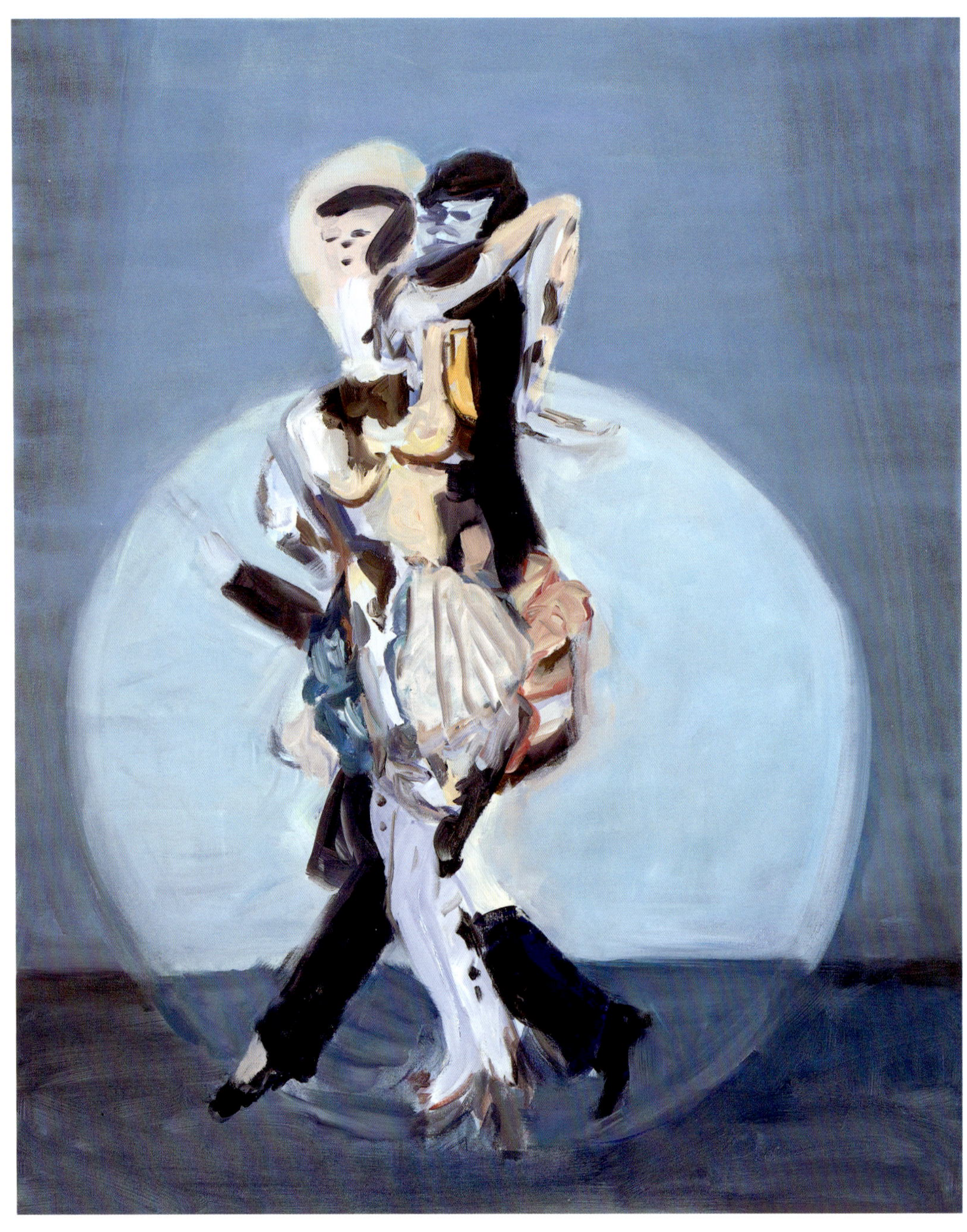

ABOVE

AFTER PICABIA 2014

38 × 32 in. / 97 × 81 cm

OPPOSITE

MHMH 2016

55 × 45 in. / 140 × 114 cm

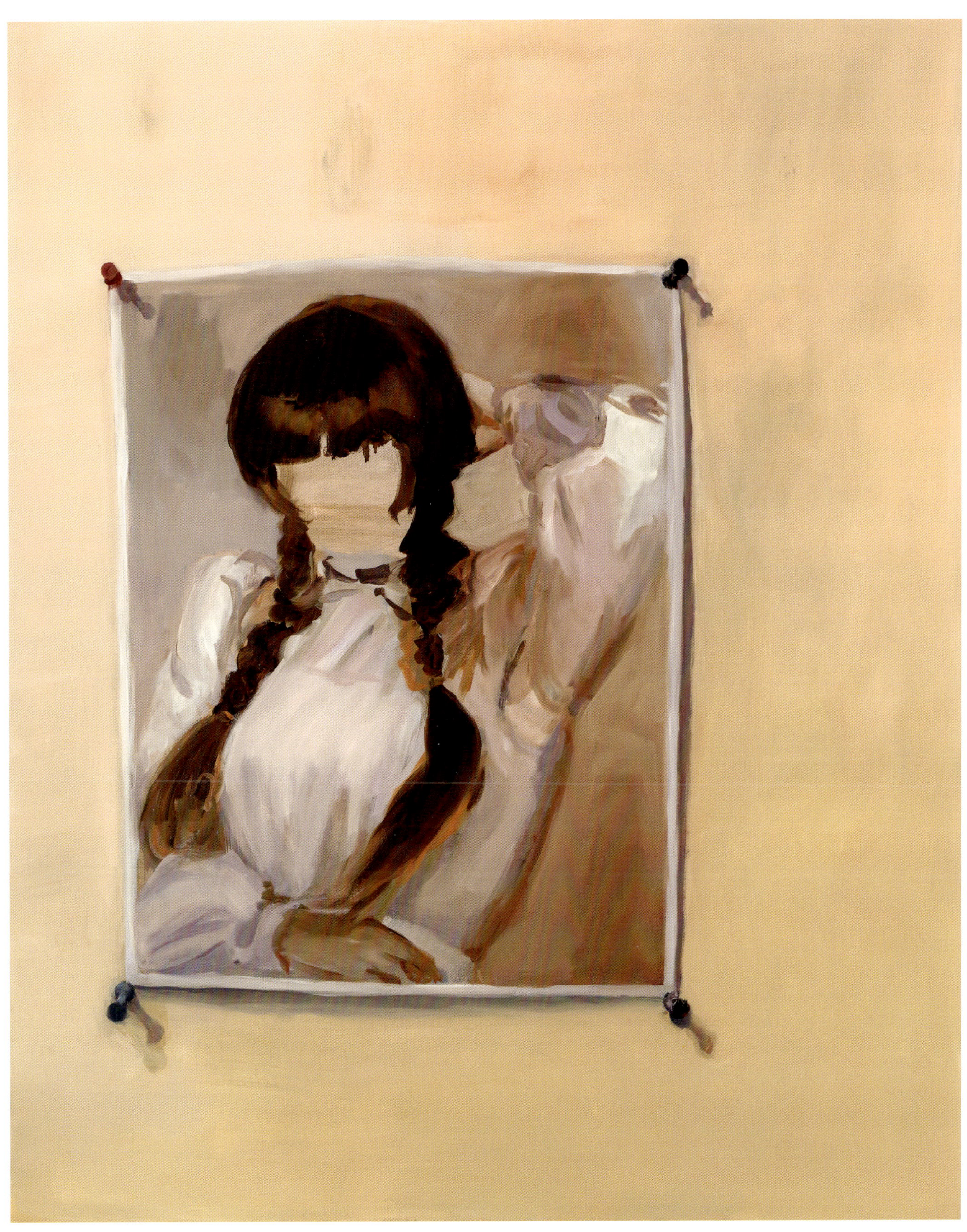

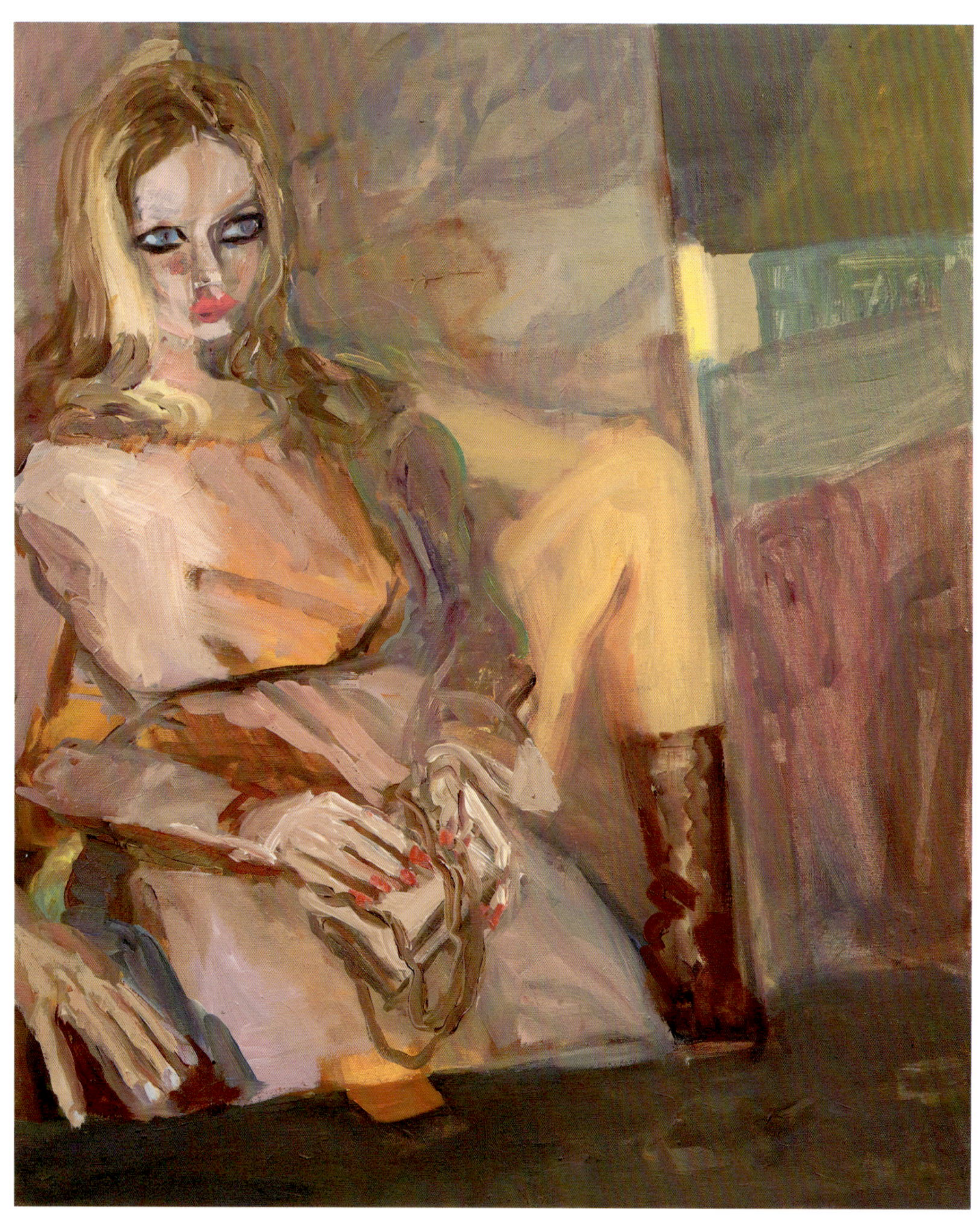

ABOVE

PORTRAIT REFLECTION 2020

24 × 20 in. / 61 × 51 cm

OPPOSITE

CINNAMON (AFTER GAINSBOROUGH) 2018

60 × 48 in. / 152 × 122 cm

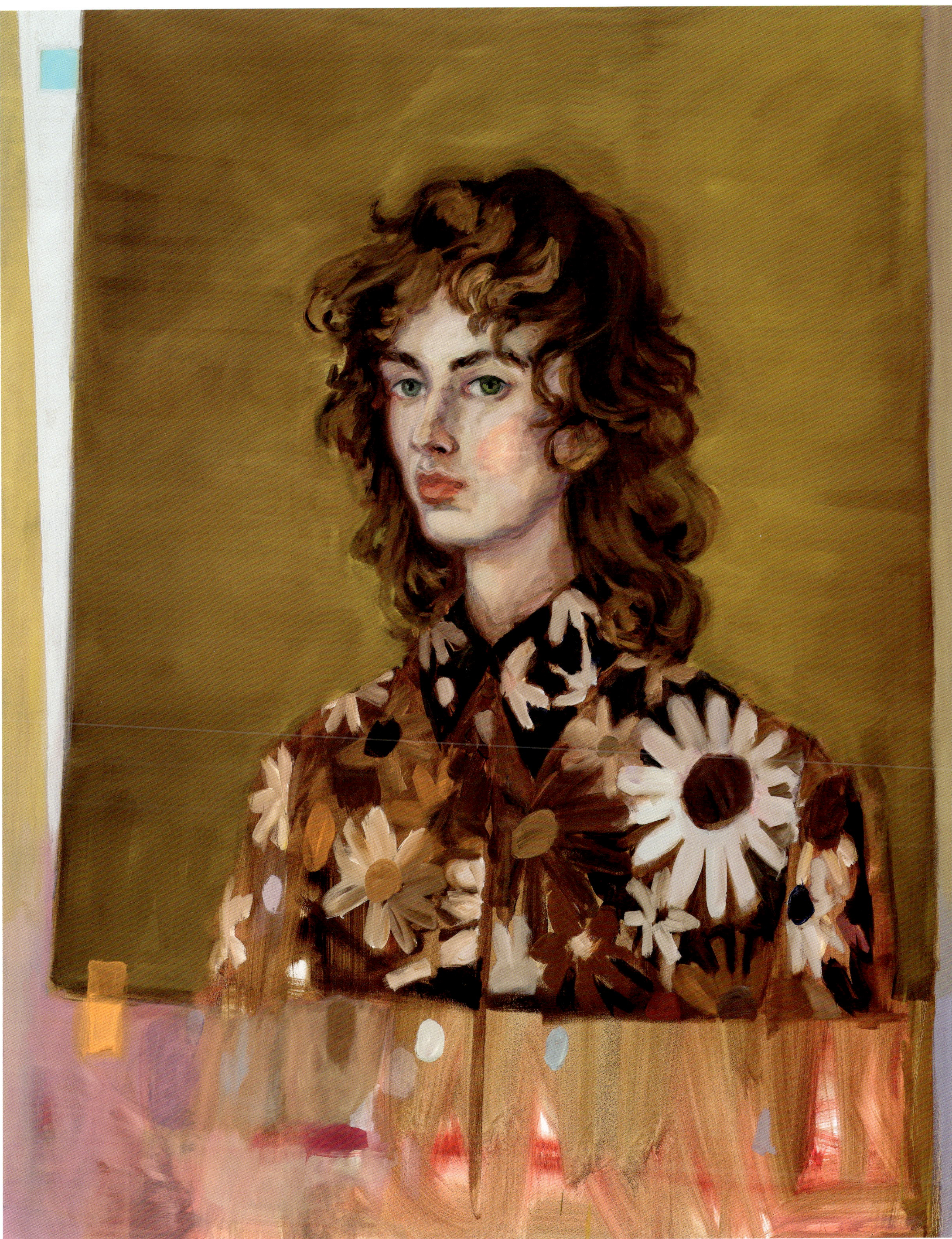

CAREY 2014

98 × 78 in. / 249 × 198 cm

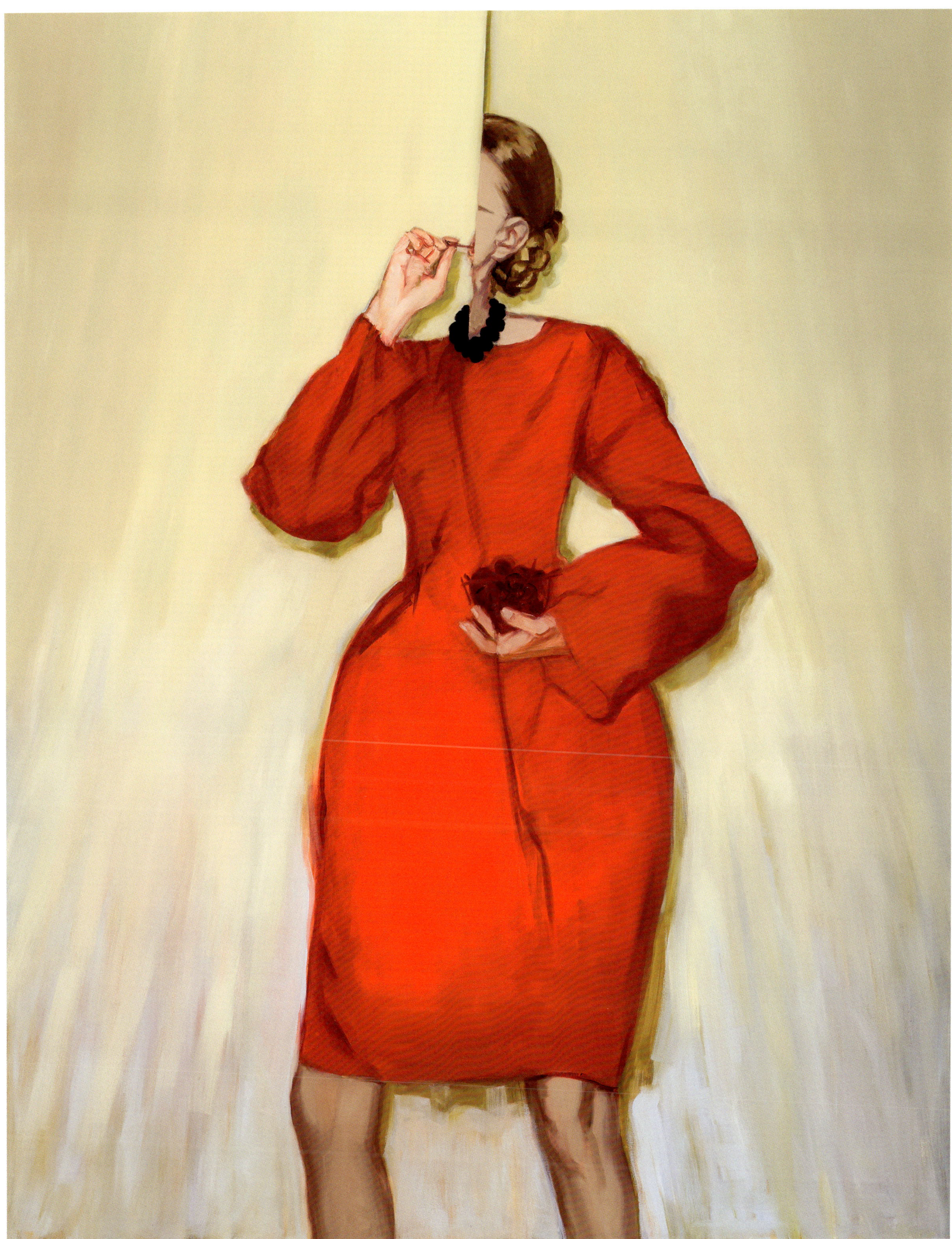

PORTRAIT (RED CURTAIN) 2019

84 × 67 in. / 213 × 170 cm

FOLLOWING SPREAD, FROM LEFT

BITTEN 2018

67 × 60 in. / 170 × 152 cm

STICKY PICTURES 2017

72 × 60 in. / 183 × 152 cm

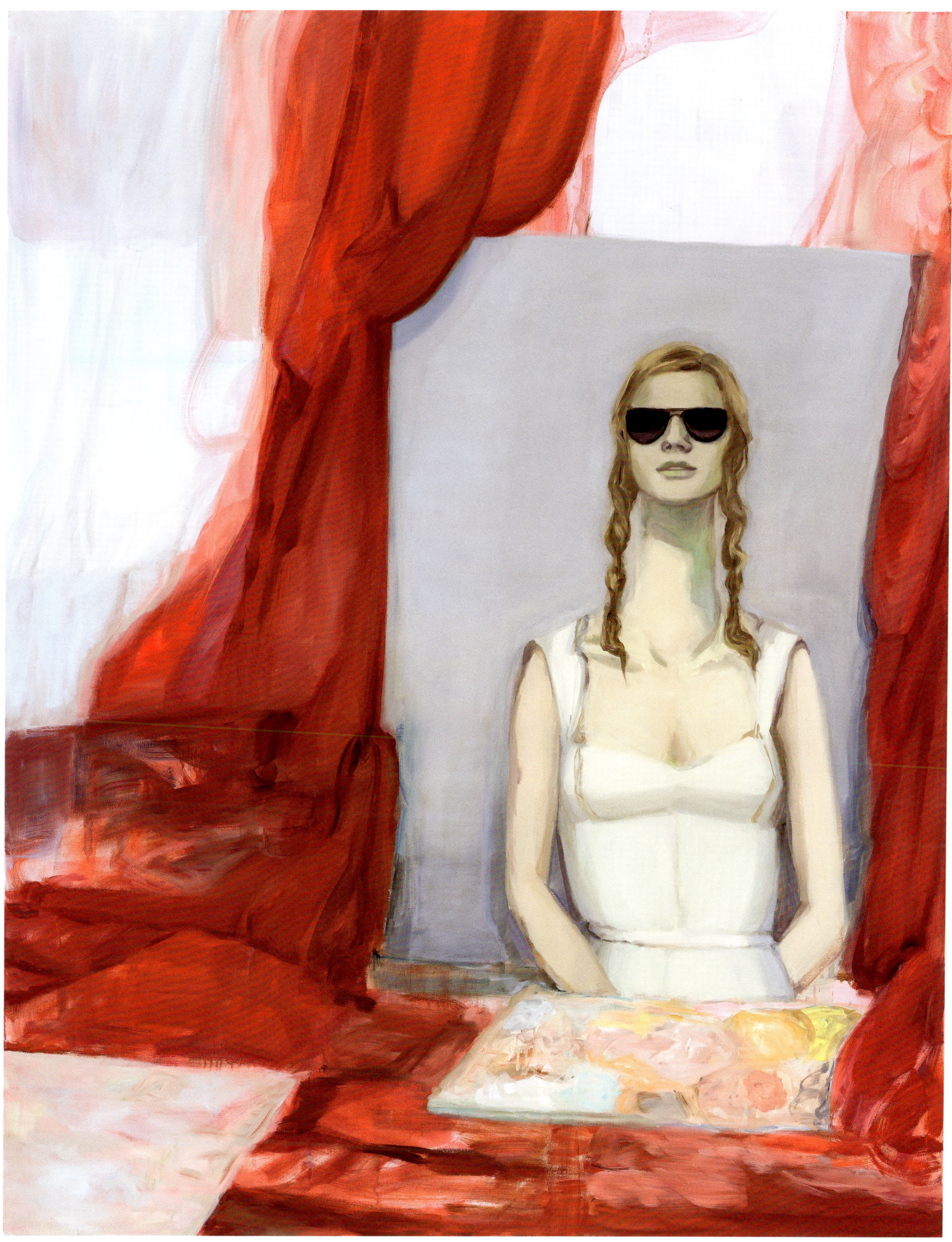

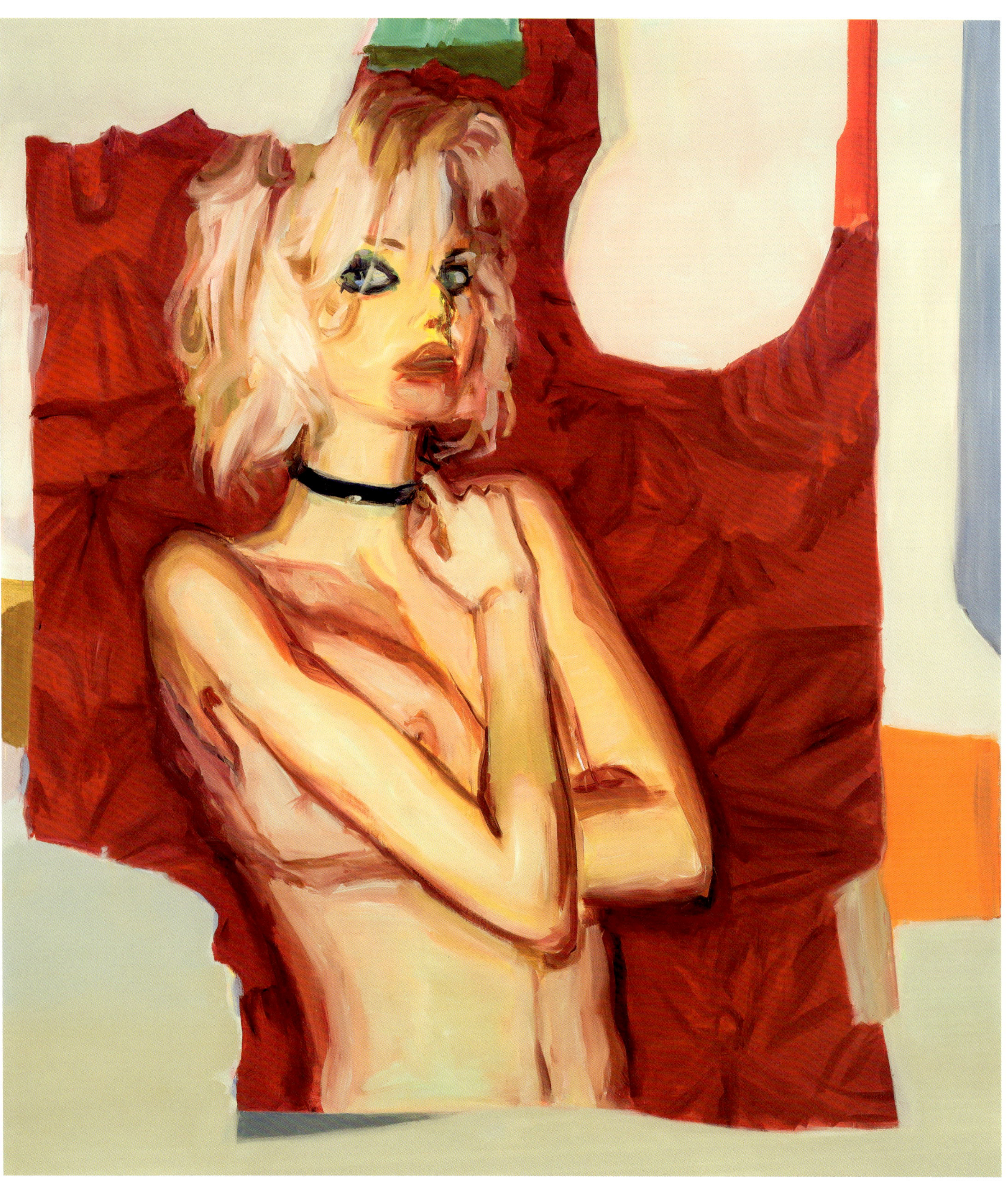

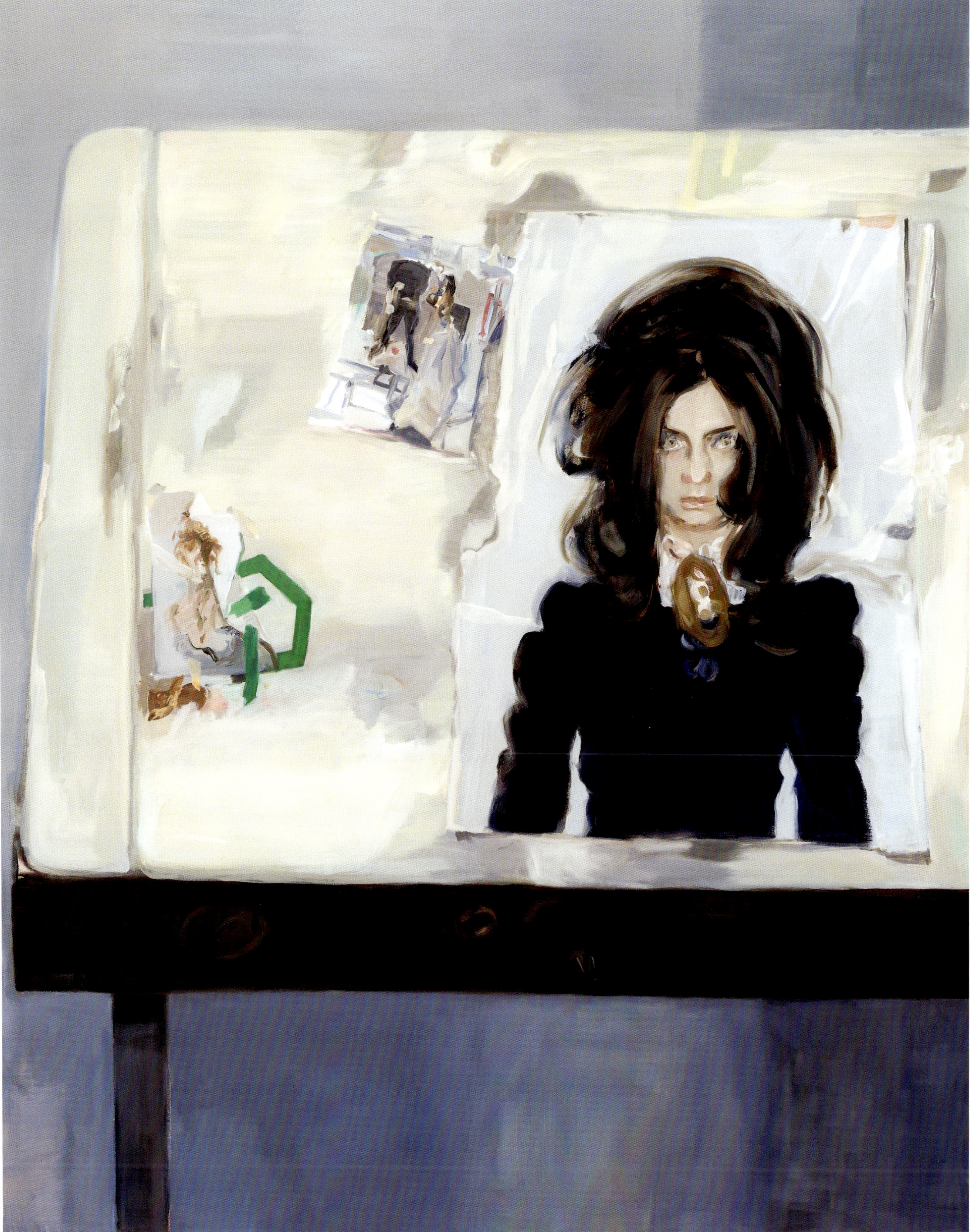

LOOP 2019

20 × 16 in. / 51 × 41 cm

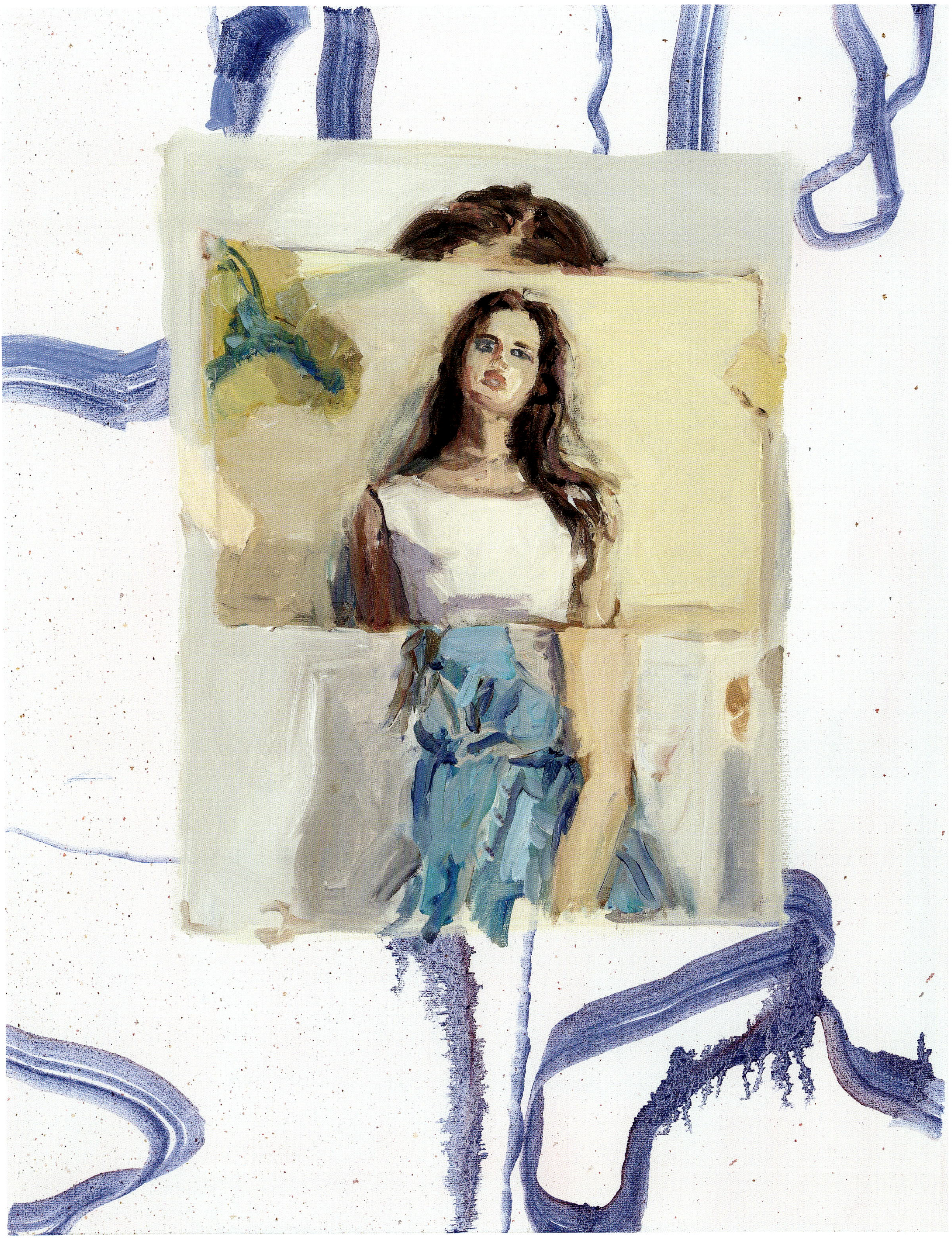

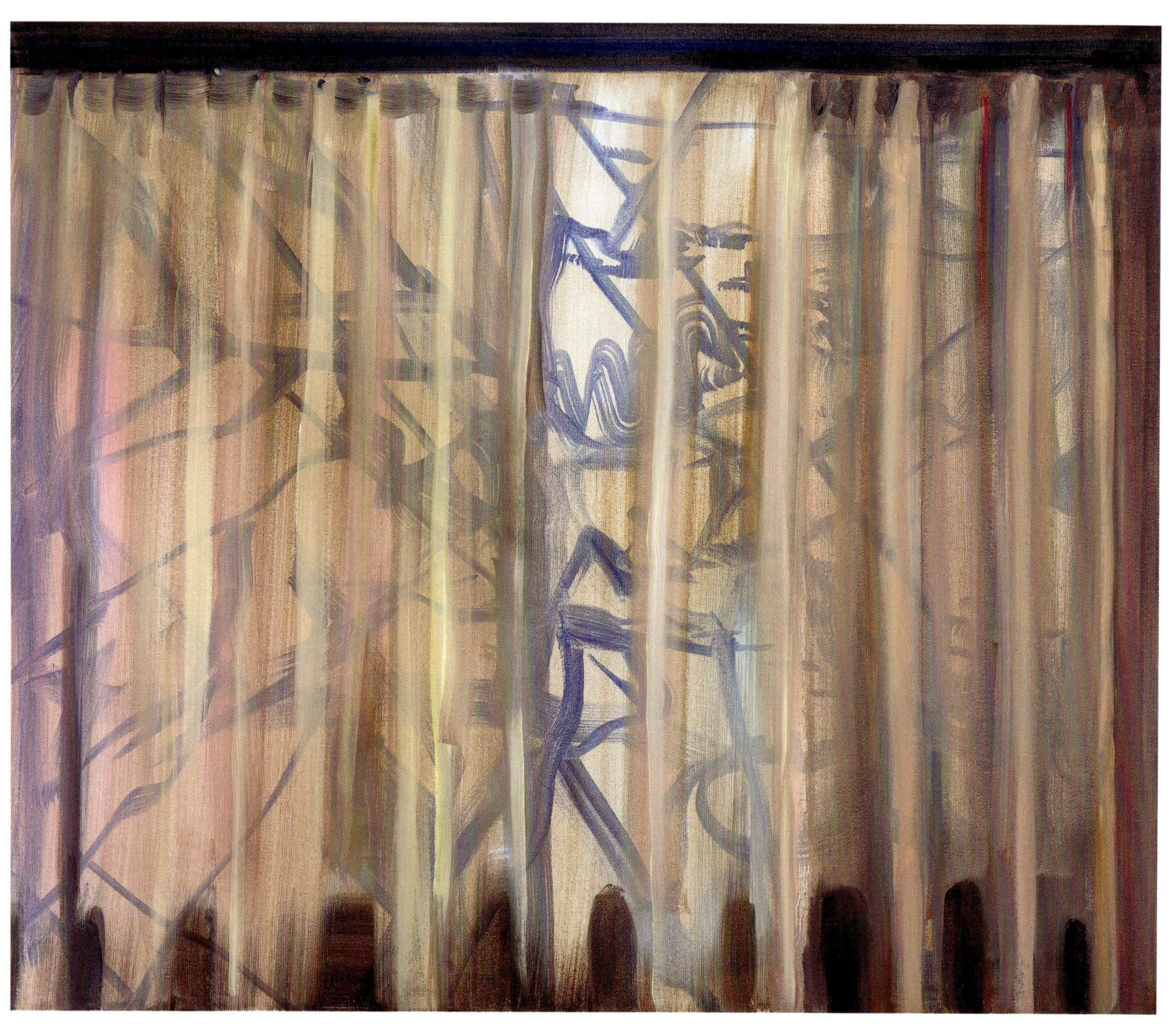

SCAR CURTAIN 2019

22 × 28 in. / 56 × 72 cm

THIS 2017

32 × 40 in. / 81 × 102 cm

DOUBLE LIPS 2018

20 × 24 in. / 51 × 61 cm

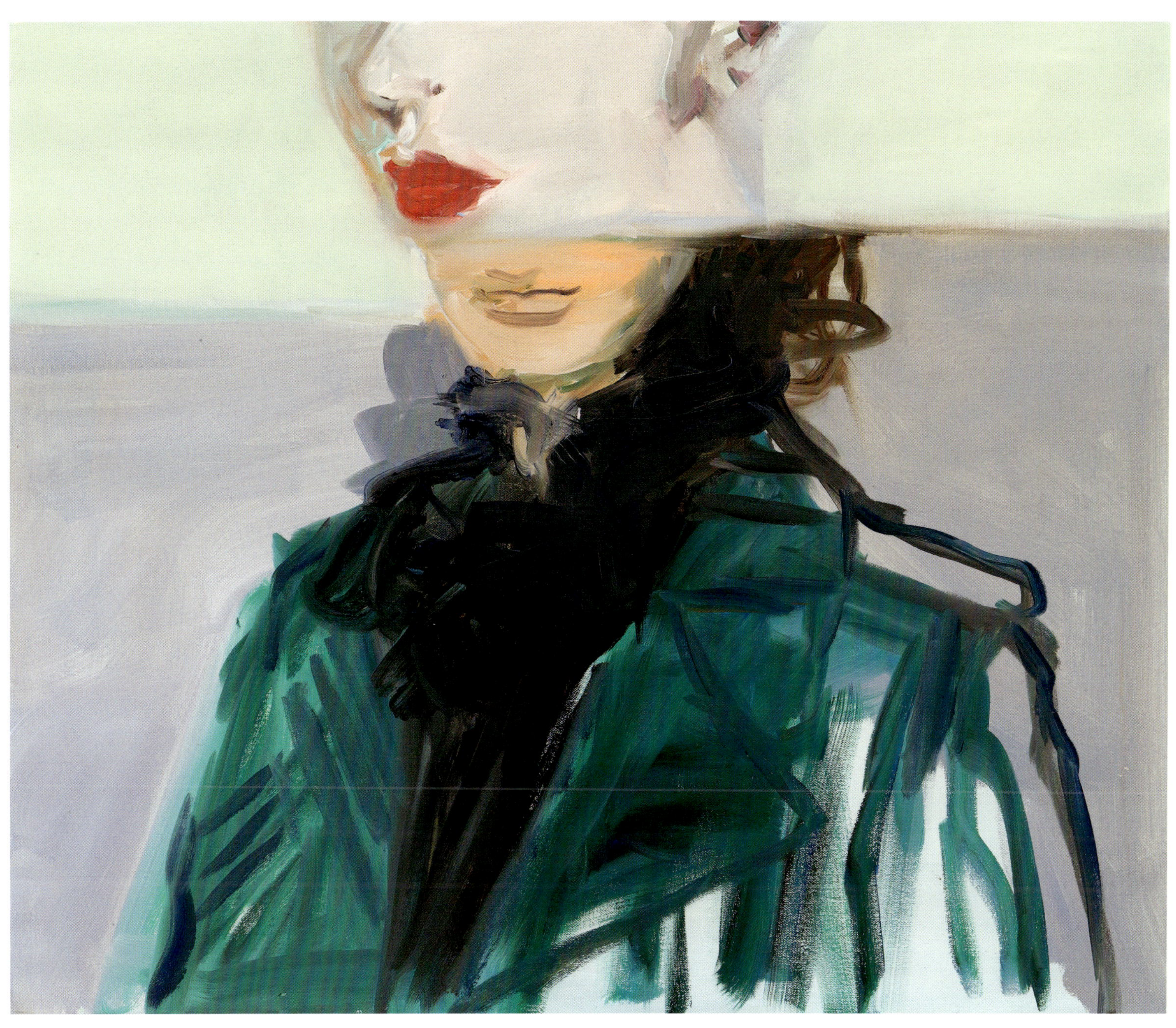

DEE (YELLOW DRESS) 2020

24 × 20 in. / 61 × 51 cm

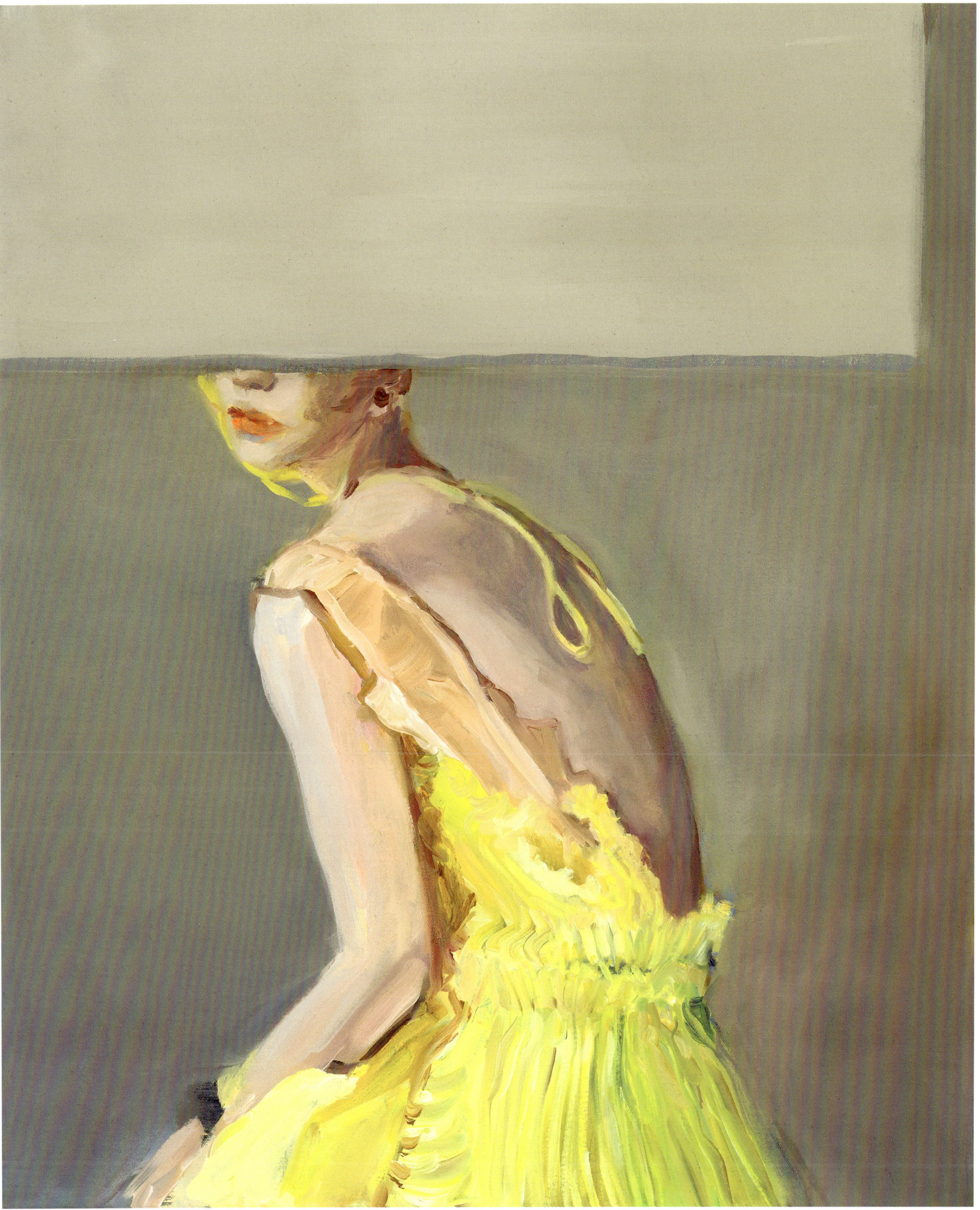

GALLERY

DOLORES 2019

55 × 45 in. / 140 × 114 cm

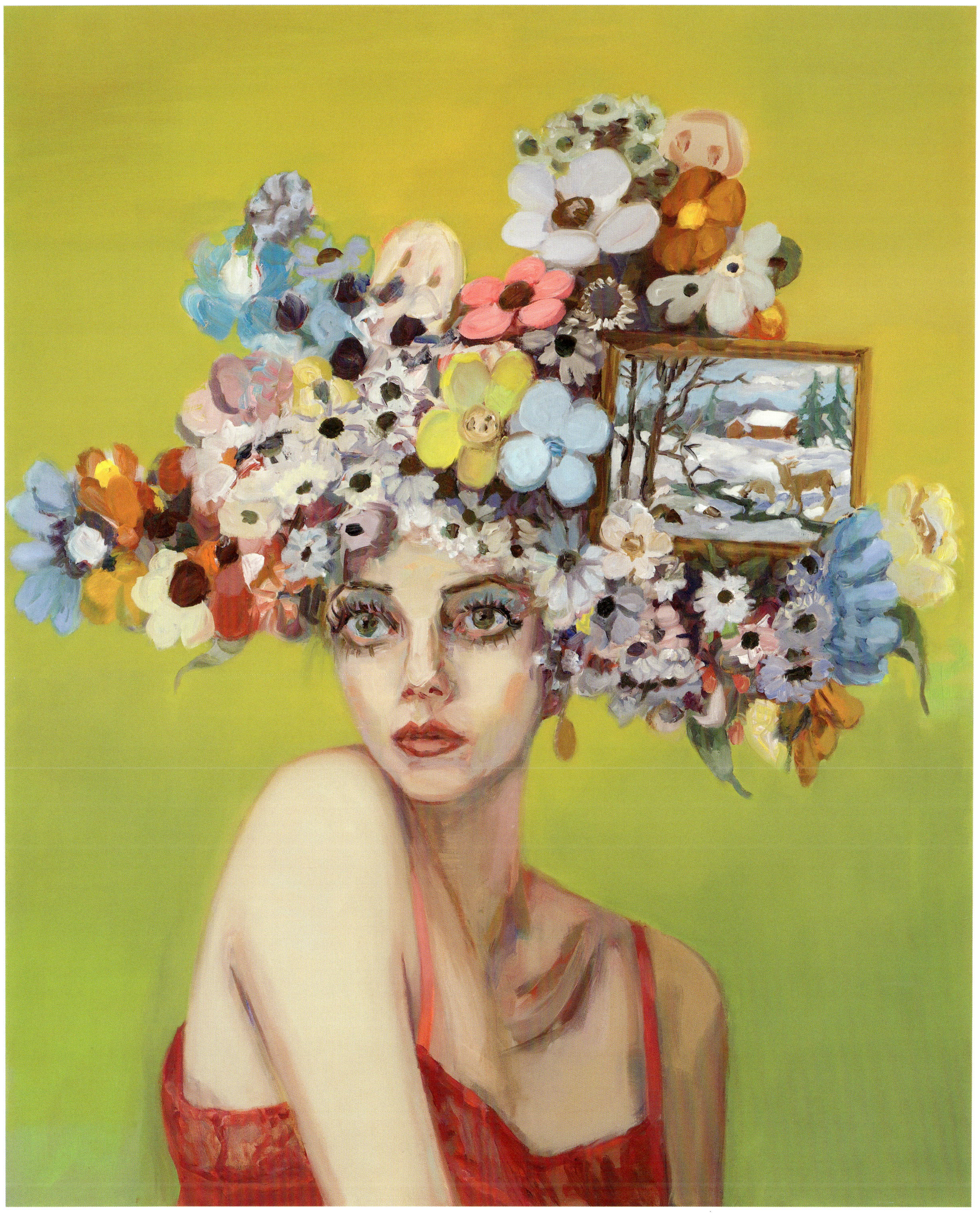

SMITH 2018

76 × 60 in. / 193 × 152 cm

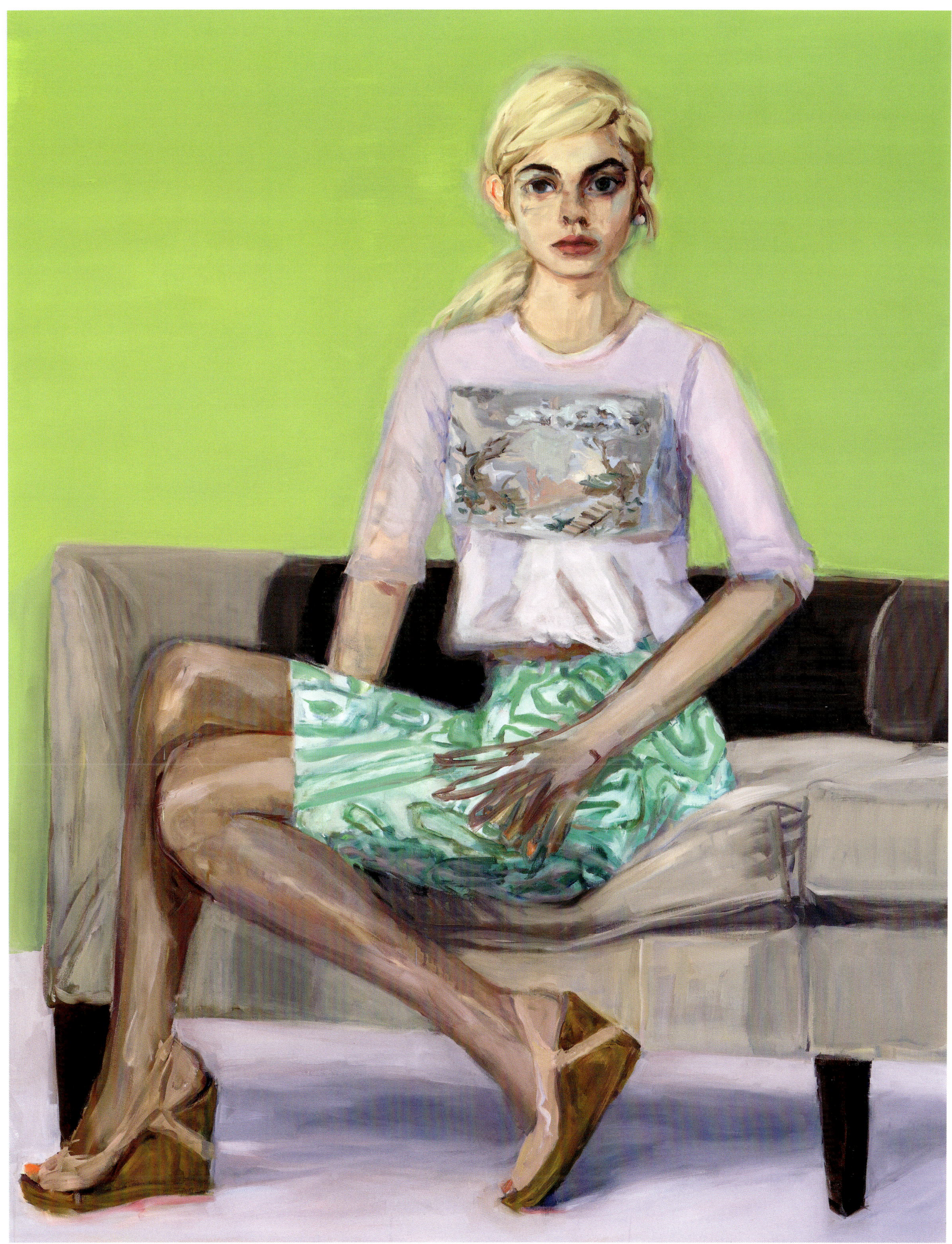

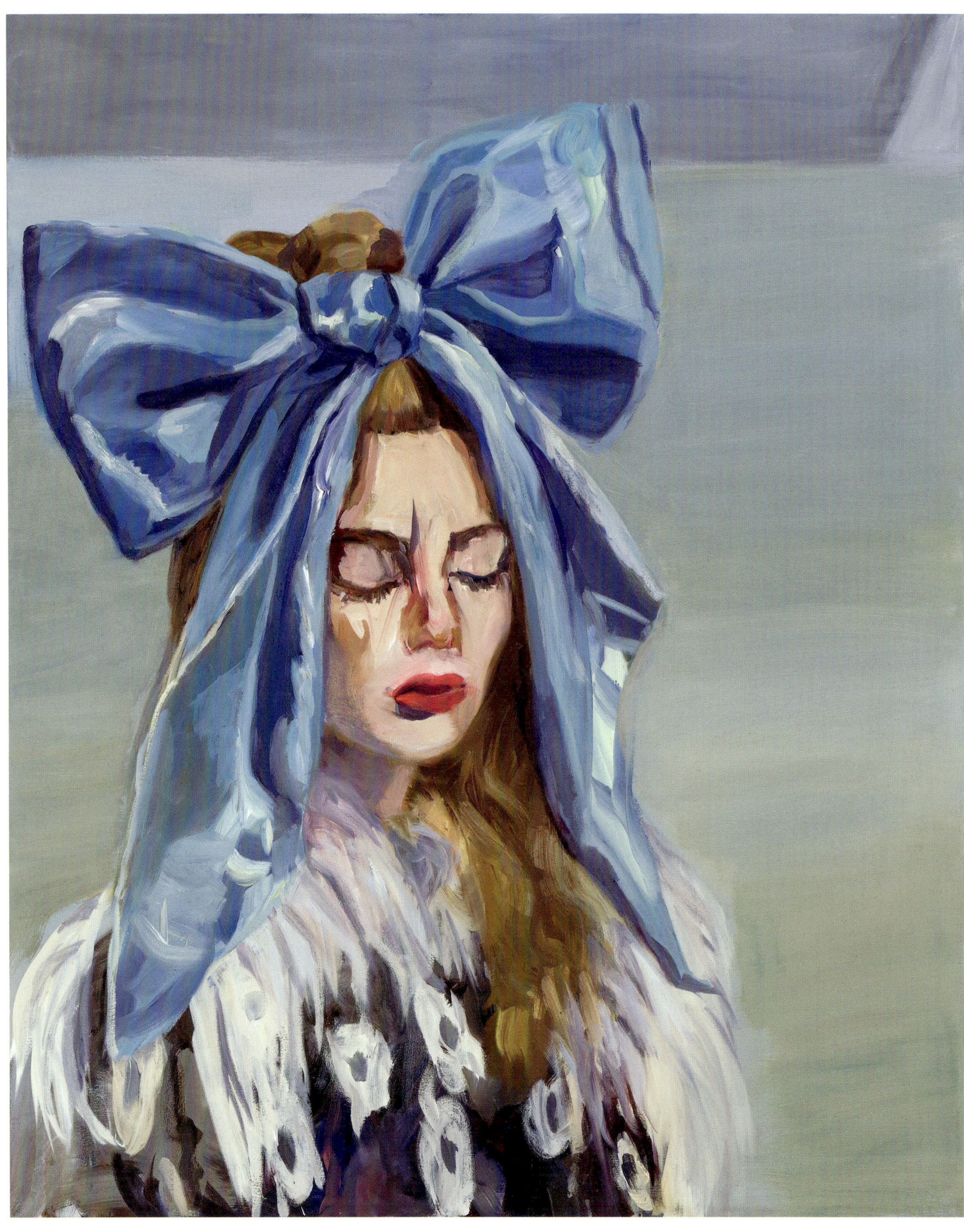

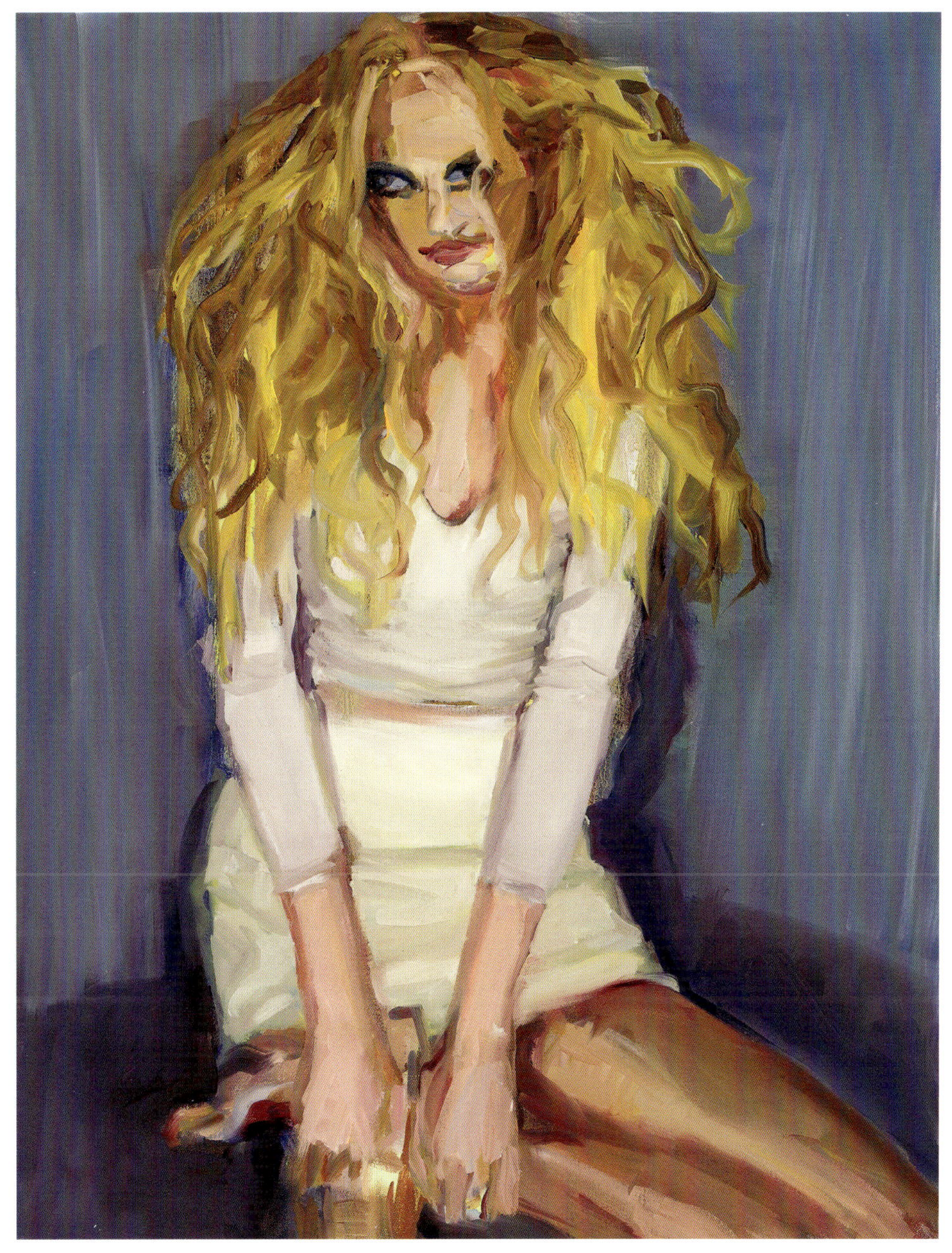

OPPOSITE

BLUE BOW 2019

44 × 36 in. / 112 × 91 cm

ABOVE

TEAZE 2018

31 × 24 in. / 79 × 61 cm

LAUREN (YELLOW SUIT) 2020

69 × 51 in. / 175 × 130 cm

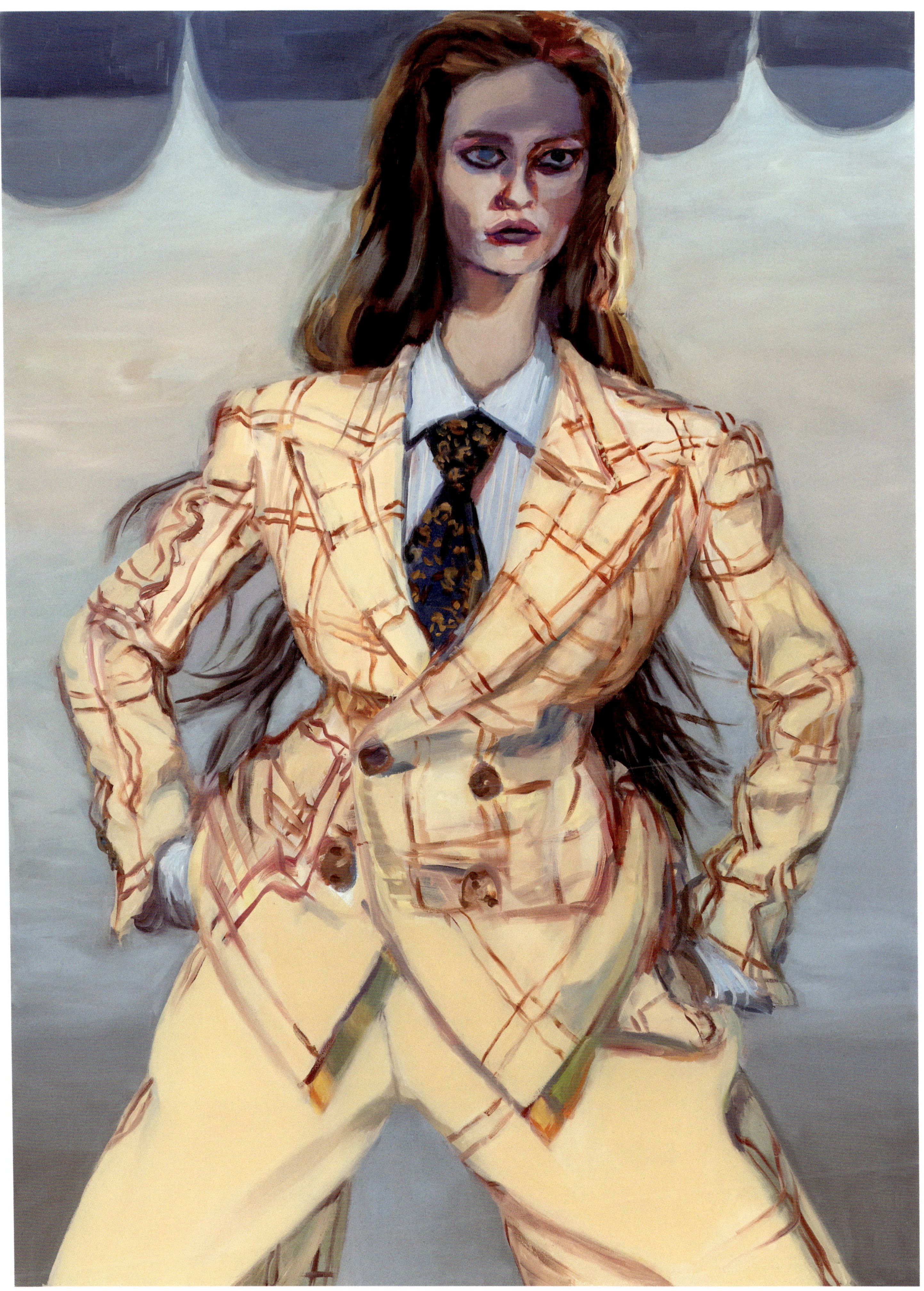

BEACON 2019

48 × 36 in. / 122 × 91 cm

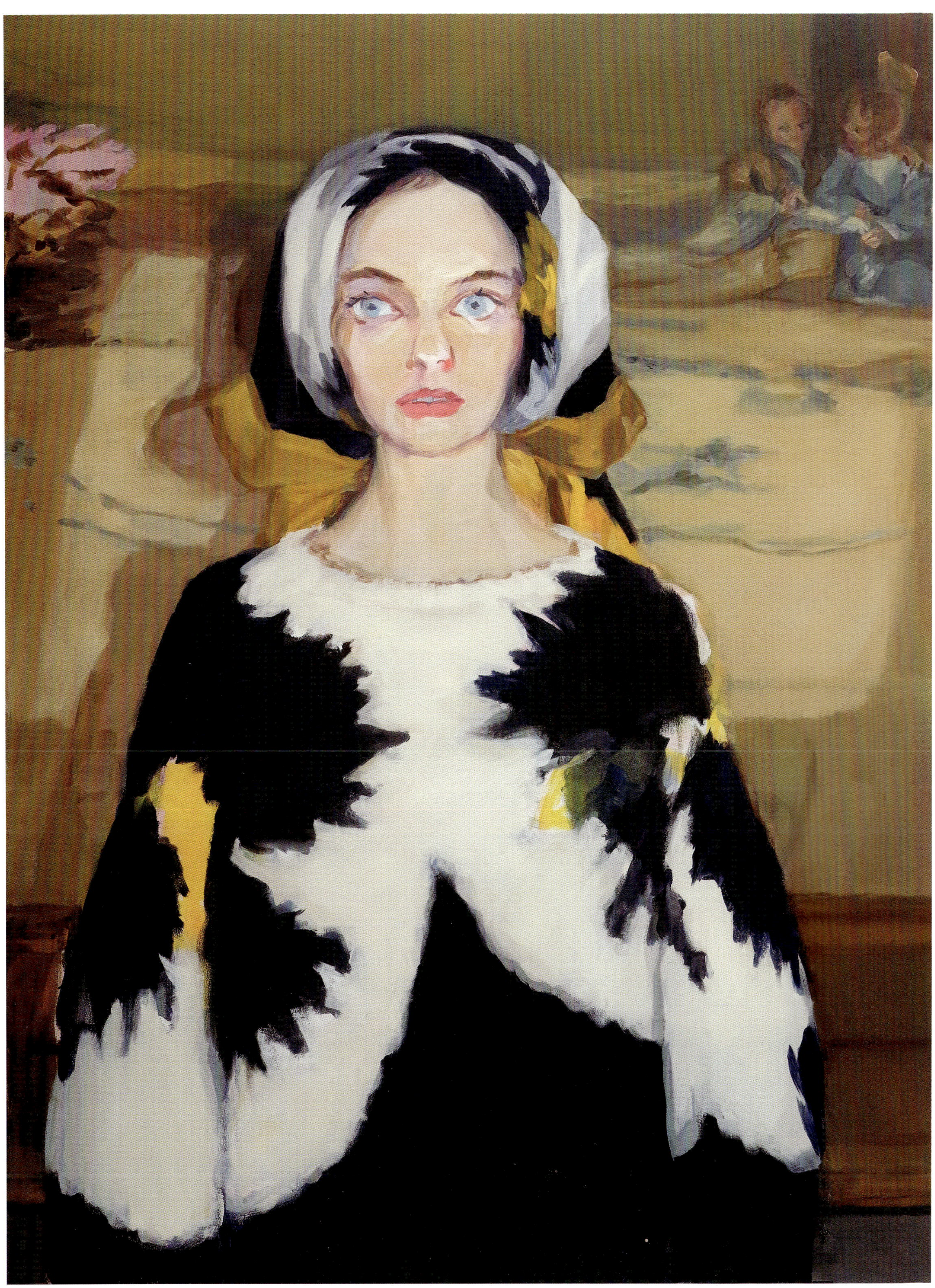

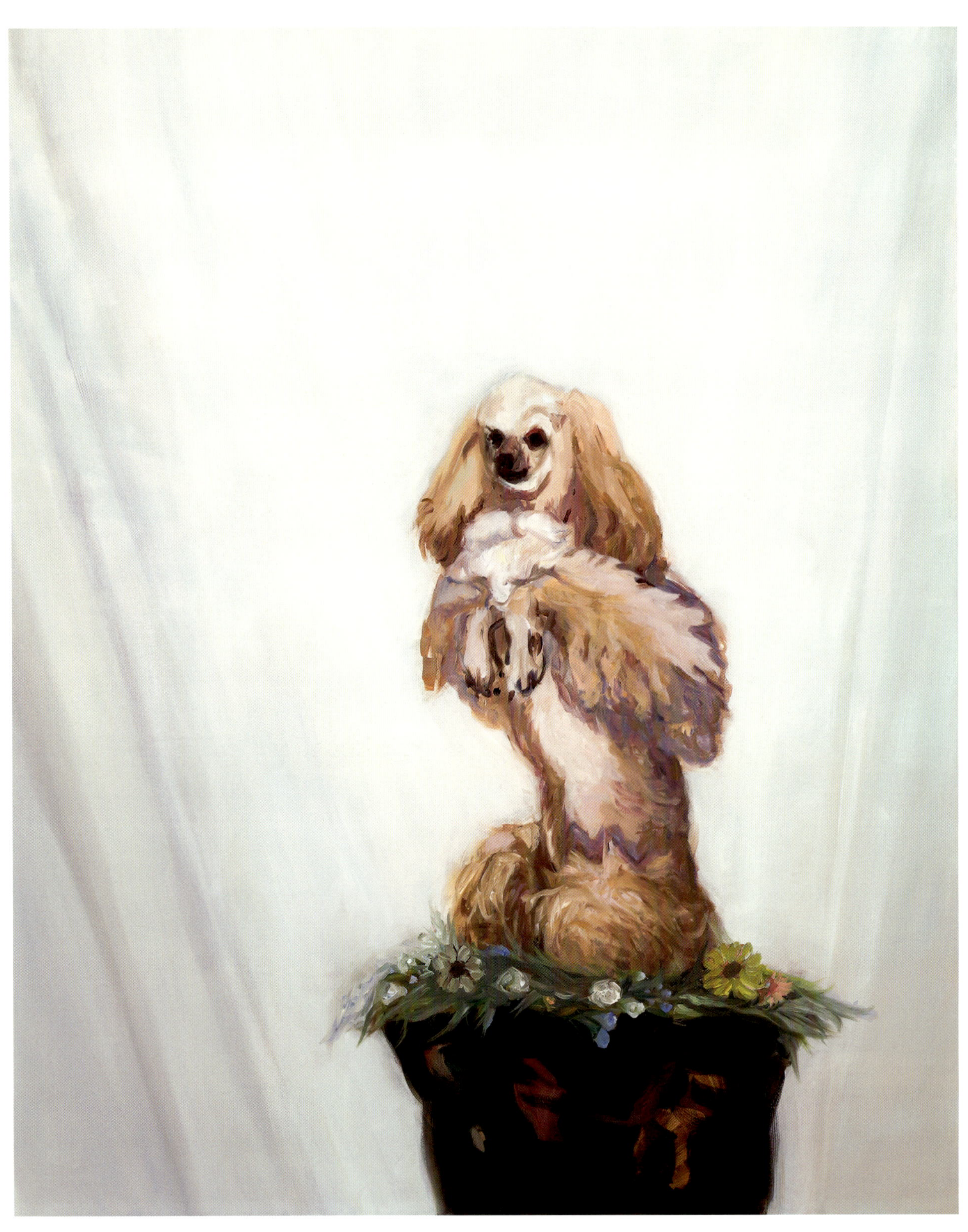

POODLE 2014

55 × 45 in. / 140 × 114 cm

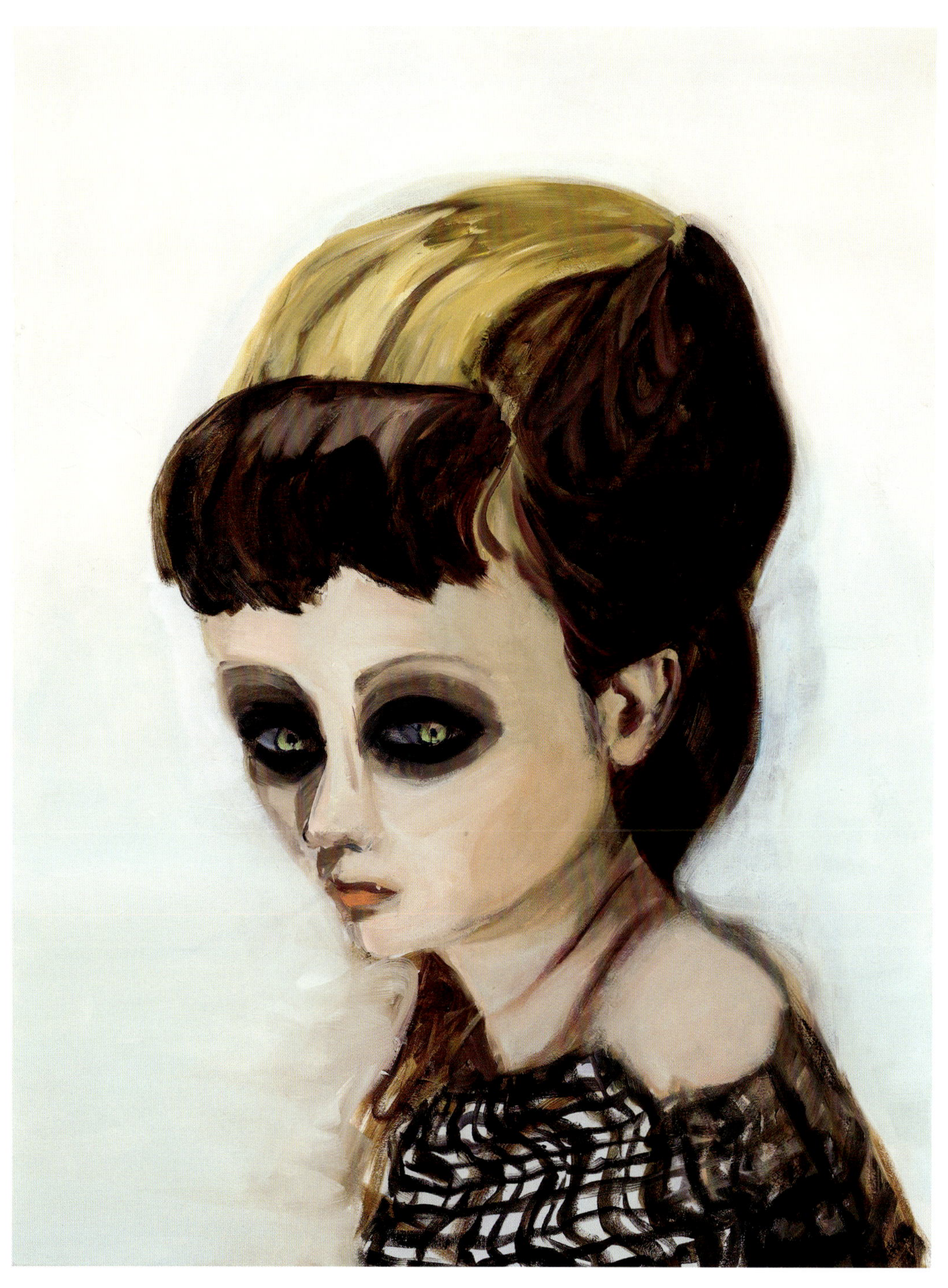

SUNDAY 2013

38 × 32 in. / 97 × 81 cm

PINKY 2019

54 × 45 in. / 137 × 114 cm

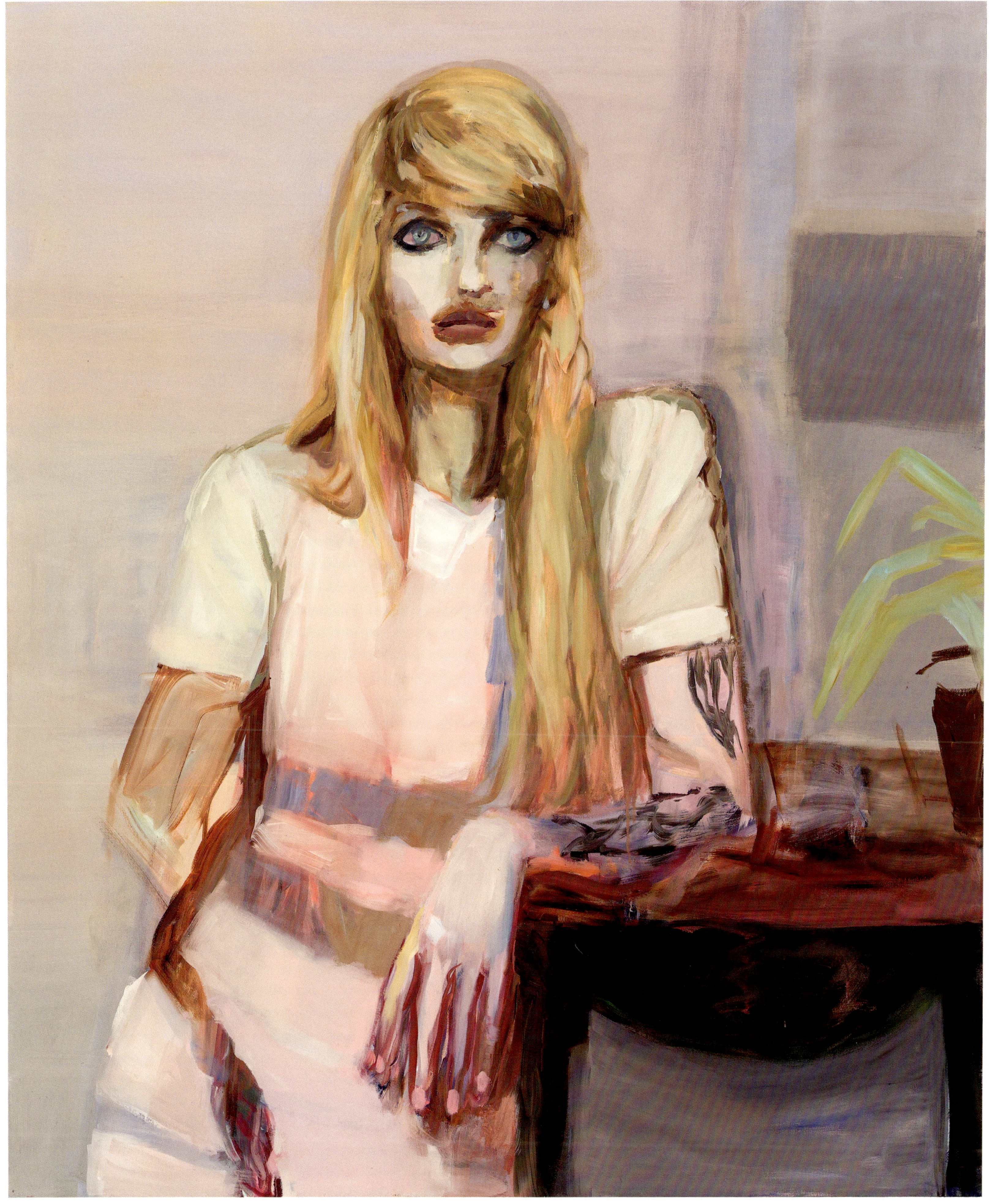

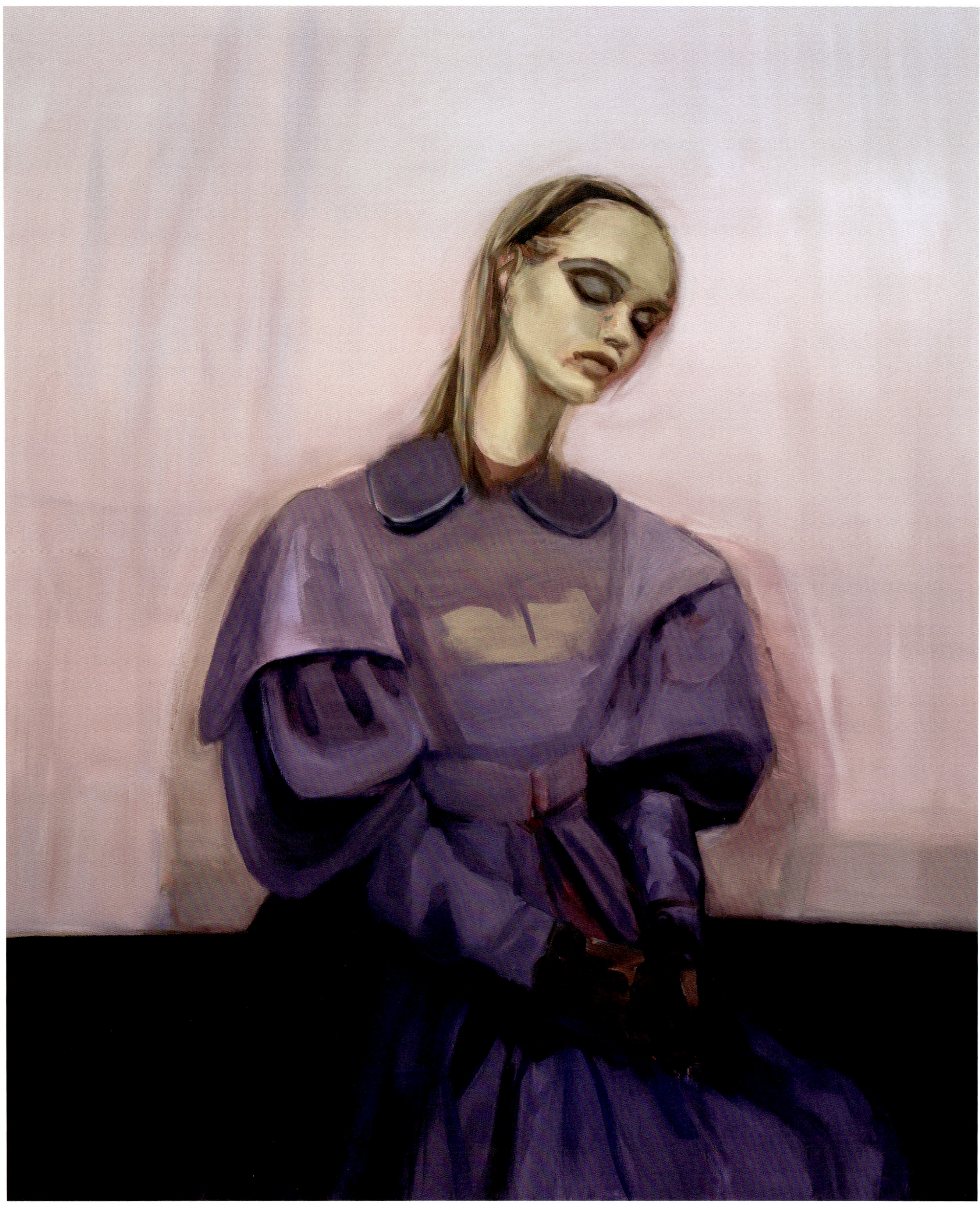

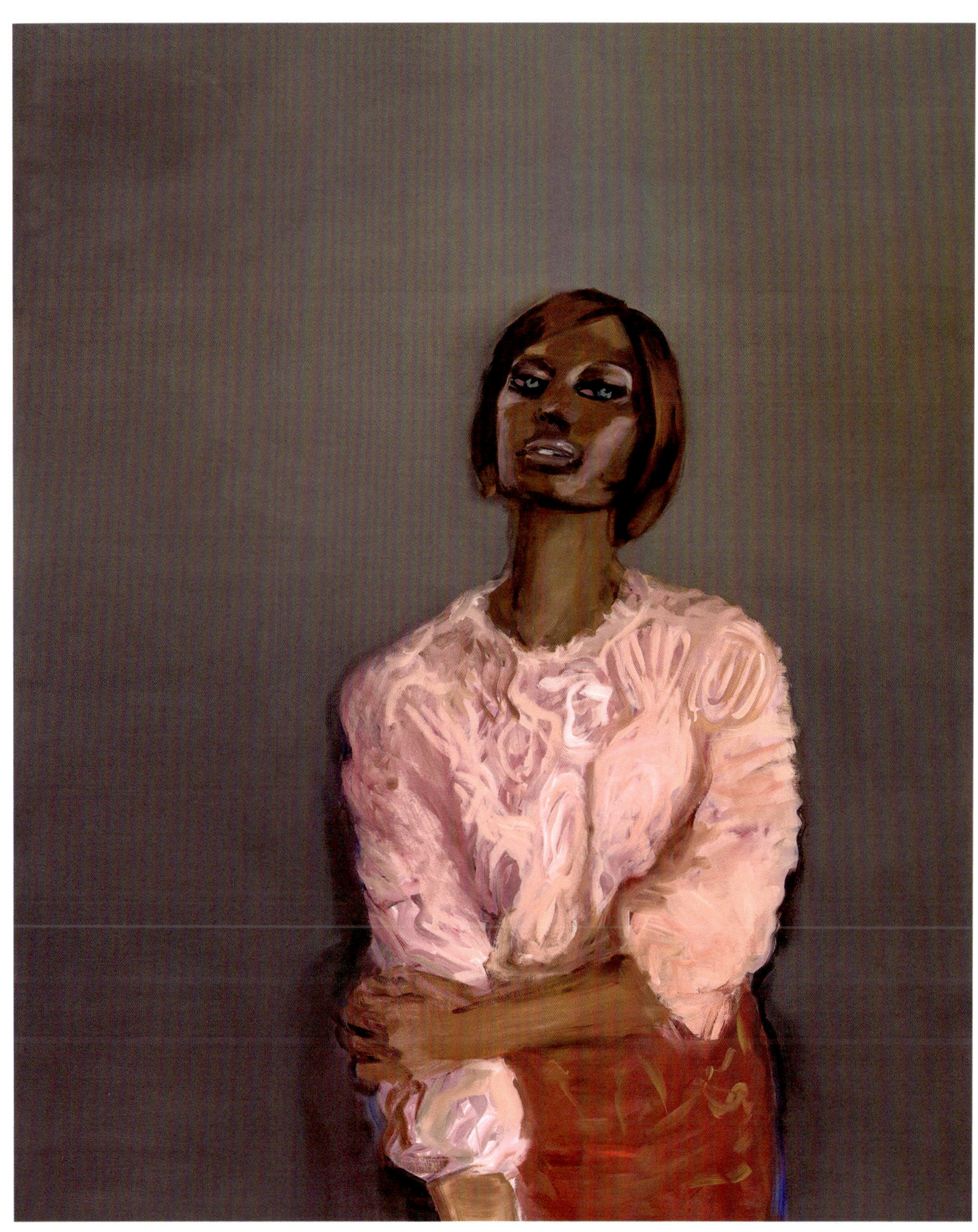

OPPOSITE

SLEEPER 2016

72 × 60 in. / 183 × 152 cm

ABOVE

RAIZIE 2014

55 × 45 in. / 140 × 114 cm

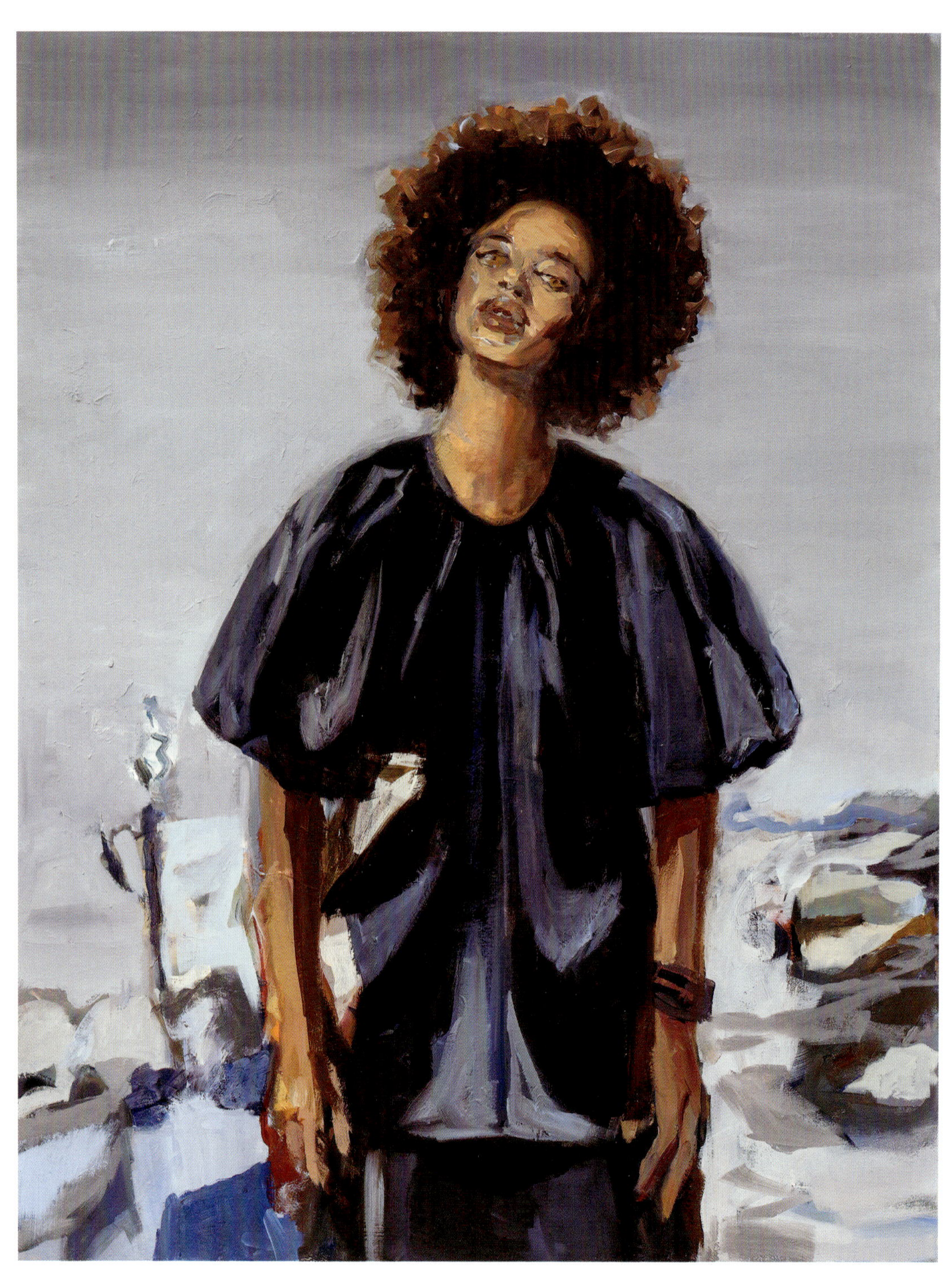

ARCTIC 2020

38 × 29 in. / 97 × 74 cm

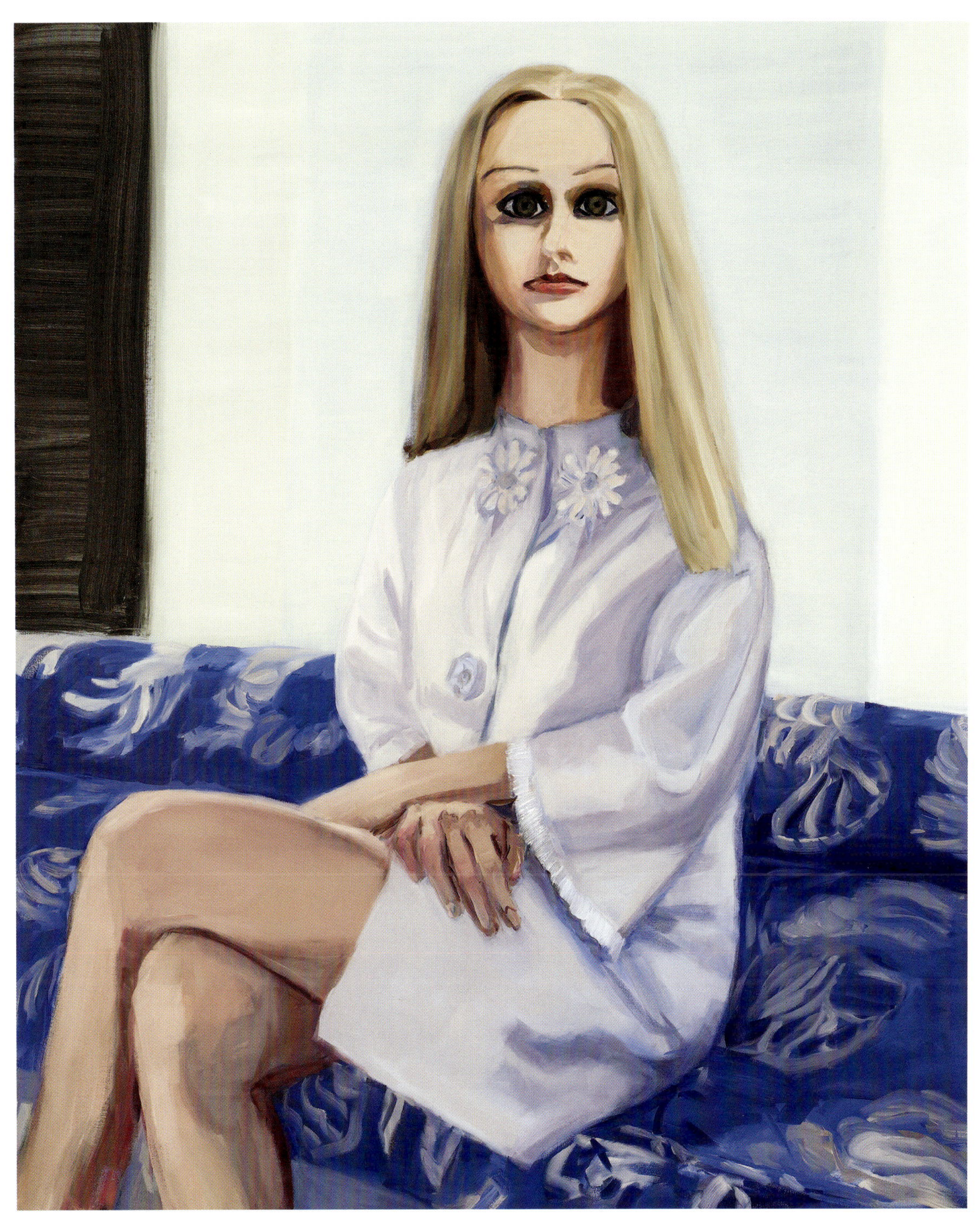

SAM 2014

55 × 45 in. / 140 × 114 cm

LUNAR 2016

77 × 66 in. / 196 × 168 cm

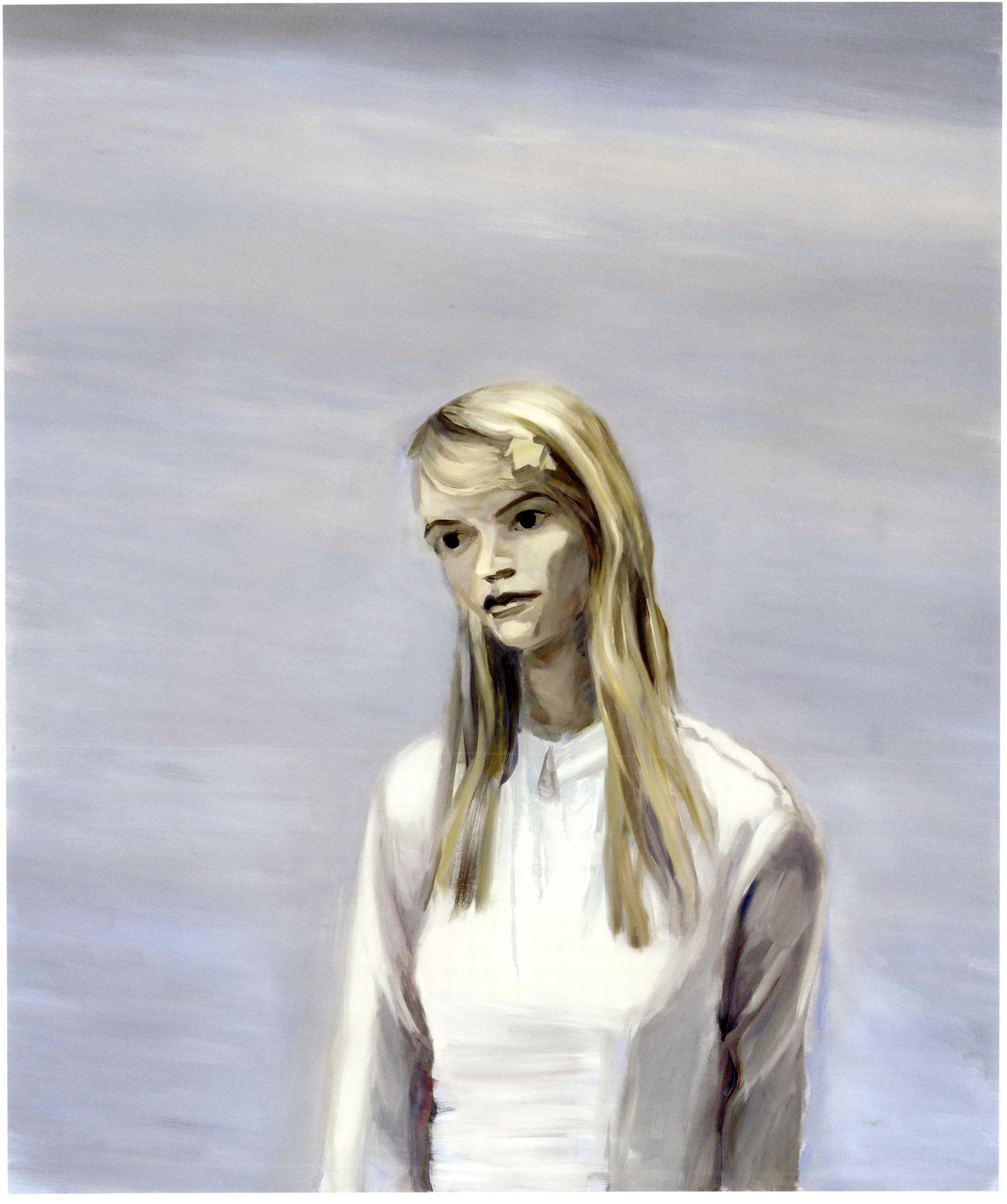

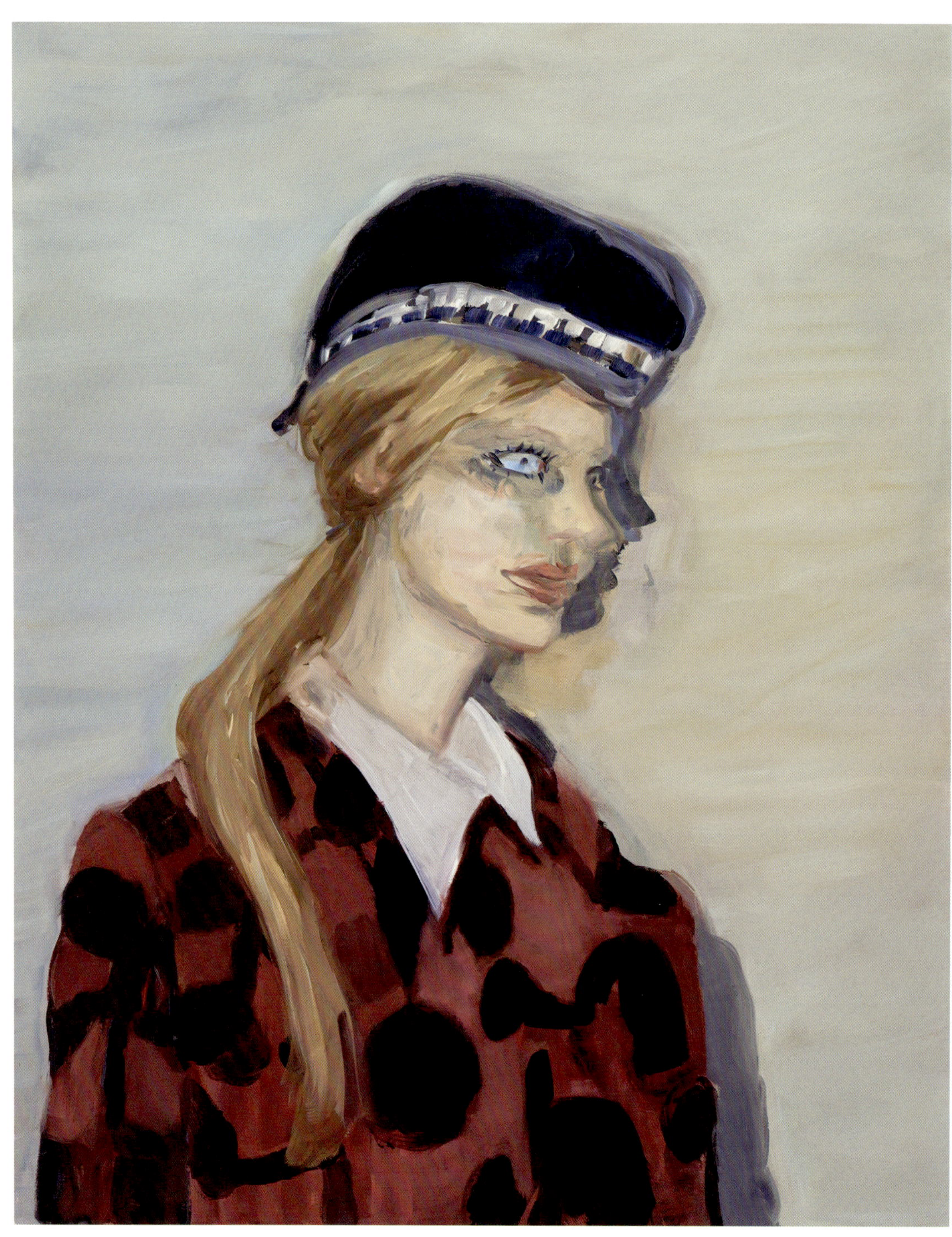

ABOVE

MEL 2017

40 × 32 in. / 102 × 81 cm

OPPOSITE

CRISS CROSS 2015

72 × 60 in. / 183 × 152 cm

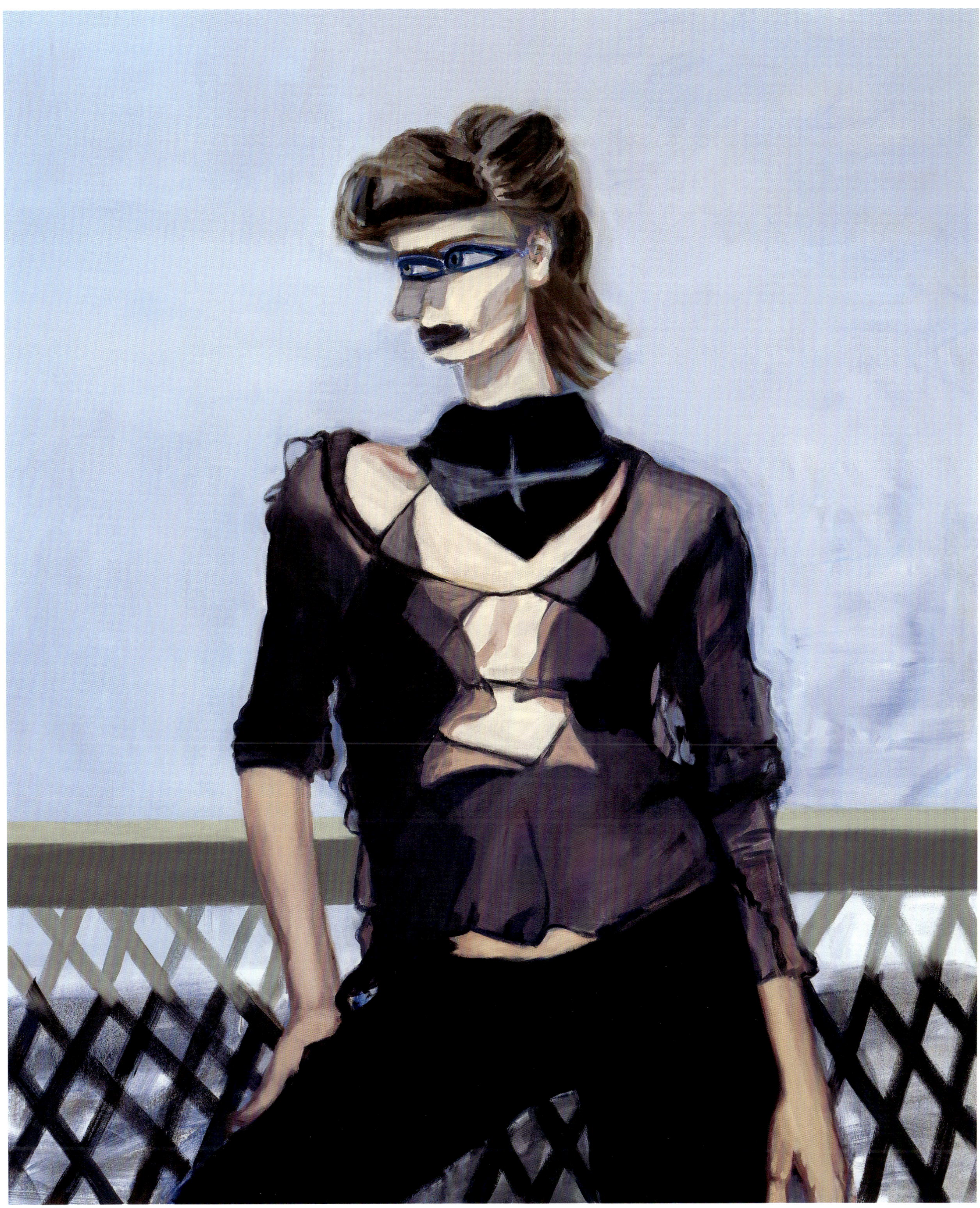

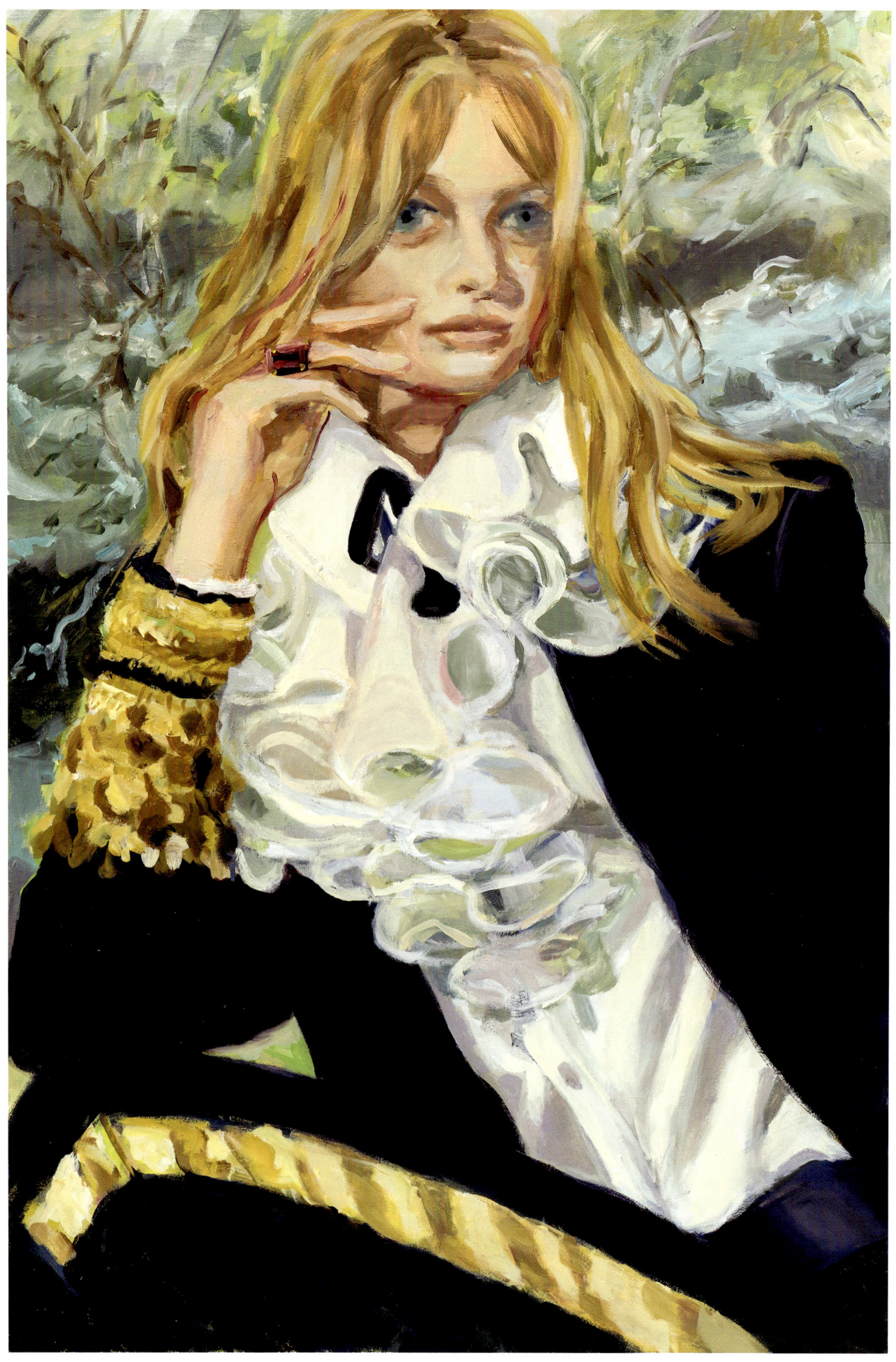

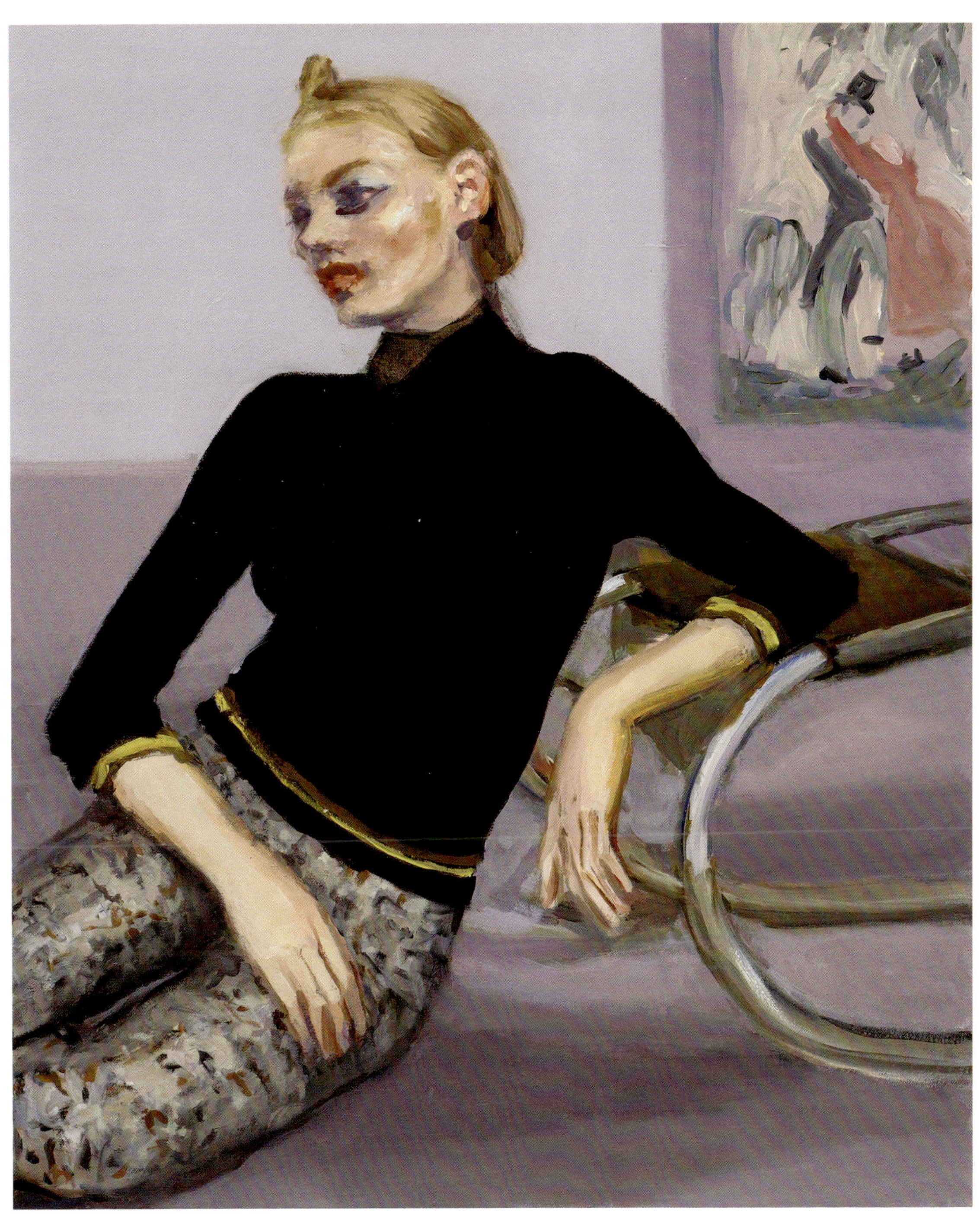

OPPOSITE

SKIPPER 2021

36 × 24 in. / 91 × 61 cm

ABOVE

BAUHAUS 2020

24 × 20 in. / 61 × 51 cm

LOU (LEAF) 2018

55 × 45 in. / 137 × 114 cm

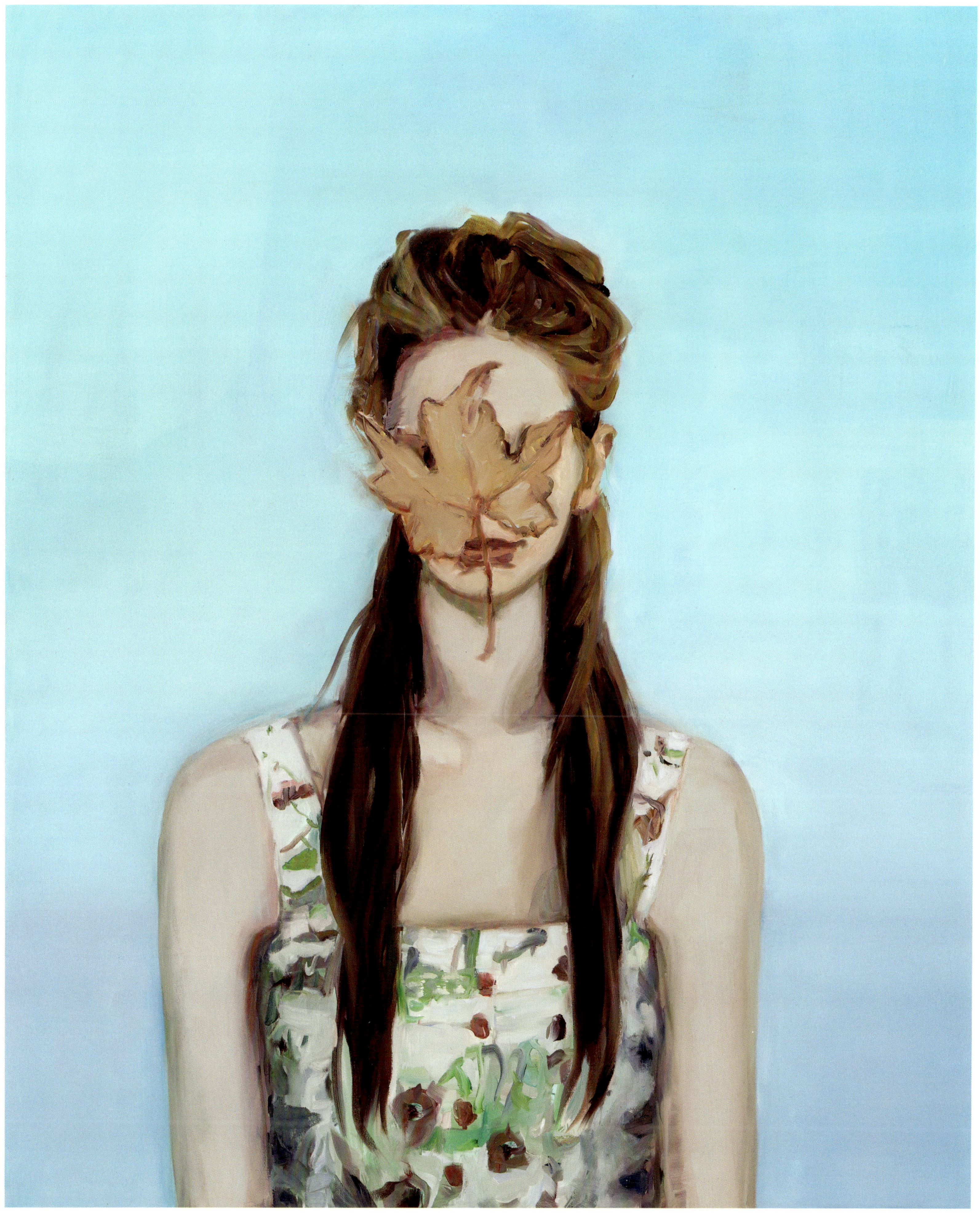

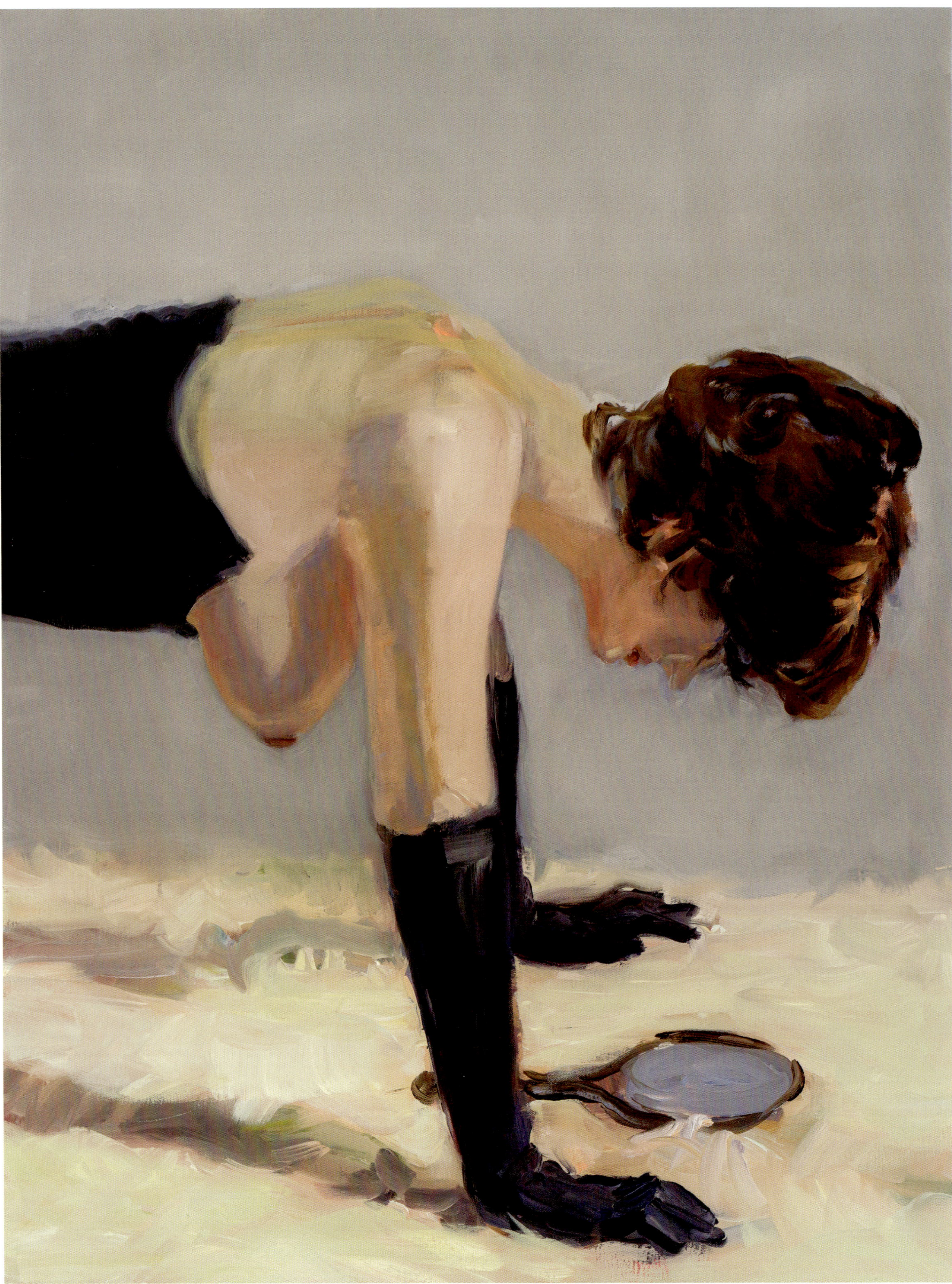

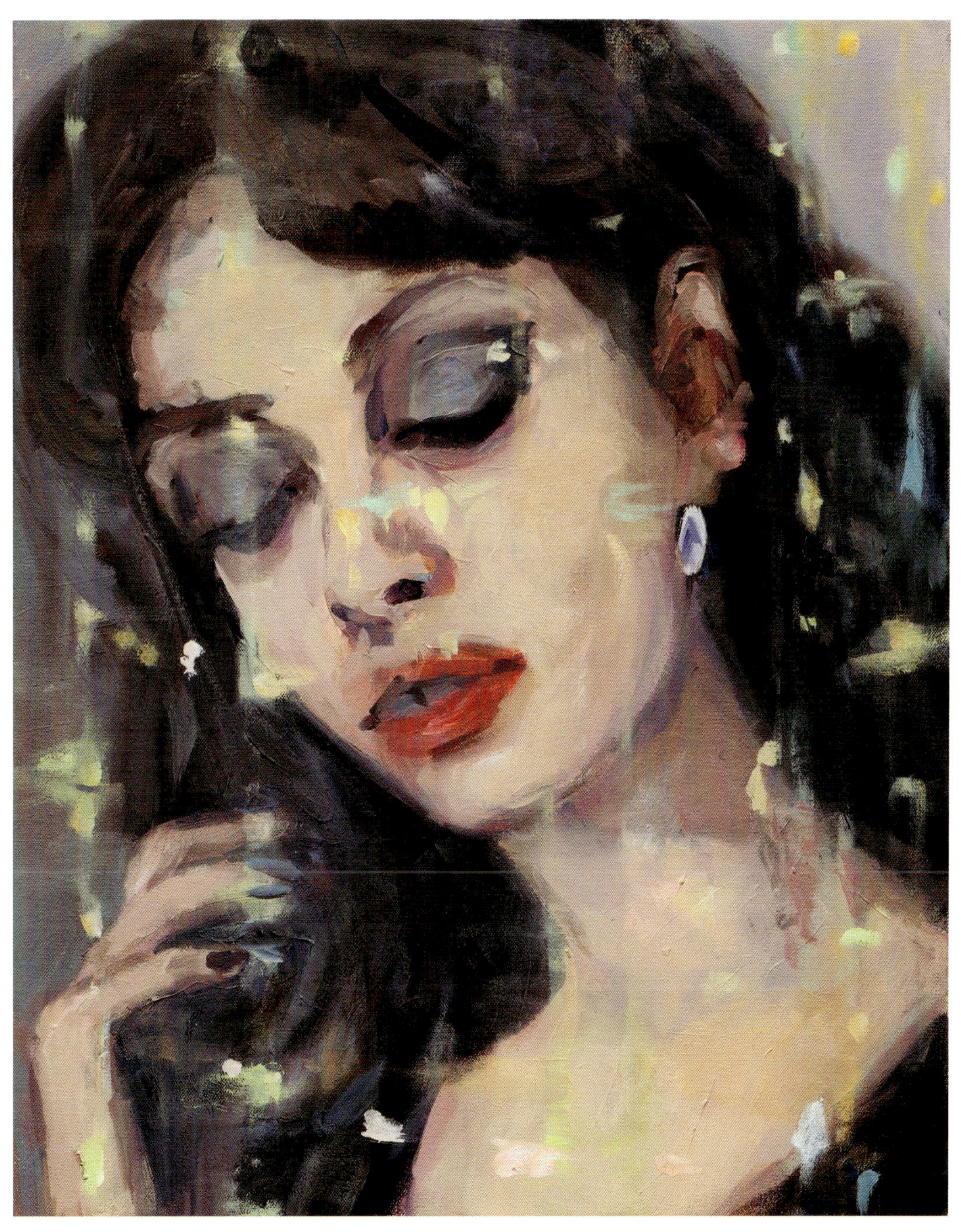

OPPOSITE

MIRROR AJ 2018

31 × 24 in. / 79 × 61 cm

ABOVE

MEDIUM 2020

20 × 16 in. / 51 × 41 cm

DOUBLE PORTRAIT
(STRAWBERRY BLONDE AND BRUNETTE) 2019

24 × 22 in. / 61 × 56 cm

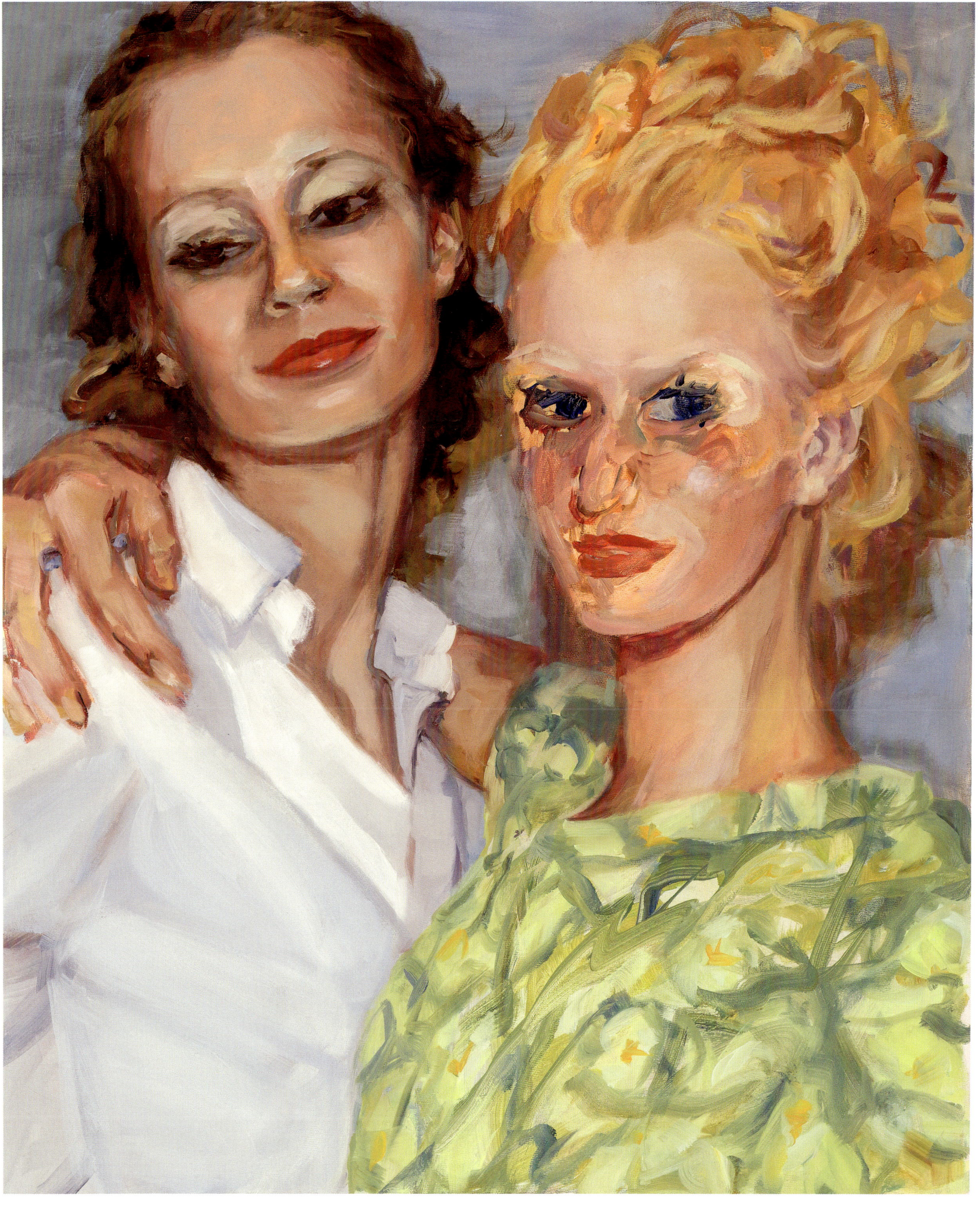

KIT 2019

24 × 22 in. / 61 × 56 cm

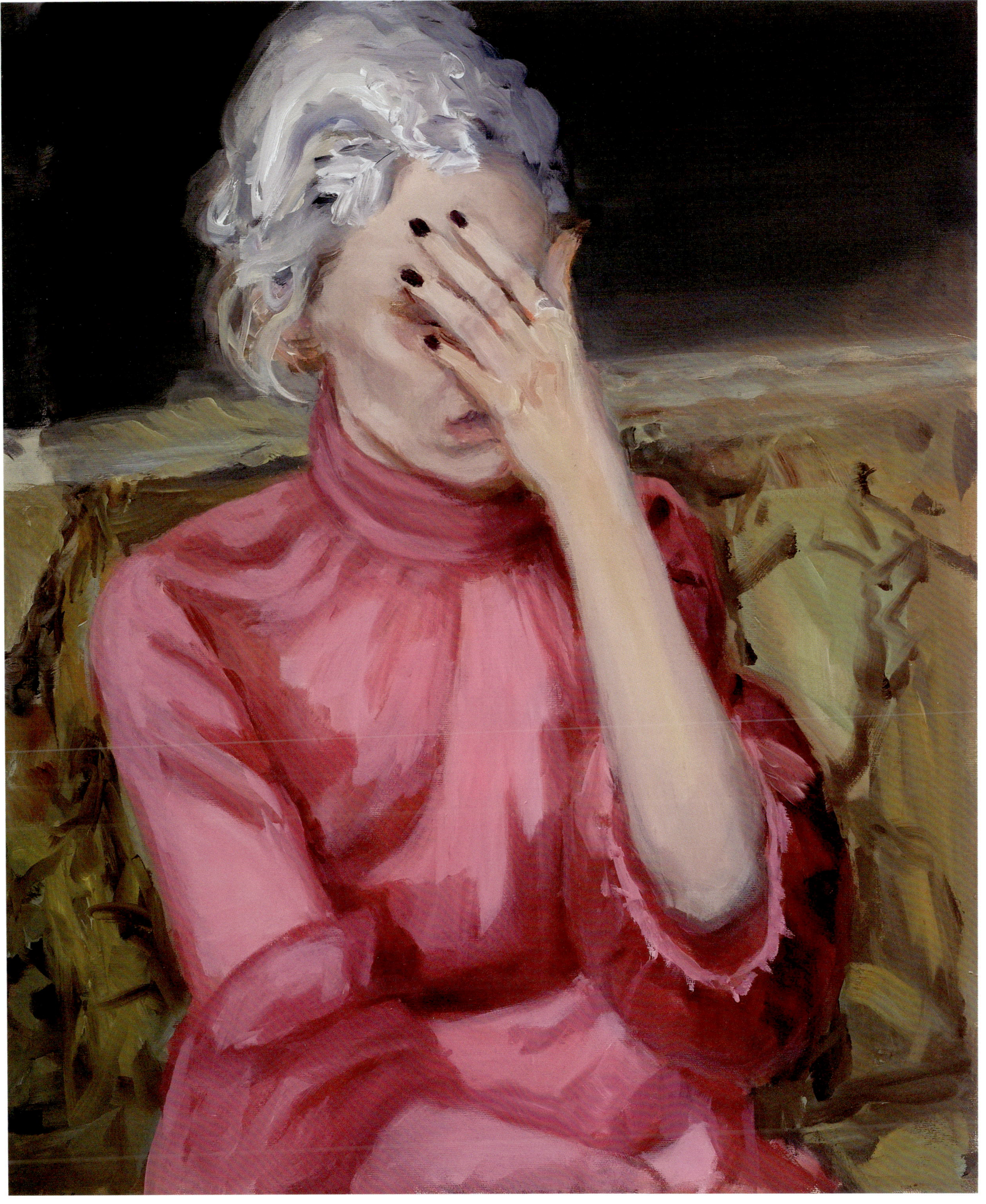

MISFITS

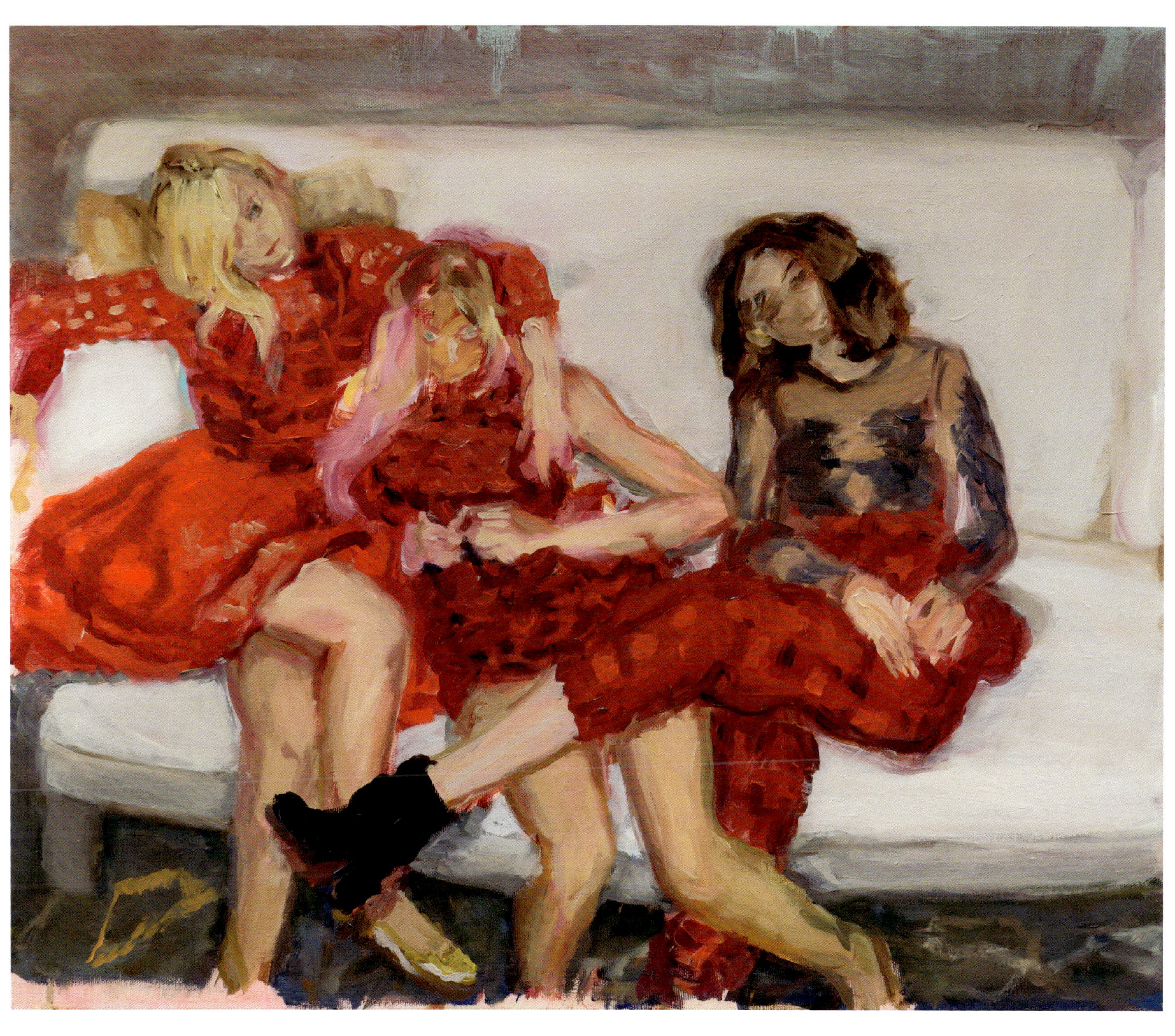

DANISH 2019

20 × 24 in. / 51 × 61 cm

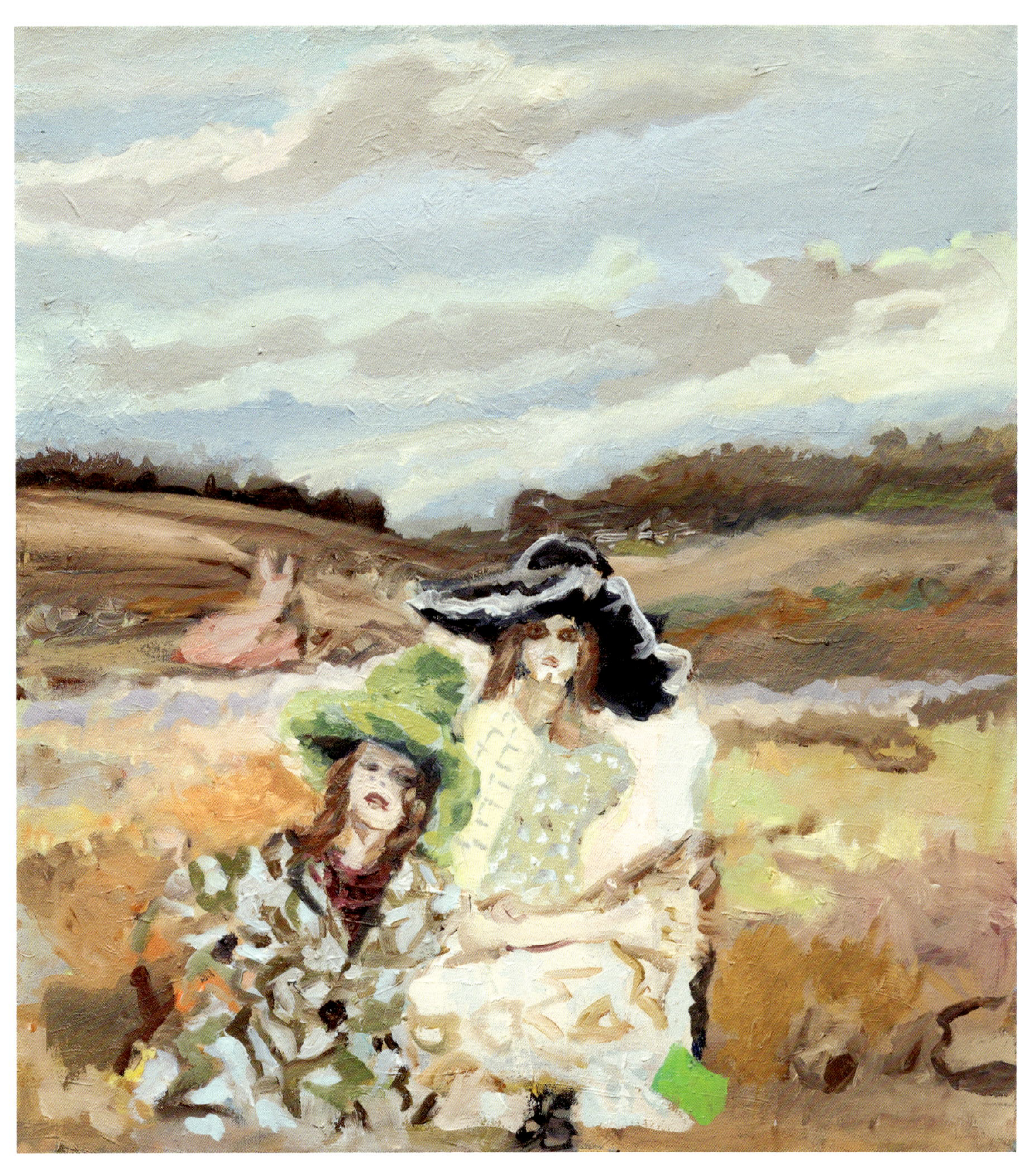

JUERGEN 2020

22 × 20 in. / 56 × 51 cm

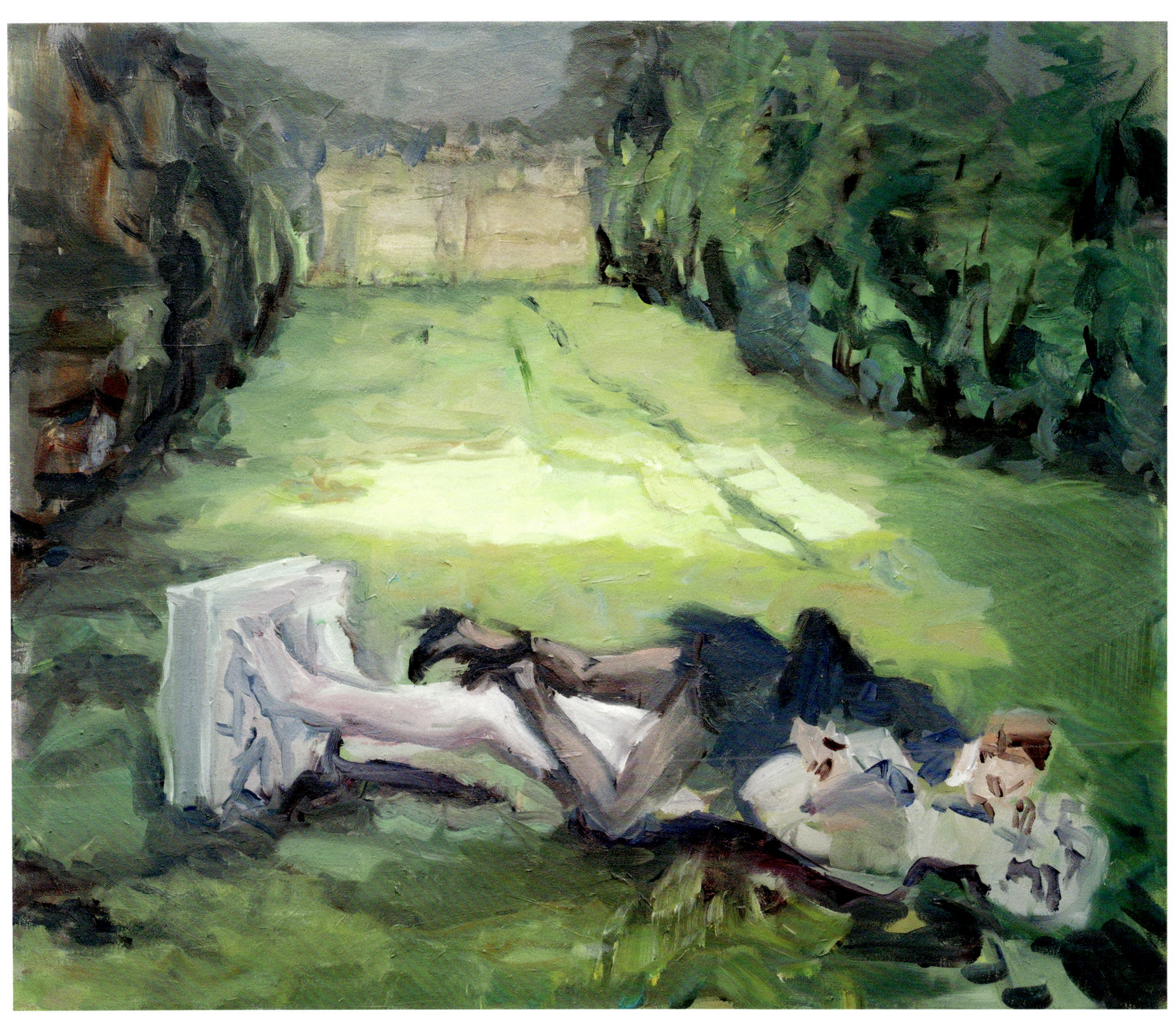

DISGRACE 2020

20 × 24 in. / 51 × 61 cm

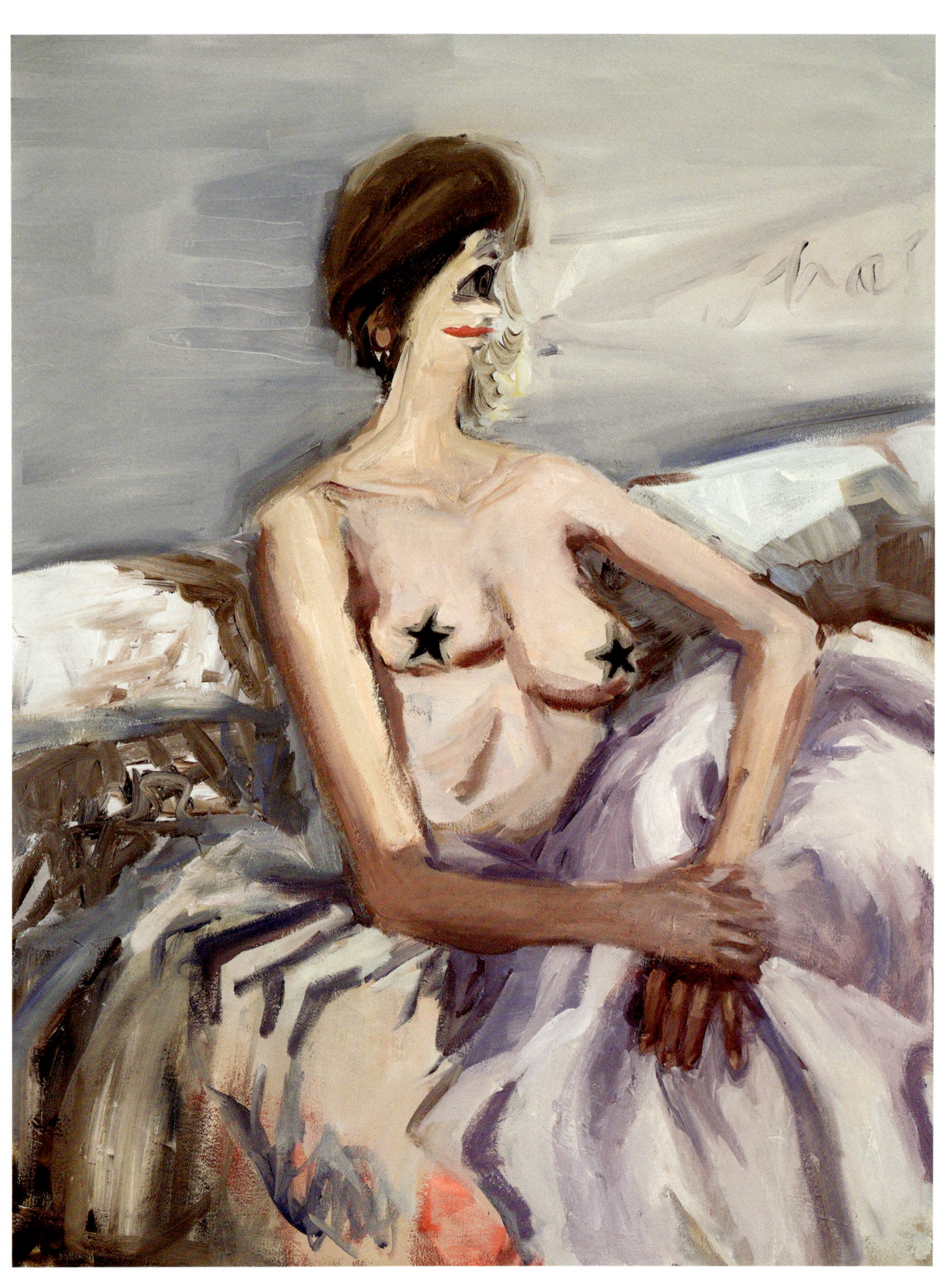

PERFORMER 2014

31 × 24 in. / 79 × 61 cm

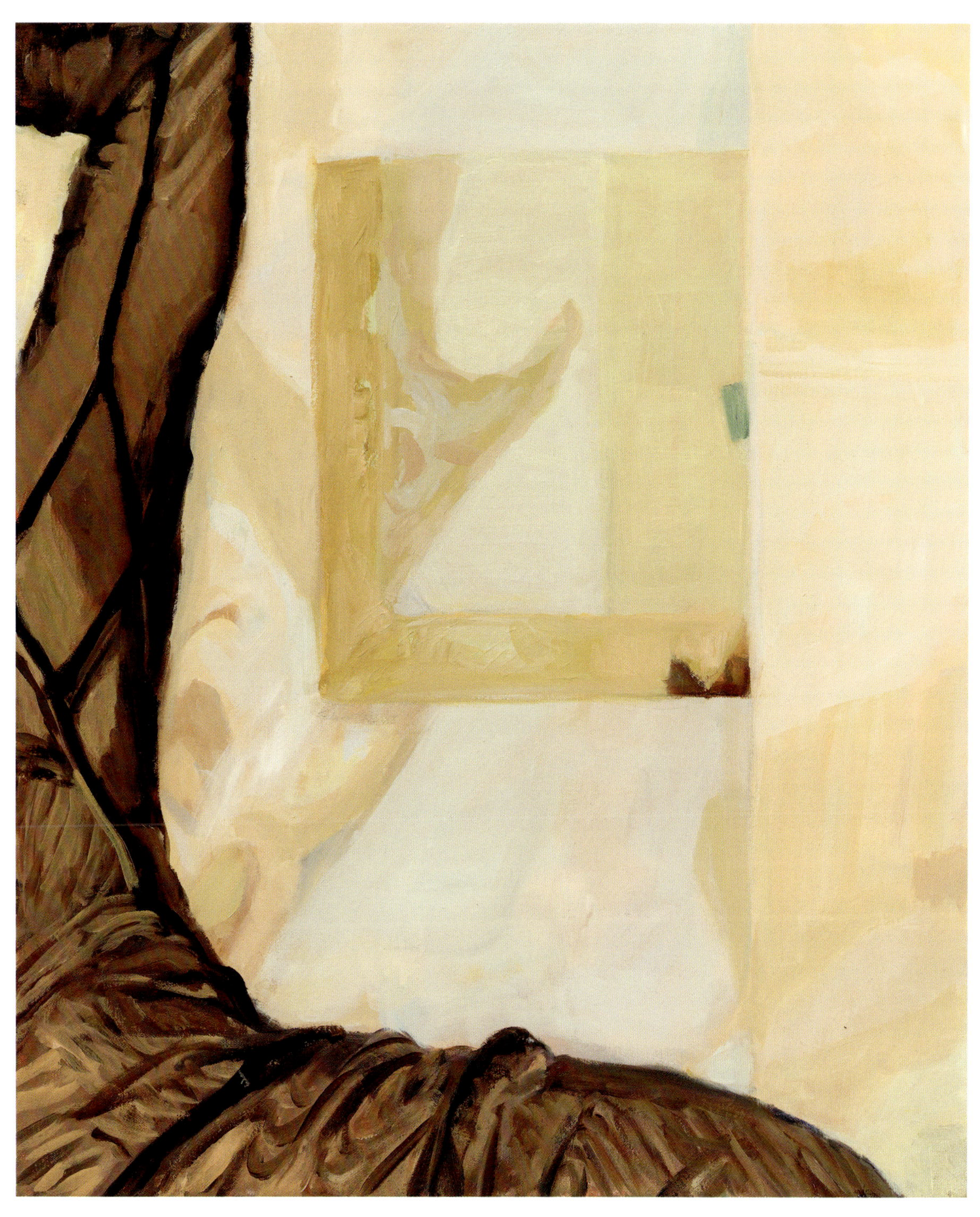

NET 2021

24 × 20 in. / 61 × 51 cm

HARP 2018

76 × 60 in. / 193 × 152 cm

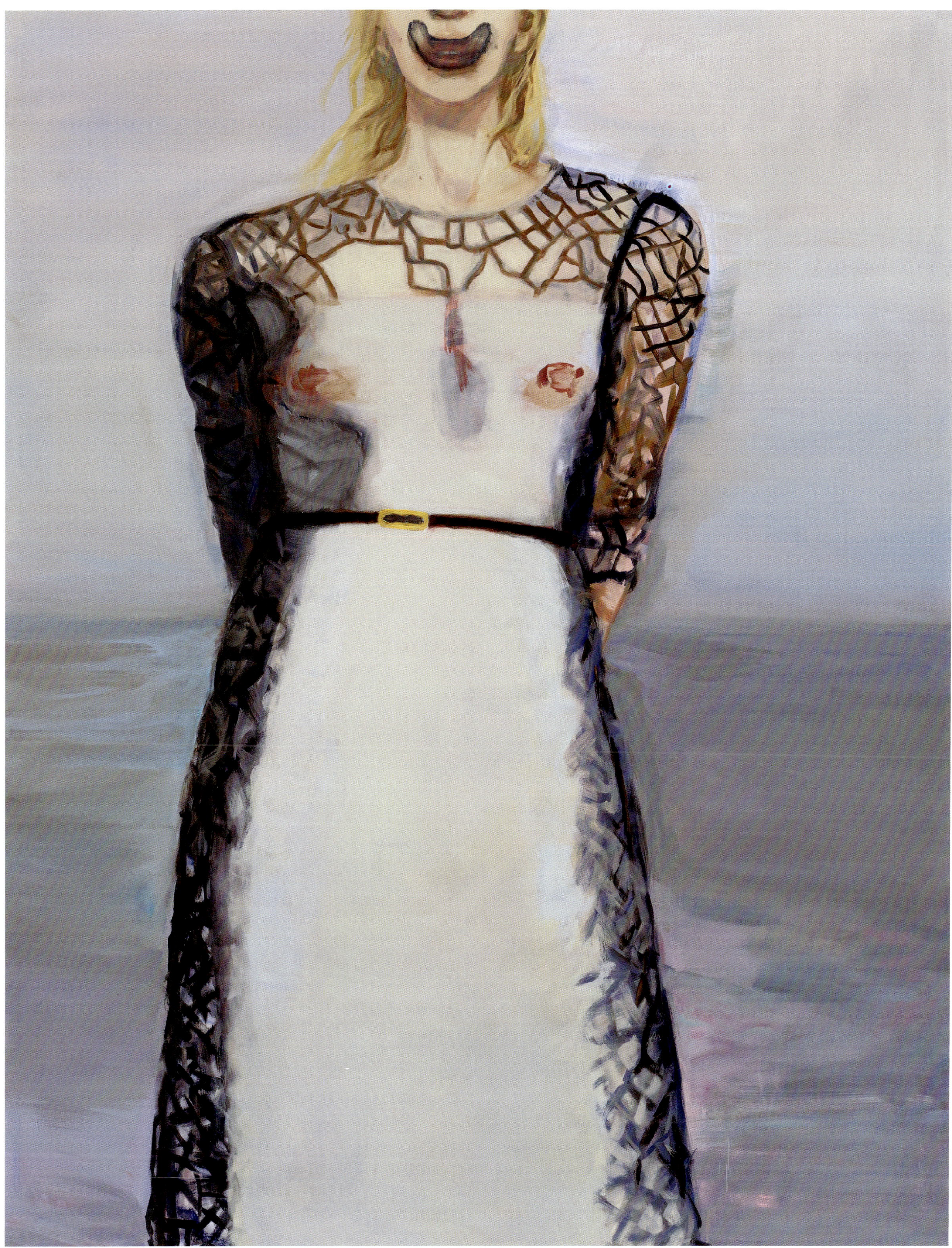

PET 2014

87 × 66 in. / 221 × 168 cm

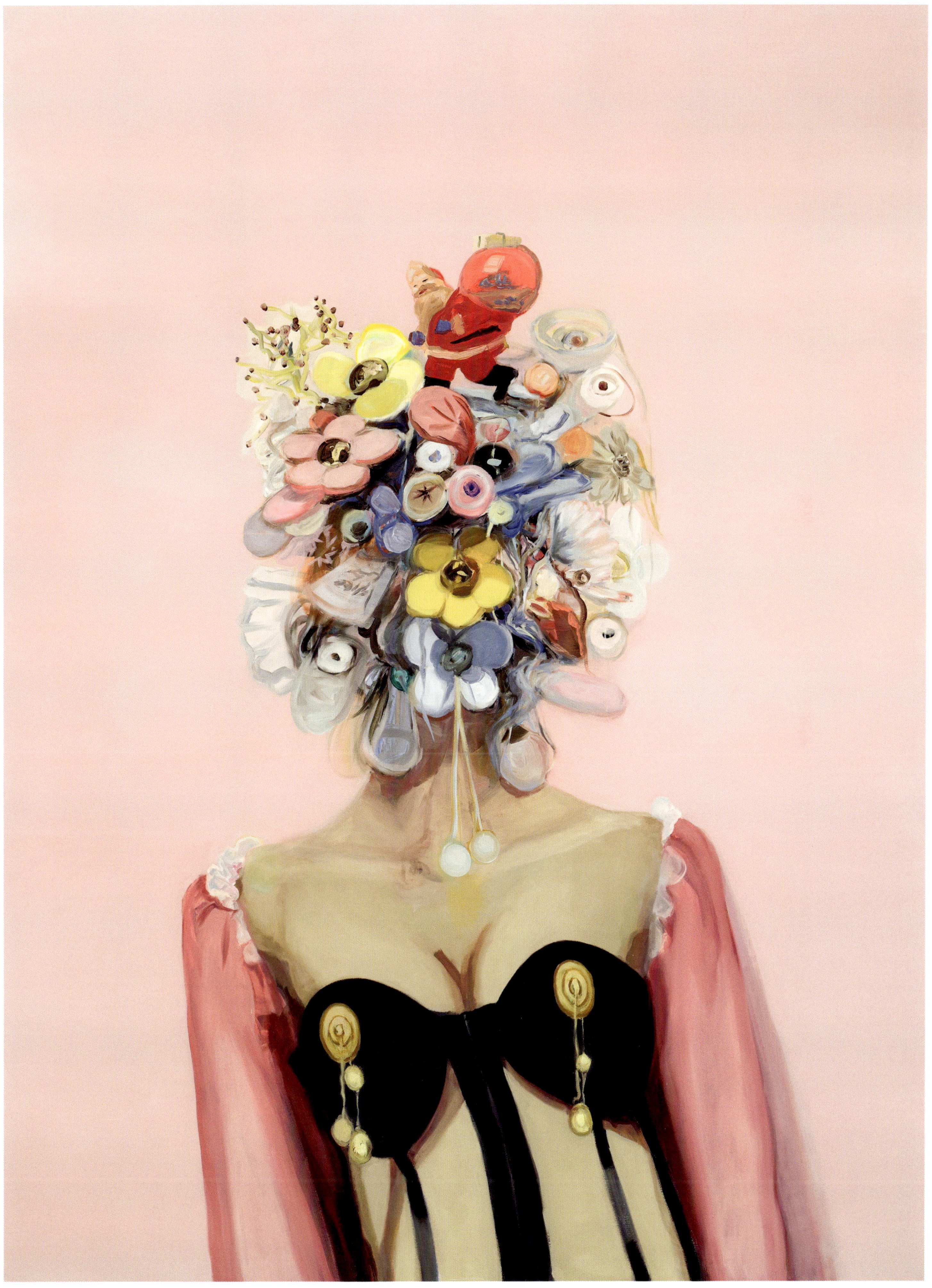

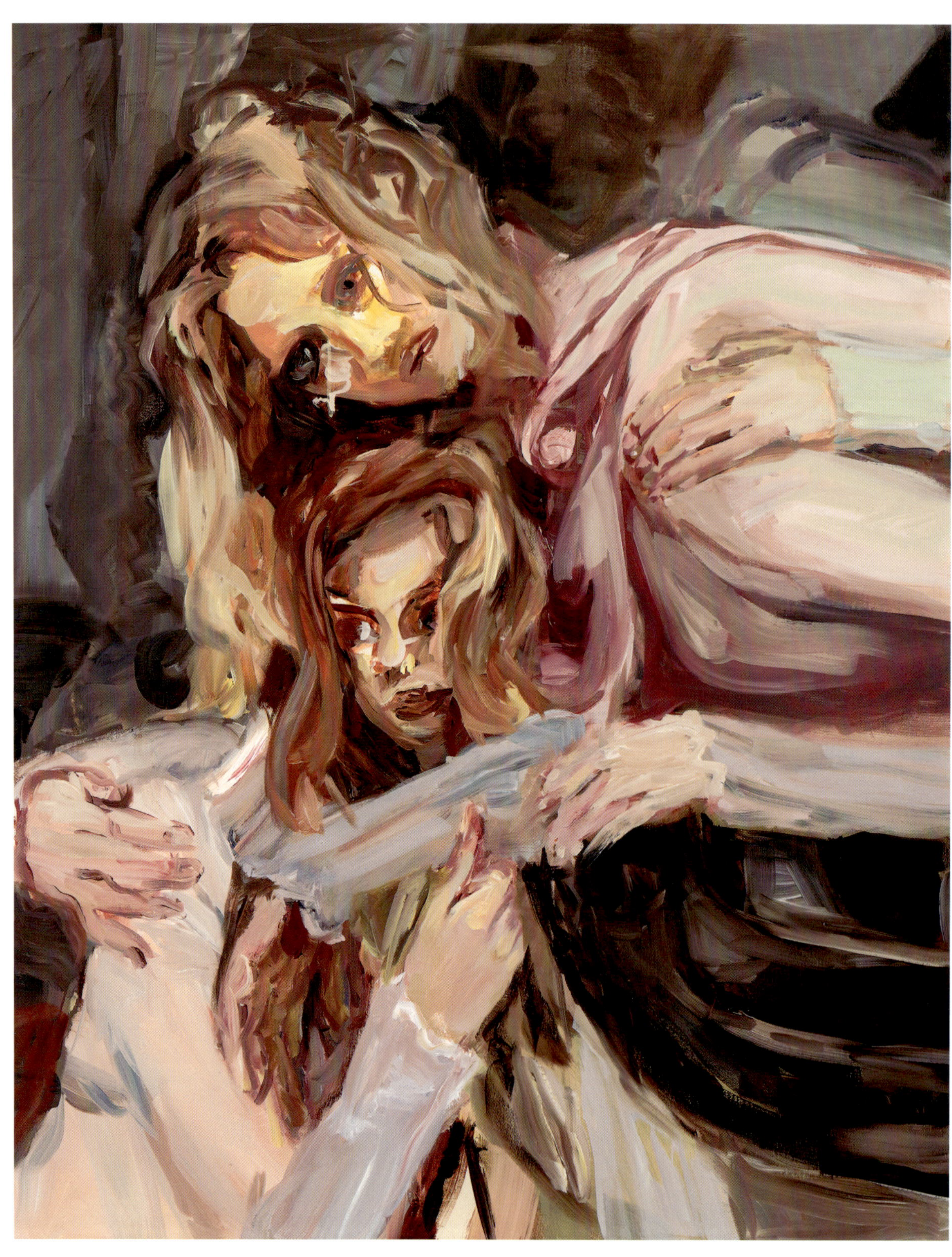

FIVE HANDS 2017

40 × 32 in. / 102 × 81 cm

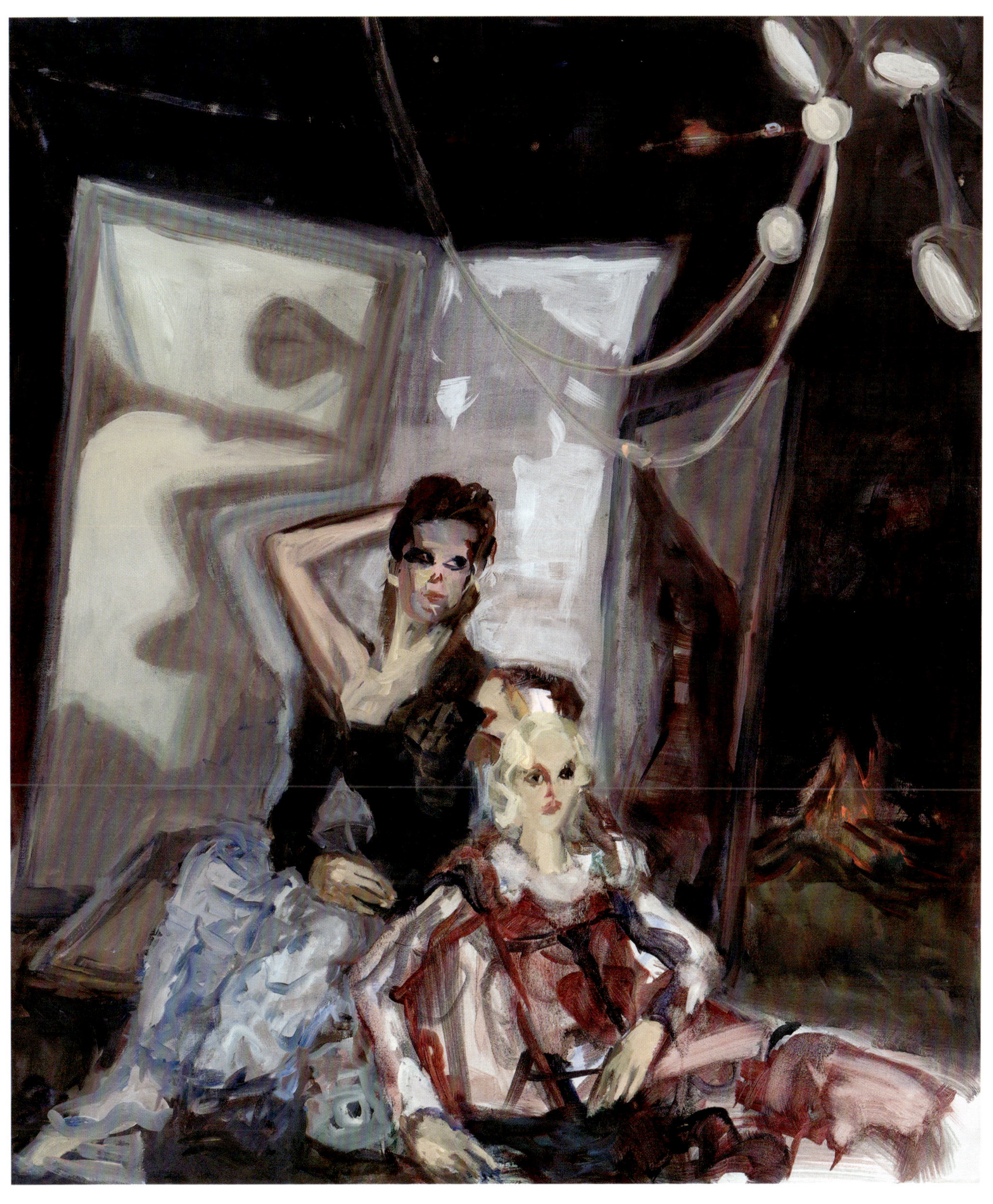

VSC (BONFIRE) 2016

42 × 36 in. / 107 × 91 cm

TWITCH (RED BOOTS) 2018

54 × 45 in. / 137 × 114 cm

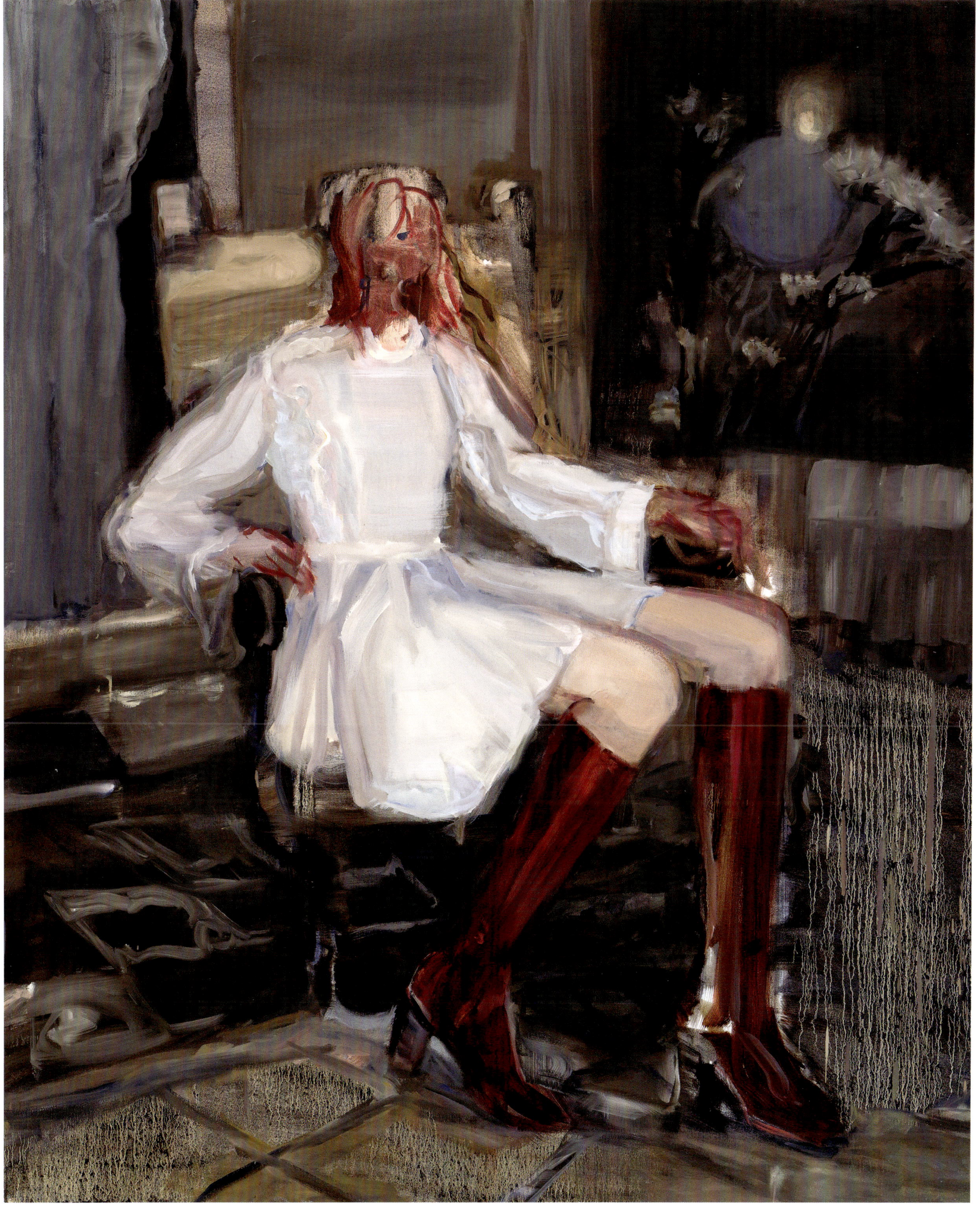

WALKER 2013

38 × 32 in. / 97 × 81 cm

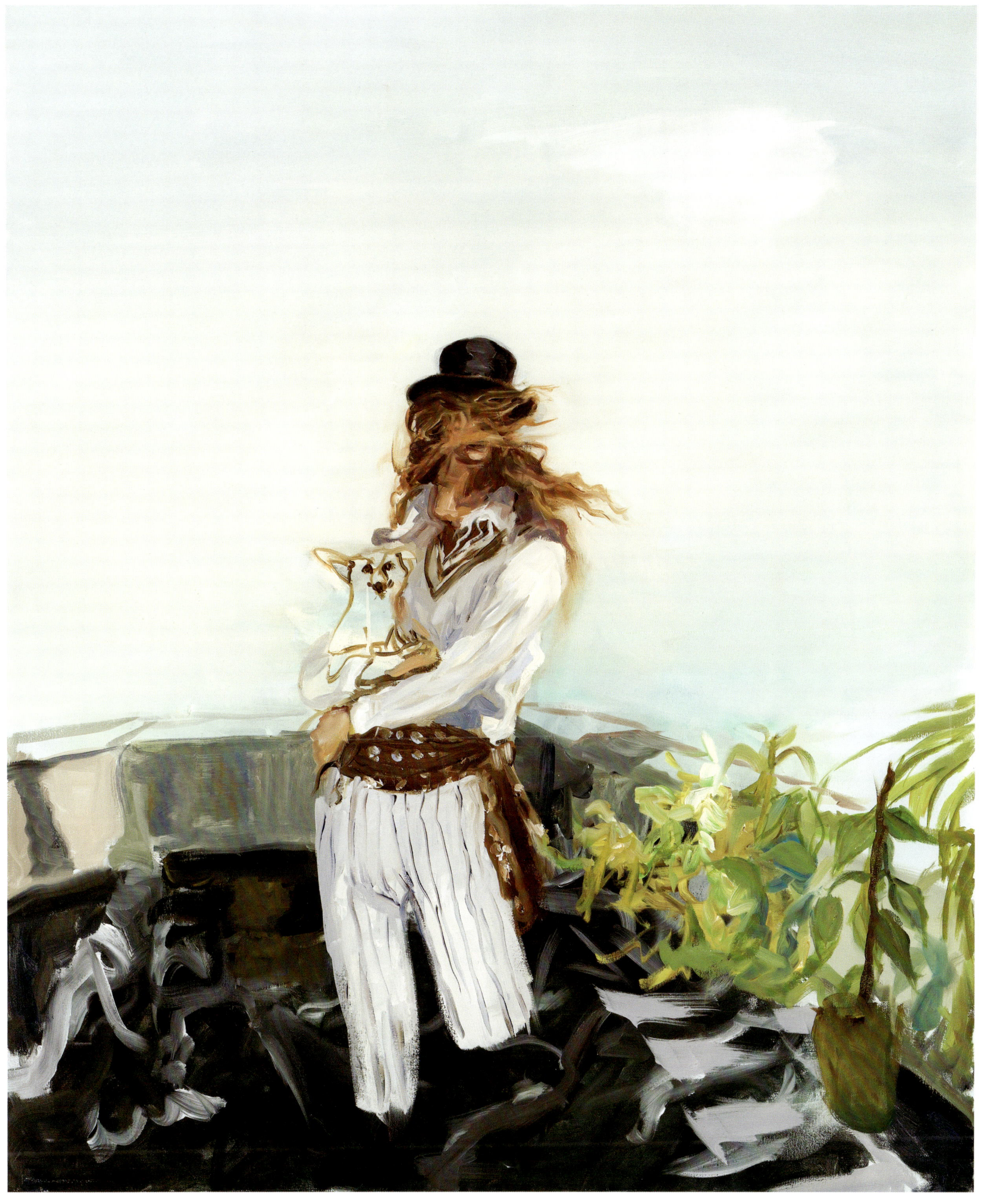

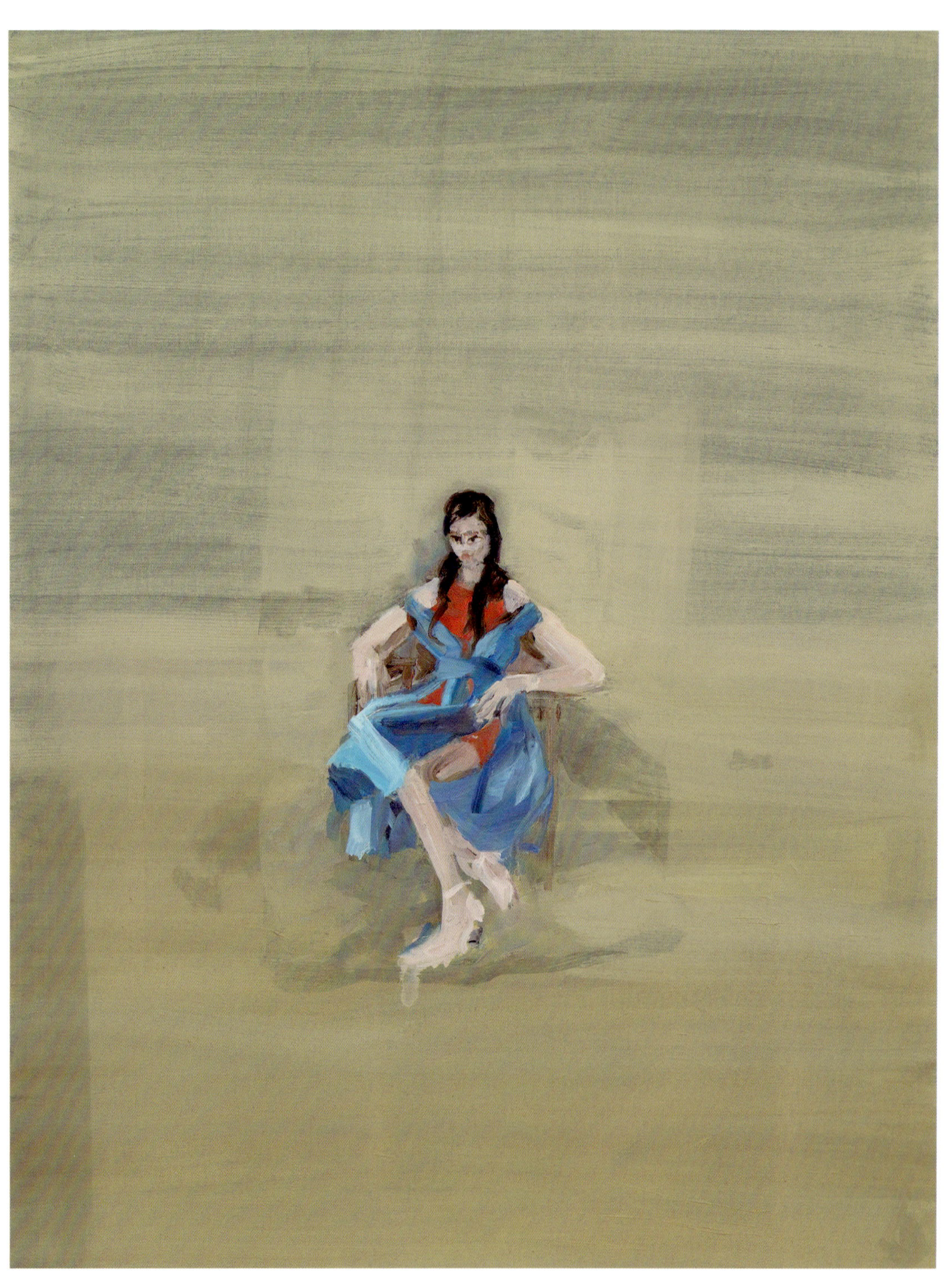

GREEN AND GOLD 2017

31 x 24 in. / 79 × 61 cm

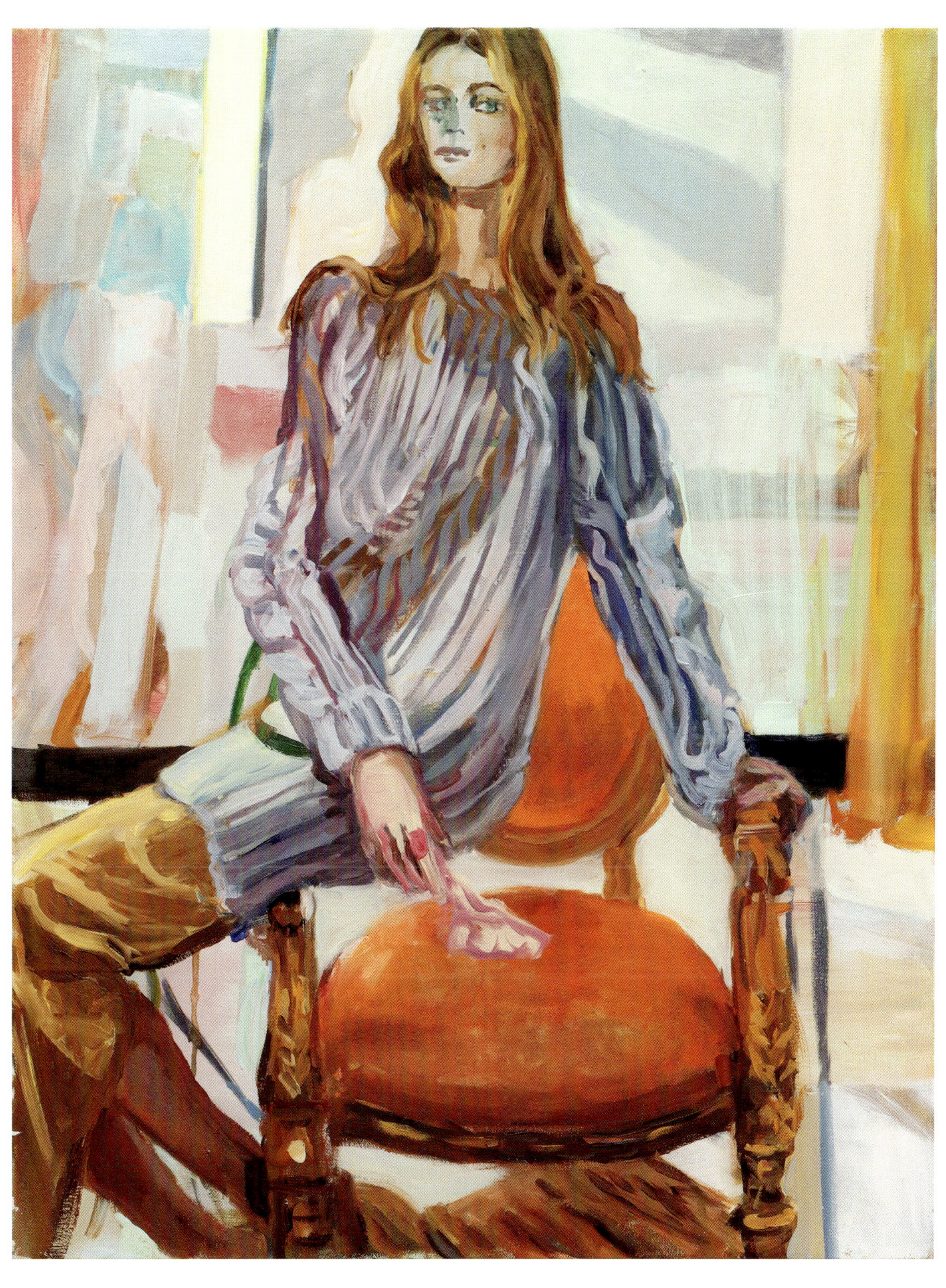

ORANGE CHAIR 2020

31 × 24 in. / 79 × 61 cm

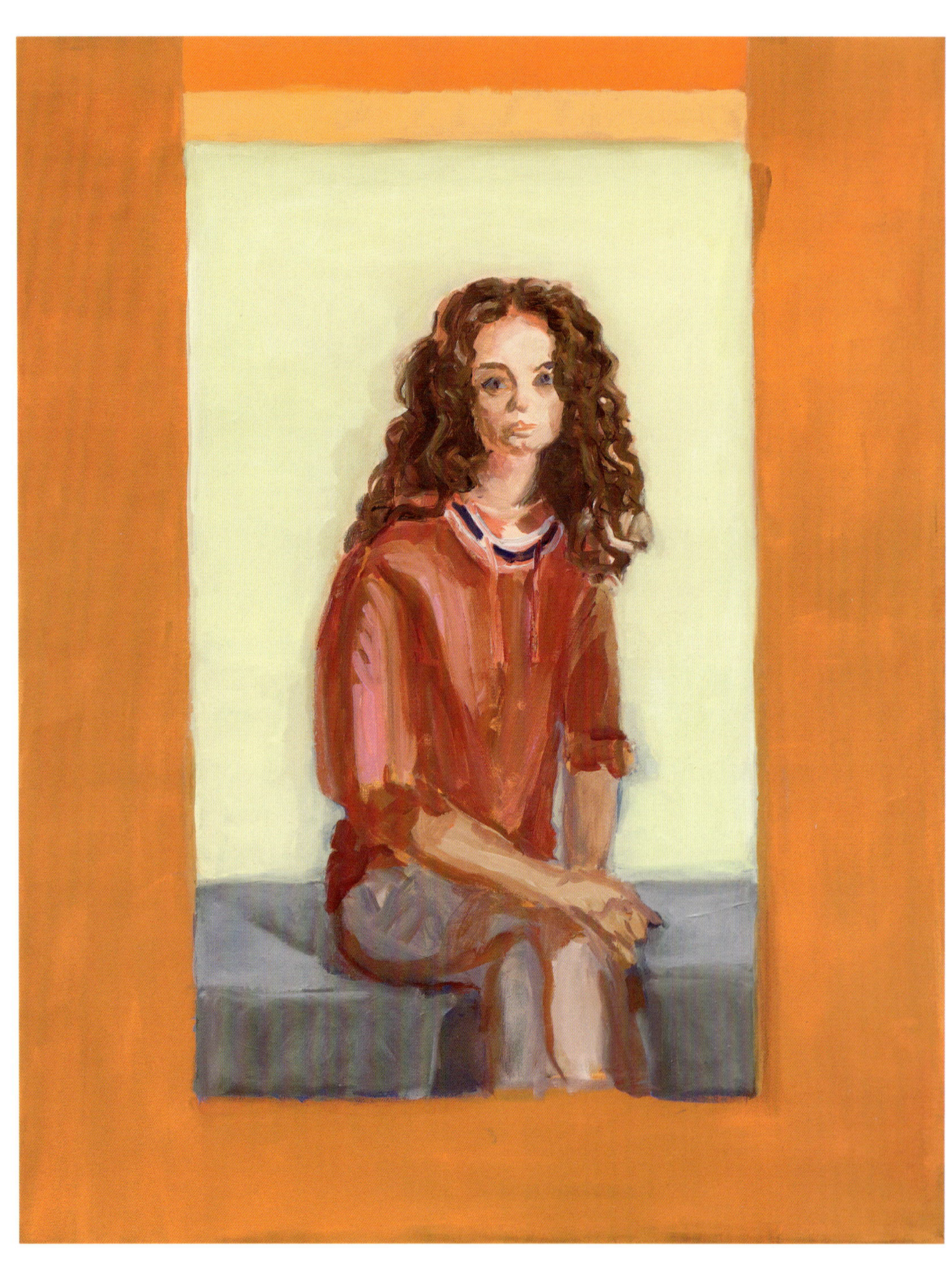

TAMMI 2020

28 × 22 in. / 71 × 56 cm

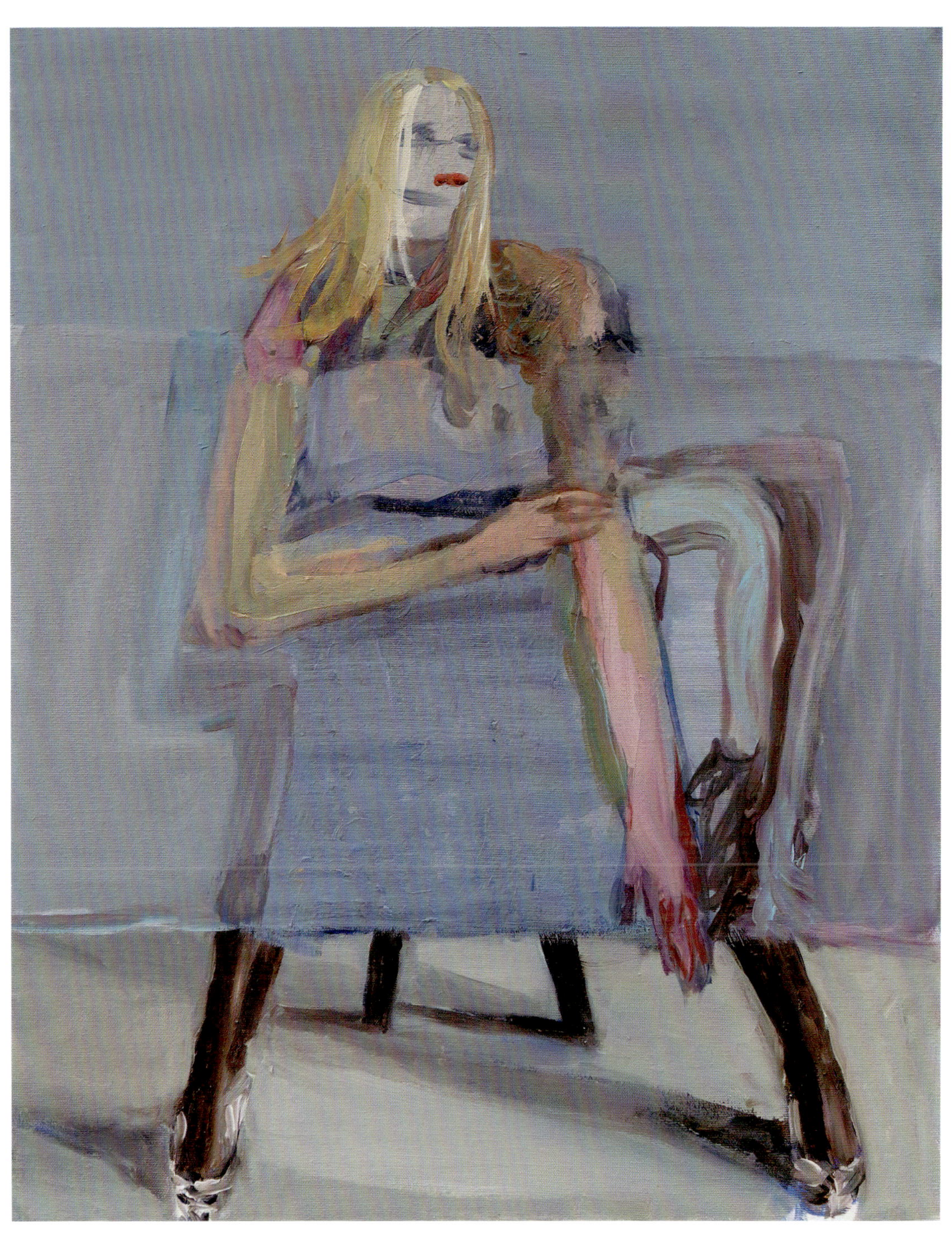

EVA 2019

20 × 16 in. / 51 × 41 cm

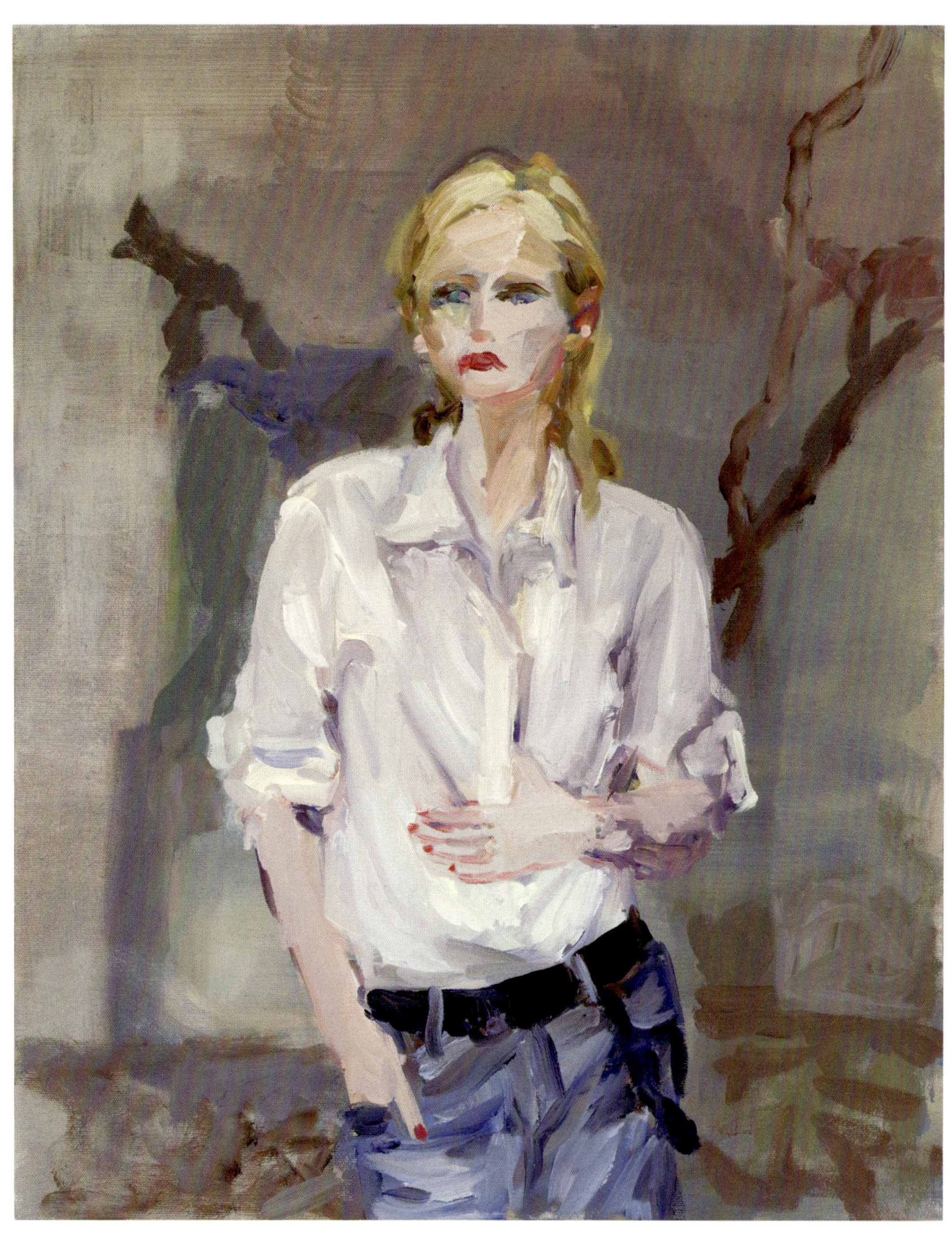

GIRL WITH WHITE SHIRT IN GRAY LANDSCAPE 2018

20 × 16 in. / 51 × 41 cm

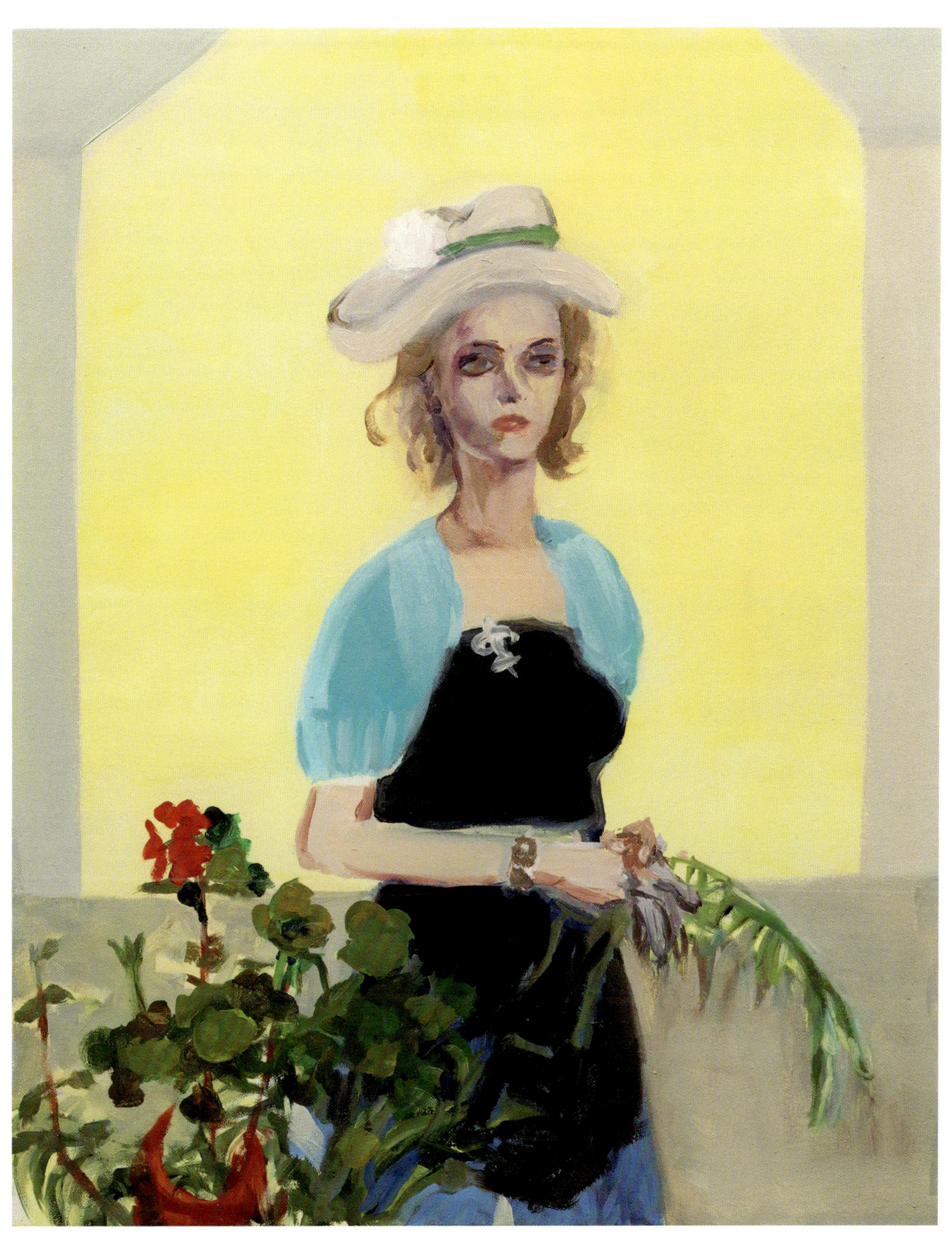

GARDENER 2020

20 × 16 in. / 51 × 41 cm

YELLOW STUDIO 2013

40 × 32 in. / 102 × 81 cm

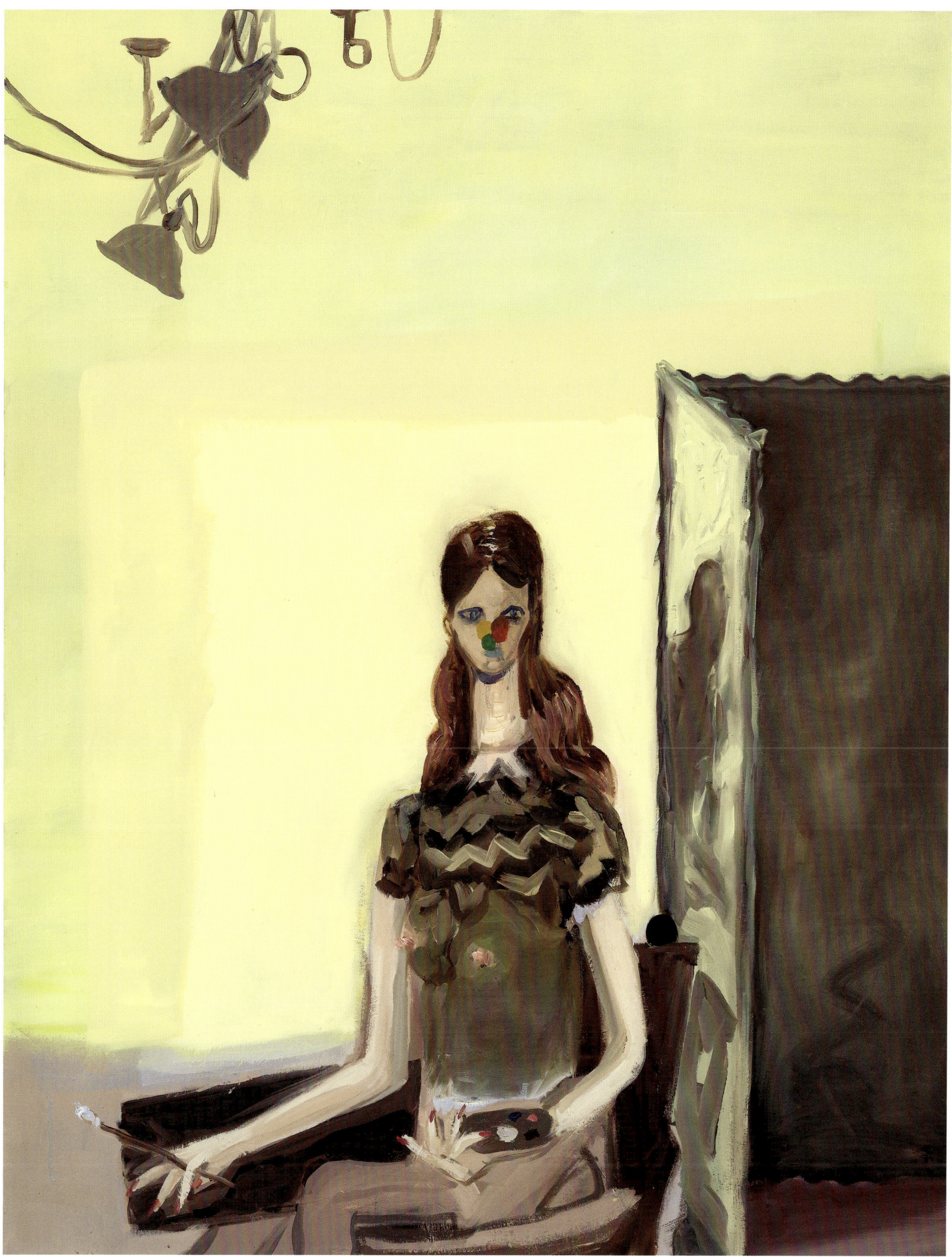

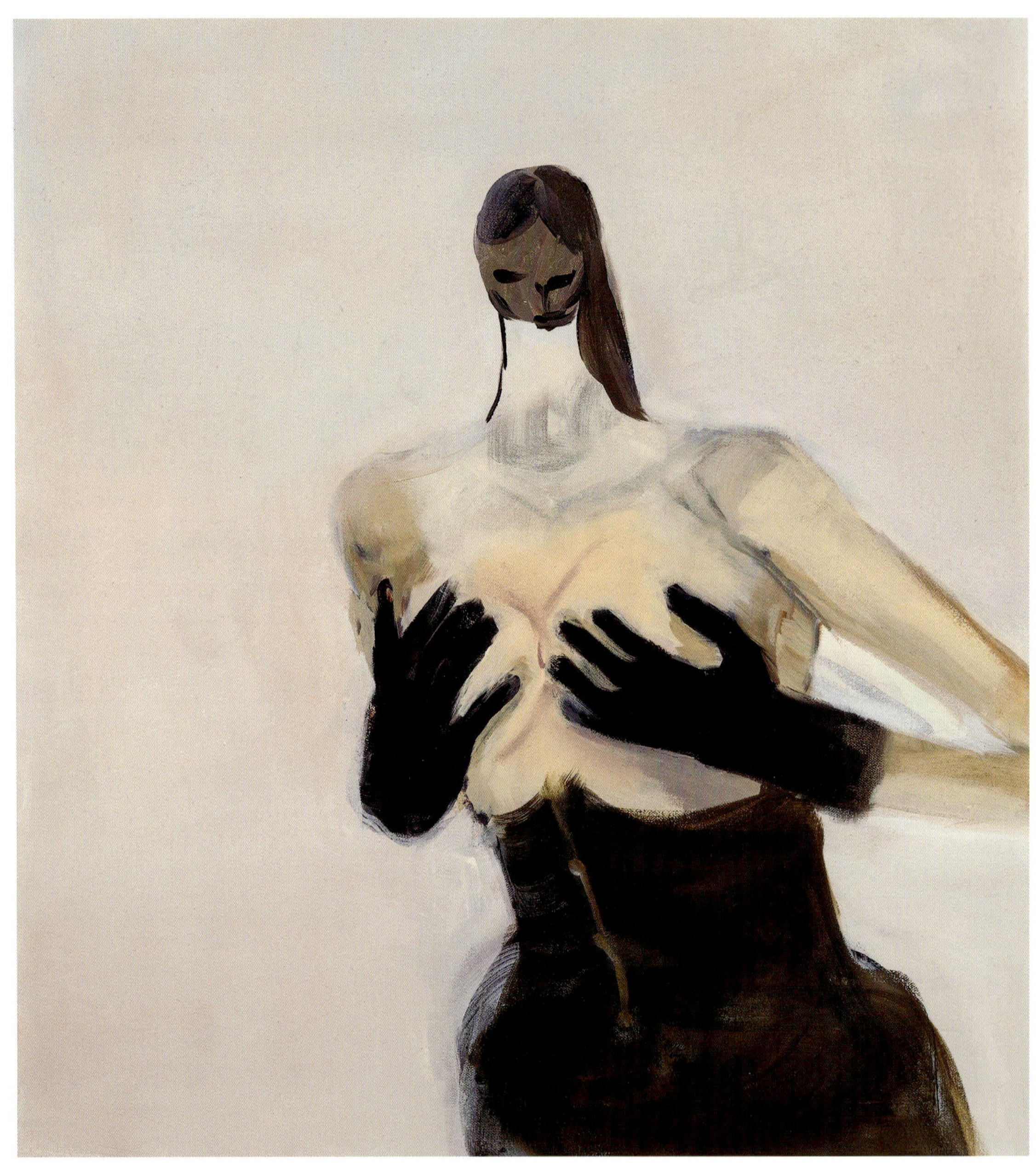

ABOVE

ELLE 2014

22 × 20 in. / 56 × 51 cm

OPPOSITE

COLLAGE FACE 2014

20 × 16 in. / 51 × 41 cm

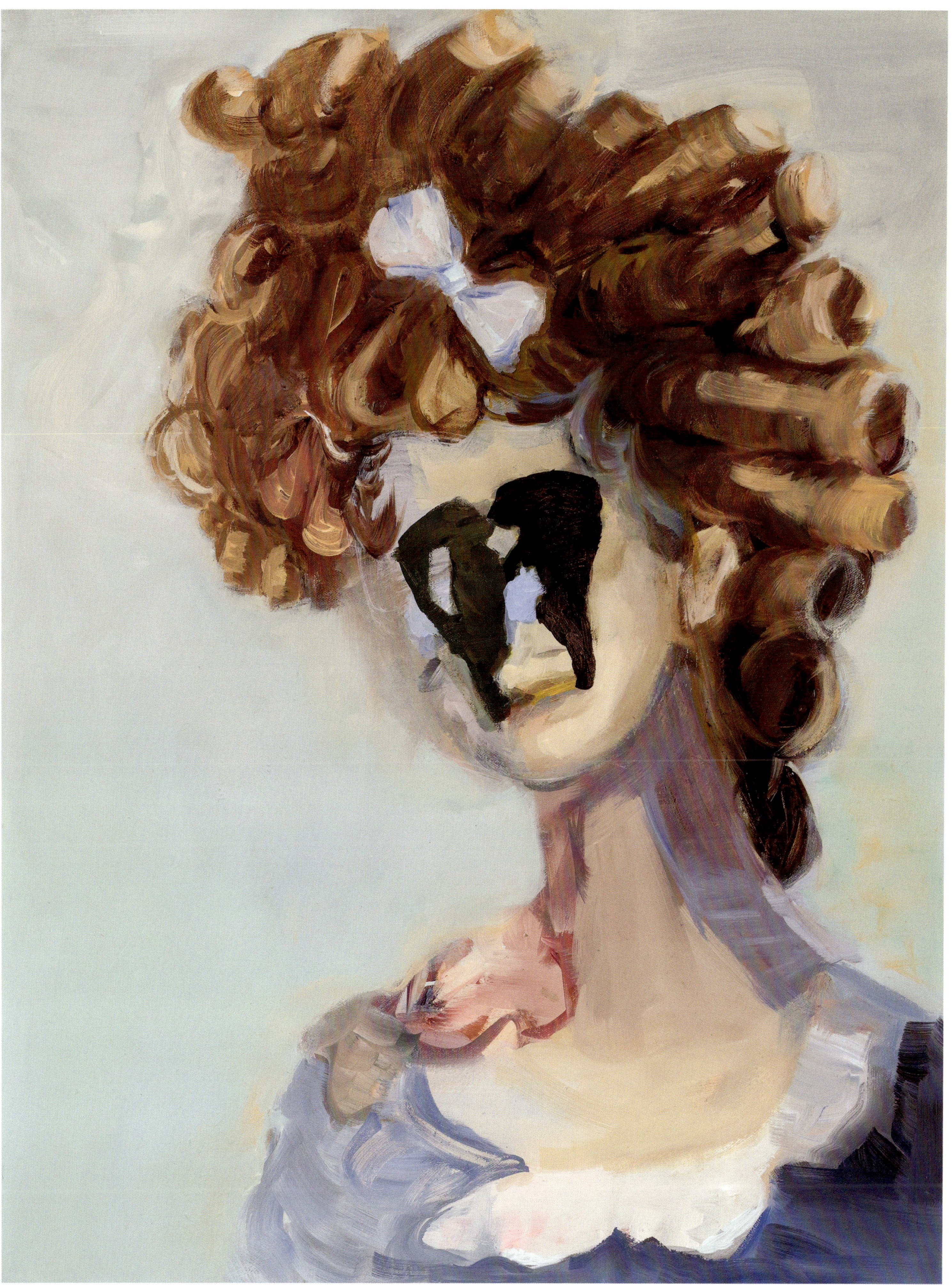

THERE
THERE

BEAST 2019

96 × 74 in. / 244 × 188 cm

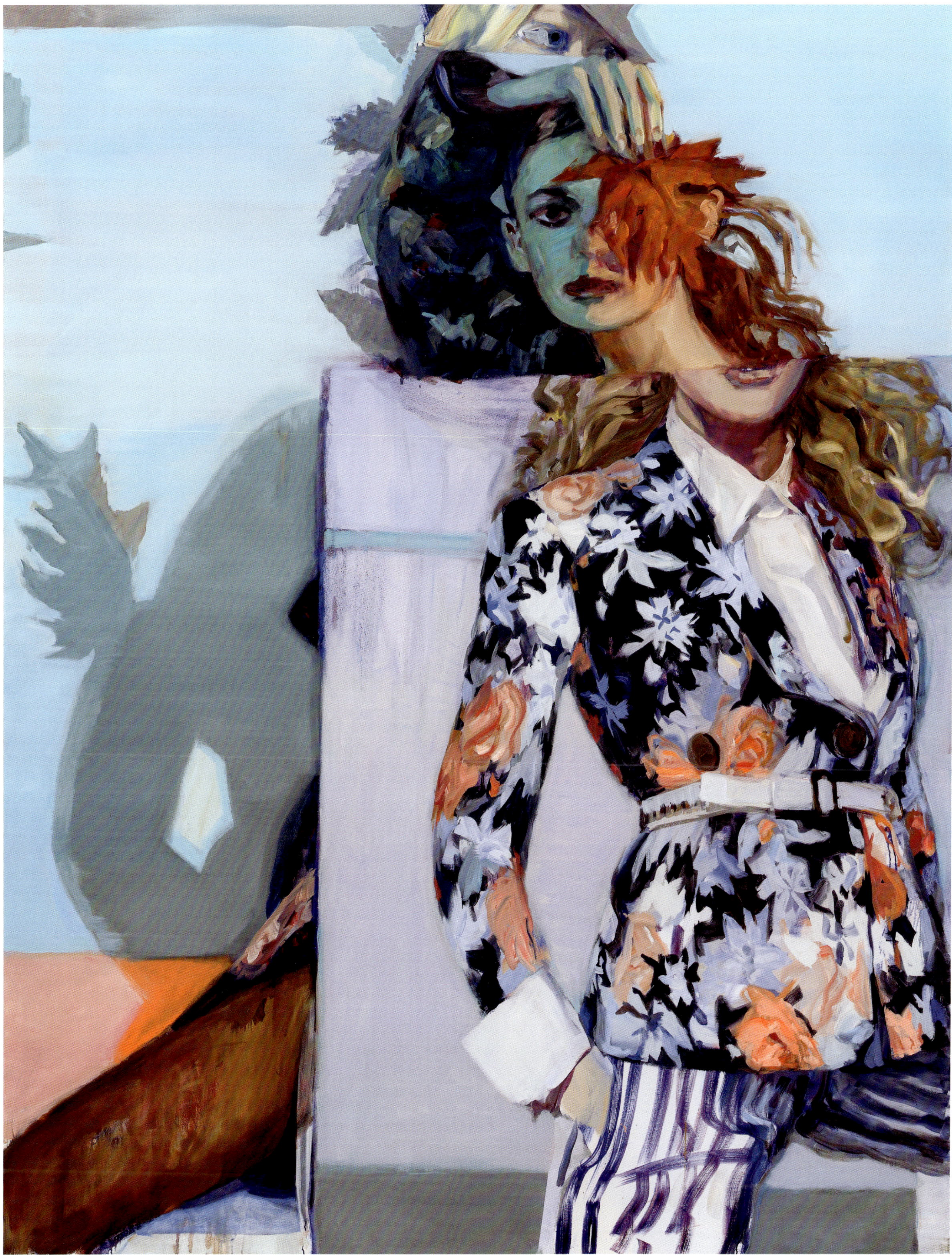

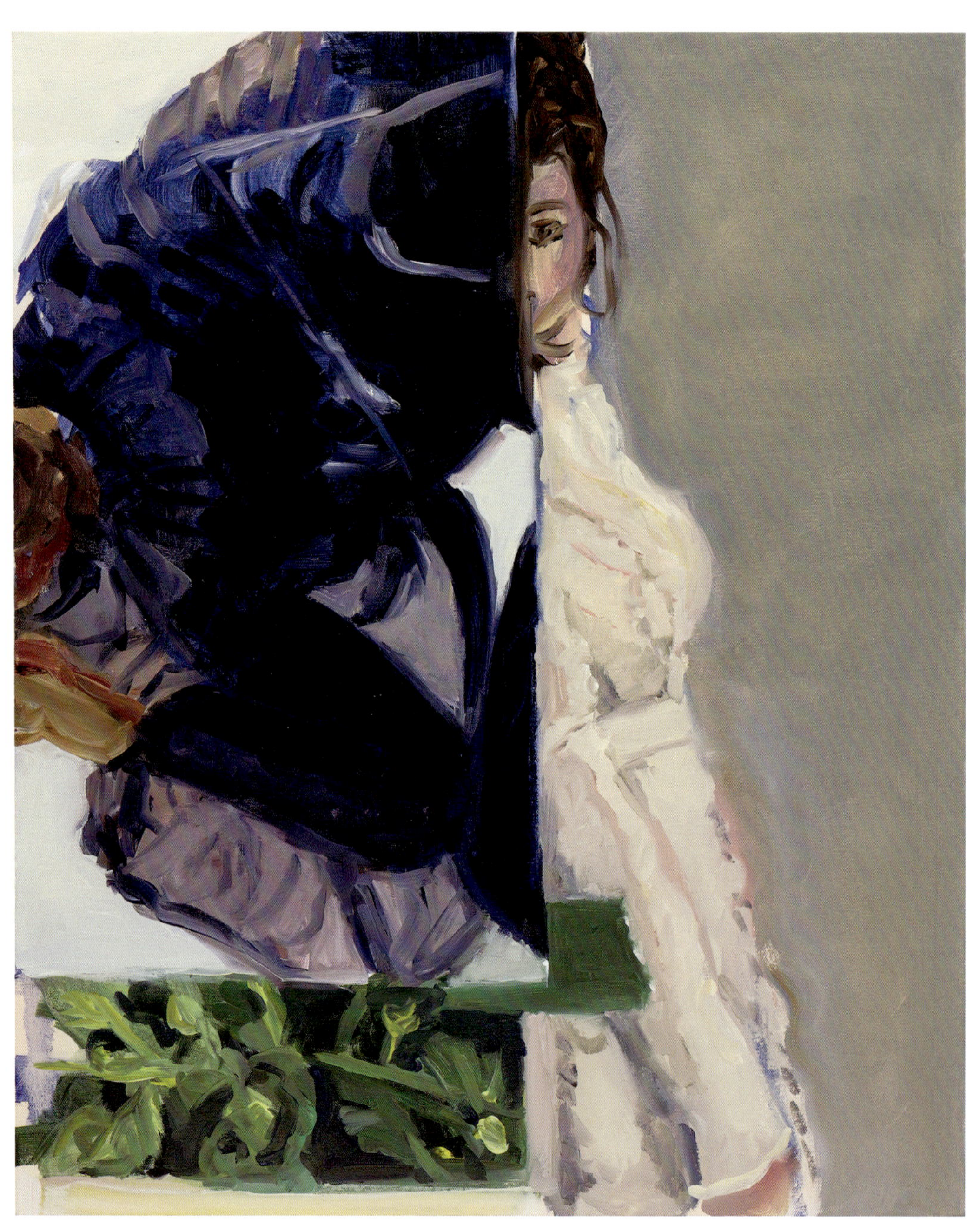

BLOOM 2022

24 × 20 in. / 61 × 51 cm

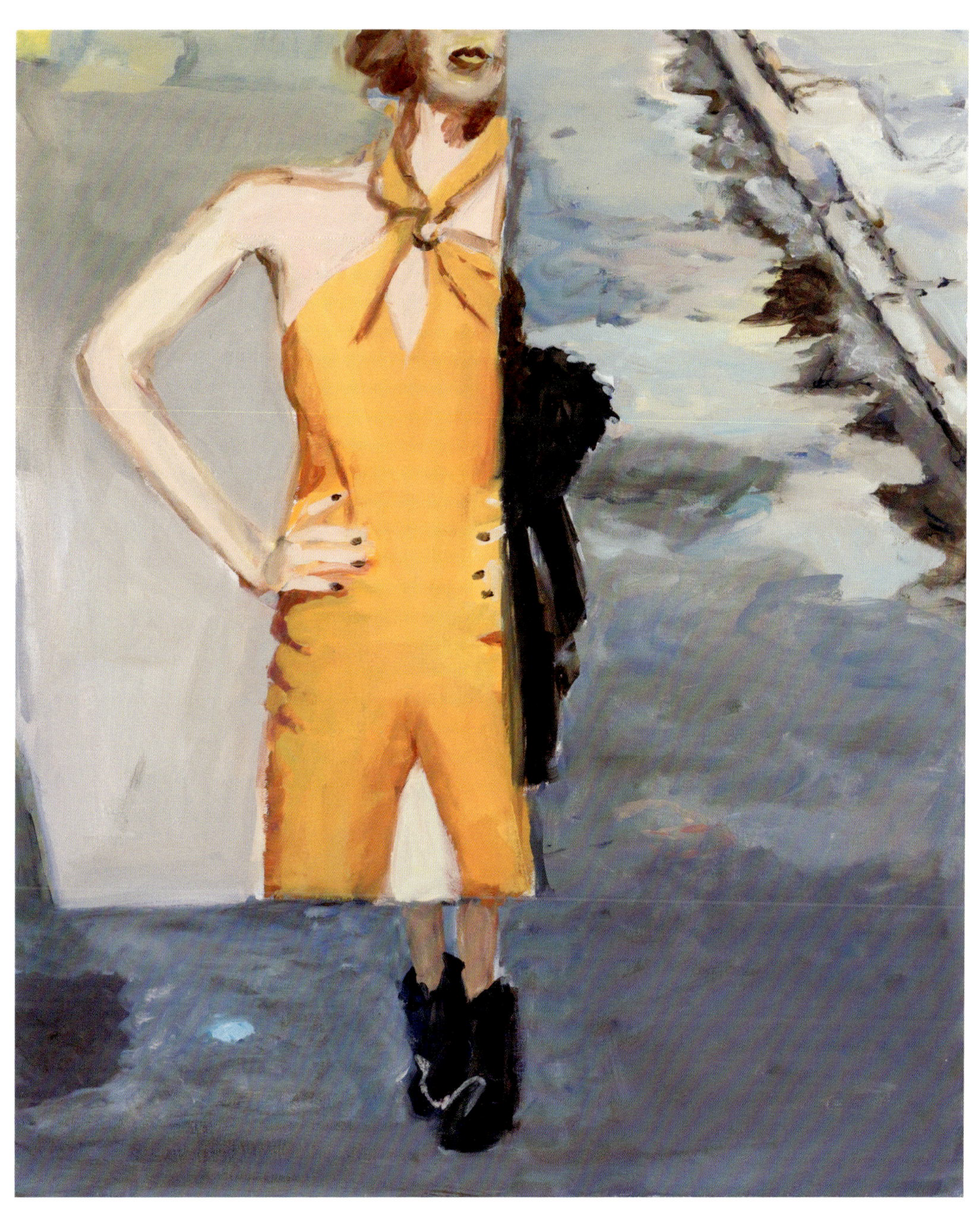

STRASSE 2021

24 × 20 in. / 61 × 51 cm

PLAZA (GOLD ROOM) 2021

76 × 60 in. / 193 × 152 cm

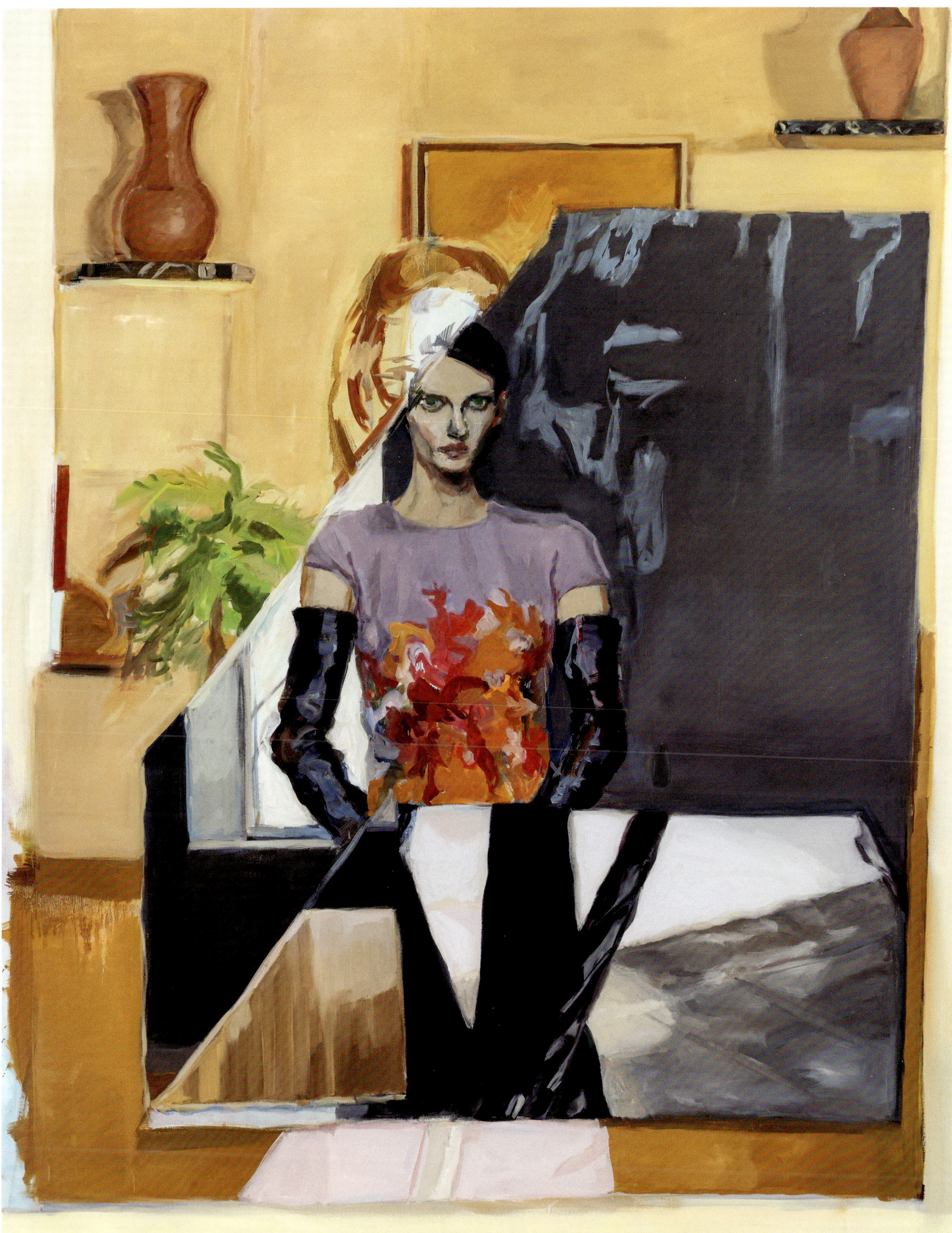

HARLEQUIN 2022

69 × 51 in. / 175 × 130 cm

FOLLOWING SPREAD, FROM LEFT

CASPAR (CDF) 2020

63 × 51 in. / 160 × 130 cm

PINK SUIT 2020

67 × 60 in. / 170 × 152 cm

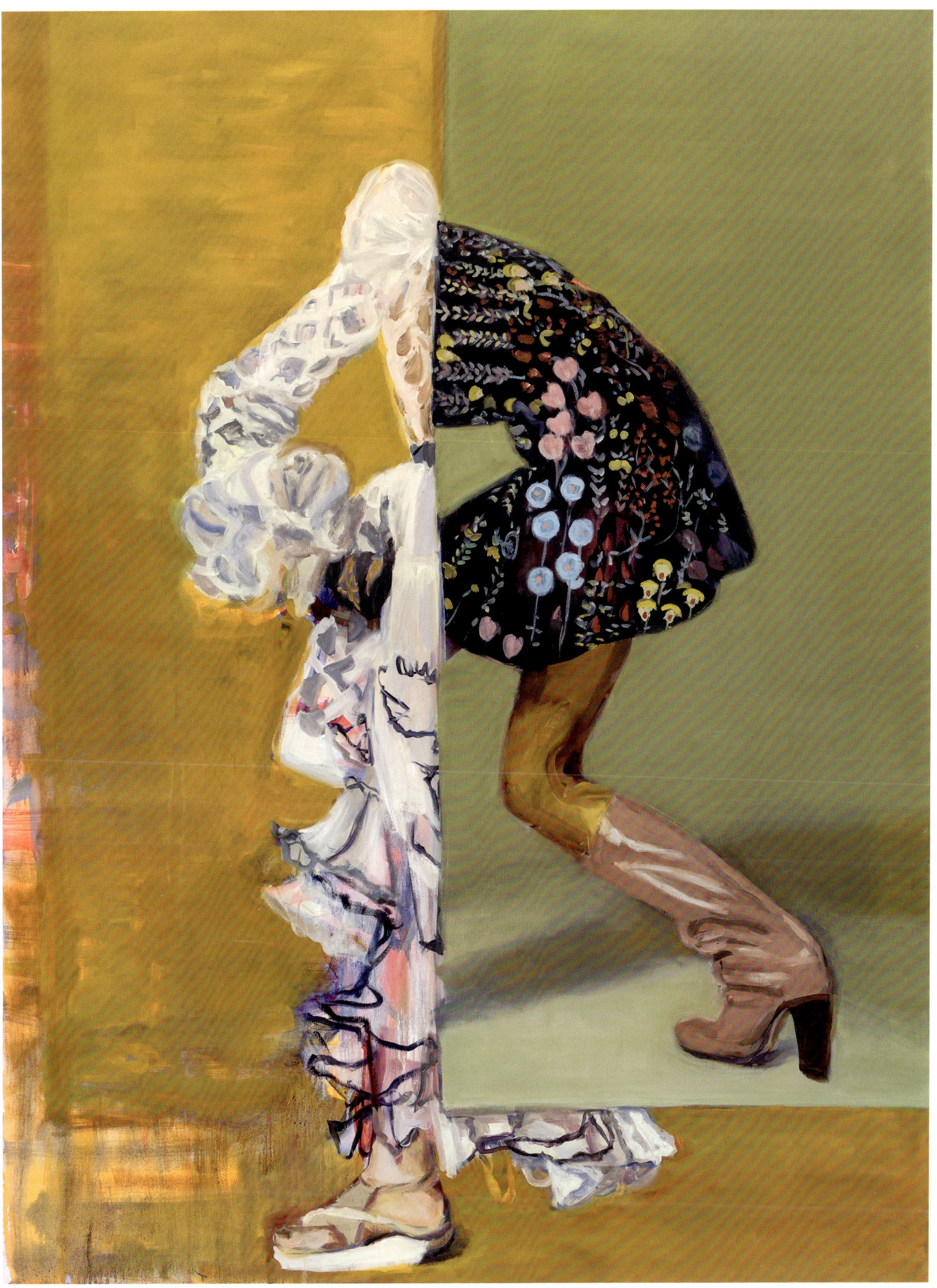

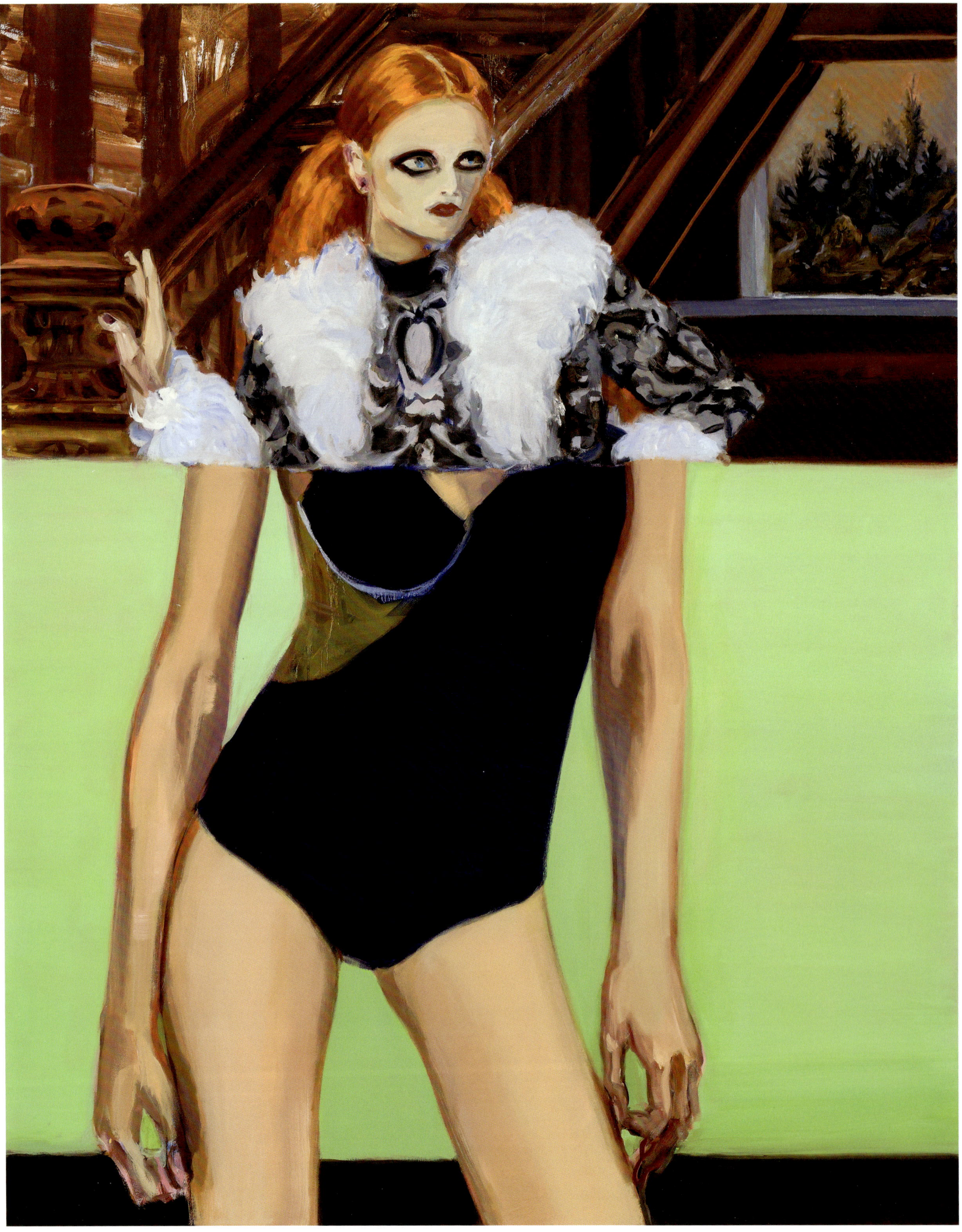

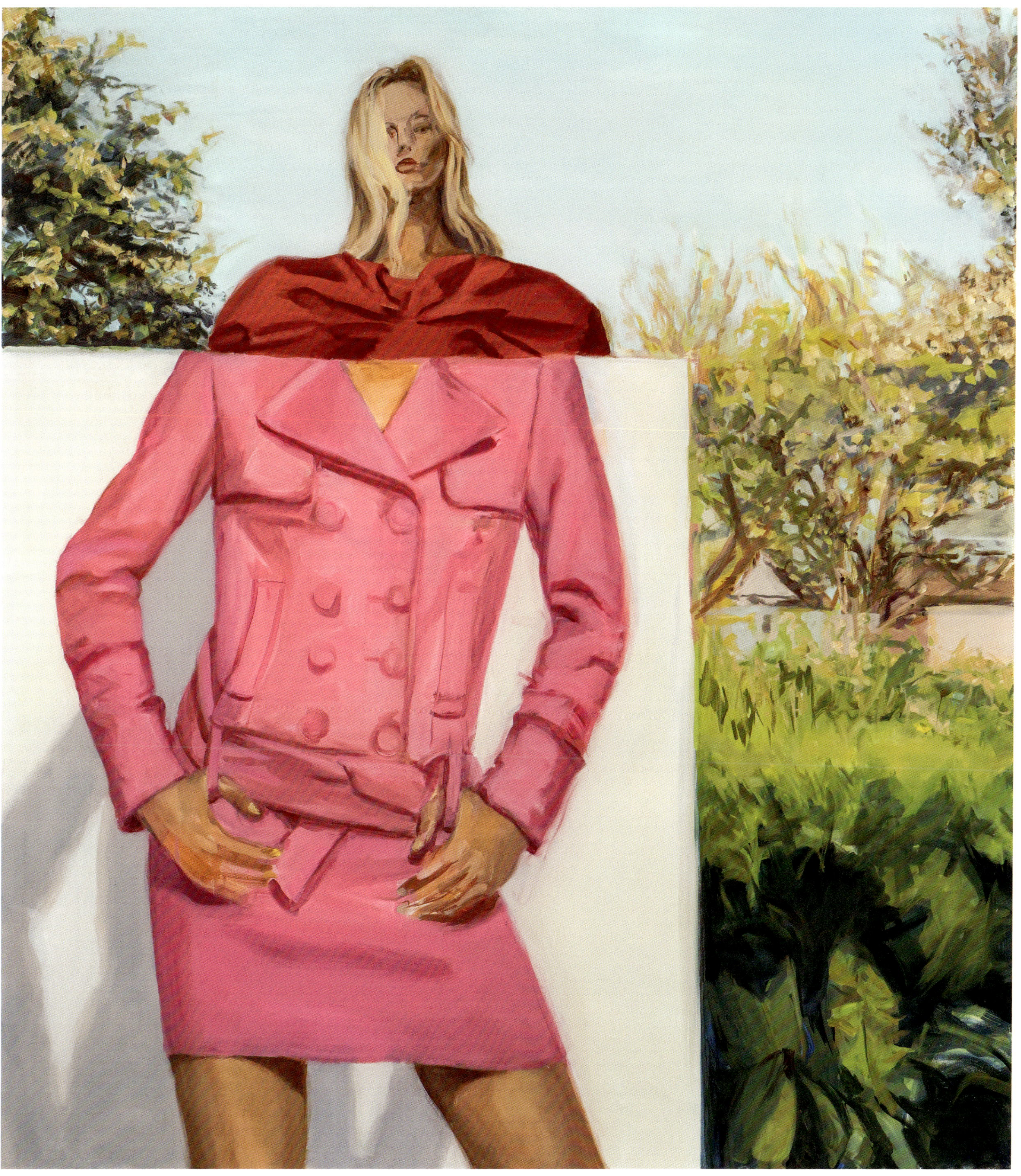

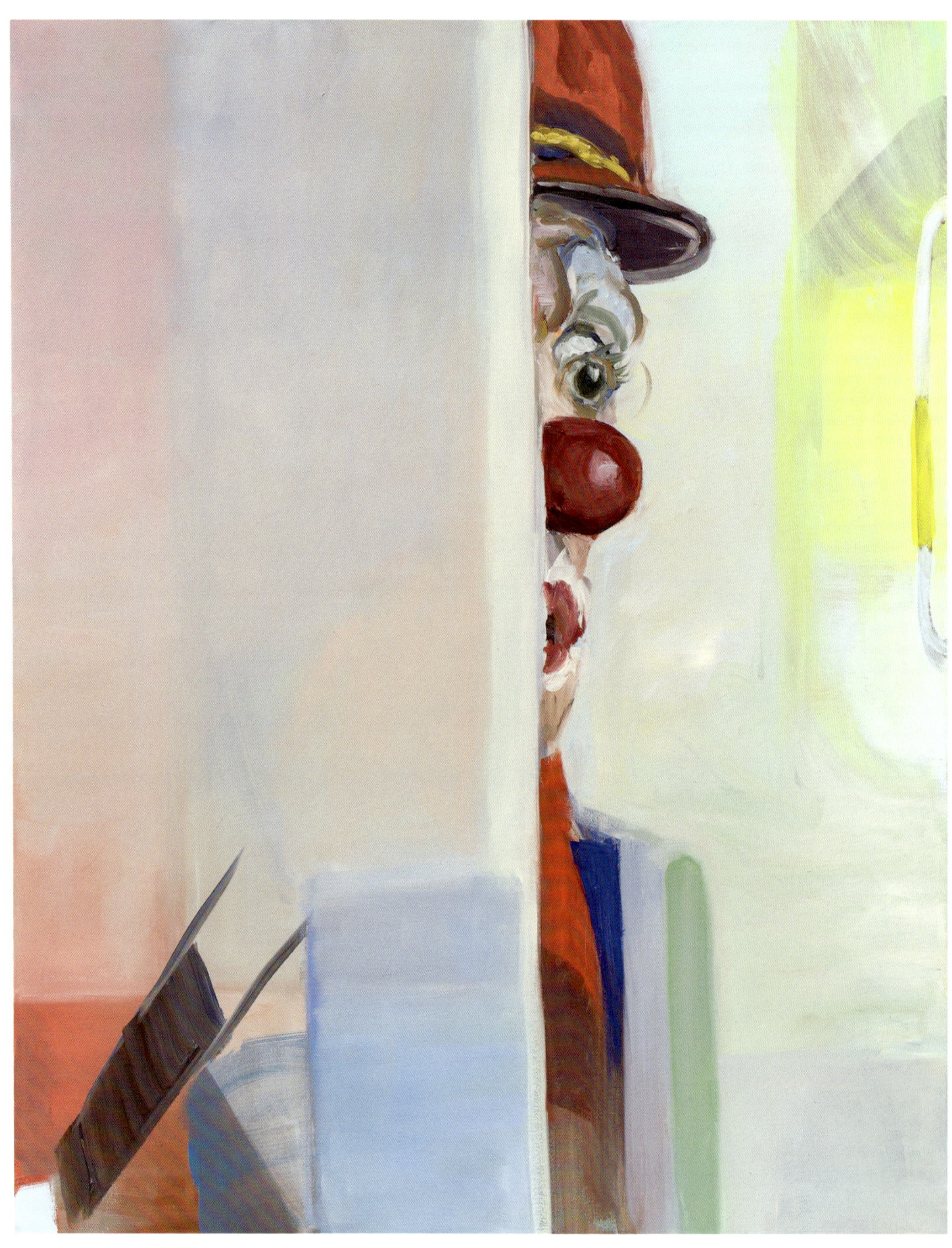

ABOVE

CLOWN 2021

33 × 26 in. / 84 × 66 cm

OPPOSITE

CLAIRE 2019

44 × 36 in. / 112 × 91 cm

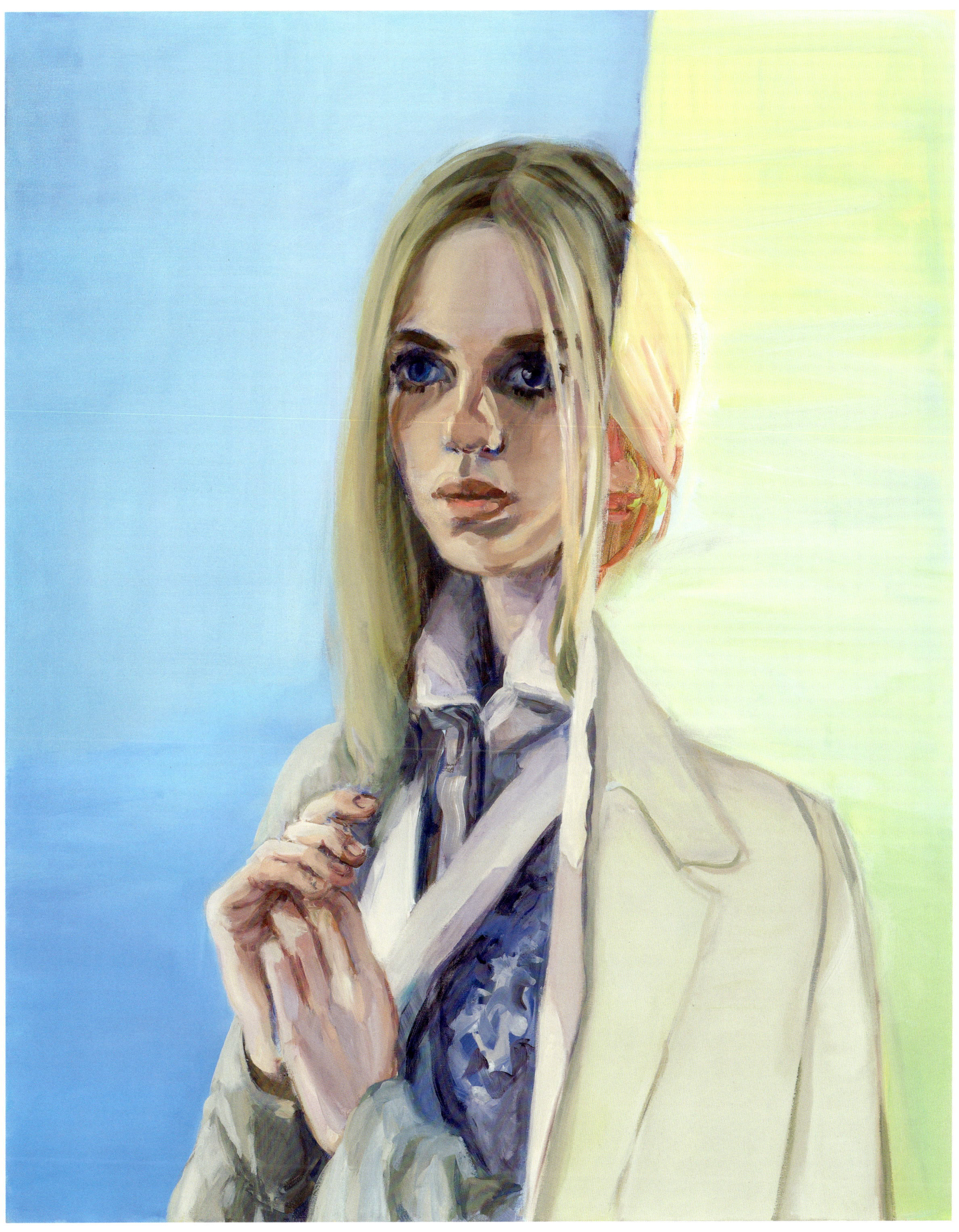

WINONA 2020

84 × 67 in. / 213 × 170 cm

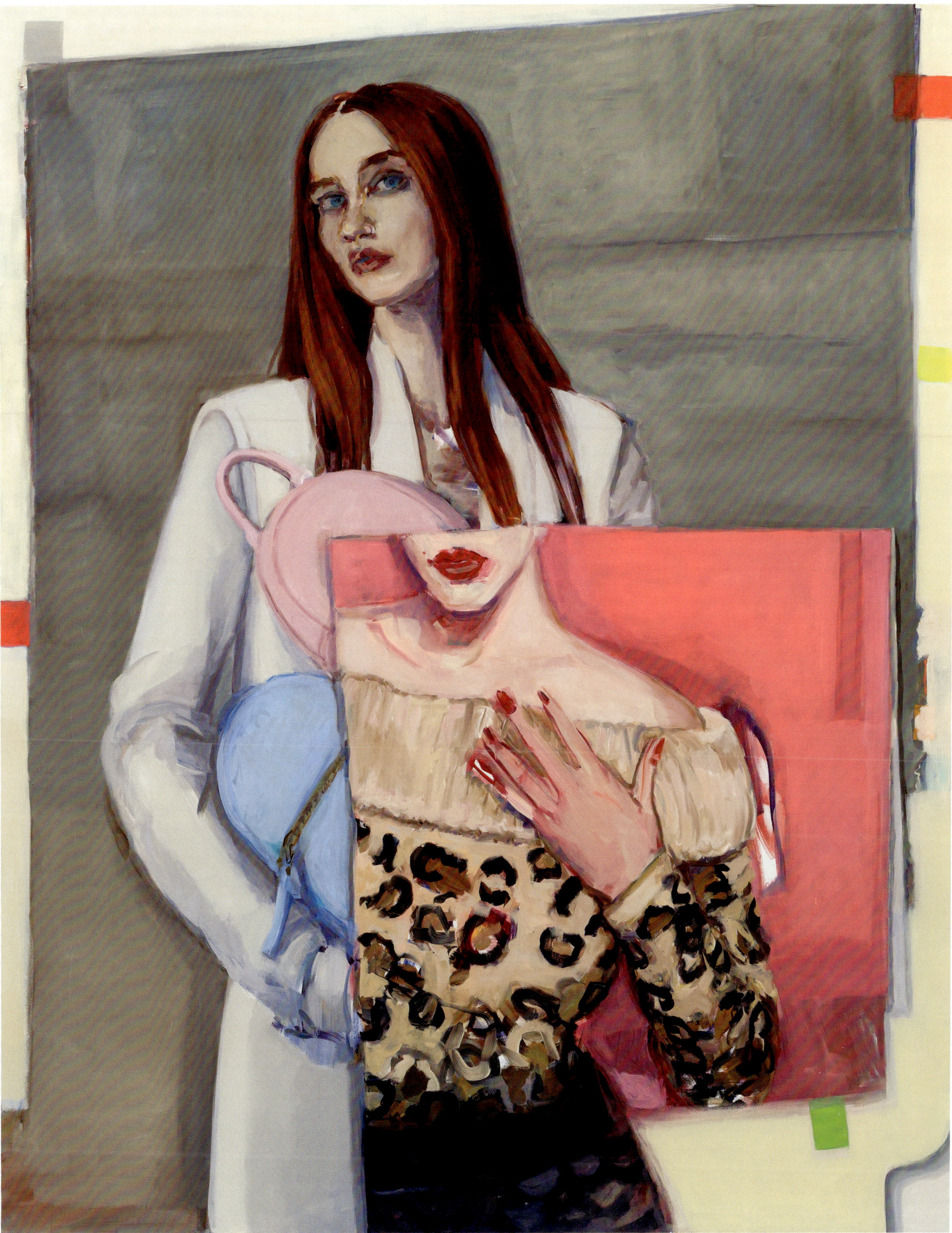

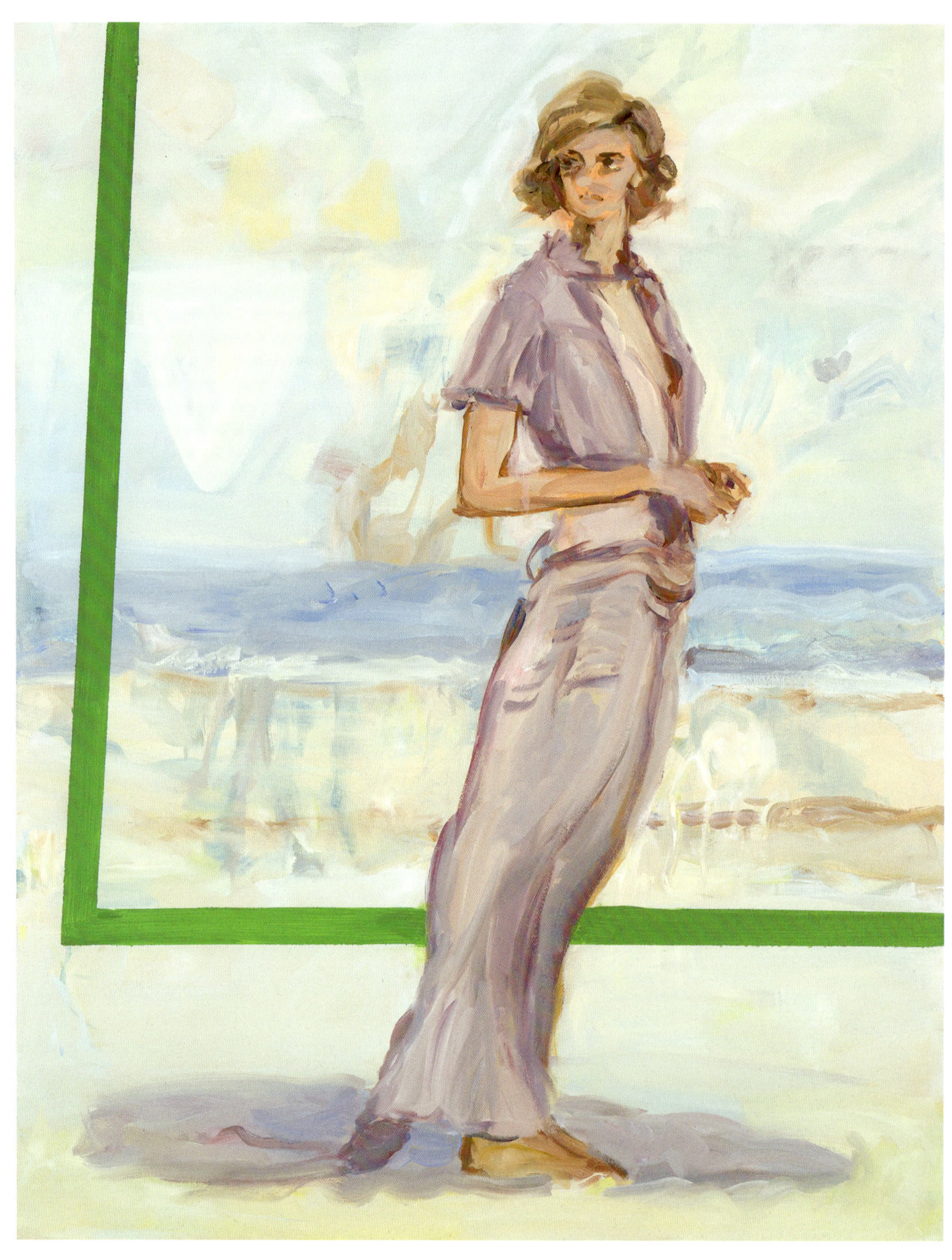

LEAN (GREEN LINE) 2019

33 × 26 in. / 84 × 66 cm

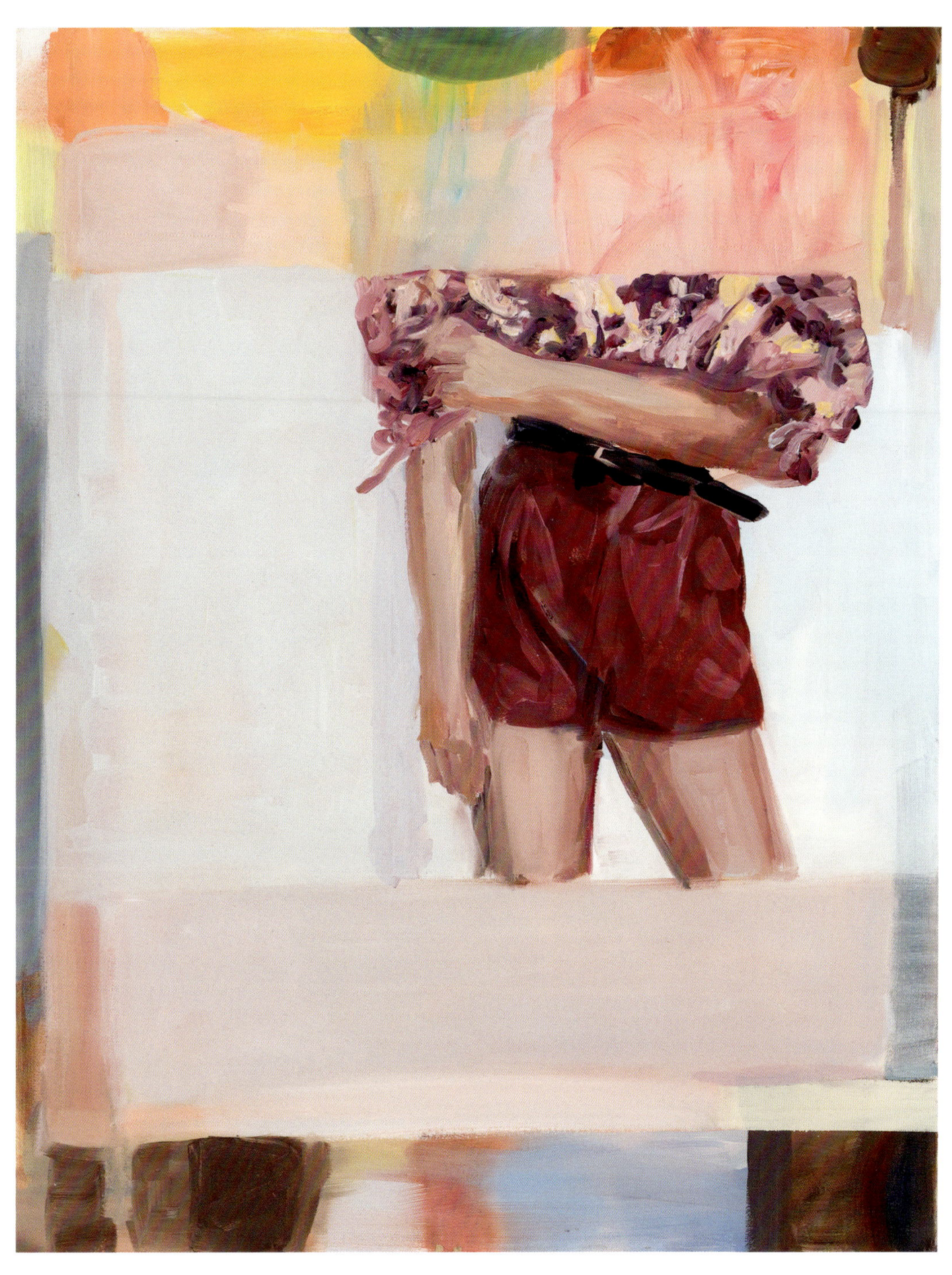

PERFORMER 2 2020

31 × 24 in. / 79 × 61 cm

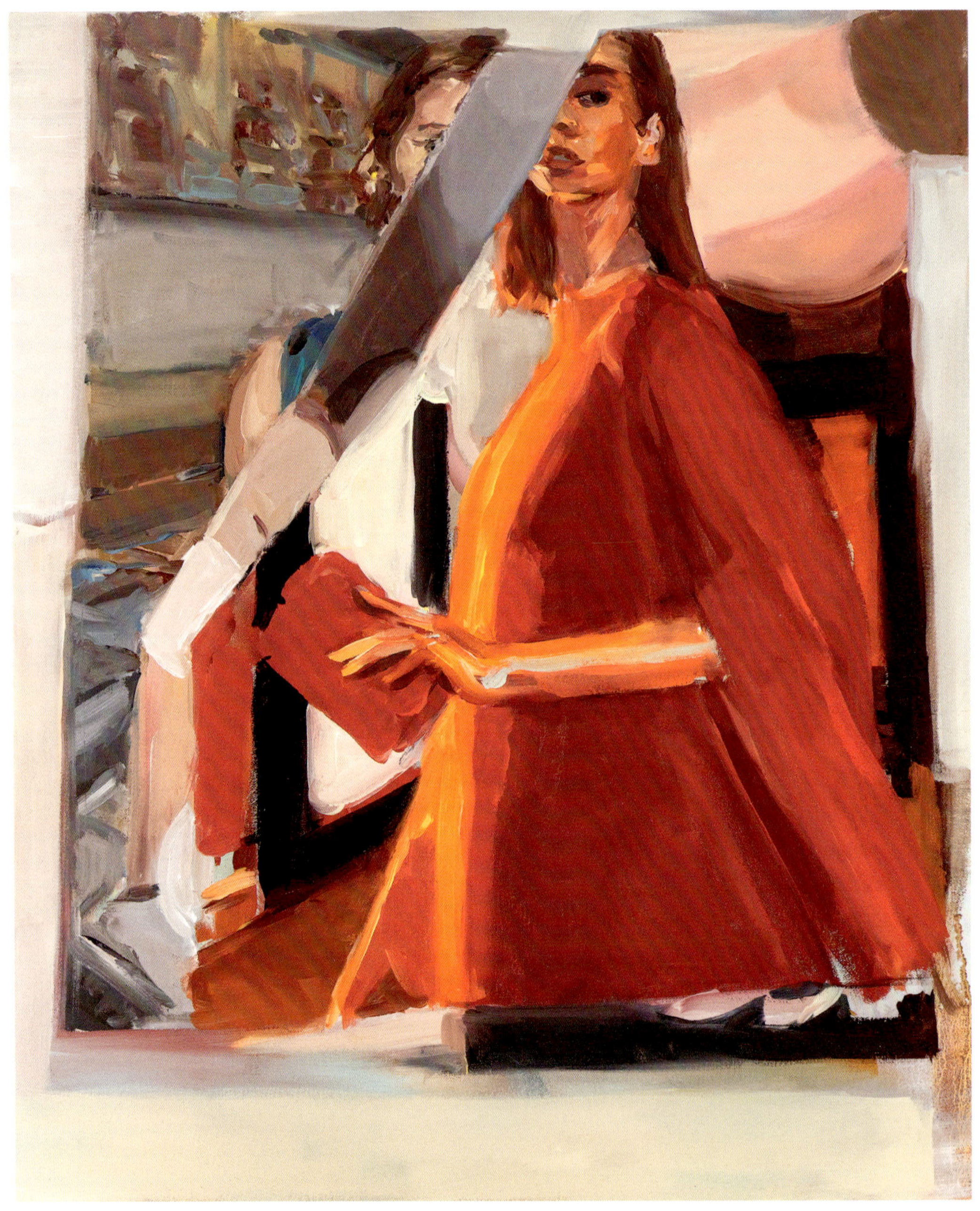

ABOVE

DALLAS 2020

24 × 20 in. / 61 × 51 cm

OPPOSITE

BROWN ROOM (TILT) 2020

40 × 24 in. / 102 × 61 cm

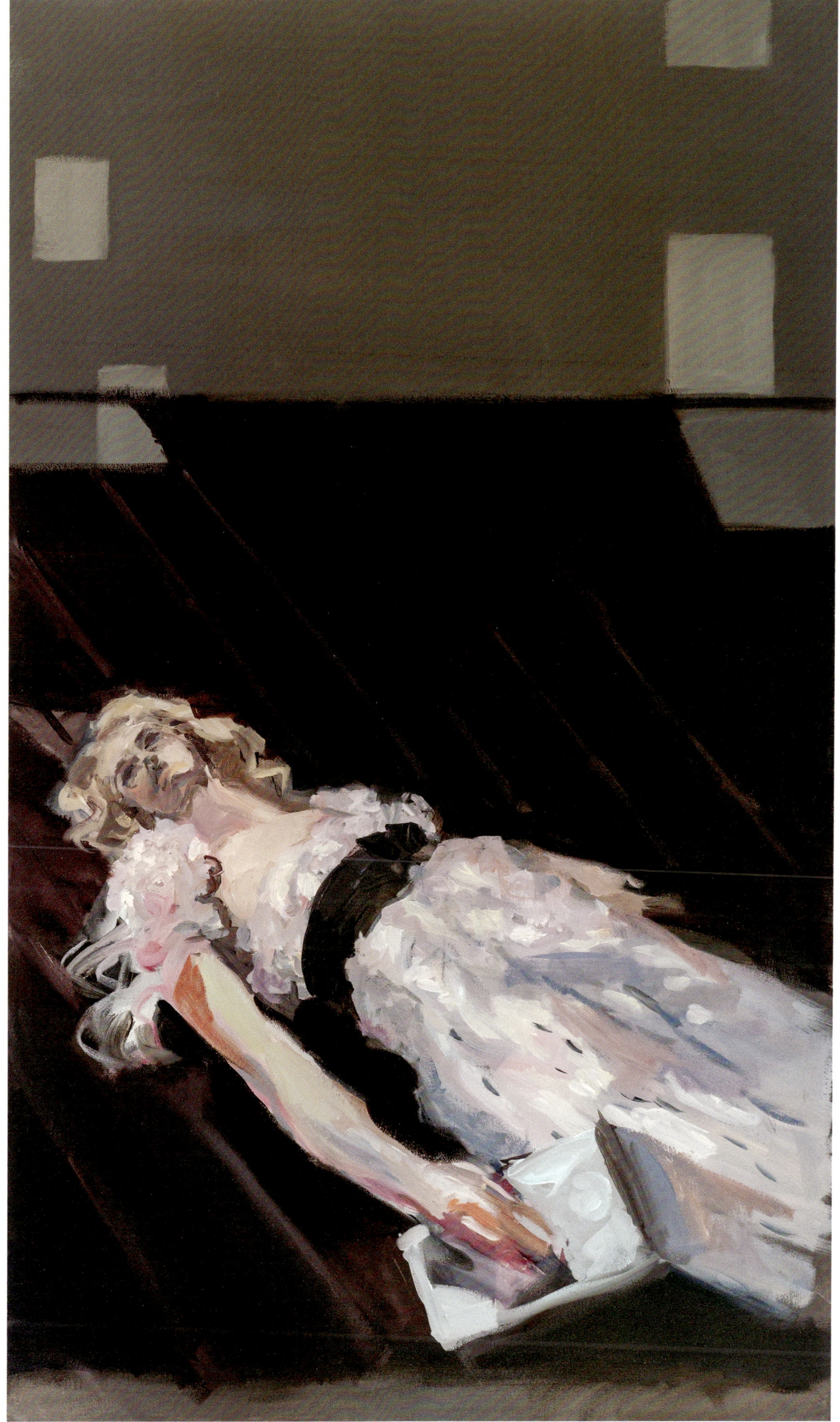

BATHER (BLUE LIPS) 2018

84 × 67 in. / 213 × 170 cm

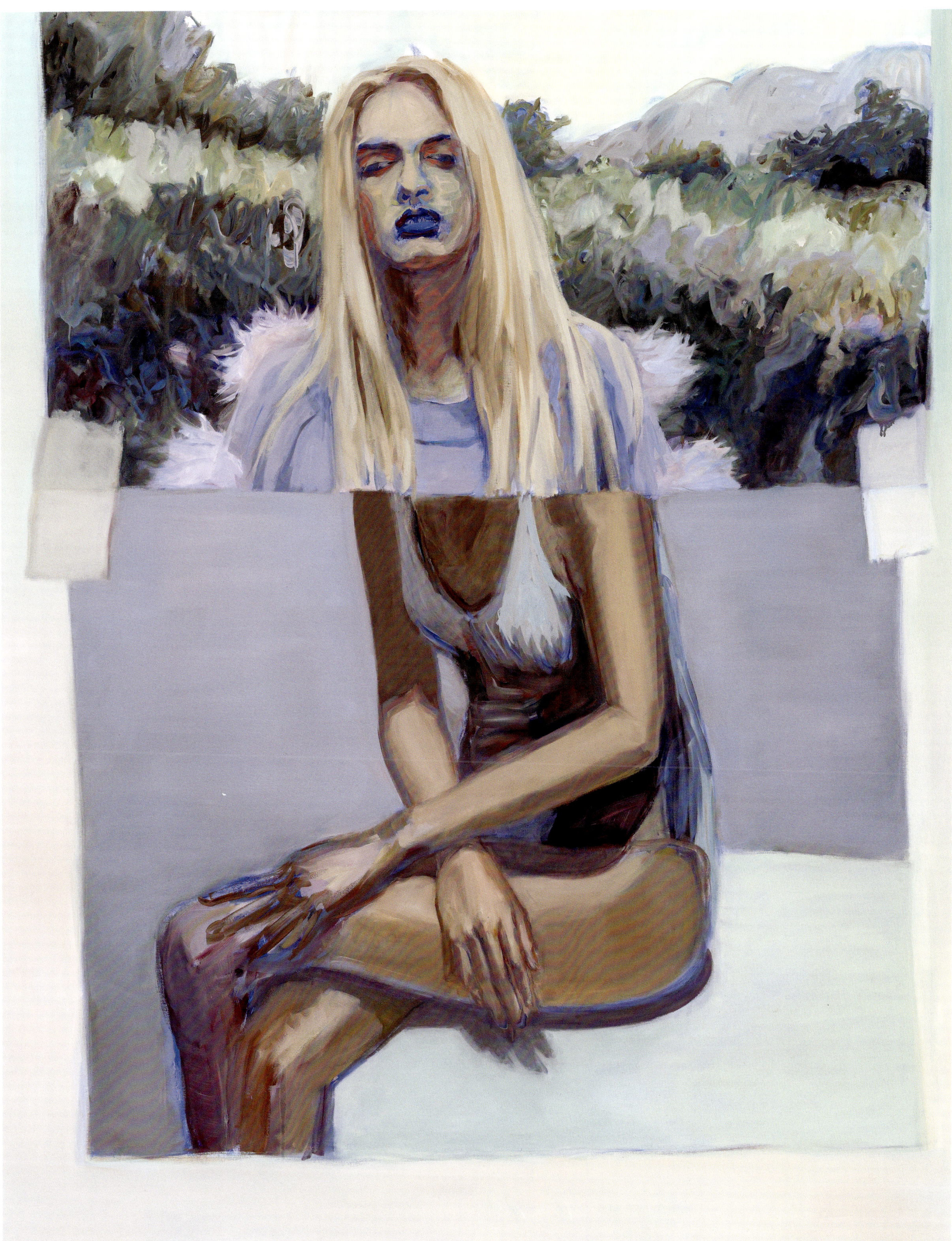

UP OVER 2021

36 × 24 in. / 91 × 61 cm

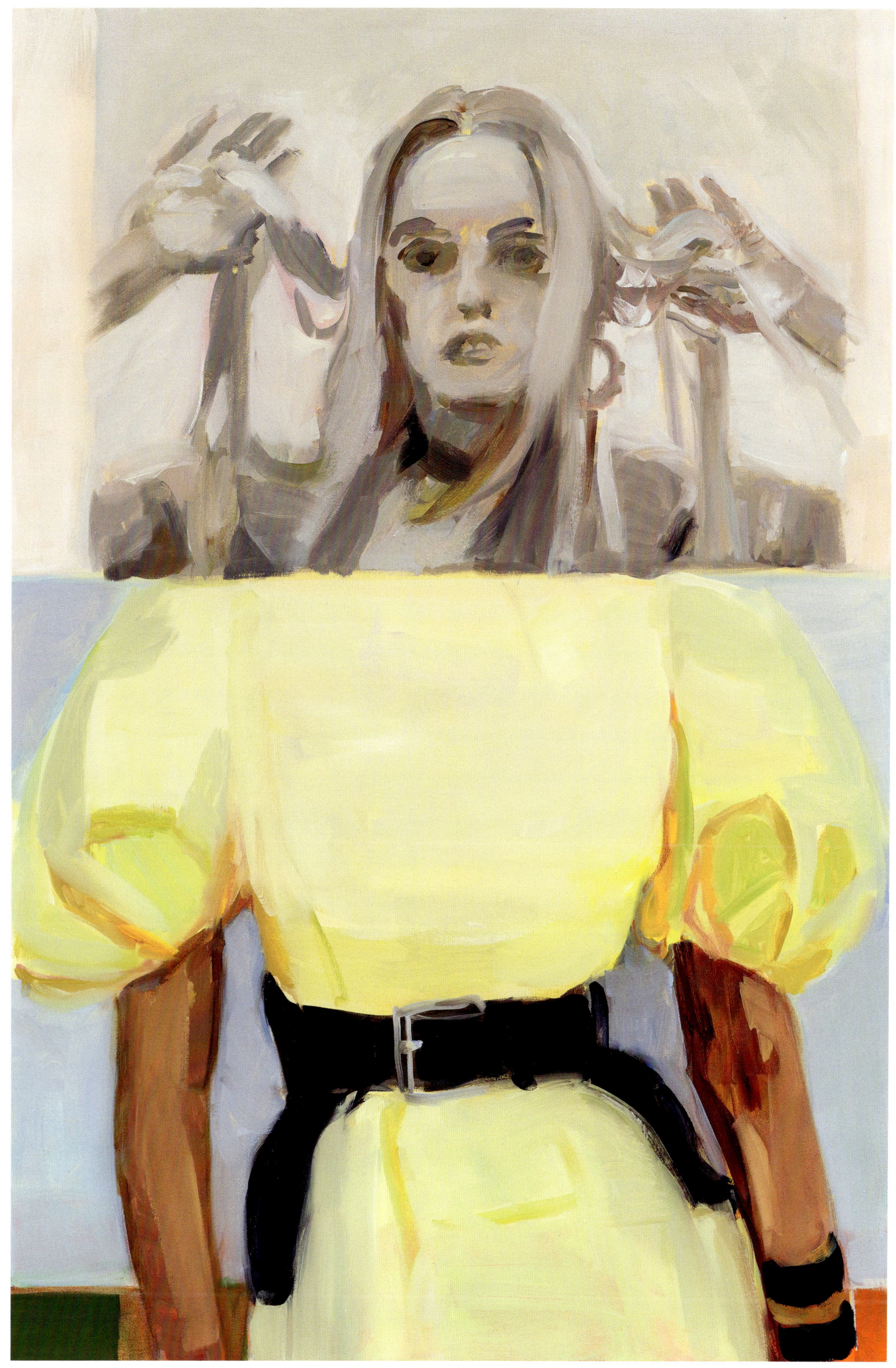

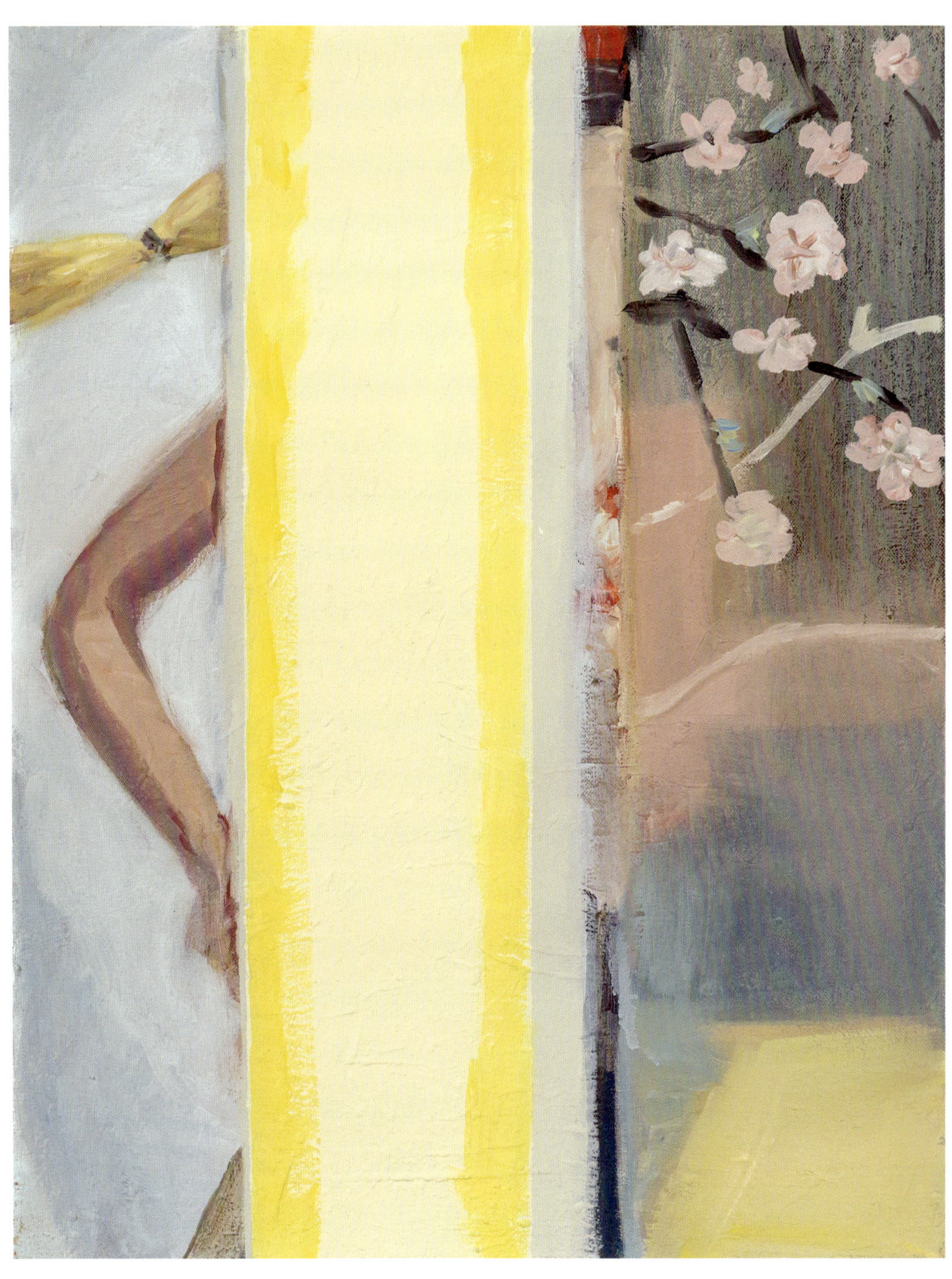

SCREEN 2020

18 × 14 in. / 46 × 36 cm

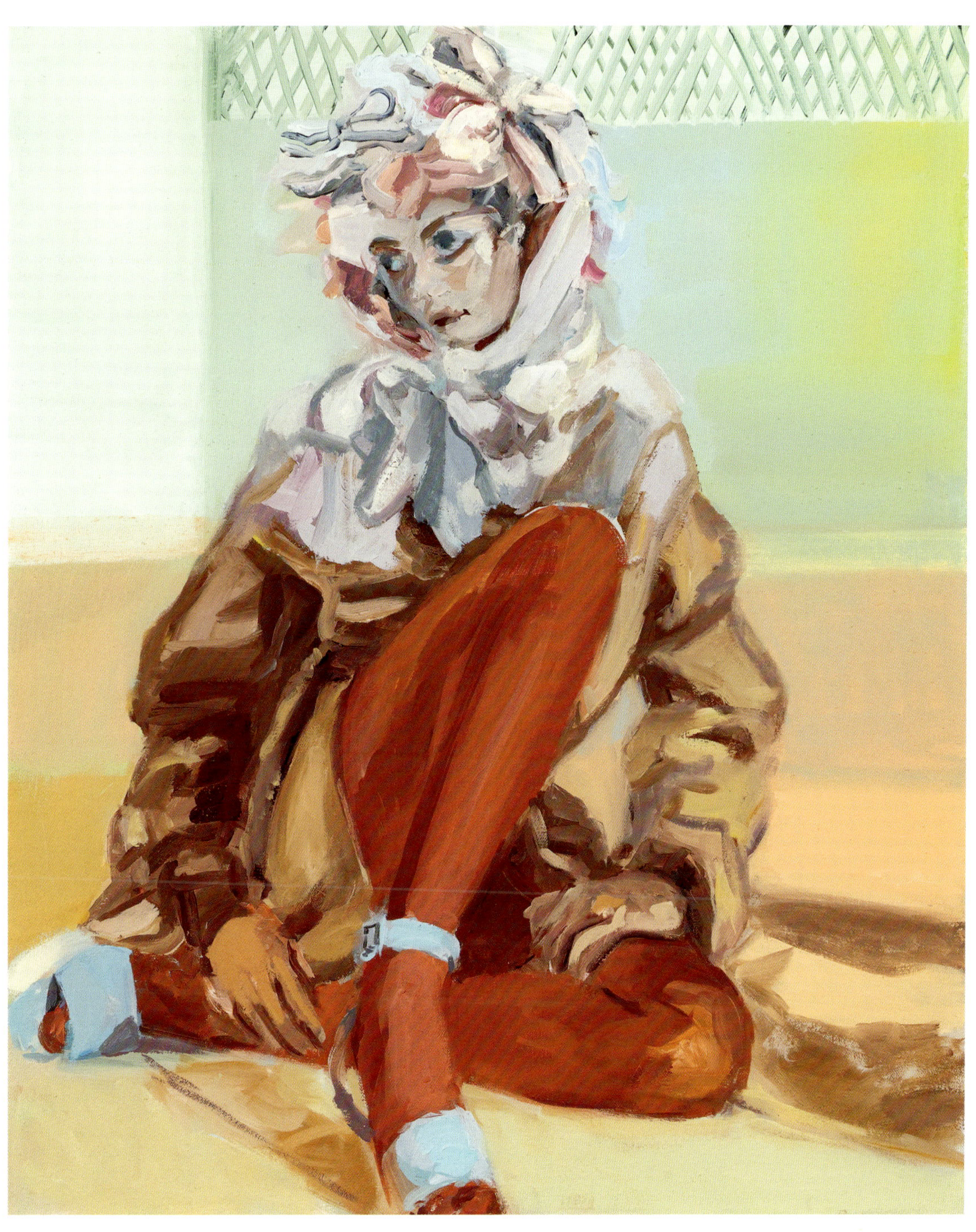

JUDY (ORANGE LEGS) 2021

24 × 20 in. / 61 × 51 cm

BREAKER 2020

60 × 48 in. / 152 × 122 cm

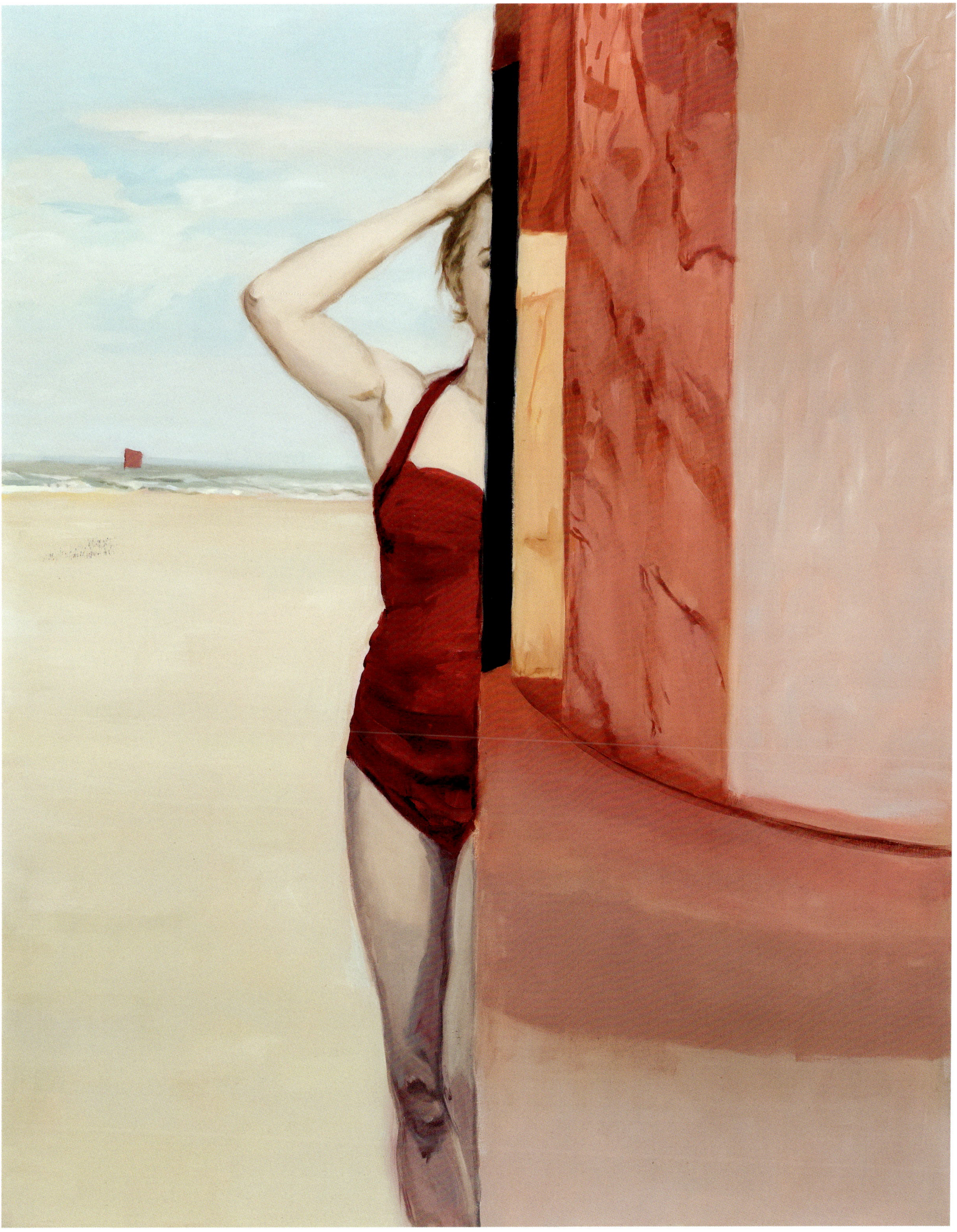

RED SHIFT 2020

54 × 45 in. / 137 × 114 cm

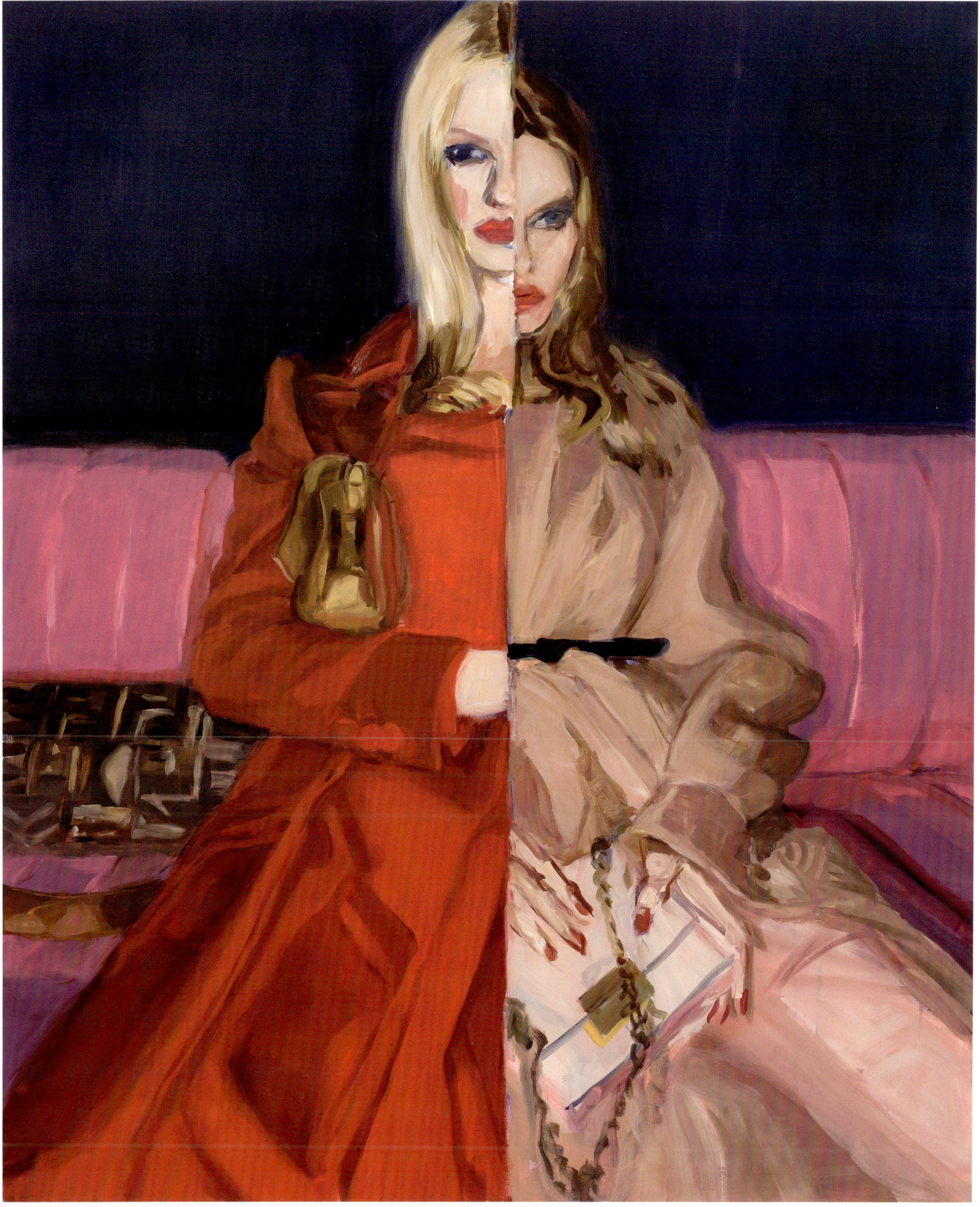

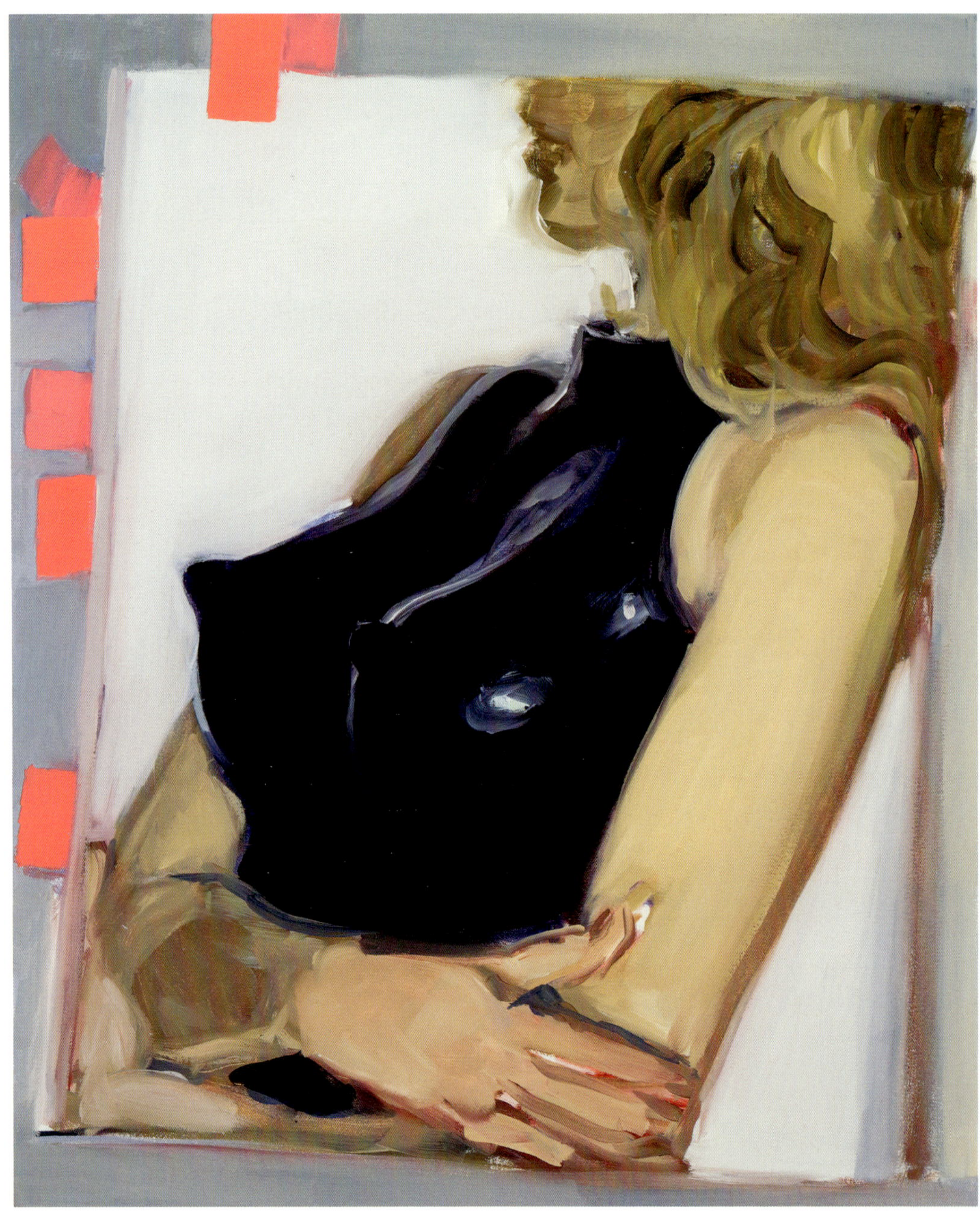

ABOVE

AJ TOP 2020

24 × 20 in. / 61 × 51 cm

OPPOSITE

KATE 2021

48 × 36 in. / 122 × 91 cm

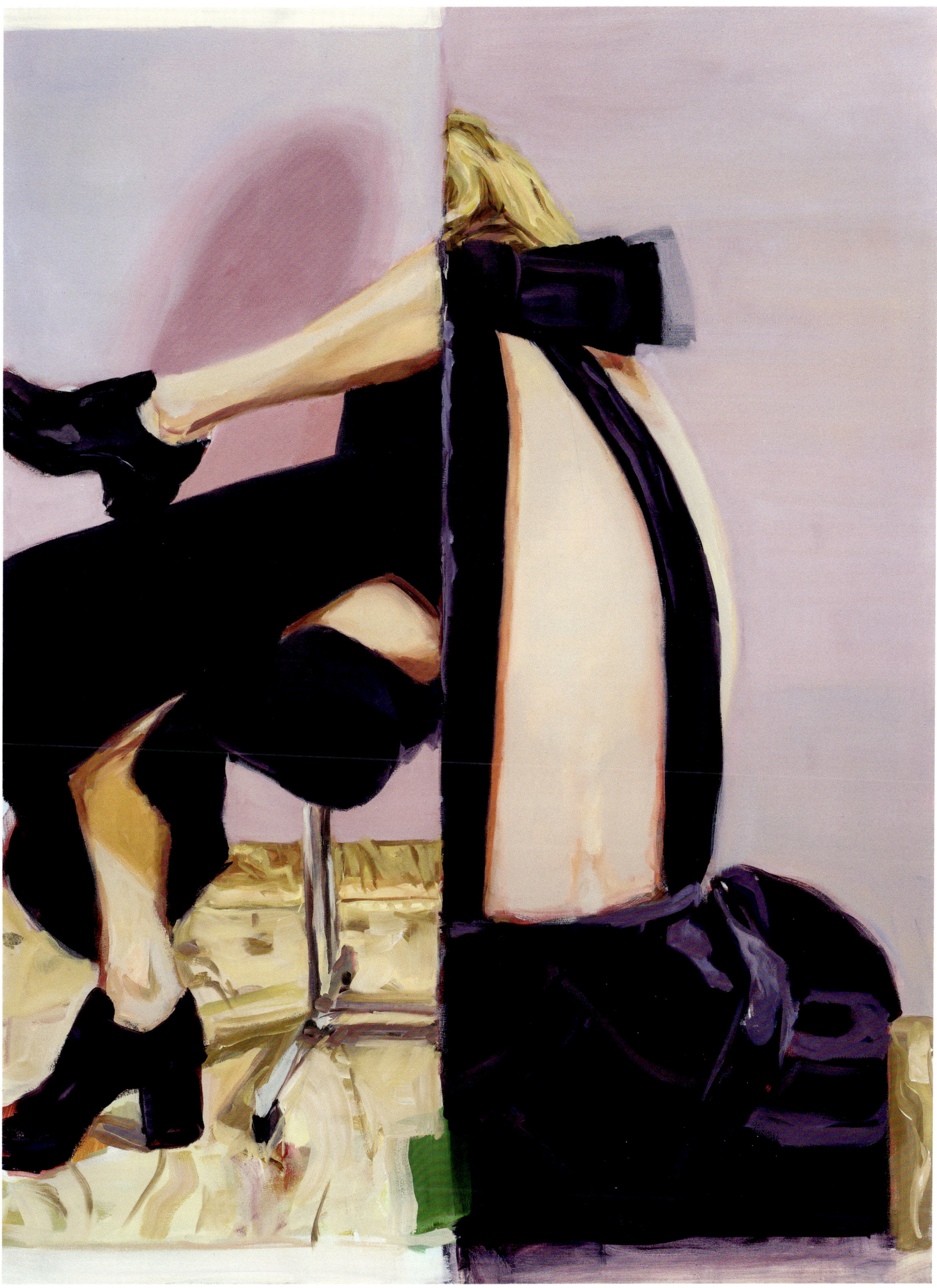

JESTER 2020

44 × 36 in. / 112 × 91 cm

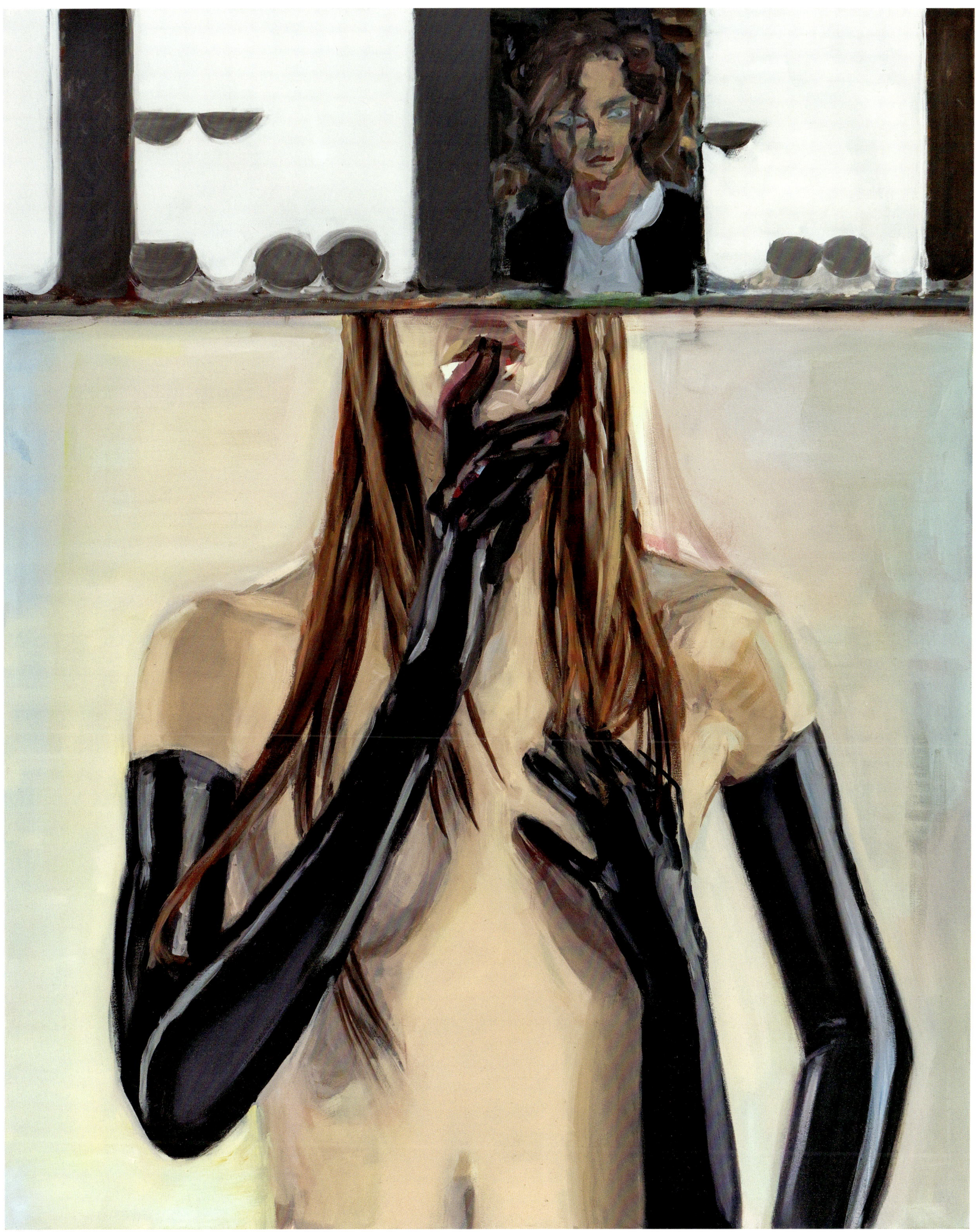

SUITE 2020

69 × 51 in. / 175 × 130 cm

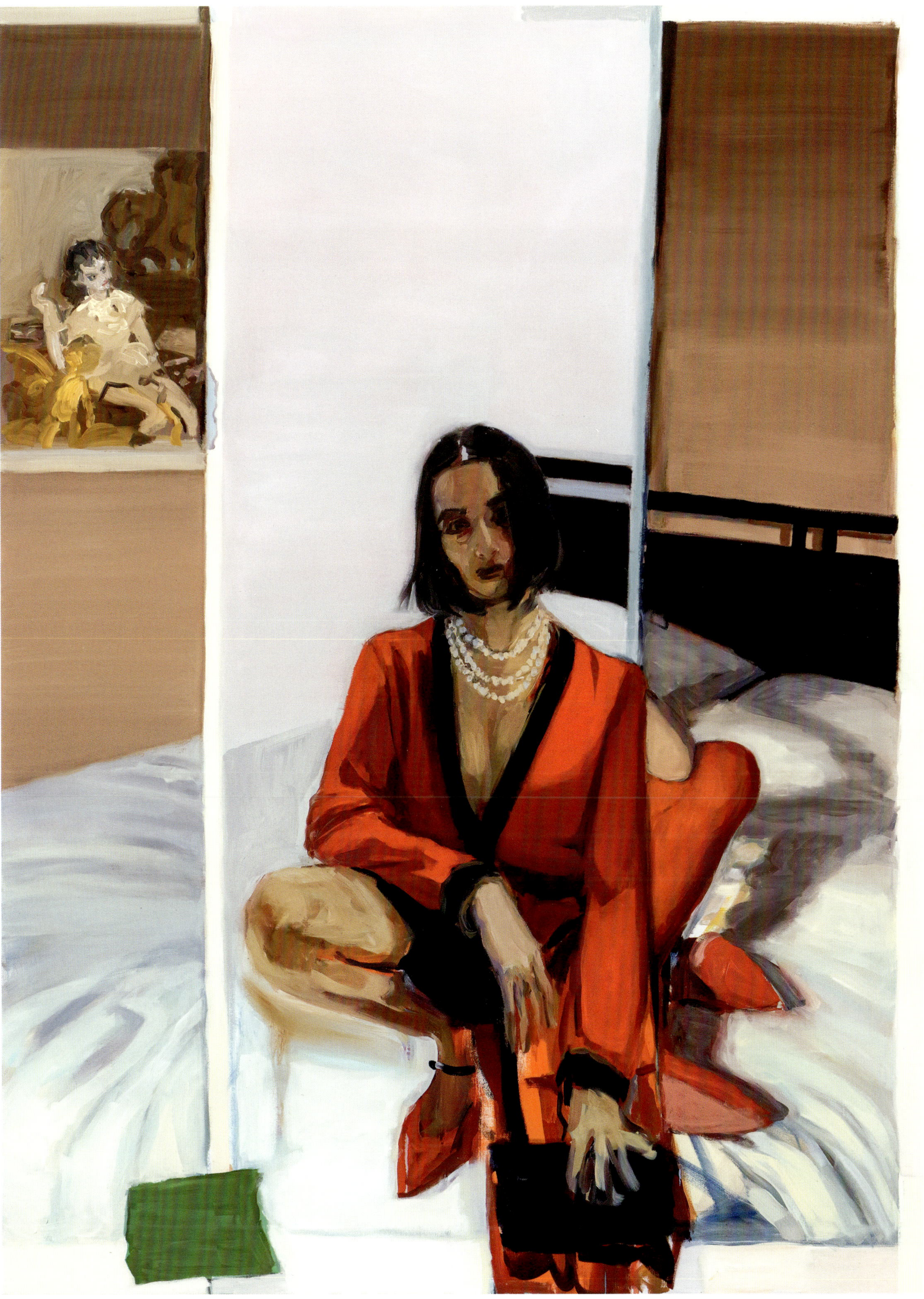

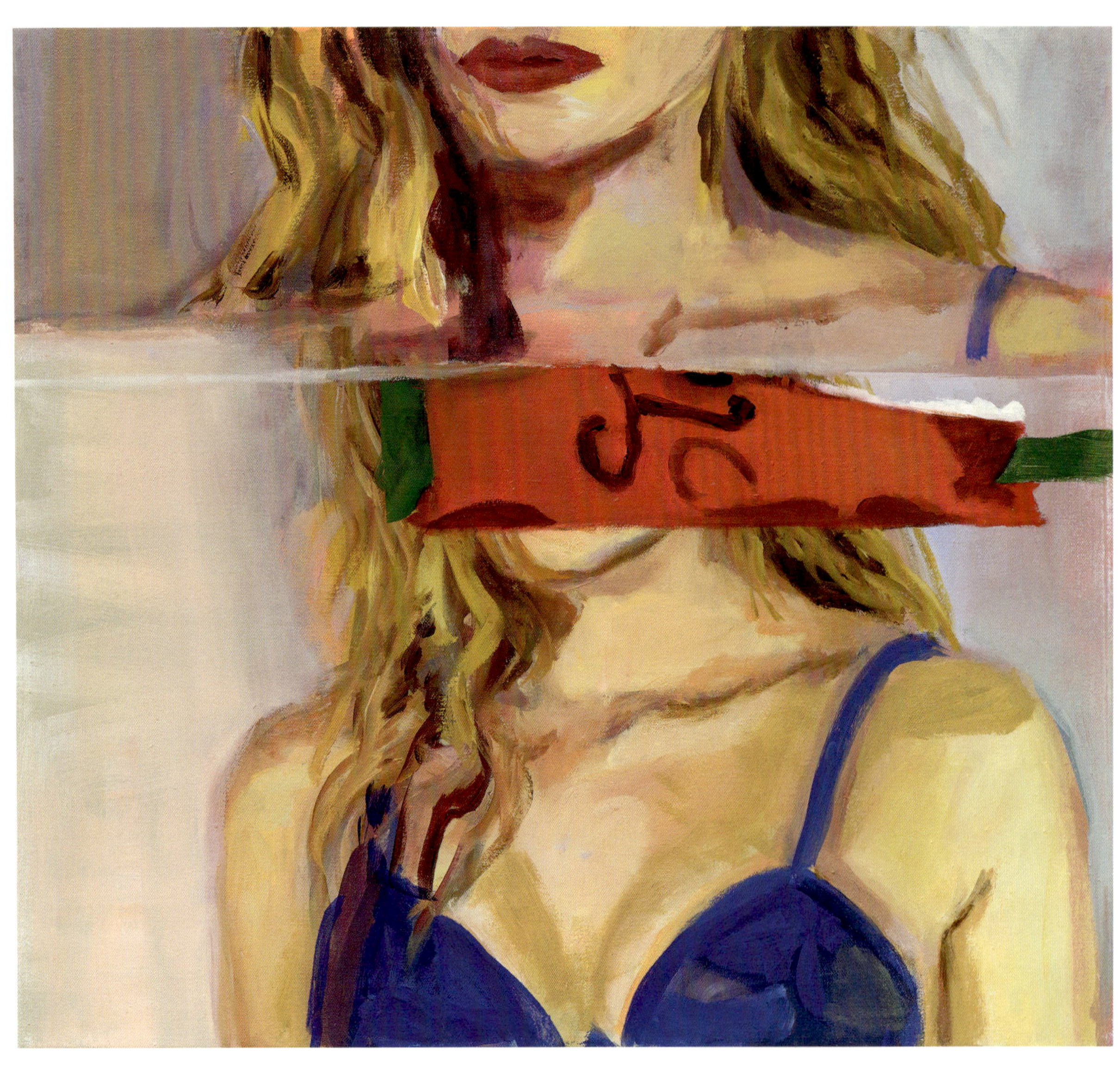

T 2021

16 × 20 in. / 41 × 51 cm

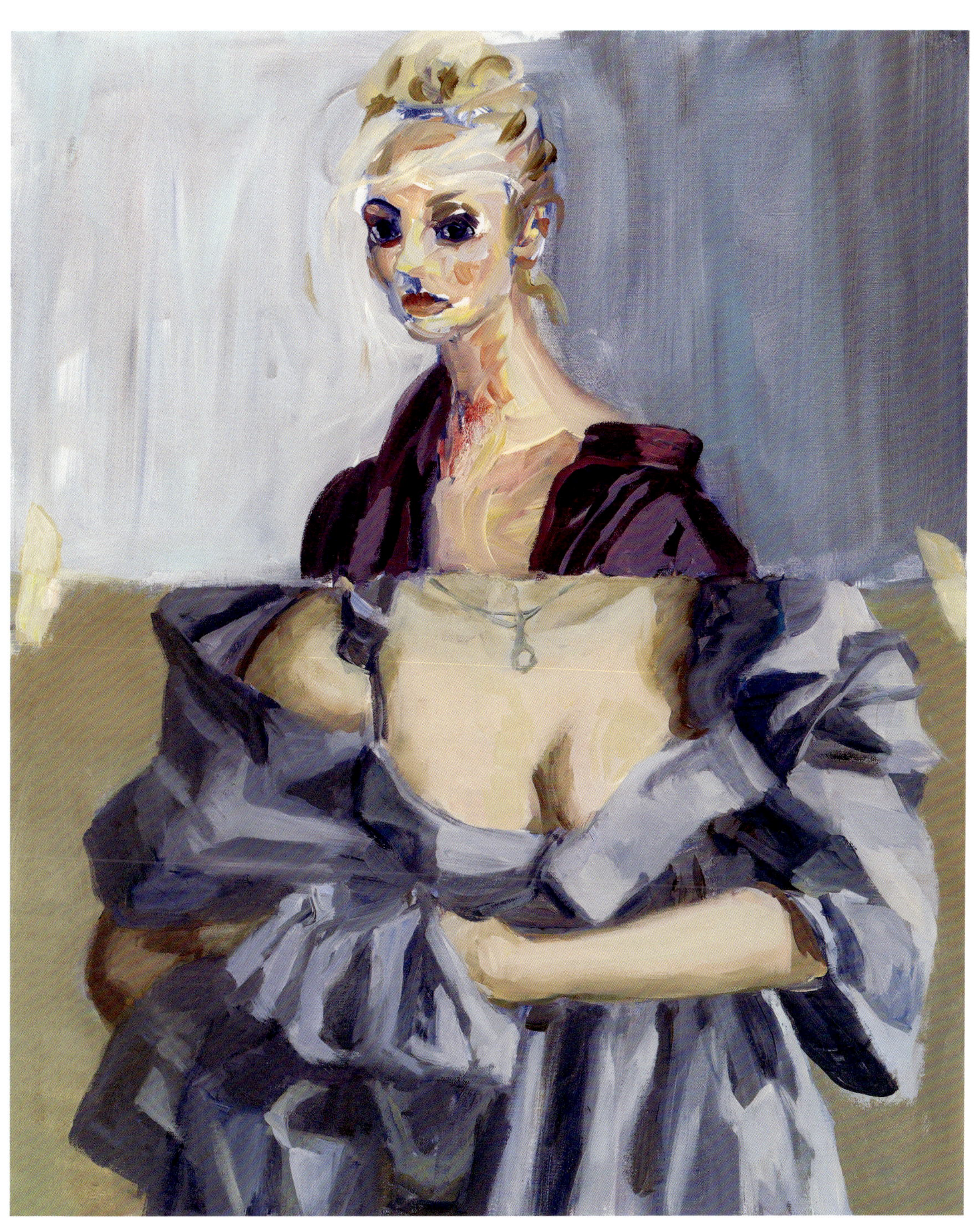

TESS (OVERLAP) 2018

22 × 20 in. / 56 × 51 cm

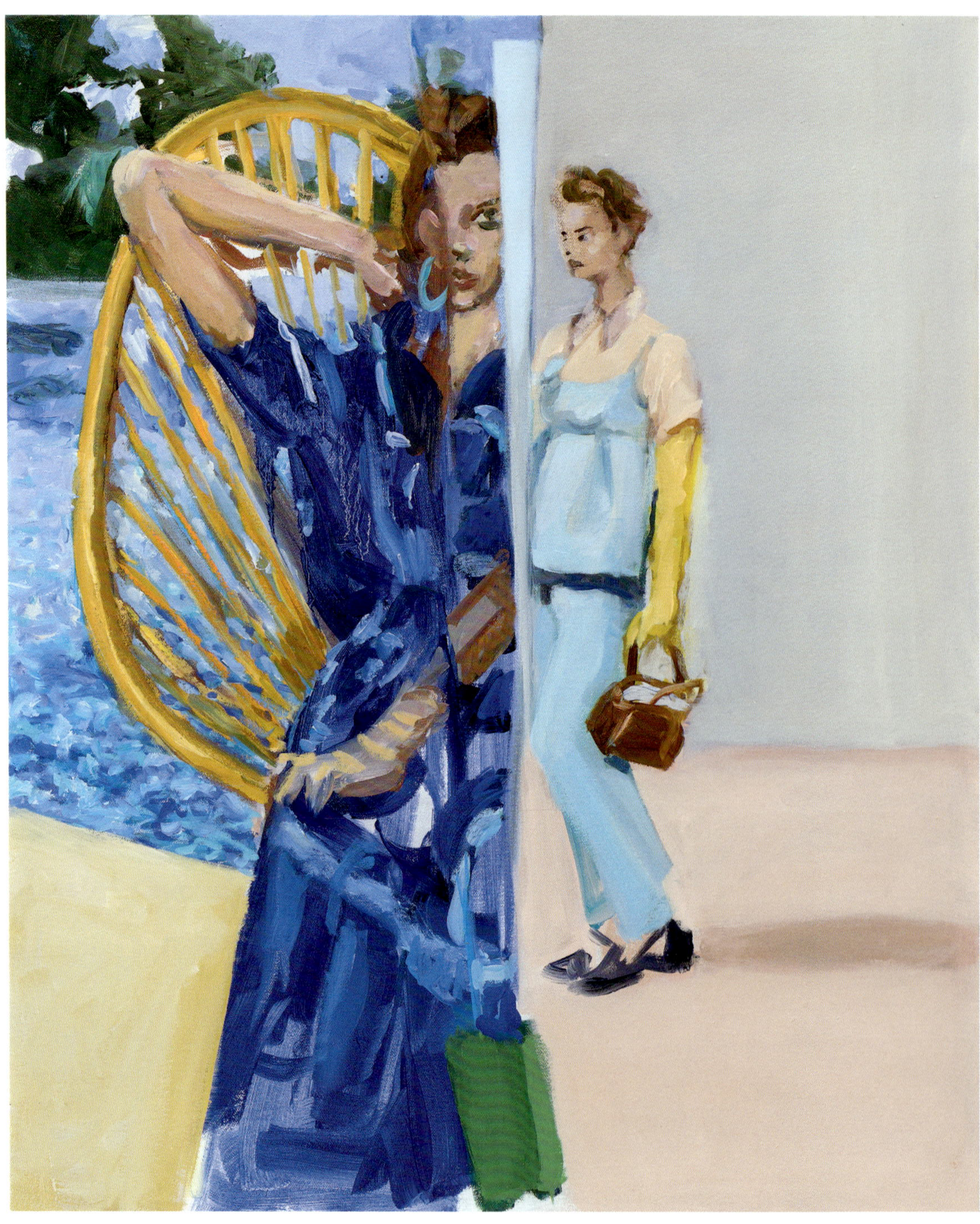

ABOVE

MIAMI 2021

24 × 20 in. / 61 × 51 cm

OPPOSITE

JULIA 2021

69 × 51 in. / 175 × 130 cm

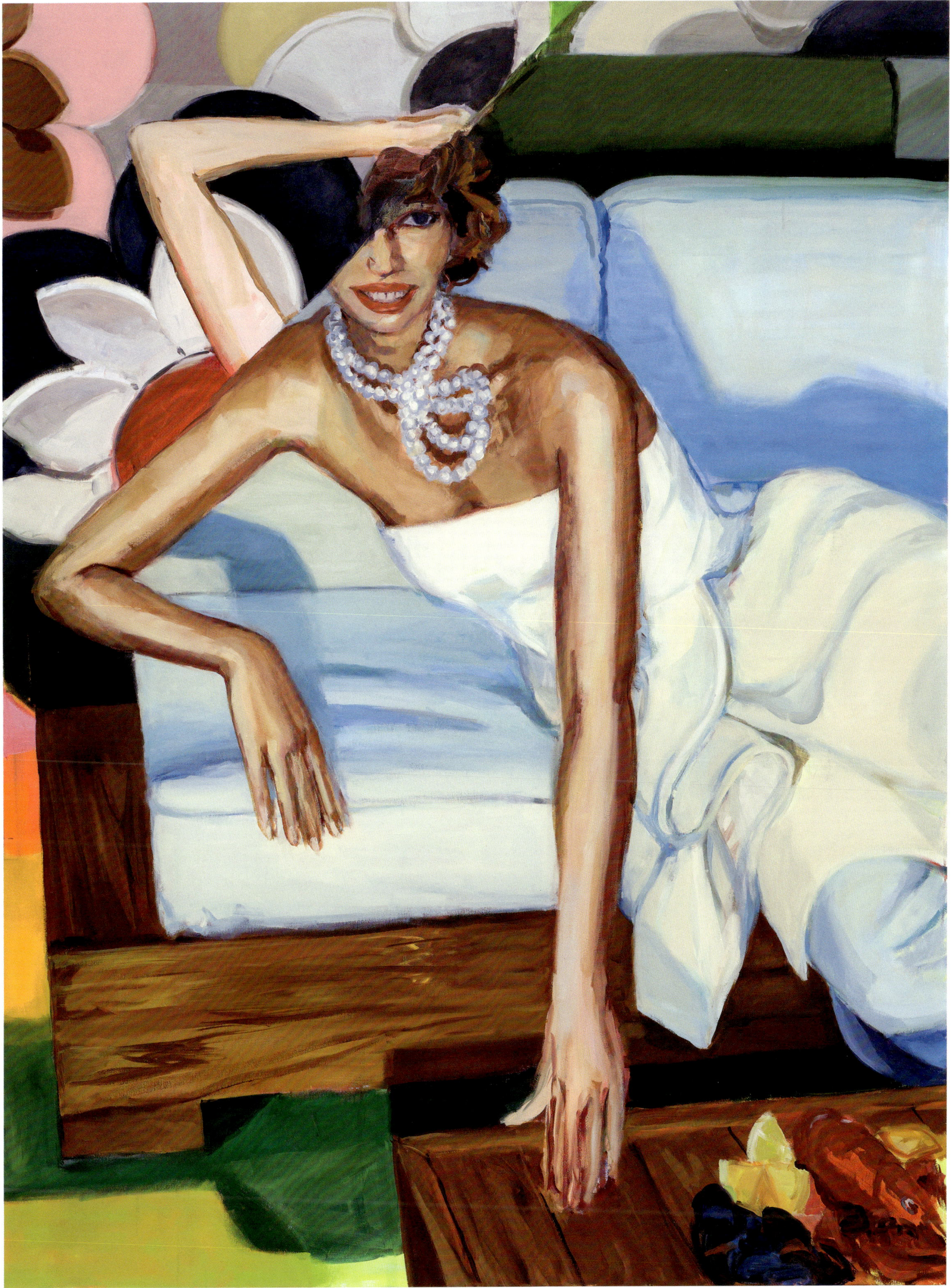

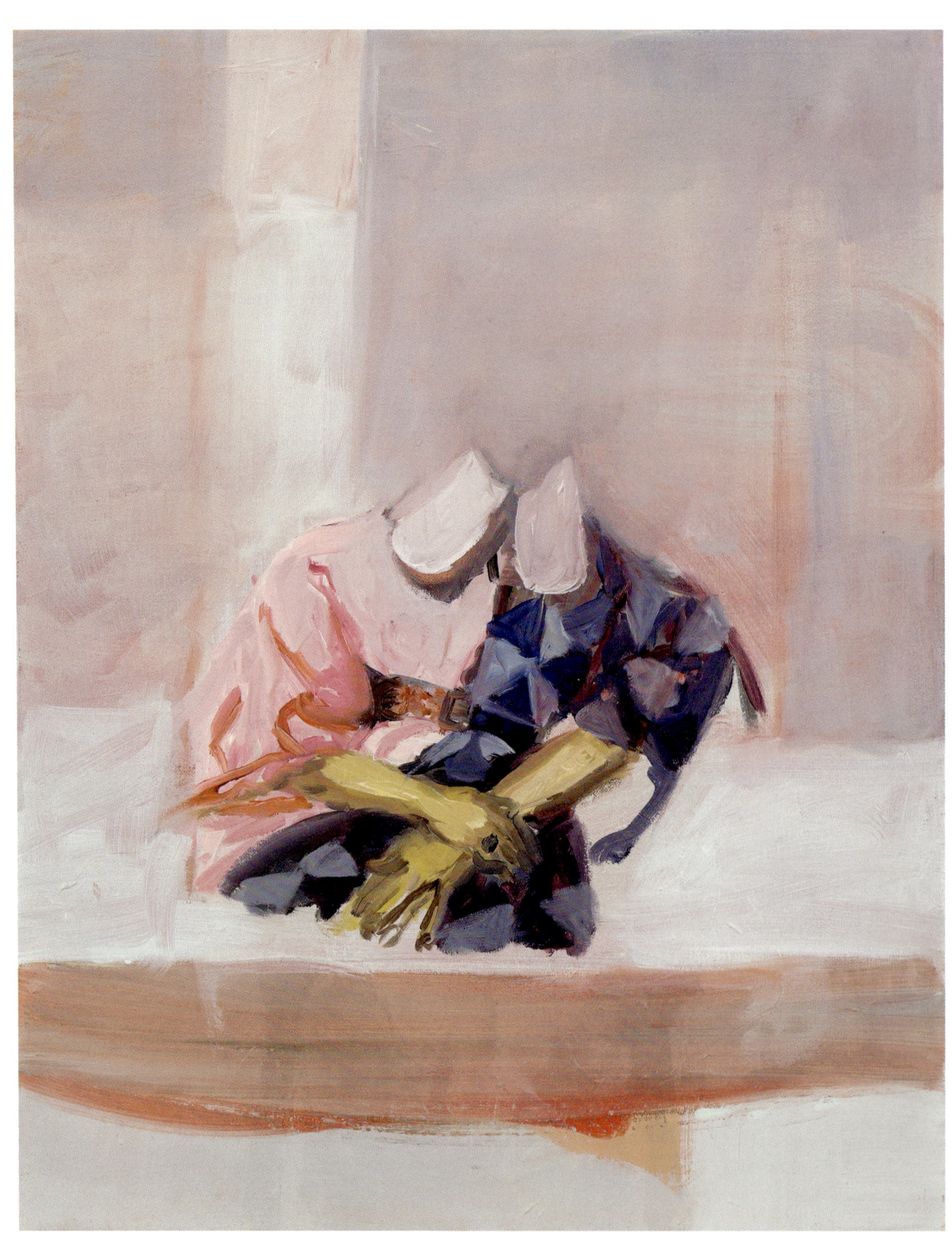

DOMINO 2020

20 × 16 in. / 51 × 41 cm

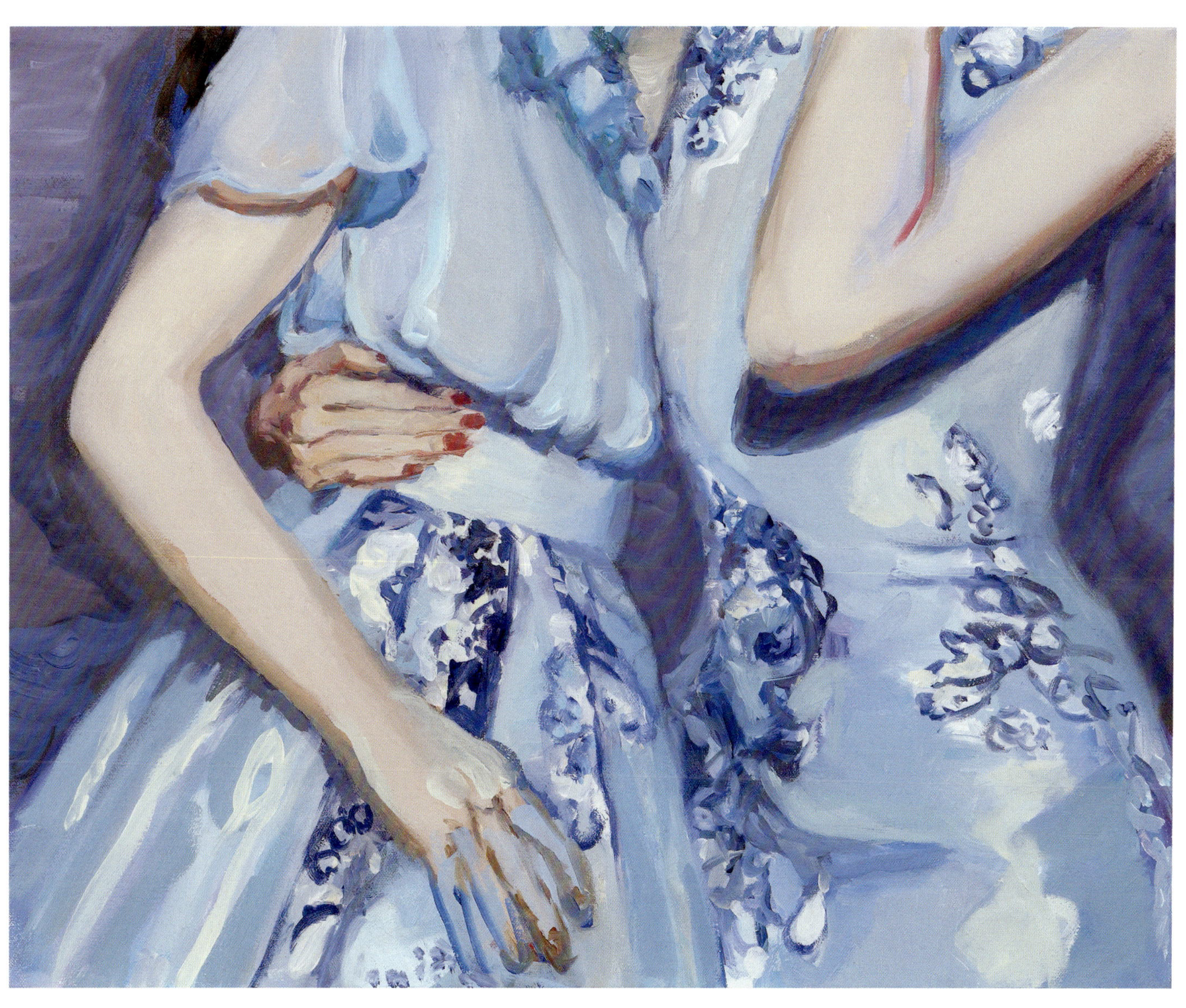

ROXY 2020

16 × 20 in. / 41 × 51 cm

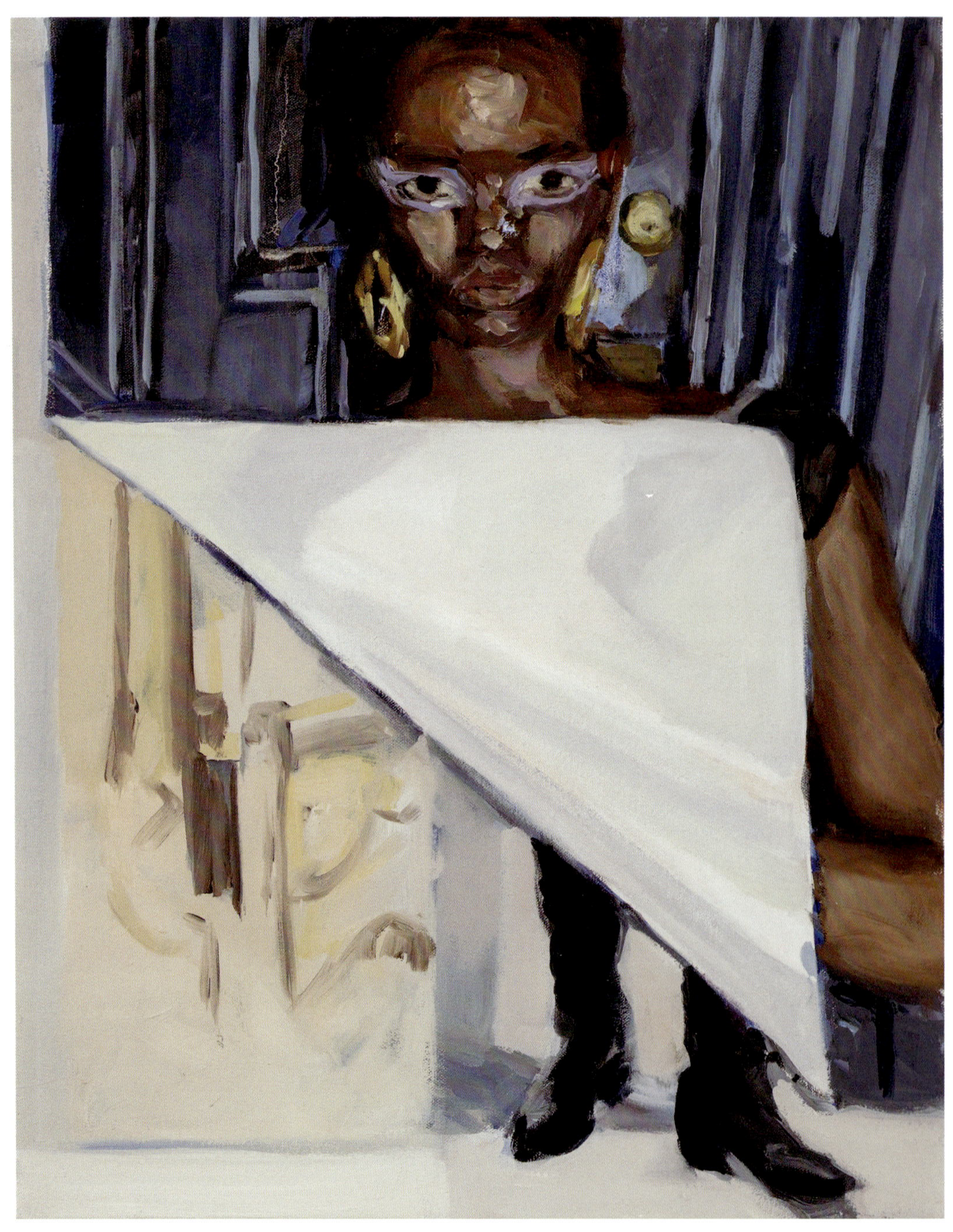

ABOVE

SCRY 2021

20 × 18 in. / 51 × 46 cm

OPPOSITE

BANDIT 2020

31 × 24 in. / 79 × 70 cm

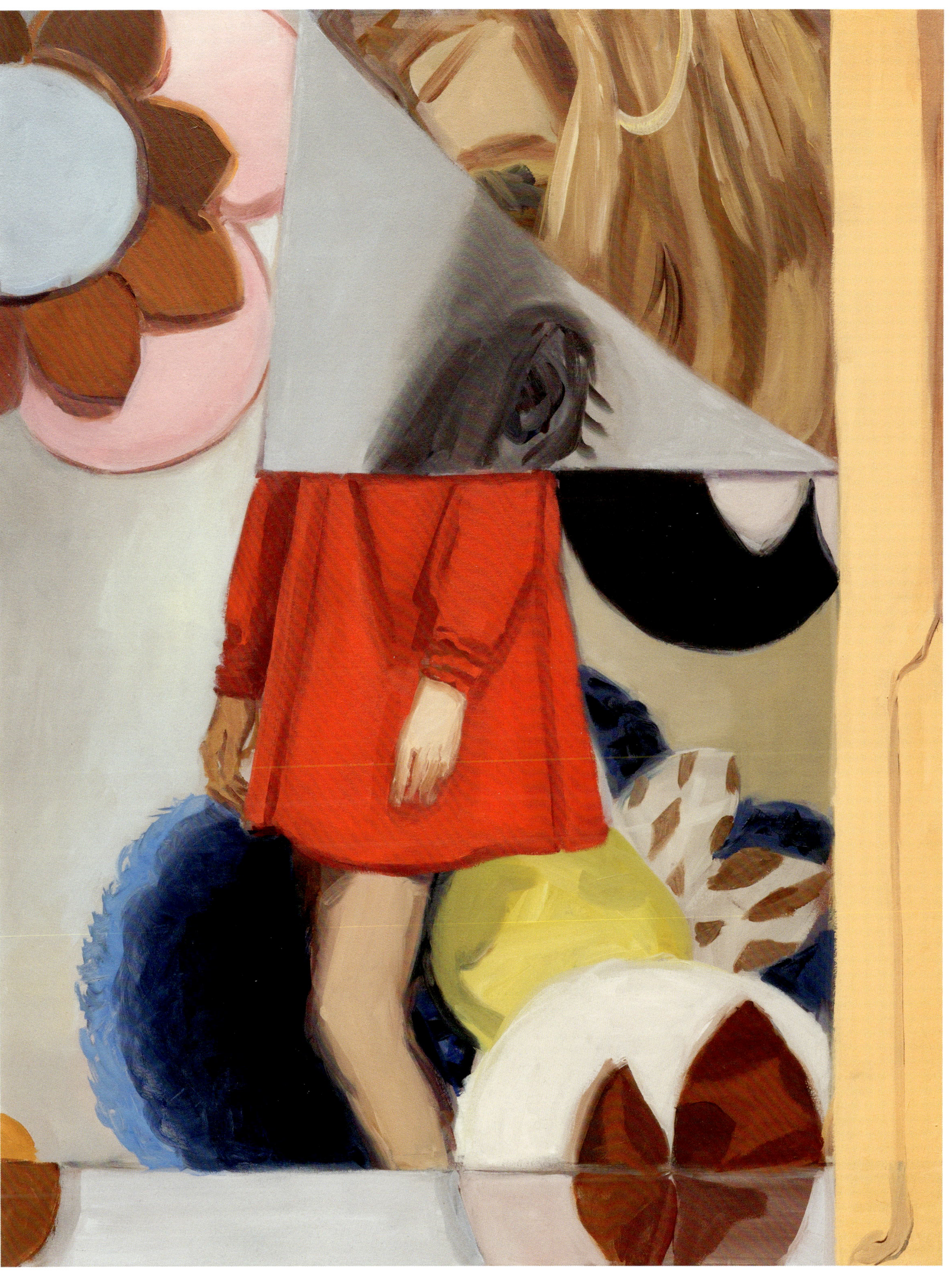

GINA 2019

84 × 67 in. / 213 × 170 cm

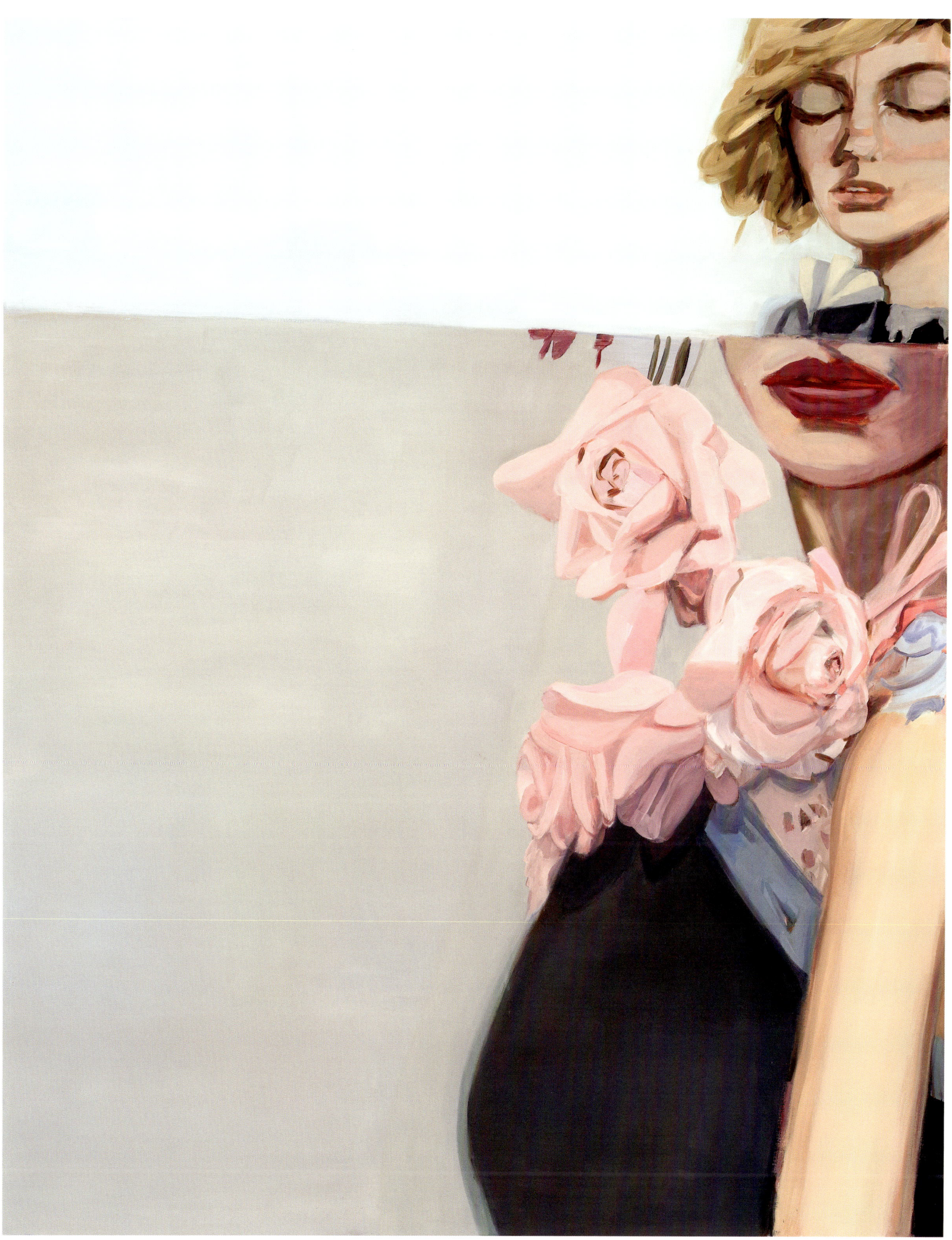

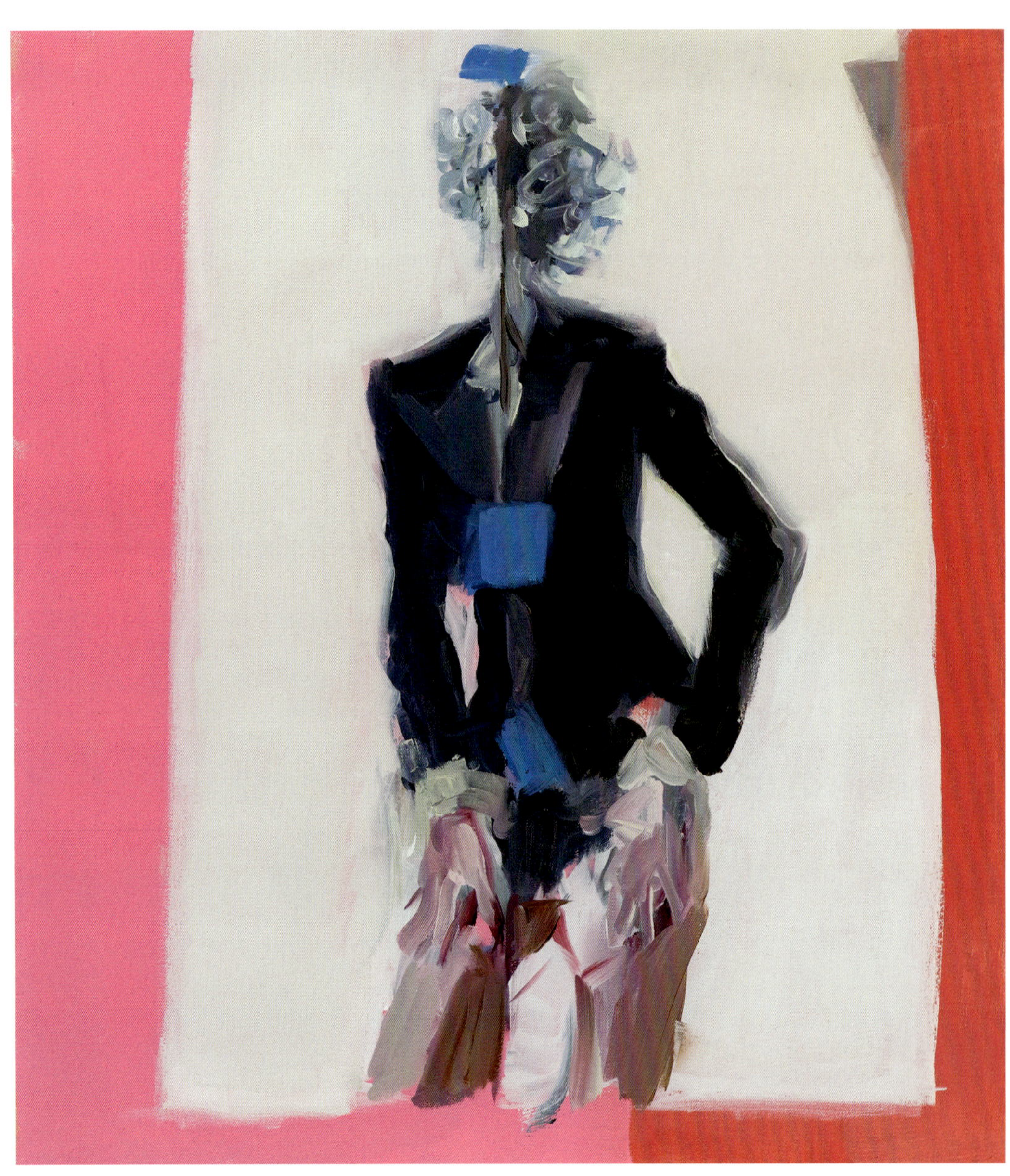

REDPINK (NICOLE) 2021

20 × 18 in. / 51 × 46 cm

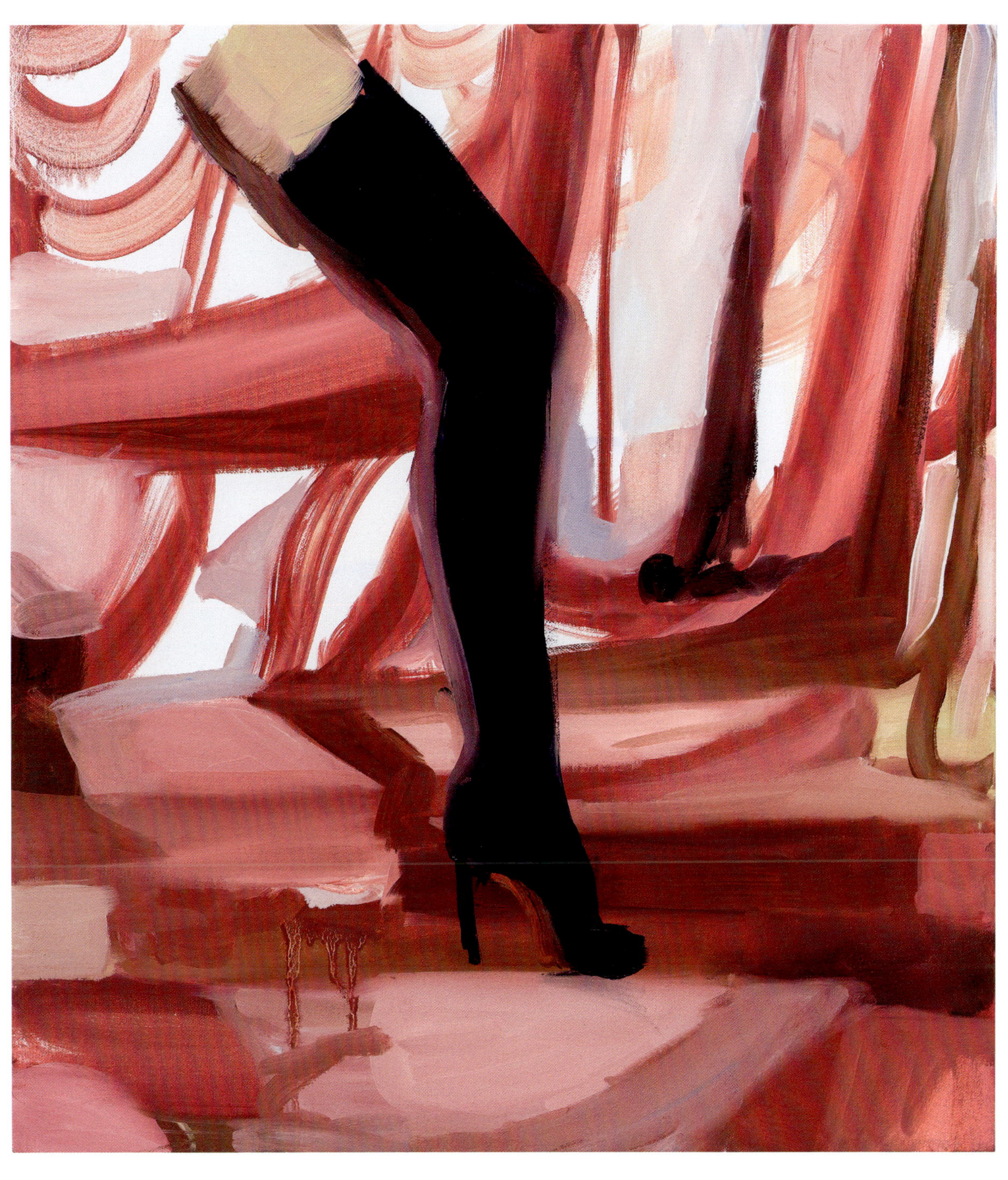

LEG 2021

20 × 18 in. / 51 × 46 cm

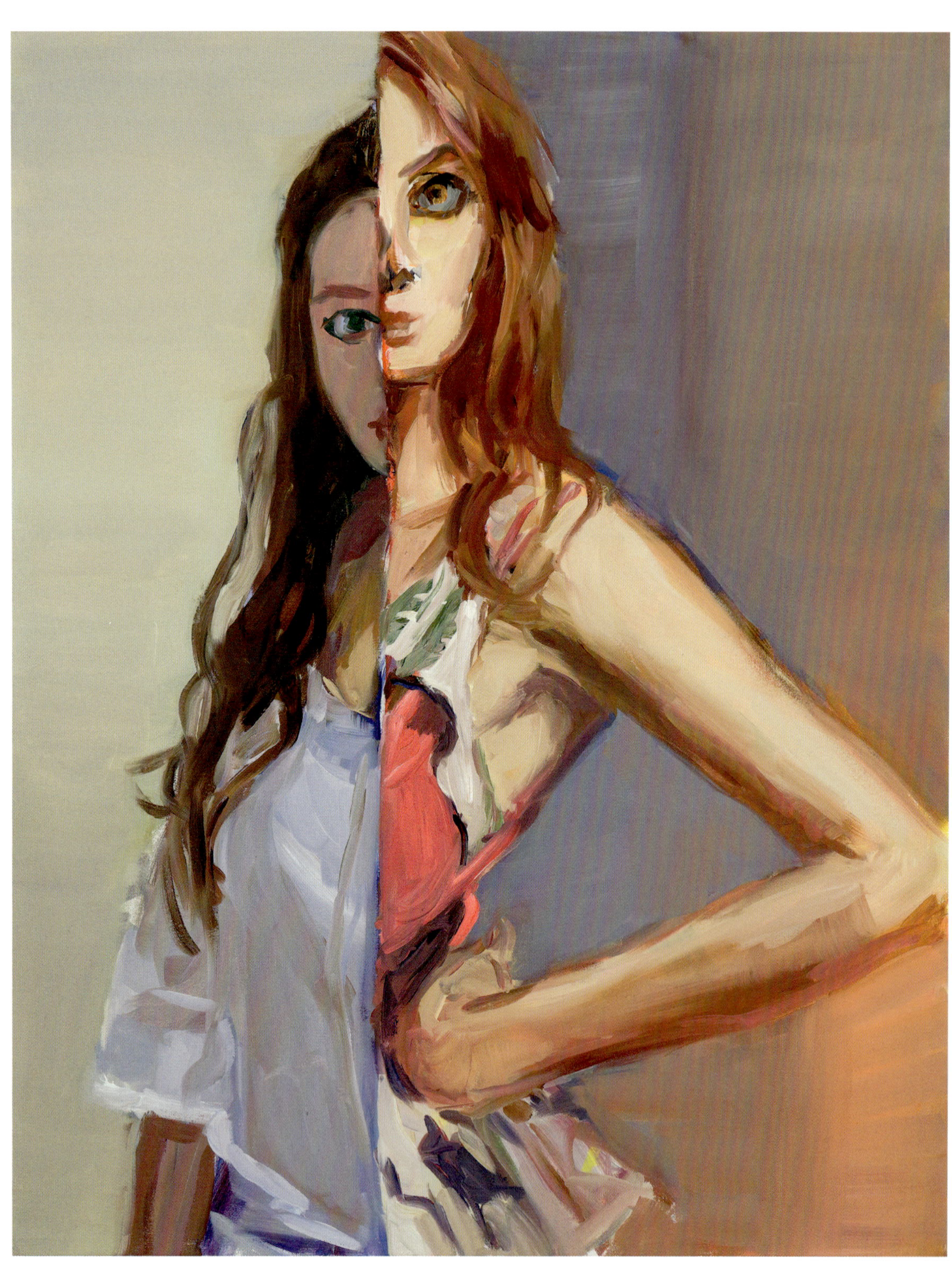

UNTITLED (ORANGE SPLIT) 2020

33 × 26 in. / 84 × 66 cm

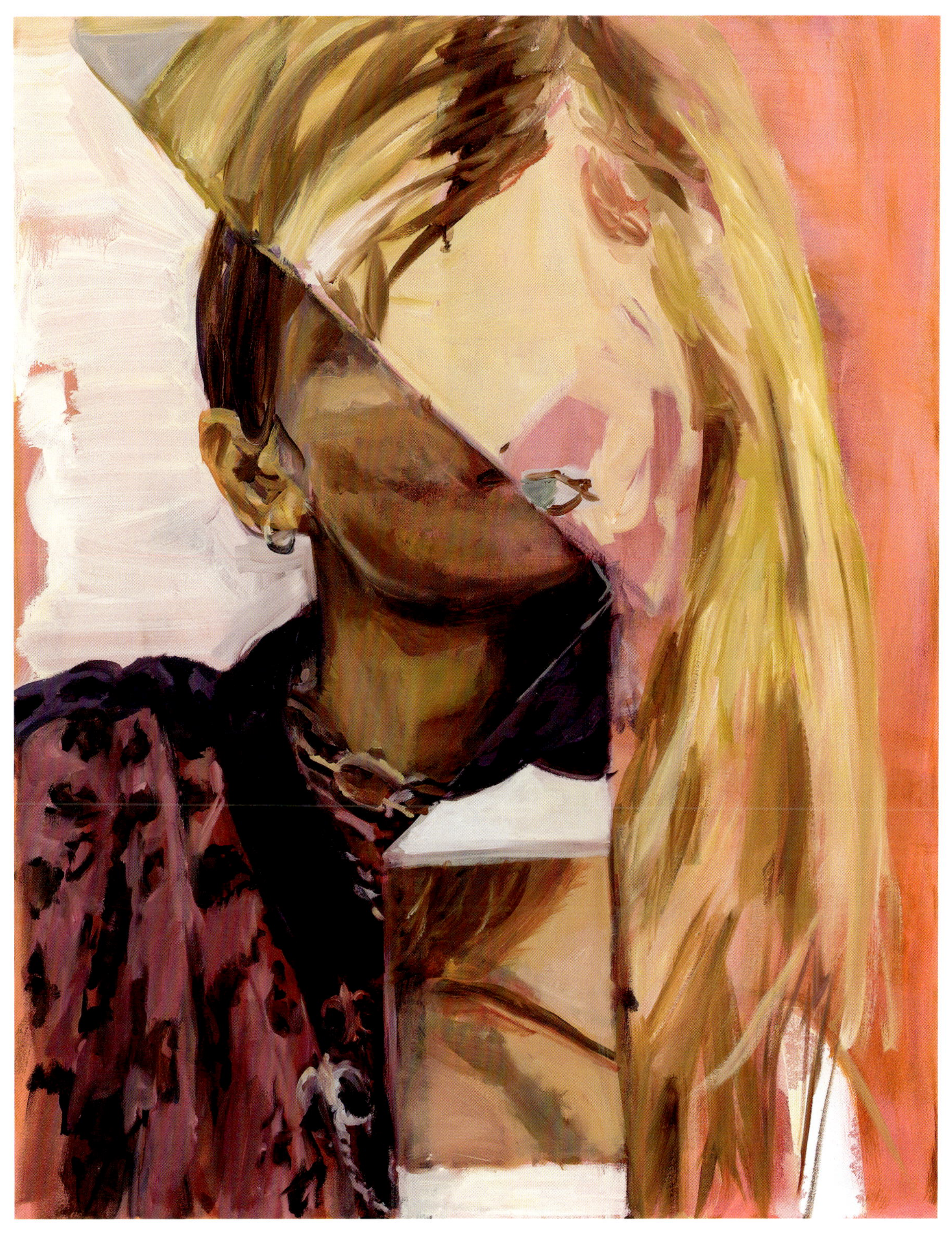

CRUSH 2 2021

33 × 26 in. / 84 × 66 cm

RABBIT 2020

51 × 69 in. / 130 × 175 cm

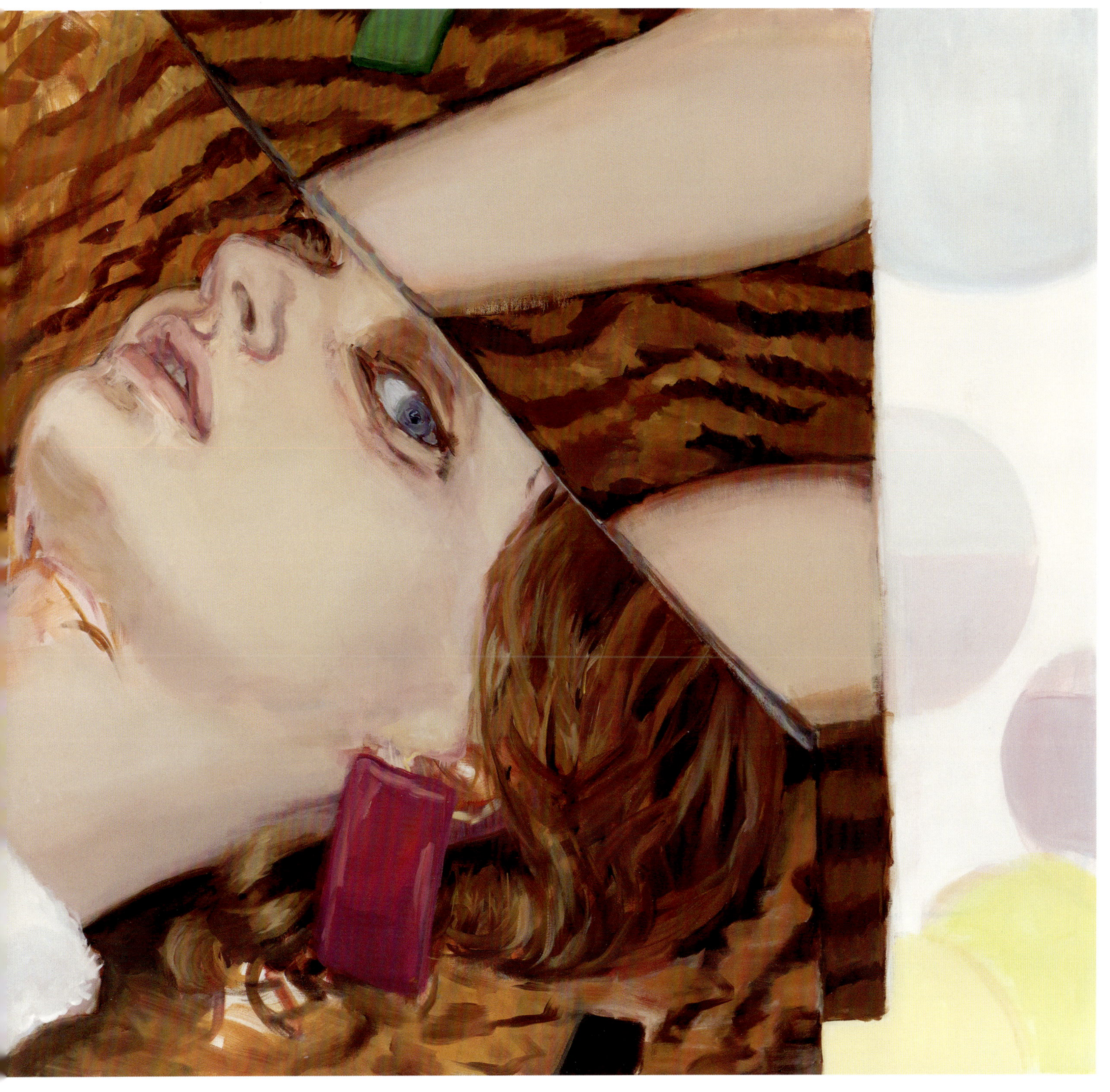

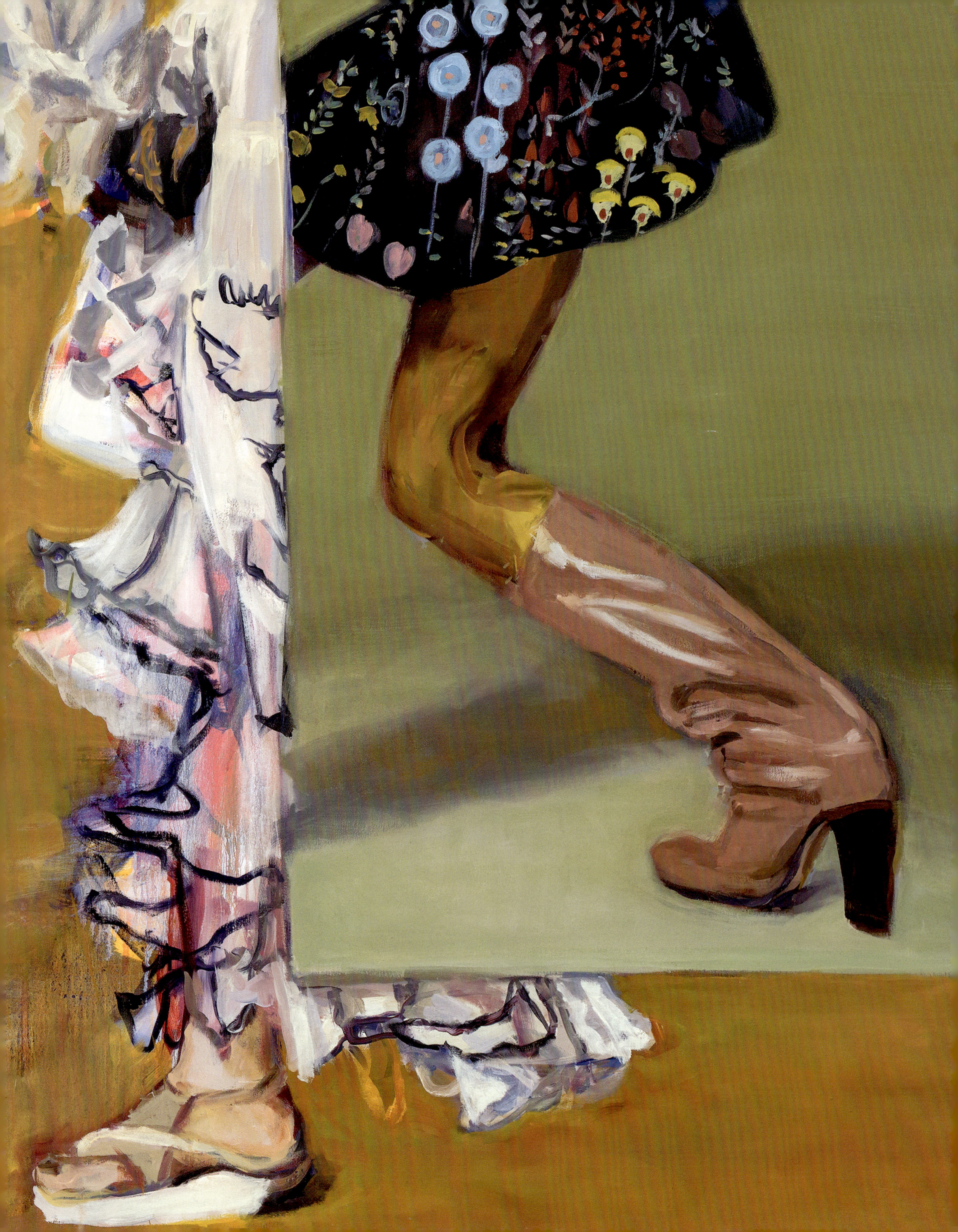

List of Works

All works are oil on canvas. Measurements of artworks are given as height × width. / Toutes les œuvres sont des huiles sur toile. Les mesures des œuvres d'art sont indiquées en hauteur × largeur.

INTRODUCTION: JANET WERNER'S WORKING GIRLS

Book 2, 2021, 20 × 24 in. / 51 × 61 cm
Collection of Jennifer Slinger, Montreal /
Collection de Jennifer Slinger, Montréal

Neapolitan, 2020, 76 × 60 in. / 193 × 152 cm
Private collection, Los Angeles /
Collection privée, Los Angeles

OBJECT RELATIONS

Abstract, 2018, 20 × 16 in. / 51 × 41 cm
Private collection, Montreal /
Collection privée, Montréal

Bear, 2010, 88 × 66 in. / 224 × 168 cm
Private collection, Montreal /
Collection privée, Montréal

Birchman, 2010, 20 × 16 in. / 51 × 41 cm
Private collection, Montreal /
Collection privée, Montréal

Curtain, 2016, 72 × 60 in. / 183 × 152 cm
Collection of the Art Gallery of Ontario, Toronto /
Collection de l'Art Gallery of Ontario, Toronto

Dreamer, 2012, 67 × 55 in. / 170 × 140 cm
Collection of Brigitte Giasson, Montreal /
Collection de Brigitte Giasson, Montréal

Float (pink trace), 2016, 60 × 48 in. / 152 × 122 cm
Collection of the artist /
Collection de l'artiste

Folding Woman, 2009, 66 × 53 in. / 168 × 135 cm
NIRO Family Collection, Montreal /
Collection de la famille NIRO, Montréal

Kinder, 2012, 55 × 45 in. / 140 × 114 cm
Collection of Colleen Pound, Calgary /
Collection de Colleen Pound, Calgary

Lexicon, 2021, 33 × 26 in. / 84 × 66 cm
Courtesy of the artist and Bradley Ertaskiran, Montreal /
Avec l'autorisation de l'artiste et de Bradley Ertaskiran, Montréal

Ohio, 2009, 66 × 55 in. / 168 × 140 cm
Private collection, Montreal /
Collection privée, Montréal

Sheila, 2011, 54 × 45 in. / 137 × 114 cm
Private collection, Quebec /
Collection privée, Québec

Sisters, 2013, 22 × 20 in. / 56 × 51 cm
Collection of the Montreal Museum of Fine Arts, Montreal /
Collection du Musée des beaux-arts de Montréal, Montréal

Smearcase, 2011, 60 × 48 in. / 152 × 122 cm
Aldo Collection, Montreal /
Collection Aldo, Montréal

Touch Hold (still life), 2019, 24 × 28 in. / 61 × 71 cm
Collection of Megan Bradley, Montreal /
Collection de Megan Bradley, Montréal

MEMBRA DISJECTA

CDF, 2020, 24 × 20 in. / 61 × 51 cm
Private collection, Dallas /
Collection privée, Dallas

Crush 2, 2021, 33 × 26 in. / 84 × 66 cm
Courtesy of the artist /
Avec l'autorisation de l'artiste

Reach, 2019, 22 × 28 in. / 56 × 71 cm
Courtesy of the artist and Bradley Ertaskiran, Montreal /
Avec l'autorisation de l'artiste et de Bradley Ertaskiran, Montréal

STICKY PICTURES

After Picabia, 2014, 38 × 32 in. / 97 × 81 cm
Courtesy of the artist and Bradley Ertaskiran, Montreal /
Avec l'autorisation de l'artiste et de Bradley Ertaskiran, Montréal

Bitten, 2018, 67 × 60 in. / 170 × 152 cm
Courtesy of the artist and Anat Ebgi, Los Angeles /
Avec l'autorisation de l'artiste et de l'Anat Ebgi, Los Angeles

Black book, 2016, 40 × 32 in. / 102 × 81 cm
Prêt d'œuvres collection of the Musée national des beaux-arts du Québec, Quebec / Collection Prêt d'œuvres du Musée national des beaux-arts du Québec, Québec

Blue Table, 2019, 76 × 60 in. / 193 × 152 cm
Majudia Collection, Montreal /
Collection Majudia, Montréal

Carey, 2014, 98 × 78 in. / 249 × 198 cm
Collection of the Montreal Museum of Fine Arts, Montreal /
Collection du Musée des beaux-arts de Montréal, Montréal

Cinnamon (after Gainsborough), 2018, 60 × 48 in. / 152 × 122 cm
McEvoy Family Collection, San Francisco /
Collection de la famille McEvoy, San Francisco

Dee (yellow dress), 2020, 24 × 20 in. / 61 × 51 cm
Collection of Anat Ebgi, Los Angeles /
Collection de l'Anat Ebgi, Los Angeles

Double (blue hat), 2019, 31 × 24 in. / 79 × 61 cm
Private collection, New York / Collection privée, New York

Double Lips, 2018, 20 × 24 in. / 51 × 61 cm
Private collection, Calgary / Collection privée, Calgary

Gallery, 2017, 88 × 67 in. / 224 × 170 cm
Collection of the National Bank, Montreal /
Collection Banque Nationale, Montréal

Green Room AJ, 2018, 48 × 60 in. / 122 × 152 cm
Majudia Collection, Montreal /
Collection Majudia, Montréal

Half Half, 2016, 20 × 24 in. / 51 × 61 cm
Ohrt-Dubuc Collection, Montreal /
Collection Ohrt-Dubuc, Montréal

Harper Valley, 2017, 40 × 32 in. / 102 × 81 cm
Ohrt-Dubuc Collection, Montreal /
Collection Ohrt-Dubuc, Montréal

Hass, 2017, 60 × 48 in. / 152 × 122 cm
Private collection, Montreal /
Collection privée, Montréal

Hover (the distance between here and there), 2017,
74 × 60 in. / 188 × 152 cm
Collection of the National Bank, Montreal /
Collection de la Banque Nationale, Montréal

Leaning In, 2016, 60 × 48 in. / 152 × 122 cm
Courtesy of the artist /
Avec l'autorisation de l'artiste

Loop, 2019, 20 × 16 in. / 51 × 41 cm
Collection of Nancy Stern and Stephen Schachter, Vancouver /
Collection de Nancy Stern et Stephen Schachter, Vancouver

MHMH, 2016, 55 × 45 in. / 140 × 114 cm
Collection of the Art Gallery of Guelph, Guelph /
Collection de l'Art Gallery of Guelph, Guelph

Portrait (red curtain), 2019, 84 × 67 in. / 213 × 170 cm
Collection of the Caisse de dépôt et placement du Québec, Quebec /
Collection de la Caisse de dépôt et placement du Québec, Québec

Portrait Reflection, 2020, 24 × 20 in. / 61 × 51 cm
Collection of Patricia Lemaire, Montreal /
Collection de Patricia Lemaire, Montréal

Recliner (death in Venice), 2018, 60 × 67 in. / 152 × 170 cm
Courtesy of the artist and Anat Ebgi, Los Angeles /
Avec l'autorisation de l'artiste et de l'Anat Ebgi, Los Angeles

Scar Curtain, 2019, 22 × 28 in. / 56 × 72 cm
Tedeschi Collection, Montreal /
Collection Tedeschi, Montréal

Slip, 2017, 20 × 16 in. / 51 × 41 cm
RBC Corporate Art Collection, Toronto /
Collection d'œuvres d'art RBC, Toronto

Someone, something, no one, 2017, 67 × 60 in. / 170 × 152 cm
Courtesy of the artist and Bradley Ertaskiran, Montreal /
Avec l'autorisation de l'artiste et de Bradley Ertaskiran, Montréal

Sorcerer, 2016, 75 × 60 in. / 191 × 152 cm
Collection of the Musée d'art contemporain de Montréal, Montreal /
Collection of Musée d'art contemporain de Montréal, Montréal

Sticky Pictures, 2017, 72 × 60 in. / 183 × 152 cm
Courtesy of the artist and Bradley Ertaskiran, Montreal /
Avec l'autorisation de l'artiste et de Bradley Ertaskiran, Montréal

Still Life with Witch, 2019, 76 × 60 in. / 193 × 152 cm
Tedeschi Collection, Montreal /
Collection Tedeschi, Montréal

Studio (Miro), 2017, 60 × 72 in. / 152 × 183 cm
Courtesy of the artist and Bradley Ertaskiran, Montreal /
Avec l'autorisation de l'artiste et de Bradley Ertaskiran, Montréal

Table with Picasso, 2018, 31 × 24 in. / 79 × 61 cm
Cogir Immobilier Collection, Montreal /
Collection Cogir Immobilier, Montréal

Theatre (the double), 2017, 40 × 32 in. / 102 × 81 cm
Majudia Collection, Montreal /
Collection Majudia, Montréal

This, 2017, 32 × 40 in. / 81 × 102 cm
Courtesy of the artist and Bradley Ertaskiran, Montreal /
Avec l'autorisation de l'artiste et de Bradley Ertaskiran, Montréal

Untitled (Di), 2018, 31 × 24 in. / 79 × 61 cm
Collection of Stephanie and Leon Vahn, Los Angeles /
Collection de Stephanie et Leon Vahn, Los Angeles

Untitled (plant), 2016, 72 × 60 in. / 183 × 152 cm
Courtesy of the artist and Bradley Ertaskiran, Montreal /
Avec l'autorisation de l'artiste et de Bradley Ertaskiran, Montréal

VO Mars, 2017, 67 × 84 in. / 170 × 213 cm
Cogir Immobilier Collection, Montreal /
Collection Cogir Immobilier, Montréal

What time is it, Mr. Wolf? 2017, 84 × 67 in. / 213 × 170 cm
Collection of the Art Gallery of Guelph, Guelph /
Collection de l'Art Gallery of Guelph, Guelph

GALLERY

Arctic, 2020, 38 × 29 in. / 97 × 74 cm
Collection of Avery Kastin, Atlanta /
Collection d'Avery Kastin, Atlanta

Bauhaus, 2020, 24 × 20 in. / 61 × 51 cm
Collection of Jay Stuckey, Los Angeles /
Collection de Jay Stuckey, Los Angeles

Beacon, 2019, 48 × 36 in. / 122 × 91 cm
Barnard Collection, Montreal /
Collection Barnard, Montréal

Blue Bow, 2019, 44 × 36 in. / 112 × 91 cm
Collection of Chris and Kari Tomaszewski, Los Angeles /
Collection de Chris et Kari Tomaszewski, Los Angeles

Criss Cross, 2015, 72 × 60 in. / 183 × 152 cm
Courtesy of the artist and Bradley Ertaskiran, Montreal /
Avec l'autorisation de l'artiste et de Bradley Ertaskiran, Montréal

Dolores, 2019, 55 × 45 in. / 140 × 114 cm
McEvoy Family Collection, San Francisco /
Collection de la famille McEvoy, San Francisco

Double Portrait (strawberry blonde and brunette), 2019,
24 × 22 in. / 61 × 56 cm
Collection of Philip Hazan architect, Montreal /
Collection de l'architecte Philip Hazan, Montréal

Kit, 2019, 24 × 22 in. / 61 × 56 cm
Private collection, Calgary / Collection privée, Calgary

Lauren (yellow suit), 2020, 69 × 51 in. / 175 × 130 cm
Courtesy of the artist and Bradley Ertaskiran, Montreal /
Avec l'autorisation de l'artiste et de Bradley Ertaskiran, Montréal

Lou (leaf), 2018, 55 × 45 in. / 137 × 114 cm
Collection of Lisa and Jordan Bender, Los Angeles /
Collection de Lisa et Jordan Bender, Los Angeles

Lunar, 2016, 77 × 66 in. / 196 × 168 cm
Collection of Mélanie Bourdeau and Philippe Meunier, Montreal /
Collection de Mélanie Bourdeau et Philippe Meunier, Montréal

Medium, 2020, 20 × 16 in. / 51 × 41 cm
Collection of Sarah Hendler and Vinny Dotolo, Los Angeles /
Collection de Sarah Hendler et Vinny Dotolo, Los Angeles

Mel, 2017, 40 × 32 in. / 102 × 81 cm
Private collection, Los Angeles /
Collection privée, Los Angeles

Mirror AJ, 2018, 31 × 24 in. / 79 × 61 cm
Private collection, Los Angeles /
Collection privée, Los Angeles

Pinky, 2019, 54 × 45 in. / 137 × 114 cm
Collection of Coralie Beauchamp, Montreal /
Collection de Coralie Beauchamp, Montréal

Poodle, 2014, 55 × 45 in. / 140 × 114 cm
Courtesy of the artist /
Avec l'autorisation de l'artiste

Raizie, 2014, 55 × 45 in. / 140 × 114 cm
Private collection, Montreal /
Collection privée, Montréal

Sam, 2014, 55 × 45 in. / 140 × 114 cm
Collection of Brian and Gail Burlant, New York /
Collection de Brian et Gail Burlant, New York

Skipper, 2021, 36 × 24 in. / 91 × 61 cm
Private collection, Beijing / Collection privée, Beijing

Sleeper, 2016, 72 × 60 in. / 183 × 152 cm
Collection of Jonathan Schurgin, Los Angeles /
Collection de Jonathan Schurgin, Los Angeles

Smith, 2018, 76 × 60 in. / 193 × 152 cm
Collection of Lynn and Craig Jacobson, Los Angeles /
Collection de Lynn et Craig Jacobson, Los Angeles

Sunday, 2013, 38 × 32 in. / 97 × 81 cm
Private collection, Toronto /
Collection privée, Toronto

Teaze, 2018, 31 × 24 in. / 79 × 61 cm
Collection of Polly Borland, Los Angeles /
Collection de Polly Borland, Los Angeles

MISFITS

Collage Face, 20 × 16 in. / 51 × 41 cm
Collection of Amanda Alvaro, Toronto /
Collection d'Amanda Alvaro, Toronto

Danish, 2019, 20 × 24 in. / 51 × 61 cm
NIRO Family Collection, Montreal /
Collection de la famille NIRO, Montréal

Disgrace, 2020, 20 × 24 in. / 51 × 61 cm
Private collection, Los Angeles /
Collection privée, Los Angeles

Elle, 2014, 22 × 20 in. / 56 × 51 cm
Private collection, Montreal /
Collection privée, Montréal

Eva, 2019, 20 × 16 in. / 51 × 41 cm
Private collection, Longueuil /
Collection privée, Longueuil

Five Hands, 2017, 40 × 32 in. / 102 × 81 cm
Collection of Raja Hanna and Marylène Debay, Montreal /
Collection de Raja Hanna et Marylène Debay, Montréal

Gardener, 2020, 20 × 16 in. / 51 × 41 cm
Courtesy of the artist and Bradley Ertaskiran, Montreal /
Avec l'autorisation de l'artiste et de Bradley Ertaskiran, Montréal

Girl with White Shirt in Gray Landscape, 2018,
20 × 16 in. / 51 × 41 cm
Collection of Dale R. Percy, Calgary /
Collection de Dale R. Percy, Calgary

Green and Gold, 2017, 31 × 24 in. / 79 × 61 cm
Collection of Jay Stuckey, Los Angeles /
Collection de Jay Stuckey, Los Angeles

Harp, 2018, 76 × 60 in. / 193 × 152 cm
Nini Family Collection, Los Angeles /
Collection de la famille Nini, Los Angeles

Juergen, 2020, 22 × 20 in. / 56 × 51 cm
Private collection, Dallas / Collection privée, Dallas

Net, 2021, 24 × 20 in. / 61 × 51 cm
Courtesy of the artist / Avec l'autorisation de l'artiste

Orange Chair, 2020, 31 × 24 in. / 79 × 61 cm
Courtesy of the artist and Gallery 12.26, Dallas /
Avec l'autorisation de l'artiste et de Gallery 12.26, Dallas

Performer, 2014, 31 × 24 in. / 79 × 61 cm
Collection of Raja Hanna and Marylène Debay, Montreal /
Collection de Raja Hanna et Marylène Debay, Montréal

Pet, 2014, 87 × 66 in. / 221 × 168 cm
Aldo Collection, Montreal / Collection Aldo, Montréal

Tammi, 2020, 28 × 22 in. / 71 × 56 cm
Private collection, Los Angeles /
Collection privée, Los Angeles

Twitch (red boots), 2018, 54 × 45 in. / 137 × 114 cm
Courtesy of the artist and Anat Ebgi, Los Angeles /
Avec l'autorisation de l'artiste et de l'Anat Ebgi, Los Angeles

VSC (bonfire), 2016, 42 × 36 in. / 107 × 91 cm
Cogir Immobilier Collection, Montreal /
Collection Cogir Immobilier, Montréal

Walker, 2013, 38 × 32 in. / 97 × 81 cm
Private collection, Toronto /
Collection privée, Toronto

Yellow Studio, 2013, 40 × 32 in. / 102 × 81 cm
Collection of Coralie Beauchamp, Montreal /
Collection de Coralie Beauchamp, Montréal

THERE THERE

AJ Top, 2020, 24 × 20 in. / 61 × 51 cm
Collection of Silvano Tardella, Toronto /
Collection de Silvano Tardella, Toronto

Bandit, 2020, 31 × 24 in. / 79 × 70 cm
Private collection /
Collection privée

Bather (blue lips), 2018, 84 × 67 in. / 213 × 170 cm
Collection of Stephanie and Leon Vahn, Los Angeles /
Collection de Stephanie et Leon Vahn, Los Angeles

Beast, 2019, 96 × 74 in. / 244 × 188 cm
Collection of the Musée d'art contemporain de Montréal, Montreal /
Collection du Musée d'art contemporain de Montréal, Montréal

Bloom, 2022, 24 × 20 in. / 61 × 51 cm
Courtesy of the artist / Avec l'autorisation de l'artiste

Breaker, 2020, 60 × 48 in. / 152 × 122 cm
Collection of Sébastien Le Sieur and Pascal de Guise, Montreal /
Collection de Sébastien Le Sieur et Pascal de Guise, Montréal

Brown Room (tilt), 2020, 40 × 24 in. / 102 × 61 cm
Private collection /
Montreal Collection privée, Montréal

Caspar (CDF), 2020, 63 × 51 in. / 160 × 130 cm
Private collection, New York /
Collection privée, New York

Claire, 2019, 44 × 36 in. / 112 × 91 cm
McEvoy Family Collection, San Francisco /
Collection de la famille McEvoy, San Francisco

Clown, 2021, 33 × 26 in. / 84 × 66 cm
Courtesy of the artist /
Avec l'autorisation de l'artiste

Dallas, 2020, 24 × 20 in. / 61 × 51 cm
Private collection, Quebec /
Collection privée, Québec

Domino, 2020, 20 × 16 in. / 51 × 41 cm
Private collection, Chagrin Falls /
Collection privée, Chagrin Falls

Gina, 2019, 84 × 67 in. / 213 × 170 cm
Courtesy of the artist and Bradley Ertaskiran, Montreal /
Avec l'autorisation de l'artiste et de Bradley Ertaskiran, Montréal

Harlequin, 2022, 69 × 51 in. / 175 × 130 cm
Courtesy of the artist /
Avec l'autorisation de l'artiste

Jester, 2020, 44 × 36 in. / 112 × 91 cm
Collection of Mr. Poplaw, Montreal /
Collection de M. Poplaw, Montréal

Judy (orange legs), 2021, 24 × 20 in. / 61 × 51 cm
Collection of Pascal Desjardins and Roxanne Arsenault, Montreal /
Collection de Pascal Desjardins et Roxanne Arsenault, Montréal

Julia, 2021, 69 × 51 in. / 175 × 130 cm
Courtesy of the artist /
Avec l'autorisation de l'artiste

Kate, 2021, 48 × 36 in. / 122 × 91 cm
Courtesy of the artist /
Avec l'autorisation de l'artiste

Lean (green line), 2019, 33 × 26 in. / 84 × 66 cm
Private collection, Miami /
Collection privée, Miami

Leg, 2021, 20 × 18 in. / 51 × 46 cm
Courtesy of the artist /
Avec l'autorisation de l'artiste

Looking Down (pink split), 2020, 16 × 20 in. / 41 × 51 cm
Private collection, Longueuil /
Collection privée, Longueuil

Miami, 2021, 24 × 20 in. / 61 × 51 cm
Courtesy of the artist /
Avec l'autorisation de l'artiste

Performer 2, 2020, 31 × 24 in. / 79 × 61 cm
Collection of Raja Hanna and Marylène Debay, Montreal /
Collection de Raja Hanna et Marylène Debay, Montréal

Pink Suit, 2020, 67 × 60 in. / 170 × 152 cm
Private collection /
Collection privée

Plaza (gold room), 2021, 76 × 60 in. / 193 × 152 cm
Bouchard/Brouillette Collection /
Collection Bouchard/Brouillette

Poppy (half face), 2021, 20 × 16 in. / 51 × 41 cm
Courtesy of the artist /
Avec l'autorisation de l'artiste

Rabbit, 2020, 51 × 69 in. / 130 × 175 cm
Courtesy of the artist and Bradley Ertaskiran, Montreal /
Avec l'autorisation de l'artiste et de Bradley Ertaskiran, Montréal

REdpink (Nicole), 2021, 20 × 18 in. / 51 × 46 cm
Collection of Polly Borland, Los Angeles /
Collection de Polly Borland, Los Angeles

Red Shift, 2020, 54 × 45 in. / 137 × 114 cm
Private collection, Quebec /
Collection privée, Québec

Roxy, 2020, 16 × 20 in. / 41 × 51 cm
Private collection, Los Angeles /
Collection privée, Los Angeles

Screen, 2020, 18 × 14 in. / 46 × 36 cm
Collection of Jennifer Slinger, Montreal /
Collection de Jennifer Slinger, Montréal

Scry, 2021, 20 × 18 in. / 51 × 46 cm
Collection of Raphael Isvy, Paris /
Collection de Raphael Isvy, Paris

Strasse, 2021, 24 × 20 in. / 61 × 51 cm
Courtesy of the artist /
Avec l'autorisation de l'artiste

Suite, 2020, 69 × 51 in. / 175 × 130 cm
Collection of Rob Dickson, Toronto /
Collection de Rob Dickson, Toronto

T, 2021, 16 × 20 in. / 41 × 51 cm
Collection of Rob Dickson, Toronto /
Collection de Rob Dickson, Toronto

Tess (overlap), 2018, 22 × 20 in. / 56 × 51 cm
Private collection, Los Angeles /
Collection privée, Los Angeles

Untitled (orange split), 2020, 33 × 26 in. / 84 × 66 cm
Collection of Dr. Jonathan Brotchie, Montreal /
Collection du Dr Jonathan Brotchie, Montréal

Up Over, 2021, 36 × 24 in. / 91 × 61 cm
Courtesy of the artist /
Avec l'autorisation de l'artiste

Winona, 2020, 84 × 67 in. / 213 × 170 cm
Private collection, Miami /
Collection privée, Miami

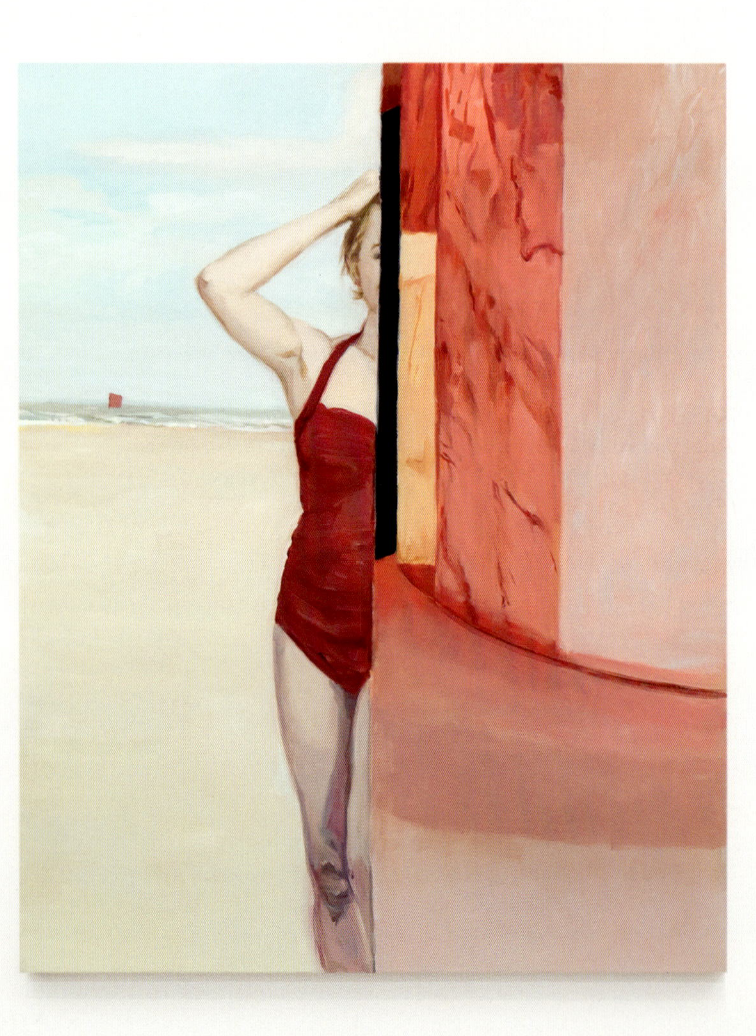

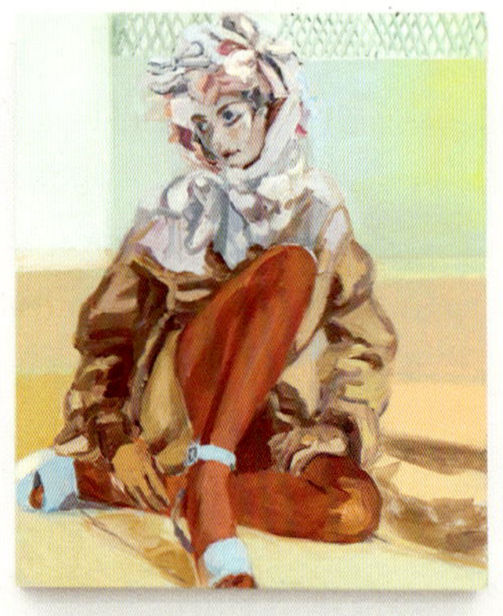

Collections

Aldo Collection, Montreal, Quebec
Art Gallery of Guelph, Guelph, Ontario
Art Gallery of Ontario, Toronto, Ontario
Battat Collection, Montreal, Quebec
Caisse de dépôt et placement du Québec collection, Quebec
Canada Council Art Bank, Ottawa, Ontario
Canadian embassy in Berlin, Germany
Cogir Immobilier Collection, Montreal, Quebec
Collection Majudia, Montreal, Quebec
Dunlop Art Gallery, Regina, Saskatchewan
Dynamite Collection, Montreal, Quebec
Galerie de l'UQAM, Montreal, Quebec
Hydro Quebec Collection, Montreal, Quebec
Kenderdine Art Gallery, Saskatoon, Saskatchewan
Leonard and Bina Ellen Art Gallery, Montreal, Quebec
Mackenzie Art Gallery, Regina, Saskatchewan
McEvoy Foundation for the Arts, San Francisco, California
Musée d'art contemporain de Montréal, Montreal, Quebec
Musée des beaux-arts de Montréal, Montreal, Quebec
Musée national des beaux-arts du Québec, Quebec City, Quebec
National Bank, Montreal, Quebec
Owens Art Gallery, Sackville, New Brunswick
RBC Corporate Art Collection, Toronto, Ontario
Remai Modern, Saskatoon, Saskatchewan
Tedeschi Collection, Montreal, Quebec
University of Lethbridge, Lethbridge, Alberta
Winnipeg Art Gallery, Winnipeg, Manitoba

Selected Exhibitions

SELECTED SOLO EXHIBITIONS

2022
Janet Werner, Arsenal Contemporary, New York

2021
There There, Bradley Ertaskiran, Montreal
Romantik, with Keer Tanchak, Gallery 12.26, Dallas

2020
Armory Show, with Amie Dicke, Anat Ebgi Booth, New York

2019
Janet Werner, Musée d'art contemporain de Montréal, Montreal
What time is it, Mr. Wolf?, Art Gallery of Guelph, Guelph
I Feel Real, with Sandra Meigs, Vivianeart, Calgary

2018
The Splits, Anat Ebgi, Los Angeles

2017
Sticky Pictures, Parisian Laundry, Montreal
Art Los Angeles Contemporary, solo booth with Parisian Laundry, Los Angeles

2015
Zero Eyes, Esther Massry Gallery, College of St. Rose, Albany
Drop, Drop Slow Tears, Parisian Laundry, Montreal

2014
Abby and Snow, Birch Contemporary, Toronto
Janet Werner, Portrait Society Gallery of Contemporary Art, Milwaukee

2013
Another perfect day, touring exhibition: Esker Foundation, Calgary; Gallery de l'UQAM, Montreal; Doris McCarthy Gallery, Toronto; Kenderdine Gallery, Saskatoon; McIntosh Art Gallery, London

2012
Mad, Bad, Sad, Glad, Whatiftheworld, Cape Town, South Africa
Earthling, Parisian Laundry, Montreal

2011
Beauty takes a holiday, Birch Libralato, Toronto

2010
Janet Werner, Galerie Julia Garnatz, Cologne, Germany
Who's Sorry Now?, Parisian Laundry, Montreal

2009
Is Anything Alright?, Art Gallery of Windsor, Windsor

2008
Too much happiness, Parisian Laundry, Montreal
New Work, Birch Libralato, Toronto

2007
Buttercup I love you, Galerie Julia Garnatz, Cologne, Germany

2006
Up here in heaven, Birch Libralato, Toronto
Misfits, Galerie Joyce Yahouda, Montreal

2005
Janet Werner, SBC Galerie d'art Contemporain, Montreal

2004
Janet Werner, Robert Birch, Toronto
Janet Werner, Tracey Lawrence, Vancouver

2002
Since first I cast eyes on you / Depuis mon premier regard sur toi, Ottawa Art Gallery, Ottawa
Janet Werner, Robert Birch, Toronto
Janet Werner, Tracy Lawrence, Vancouver

2001
Janet Werner, Paul Kuhn, Calgary
Janet Werner, The GALLERY / Art Placement, Saskatoon

2000
Beautiful Losers, with Michael Fernandes, Dunlop Art Gallery, Regina
New Work, Robert Birch, Toronto
Trust, Thames Art Gallery, Chatham
Trust, Estevan National Exhibition Center, Estevan

1999
Trust, Contemporary Art Gallery, Vancouver
Portraits, MacLaren Art Centre, Barrie
Trance, with Patrick Traer, Plug In Contemporary Art, Winnipeg
Trust, Art Gallery of Mississauga, Mississauga
New Paintings, Paul Kuhn, Calgary
Portraits, Tableau Vivant, Toronto

1998
Trust, Optica, Montreal
Lucky, Owens Art Gallery, Sackville

1997
Lucky, Southern Alberta Art Gallery, Lethbridge
Trance, Mendel Art Gallery, Saskatoon
Listen, with Beaty Popescu, AKA, Saskatoon

1996
Slow Pictures, Robert Birch Gallery, Toronto

1995
Janet Werner / Kathleen Sellars, Eye Level, Halifax
Figures and Fields, Sir Wilfred Grenfell Gallery, Corner Brook
Scat, Axe NEO 7, Gatineau

1994
Lingua, La Centrale, Galerie Powerhouse, Montreal

1992
Reflections on Language and the Appearance of Things, Dunlop Art Gallery, Regina

1991
Reflections on Language and the Appearance of Things, Mendel Art Gallery, Saskatoon, and Illingworth Kerr Gallery, Calgary

1990
Paintings, Garnet Press Gallery, Toronto

1989
Rehearsing the World, Plug In Contemporary Art, Winnipeg

SELECTED GROUP EXHIBITIONS

2021
North by Northeast: Contemporary Canadian Painting, Kasmin, New York
NADA Miami, with Bradley Ertaskiran
Frieze New York, with Anat Ebgi
Quarante, Blouin/Division, Montreal
In Good Company, Anat Ebgi, Los Angeles

2019
Person/ne, Griffin Art Projects, Vancouver
The Conversation, Minnesota Street Project, San Francisco
Heads, McIntosh Gallery, London, Ontario
Frieze Los Angeles, with Anat Ebgi

2018
Flower, Petal, Tongues, Griffin Art Projects, Vancouver

2017
How the light gets in, Musée d'art contemporain de Montréal, Montreal
PDA Lovers, Four Six One Nine Gallery, Los Angeles
Industry, DC3 Projects, Edmonton

2016
De Ferron a BGL, Musée national des beaux arts du Québec, Quebec
Art Toronto, Parisian Laundry and Birch Contemporary, Toronto
Silhouettes and Other Shadows, Owens Art Gallery, Sackville
Jupe Bleue, Une Blonde, Des Calculatrices et un nu couché, Parisian Laundry, Montreal

2015
Elles Aujhourd'hui, Montreal Museum of Fine Arts, Montreal
L'Œil et l'Esprit, Musée d'art contemporain de Montréal, Montreal
Sexish, Birch Contemporary, Toronto
Oh, Canada, Glenbow Museum, Calgary
Side Project, Pop Montreal, Montreal

2014
Portrait, Trépanier Baer Gallery, Calgary
The Portrait Society Gallery, Milwaukee
Masquerade, Musée du Bas St. Laurent, Rivière-du-Loup

2013
The Painting Project/Projet Peinture, Galerie de l'UQAM, Montreal
Painting Perspectives, AXE NEO7, Gatineau
Perfect Imperfections, School of Art Gallery, University of Manitoba, Winnipeg

2012
The Winnipeg Alphabestiary, Simon Fraser University Gallery, Burnaby, and University of Lethbridge Art Gallery, Lethbridge
Oh, Canada, Mass MoCa, North Adams

2011
Bestial Encounters, Winnipeg Art Gallery, Winnipeg

2010
Extreme Painting, Parisian Laundry, Montreal

2009
Added Value, Platform Gallery, Winnipeg

2008
Intrus/Intruders, Musée national des beaux-arts du Québec, Quebec
Generation, Art Gallery of Alberta, Edmonton
Entre/Voir, Galerie de l'UQAM, Montreal

2007
Some Girls, McClure Gallery, Montreal
Framed: The art of the portrait, Art Gallery of Hamilton, Hamilton

2006
Peindre, Centre d'Exposition de Baie-Saint-Paul, Baie-Saint-Paul

2005
Individuation, Galerie Esthésio, Quebec City

2004
Sweet and Sour, Tracey Lawrence Gallery, Vancouver

2003
Lazarus Effect, Prague Biennale, Prague, Czech Republic
Dog Days, Tracey Lawrence Gallery, Vancouver
Woman, James Baird Gallery, St. John's

2002
Posers, St. Mary's University Art Gallery, Halifax
Beautiful Stranger, The Physics Room, Christchurch, New Zealand
Portraits - Robots, Galerie Graff, Montreal

2001
Defining the Portrait, Ellen Art Gallery, Montreal

2000
Small Craft Warning, Gallery 101, Ottawa

1999
Les Peintures, Galerie René Blouin, Montreal

1998
Mixed Messages, Kenderdine Gallery, Saskatoon

1993
Anima <-> Materia, Kenderdine Gallery, Saskatoon
The Heliotropic, I, Mercer Union, Toronto

1992
Propositions/Painting, Charles Scott Gallery, Vancouver

1991
Remembering and Telling: Reflections on Identity and Location, Mackenzie Art Gallery, Regina

1990
Memory and Subjectivity, touring exhibition: Garnet Press Gallery, Toronto; Tom Thomson Memorial Art Gallery, Owen Sound; Thunder Bay Art Gallery, Thunder Bay Laurentian University, Thunder Bay; and Museum and Art Centre, Sudbury

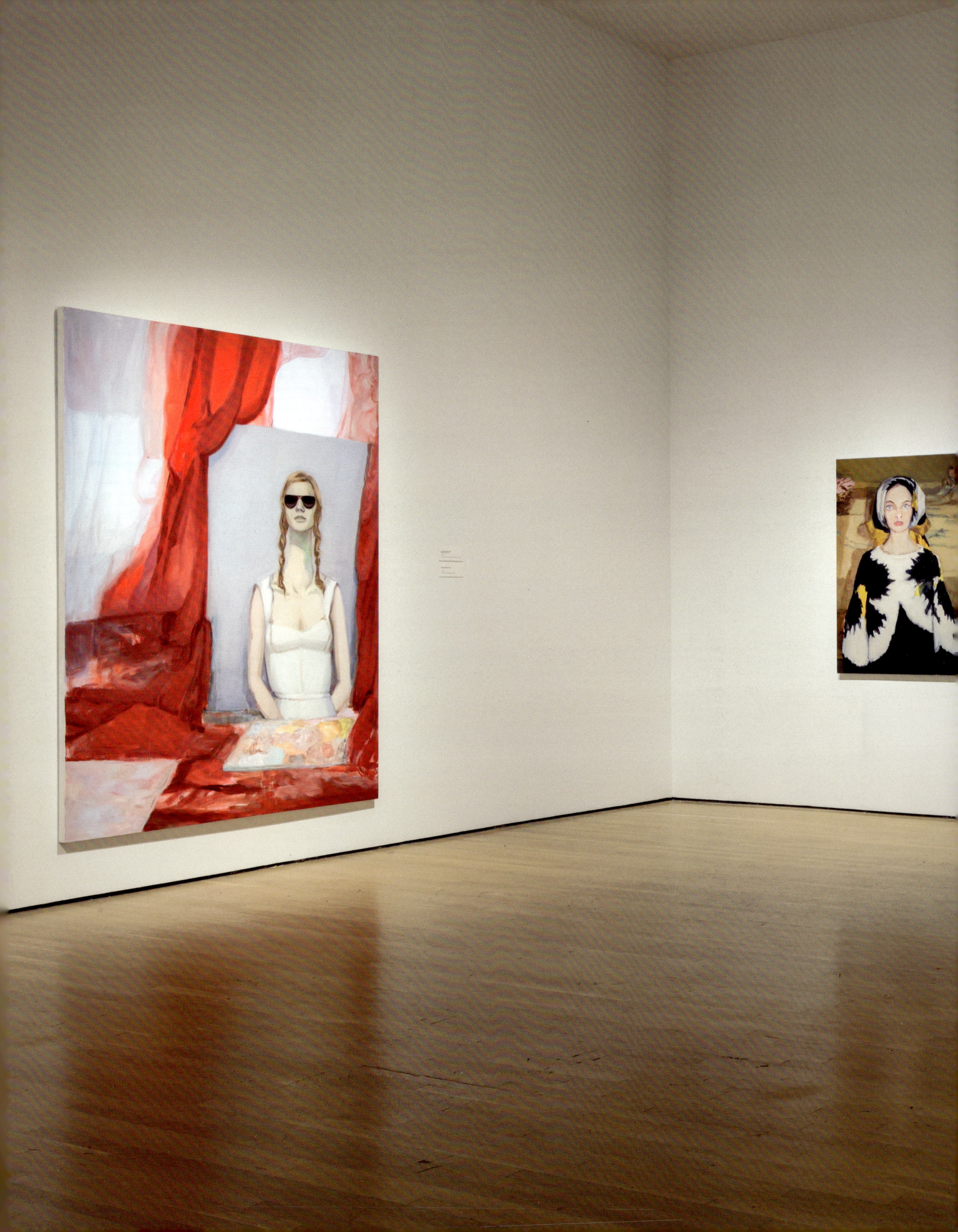

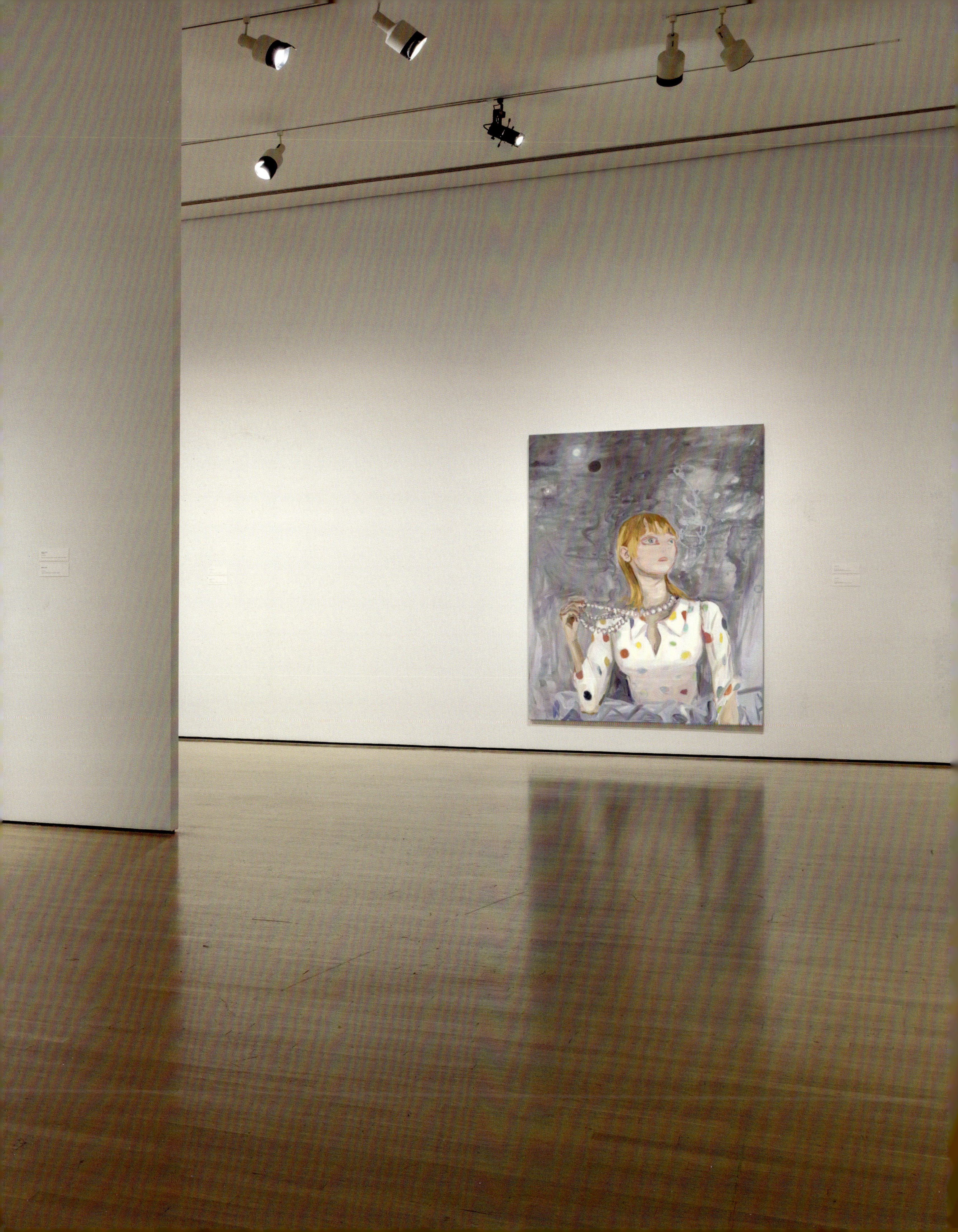

Selected Bibliography

Baert, Renee. "Real Enough." *Janet Werner*. Montreal: SBC Gallery, 2008. Exhibition catalog.

Baert, Renee. *Since First I Cast Eyes on You / Depuis mon premier regard sur toi*. Ottawa: Ottawa Art Gallery / Galerie d'art d'Ottawa, 2002. Exhibition catalog.

Baerwaldt, Wayne. *Trance*. Saskatoon, Saskatchewan: Mendel Art Gallery, 1998. Exhibition catalog.

Balzer, David. "Janet Werner." *Modern Painters*, July/August 2012.

Balzer, David. "Real Fakery: Janet Werner and Company." *Another Perfect Day*, edited by Meeka Walsh. Saskatoon, Saskatchewan: Kenderdine Art Gallery, 2013.

Balzer, David. "Up Here in Heaven." *Canadian Art* 24, no. 1, spring 2007.

Blatherwick, David. "Peindre les failles du langage." *Spirale*, no. 140, March 1995.

Budney, Jen. "Small Craft Warnings." *Parachute* 100, 2000.

Campbell, James. "Janet Werner." *Border Crossings* 24, no. 4, November 2005, 90–91.

Campbell, James. "Janet Werner." *Frieze* 192, January/February 2018.

Carson, Anne. "Flotage (Border)." *Another Perfect Day*, edited by Meeka Walsh. Saskatoon, Saskatchewan: Kenderdine Art Gallery, 2013.

Charron, Marie-Eve. "Secrets d'atelier avec Janet Werner et Anthony Burnham." *Le Devoir*, October 7, 2017.

Côté, Nathalie. "Et moi et moi et moi." *Voir Quebec*, July 7, 2005.

Crevier, Lyne. "Tout sucre." *Ici Montréal*, July 14, 2005.

Dault, Gary Michael. "Paint-by-Numbers Portraits Hide Disturbing Details." *Globe and Mail*, December 20, 2008.

Dault, Gary Michael. "Painting as Patchwork," *Globe and Mail*, September 23, 2000.

Dault, Gary Michael. "Portraits that Hide Much More than They Reveal." *Globe and Mail*, April 17, 1999.

Dault, Gary Michael. "Tawdry, Exhausting and Possibly Brilliant." *Globe and Mail*, May 1, 2004.

Dault, Julia. "Portraits of Pretend People." *National Post*, December 30, 2004.

Elliott, David. "Paint Person." *Canadian Art* 19, no. 2, summer 2002.

Enright, Robert. "Head Games." *Globe and Mail*, November 20, 1999.

Enright, Robert. "Mute Ability: Janet Werner Changes the Face of Portraiture." *Border Crossings* 21, no. 3, August 2002, 20–31.

Enright, Robert. "Unmasking Self-Portraiture." *Another Perfect Day*, edited by Meeka Walsh. Saskatoon, Saskatchewan: Kenderdine Art Gallery, 2013

Ghaznavi, Corinna. "Surfacing: Janet Werner at Robert Birch." *Dart*, fall 2002.

Gillmor, Alison. "Added Value." *Border Crossings* 29, no. 1, March 2010, 92–93.

Grenville, Bruce. *Reflections on Language and the Appearance of Things*. Saskatoon, Saskatchewan: Mendel Art Gallery, 1991.

Hartland-Rowe, Sara, "Around and About Painting." *Border Crossings* 22, no.1, February 2003, 65–67.

Hogg, Lucy. *Propositions/Painting*. Vancouver: Charles Scott Gallery, 1992. Exhibition catalog.

Keindl, Anthony. *Beautiful Losers*. Regina, Saskatchewan: Dunlop Art Gallery, 2000. Exhibition catalog.

Kissick, John, "Someone/Something/Nothing." *Another Perfect Day*, edited by Meeka Walsh. Saskatoon, Saskatchewan: Kenderdine Art Gallery, 2013.

Kissick, John, "Someone/Something/Nothing: Some Thoughts on Janet Werner's Recent Paintings." *Border Crossings* 32, no. 2, June 2013, 46.

Laing, Carol. "The Silence of the World." *Lucky*. Lethbridge, Alberta: Southern Alberta Art Gallery, 1997. Exhibition catalog.

Lamarche, Bernard. "Portraits d'idéaux." *Le Devoir*, August 14, 2005.

Laurence, Robin. "Face Off." *Border Crossings* 18, no. 4, November 1999, 67–70.

Lee, James-Jason. "Trust Puts Gallerygoers' Faith to Test." *Georgia Straight*, August 5–12, 1999.

Lehmann, Henry. "A Probing Look at Portraits." *Montreal Gazette*, July 16, 2005.

Lilburn, Tim. "Angels of History." *Border Crossings* 16, no. 4, November 1997, 64–65.

Lilburn, Tim. "Clear Suspicions." *Border Crossings* 11, no. 1, January 1992, 55–56.

Liss, David. "La Centrale/Galerie Powerhouse..." (review). *Montreal Gazette*, November 26, 1994.

Maclear, Kyo. "Blurred Vision." *Toronto Life*, April 1999.

Mark, Lisa. "Getting Our Hands Dirty." *C Magazine* 59, September–November 1998.

Mark, Lisa. "The Language of Eyes." *Trust*. Mississauga, Ontario: Art Gallery of Mississauga, 2000. Exhibition catalog.

Markonish, Denise. *Oh, Canada*. Cambridge, Massachusetts: MIT Press, 2012.

Massier, John. "Trust." *Lola* 4, summer 1999.

McMackon, Jennifer. *The Heliotropic*. Toronto: Mercer Union, 1993. Exhibition catalog.

Mendritzki, Erica. "Janet Werner," *Border Crossings* 37, no. 1, March 2018, 109–110.

Miller, Marcus. "Janet Werner, Melanie Rocan, Tammy Salzl." *Border Crossings* 32, no. 3, August 2013, 84–85.

Morin, Manon. *Lingua*. Montreal: La Centrale, Galerie Powerhourse, 1994. Exhibition catalog.

O'Neill, Colleen. "Figures and Fields." *Janet Werner*. Corner Brook, Newfoundland: Sir Wilfred Grenfell Art Gallery, 1998. Exhibition catalog.

Osborne, Catherine. "Painter Gets Down to Basics." *National Post*, April 17, 2004.

Osterweil, Ara, "Between the Glossies and the Grotesque Janet Werner Paints a World." *Border Crossings* 39, no. 1, March 2020, 46–54.

Osterweil, Ara. "Janet Werner: Sticky Pictures." *Artforum*, December 2017.

Redfern, Christine, "Seeking to Put a Different Perspective on Beauty." *Montreal Gazette*, March 15, 2008.

Reichertz, Mathew. *Posers*. Halifax: St. Mary's University Art Gallery, 2002. Exhibition catalog.

Ring, Dan. *Trance*. Saskatoon, Saskatchewan: Mendel Art Gallery, 1998. Exhibition catalog.

Ring, Nancy. "Awkward Beauty." *Too Much Happiness*. Montreal: Parisian Laundry, 2008. Exhibition catalog.

Roenish Clint and Jane Urquhart. *Carte Blanche 2: Volume 2, Painting*. Toronto: Magenta Publishing for the Art, 2008.

Rosenberg, Karen. "Border Crossing Identity Crisis: Oh, Canada Exhibition at Mass MoCa." *New York Times*, August 30, 2012.

Sandals, Leah. "All the Pretty Horses and Women." *National Post*, November 19, 2009.

Severson, Anne. "Unusual Portraits of Our Time." *Fast Forward Weekly* (Calgary), June 3–9, 1999.

Sherlock, Diana. *I Feel Real*. Calgary: Vivaneart Gallery, 2019. Exhibition catalog.

Skene, Cameron. "Janet Werner." *Border Crossings* 29, no. 3, September 2010, 129–130.

Sloan, Johanne. "Janet Werner and the Surface of Things." *Too Much Happiness*. Montreal: Parisian Laundry, 2008. Exhibition catalog.

Sorenson, Oli, "Flirting with Death: Dispatches Along 19th to 20th Century Painting." *Esse Arts + Opinions* 76, autumn 2012, 4–11.

Tousignant, Isa, "Piece and Parcel: Janet Werner Splits Her Portraits Back into Pieces." *Hour*, July 28, 2005.

Tousley, Nancy. "First Language." *Canadian Art 14, no. 3*, fall 1997.

Walsh, Meeka. *The Winnipeg Alphabestiary*. Winnipeg: Border Crossings/Arts Manitoba Publications Inc., 2008.

Warland, Betsy. "Patrick Traer and Janet Werner." *C Magazine* 57, February–April 1998.

Williamson, Janice. "Scat." *Janet Werner*. Corner Brook, Newfoundland: Sir Wilfred Grenfell Art Gallery, 1998. Exhibition catalog.

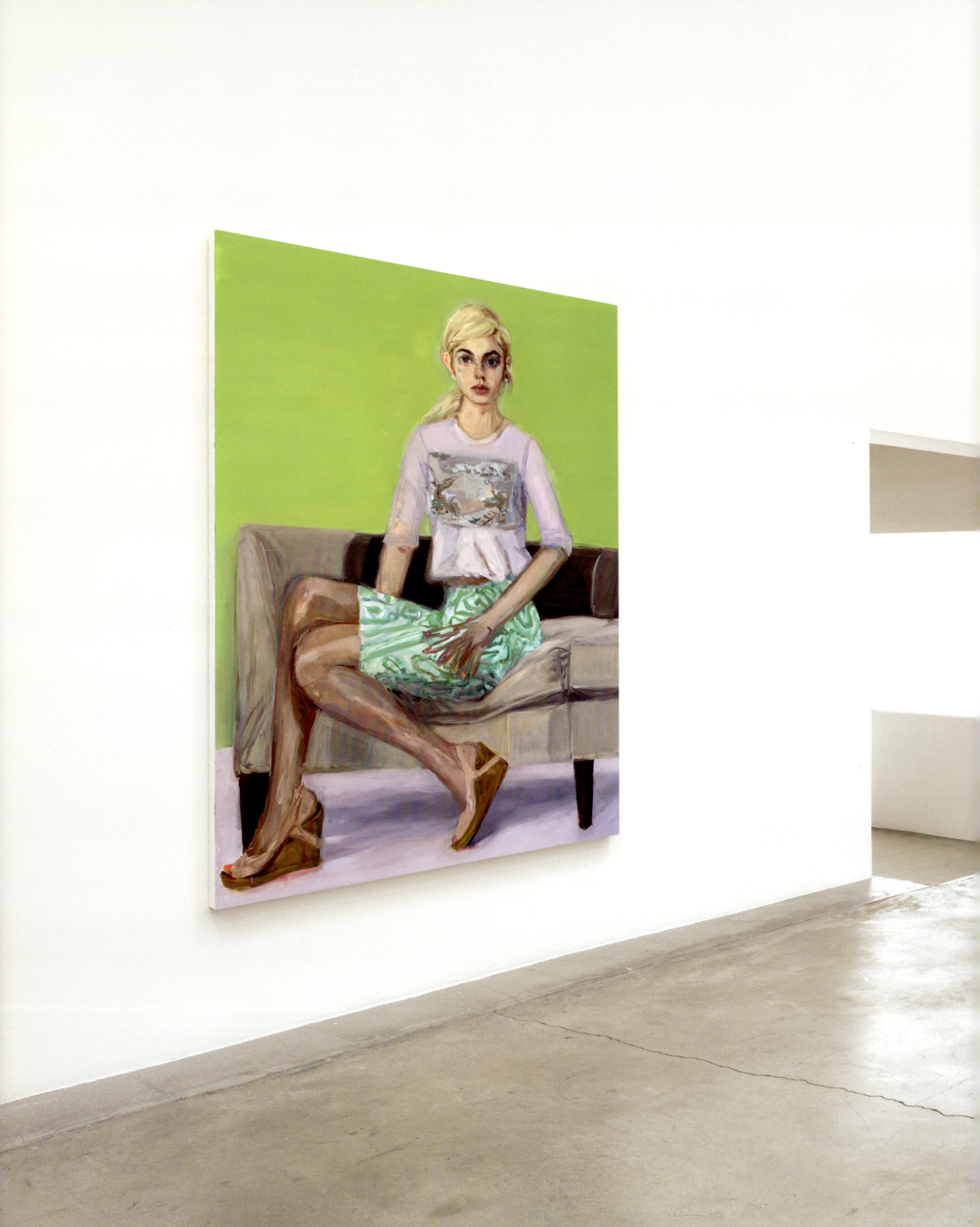

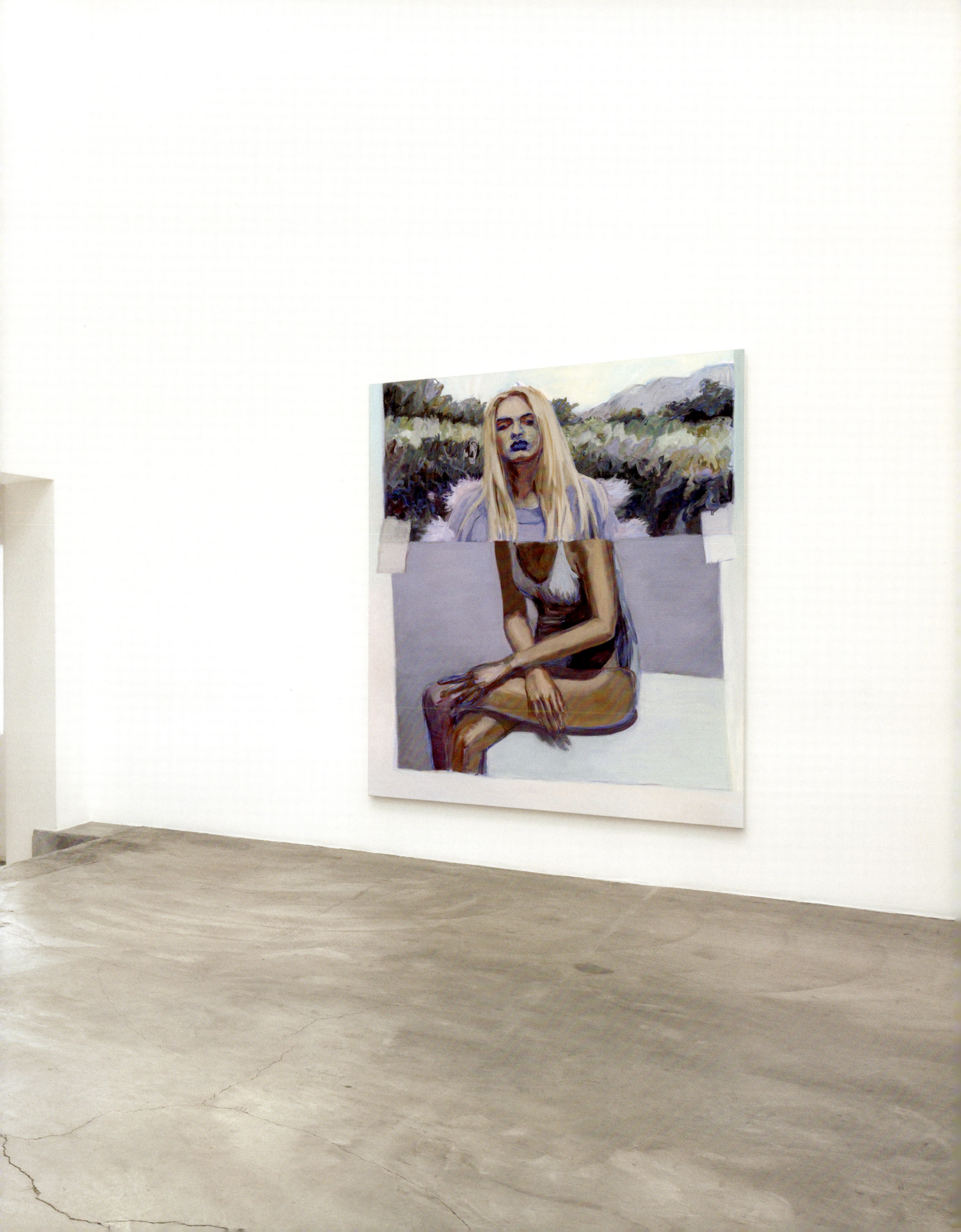

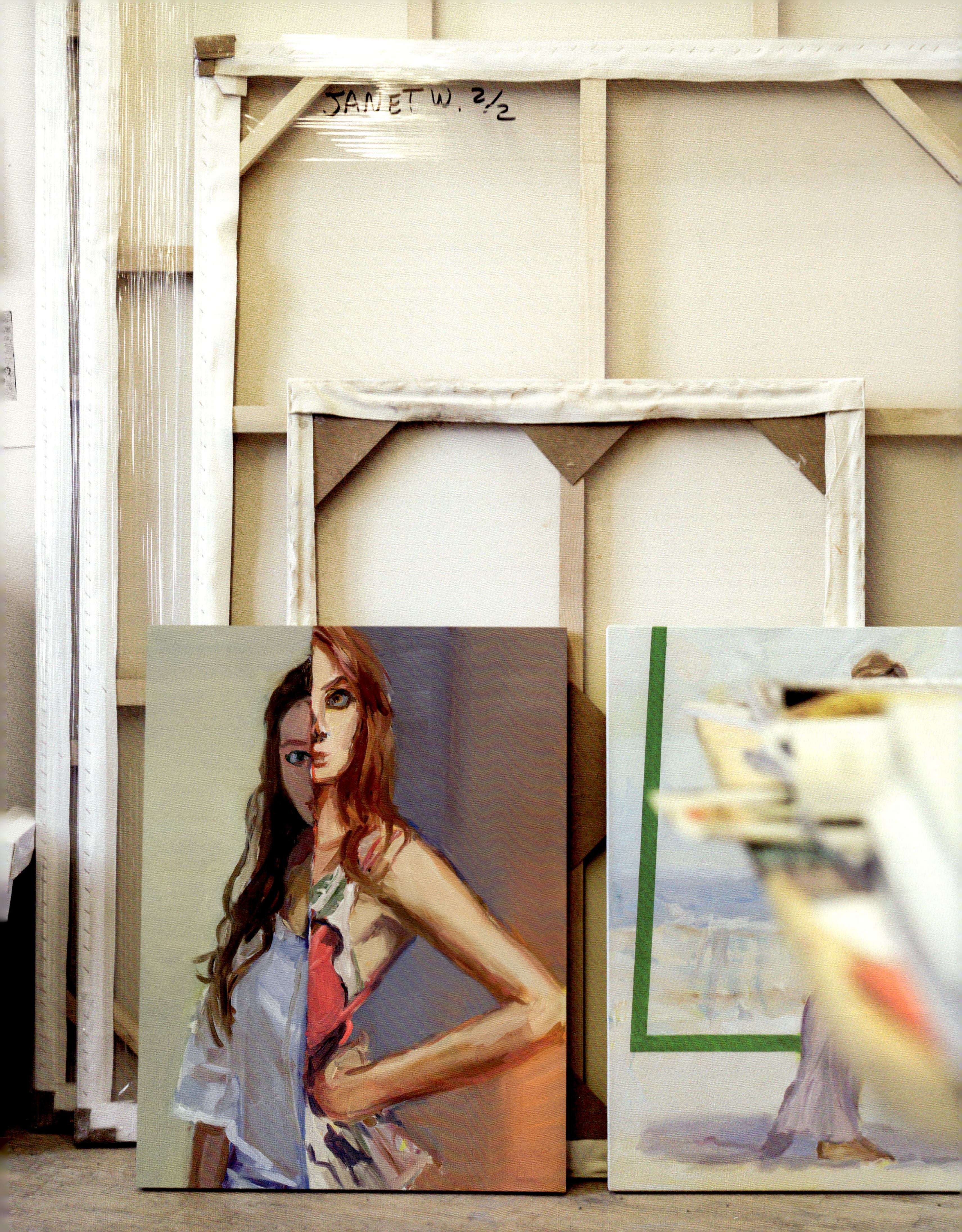
JANET W. 2/2

List of Contributors

LISA BALDISSERA is the director of Griffin Art Projects and has worked in curatorial roles in public art galleries in Western Canada since 1999, including senior curator at Contemporary Calgary (2014–16) and chief curator at the Mendel Art Gallery in Saskatoon (2012–14). She was curator of contemporary art at the Art Gallery of Greater Victoria from 1999 to 2009, where she produced more than fifty exhibitions of local, Canadian, and international artists. She holds MFAs in Creative Writing (UBC) and Art (University of Saskatchewan) and a PhD from Goldsmiths College, University of London. Baldissera is non-regular faculty at the Emily Carr University of Art and Design in the graduate program and has served on contemporary art juries across Canada and internationally, including the Alvin Balkind Curator's Prize (the Doris and Jack Shadbolt Foundation), the Canada Council for the Arts, the Saskatchewan Arts Board, the Royal Bank of Canada Canadian Painting Competition, the Hnatyshyn Foundation Visual Arts Awards, the Sobey Art Award, the British Columbia Arts Council, the Prix Pierre-Prince-de-Monaco jury, and as a guest of the British Arts Council outreach program.

MELISSA E. FELDMAN is an American independent curator and writer specializing in contemporary art in relation to art and cultural history. Her recent projects include *Indie Folk: New Art and Sounds from the Pacific Northwest*, organized by the Jordan Schnitzer Museum of Art, Pullman, Washington, and touring through 2025, as well as: *Free Play*, organized by Independent Curators International; *A Cool Breeze: L.A. and Vancouver Art in the 1960s and Beyond* at Griffin Art Projects, Vancouver; and *Dance Rehearsal: Karen Kilimnik's World of Ballet and Theatre* at Mills College Art Museum, Oakland, California, and the Museum of Contemporary Art, Denver. Feldman also writes for publications such as *Art in America*, *Frieze* and *Third Text*, and she has taught in the United Kingdom, at the Cornish College of the Arts and Goldsmith's College, London, and on the West Coast in Seattle and at the California College of the Arts, San Francisco.

FRANÇOIS LETOURNEUX is a curator at the Musée d'art contemporain de Montréal. He has curated solo exhibitions devoted to the artists Etienne Zack (2010), Jon Pylypchuk (2011), Lynne Cohen (2013–2015) and Janet Werner (2019–2020), in addition to cocurating *Quebec Triennial* (2011), *Zoo* (2012), *Rafael Lozano-Hemmer: Unstable Presence* (2018, in collaboration with SFMOMA), and *La machine qui enseignait des airs aux oiseaux* (2020–2021). As part of his public programs mandate, he also organizes the annual Max and Iris Stern International Symposium. LeTourneux holds a PhD in art history from the Art History and Film Studies Department of the Université de Montréal, where he taught as a visiting professor from 2014 to 2016.

ARA OSTERWEIL is an abstract painter, writer, and scholar of postwar film and art as well as an associate professor of cultural studies in the English Department at McGill University. She is a regular contributor at *Artforum* and has also published essays in the *Los Angeles Review of Books*, *Art Journal*, *Film Quarterly*, *Film Culture*, *Border Crossings*, *Camera Obscura*, *C Magazine*, *Little Joe*, *Framework*, *The Brooklyn Rail*, and *Millennium Film Journal*. Her first book, *Flesh Cinema: The Corporeal Turn in American Avant-Garde Film* (Manchester University Press, 2014), examines the representation of sexuality in experimental film of the 1960s and 1970s. She is currently working on two books: *The Pedophilic Imagination: A History of American Film* and a collection of experimental prose entitled *Stains & Fragments*.

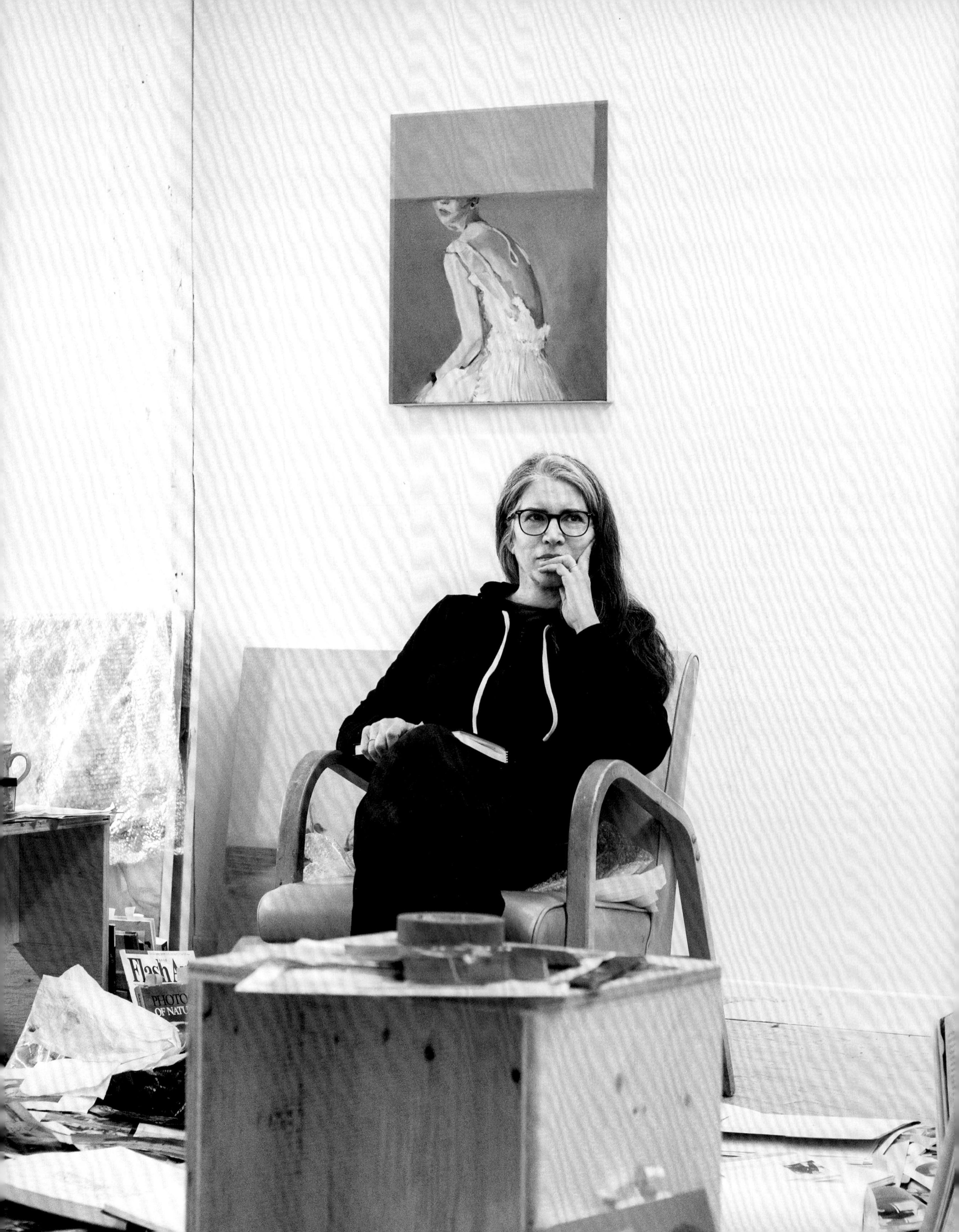
Flash

Artist's Biography

Janet Werner (b. 1959, Winnipeg) received her MFA from Yale University (1987) and her BFA from the Maryland Institute College of Art (1985). She returned to Canada to teach at the University of Saskatchewan from 1987 to 1999 and is Professor Emerita at Concordia University, Montreal, where she taught from 1999 to 2019.

Werner's work has been shown extensively in Canada, including monographic exhibitions at the Musée d'art contemporain de Montréal; the Art Gallery of Guelph; the Mendel Art Gallery, Saskatoon; the Ottawa Art Gallery; Saidye Bronfman Centre (SBC) and Bradley Ertaskiran, Montreal. Internationally, Werner's work has been featured in the Armory Show NY, Frieze LA, NADA Miami and in solo presentations at Anat Ebgi, Los Angeles; Galerie Julia Garnatz, Cologne; Whatiftheworld Gallery, Cape Town; and Arsenal Contemporary, New York. Group exhibitions include *Oh, Canada* (Mass MoCa, 2012); *North by Northeast: Contemporary Canadian Painting* (Kasmin, New York); *Lazarus Effect*, the Prague Biennale (2003); *The Painting Project* (Galerie de l'UQAM, Montreal, 2013); and Person/ne (Griffin Art Projects, Vancouver, 2019). A survey exhibition of Werner's work entitled *Another perfect day* traveled to five locations in Canada from 2013 to 2015, including the Esker Foundation (Calgary), McIntosh Art Gallery (London), and the Doris McCarthy Gallery (Toronto). Previous monographs include *Another perfect day* (Kenderdine Art Gallery, 2013) and *Too Much Happiness* (Parisian Laundry, 2008).

Werner's work is in the collections of the Musée d'art contemporain de Montréal; the Art Gallery of Ontario (AGO), Toronto; the McEvoy Foundation for the Arts, San Francisco; the Canadian Embassy in Berlin; the Musée national des beaux-arts du Québec; the Winnipeg Art Gallery; the Remai Modern, Saskatoon; the Mackenzie Art Gallery, Regina; and the Montreal Museum of Fine Arts as well as in numerous private and corporate collections. Werner lives and works in Montreal.

Artist's Acknowledgments

A solo exhibition at the Musée d'art contemporain in Montreal, curated by François LeTourneux, provided the impetus for this publication. The exhibition hinged around a shift in my practice that is reflected in the structure of this book. Deepest thanks to François for his very thoughtful and insightful text, and thank you to the MAC team, Lesley Johnstone, John Zeppetelli, and Marie-Eve Beaupré for their generous collaboration.

I am grateful to Griffin Art Projects and to Henning and Brigitte Freybe for the gift of a residency in the spring of 2019. The idea for this publication took root during the residency and would not have come to fruition without the support and guidance of director Lisa Baldissera, who collaborated with me on all aspects of this project. Thank you for your intelligence, grace, and editorial input.

Many thanks to Ara Osterweil for her close reading of the work and her incisive essay, and to Melissa Feldman for her thoughtful interview and critical input on the selection of images. Thank you to Kelsey Blackwell for the beautiful design of this book and to Rachel Topham for her careful image preparation. Madeline Richards, Lara Smith, Amanda McMorran, Nancy Foran, and Steve Cameron provided essential assistance with the details of the publication. Thanks also to Genevieve Landreville, Todd Bradway, Hilary Fagadau, and Anais Castro for early discussions around this project.

I am grateful to Bradley Ertaskiran and Anat Ebgi galleries for their ongoing support and to Arsenal Contemporary NY, Gallery 12.26, and Vivianeart, where some of the works in this book were first exhibited. Special thanks to Megan Bradley, Antoine Ertaskiran, Anat Ebgi, and Stefano Di Paola, as well as the collectors who have supported my work.

Lastly, as always, I thank Adrian Norvid for his patience, support, and good humor throughout the making of this book.

GRIFFIN ART PROJECTS ACKNOWLEDGMENTS

A publication like this is not possible without the vision of many. We would like to express our gratitude to François LeTourneux and Ara Osterweil, for their thoughtful essays that provide an overview of Janet Werner's work not only from the past decade but also chart the conceptual and formal maps that have shaped her work. Sincere thanks to Melissa E. Feldman, whose insightful interview invites the reader into Werner's personal process. We are also grateful to the team at Figure 1 for their energy and enthusiasm for this project and to Kelsey Blackwell for her brilliant design. Thanks to our editors, Nancy Foran and, for the LeTourneux essay and translation, Judith Terry. Thanks to Rachel Topham for her keen photo-editorial eye. Griffin is also grateful to the Canada Council for the Arts and the Freybe Foundation for their support of this project. Finally, I would like extend my hearfelt gratitude to the artist, Janet Werner, whose exceptional insight, professionalism, and artistic excellence have guided us at every turn in the process of making this book and has resulted in a beautiful journey through the world of her paintings.

— Lisa Baldissera, Director

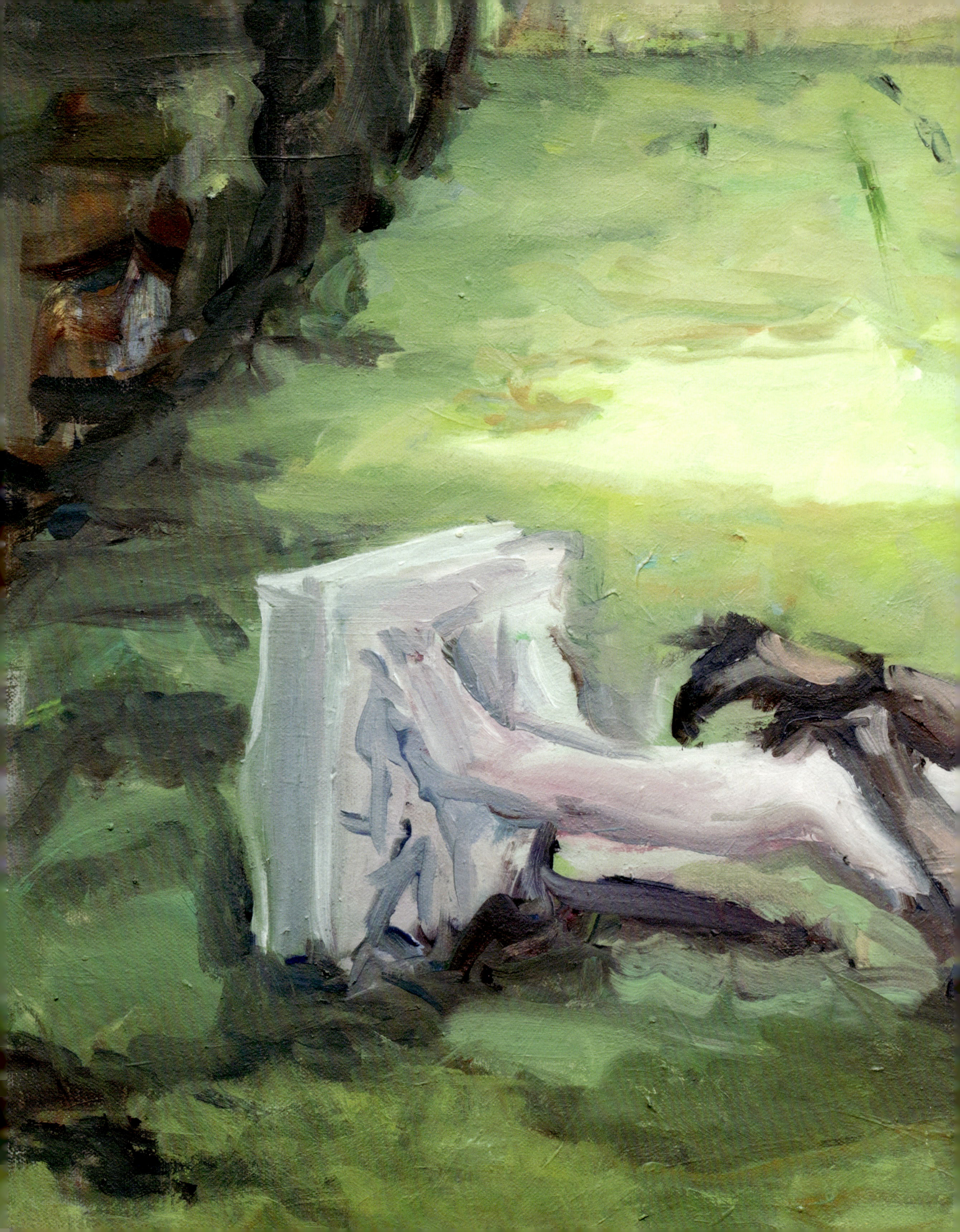

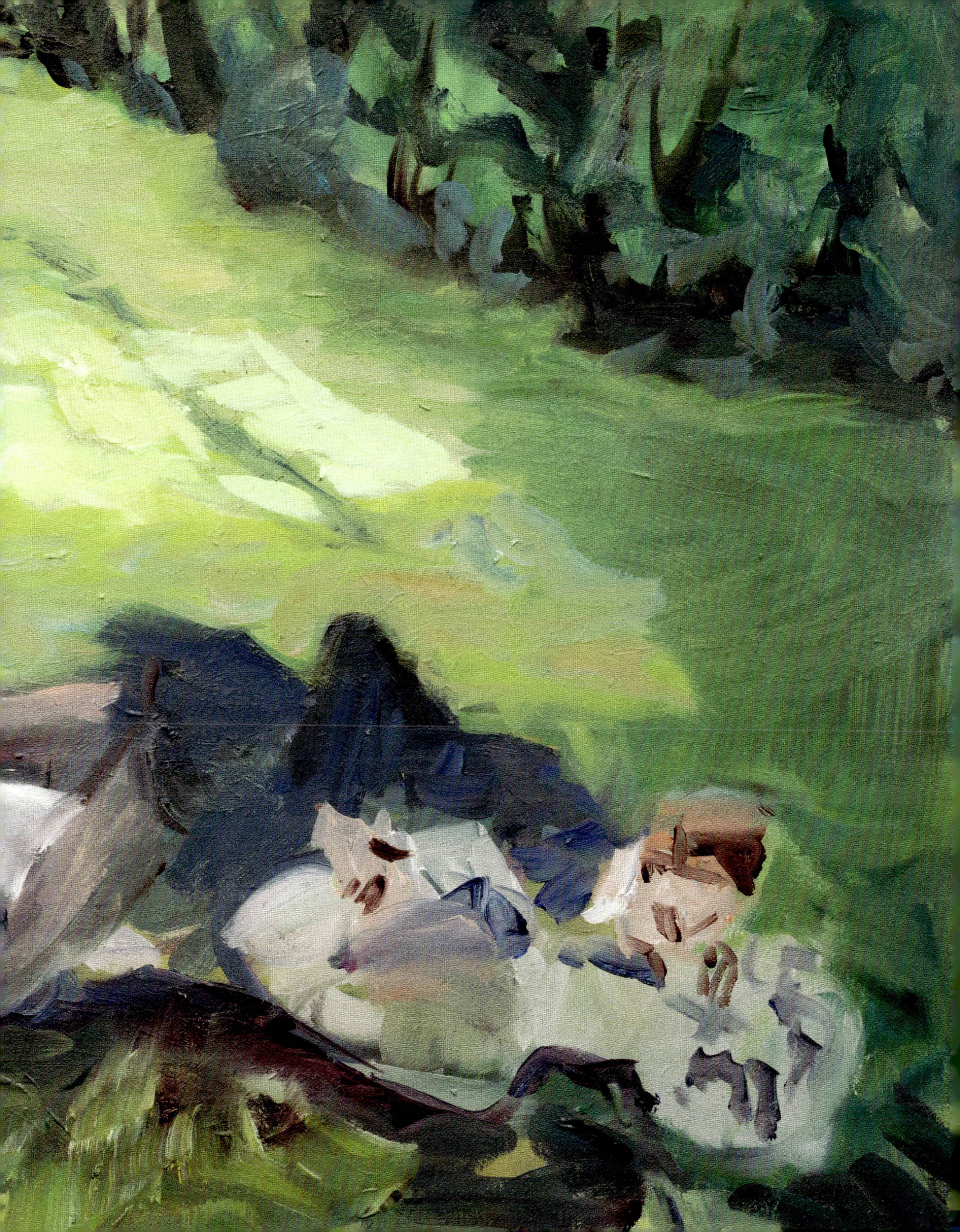

22 23 24 25 26   5 4 3 2 1

Cataloging data is available from Library and Archives Canada. / Les données de catalogage sont disponibles de Bibliothèque et Archives Canada.

ISBN 978-1-77327-202-3 (hbk.)

Photography of individual works by / Photographies d'œuvres individuelles par Guy L'Heureux, Paul Litherland. Gallery installation views / Vues d'installations: Richard-Max Tremblay (p. 228–9), Maxime Brouillet (p. 30), Michael Underwood (p. 232–3). Studio shots / Photos en studio: Sandra Lorochelle (p. 234, p. 236), Guy L'Heureux (p. 1, p. 27, p. 32)

Image file preparation / Préparation des fichiers d'images: Rachel Topham
Design: Studio Blackwell
General editor / Réviseure en chef: Lisa Baldissera
Translator of / Traductrice de *Membra Disjecta*: Judith Terry
Copy editor and proofreader / Réviseure de forme et correctrice des épreuves: Nancy Foran

Printed and bound in Canada by / Imprimé et relié au Canada par Friesens
Distributed internationally by / Distribué internationalement par Publishers Group West

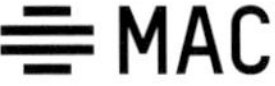

Published in collaboration with / Publié en collaboration avec le Musée d'art contemporain de Montréal

This publication has been generously supported by the Canada Council for the Arts / Cette publication a été généreusement soutenue par le Conseil des Arts du Canada

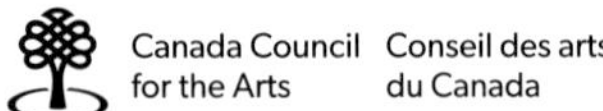

Cover images / Images en couverture:
Front / Devant: *Dee (yellow dress)*, 2020, 24 × 20 in. / 61 × 51 cm (detail/détail); Front flap / Rabat avant: *Up Over*, 2021, 36 × 24 in. / 91 × 61 cm; Back / Arrière: *Touch Hold (still life)*, 2019, 24 × 28 in. / 61 × 71 cm (detail/détail); Back flap / Rabat arrière: *VO Mars*, 2017, 67 × 84 in. / 170 × 213 cm (detail/détail)

Images in front matter / Images dans les textes préliminaires:
p. 1: Janet Werner's studio / Atelier de l'artiste, Montreal/Montréal, 2022; p. 2–3: *Portrait Reflection*, 2020, 24 × 20 in. / 61 × 51 cm (detail/détail)

Images in back matter / Images dans les parties complémentaires:
p. 218: *Harlequin*, 2022, 69 × 51 in. / 175 × 130 cm (detail/détail); p. 224: installation view / vue d'installation, Bradley Ertaskiran, Montreal, 2021; p. 228–9: installation view / vue d'installation, Musée d'art contemporain de Montréal, 2019; p. 232–3: installation view / vue d'installation, Anat Ebgi, Los Angeles, 2018; p. 234: Janet Werner's studio / Atelier de l'artiste, Montreal/Montréal, 2022; p. 238–9: *Disgrace*, 2020, 20 × 24 in. / 51 × 61 cm (detail/détail)

p. 29, clockwise from top left:
Allen Jones, *Table*, 1969. Mixed media / Techniques mixtes, 24 × 51 × 30 in. / 61 × 130 × 76 cm. Museum Ludwig, Cologne, with permission of the artist / avec la permission de l'artiste

Caspar David Friedrich, *Chalk Cliffs on Rügen*, 1818. Oil on canvas / Huile sur toile, 35.6 × 27.9 in. / 91 × 71 cm. Kunst Museum Winterthur, Stiftung Oskar Reinhart. Photo © SIK-ISEA, Zürich (Philipp Hitz)

Francis Picabia, *Bird and Turtle*, ca./v. 1927. Gouache, watercolor, graphite, and Conté crayon on paper / Gouache, aquarelle, graphite et crayon Conté sur papier, 25.6 × 19.8 in. / 65 × 50 cm. Alfred Stieglitz Collection, 1949. Photo © ADAGP, Paris / SOCAN, Montreal (2022) / The Metropolitan Museum of Art; Art Resource, NY

Thomas Gainsborough, *Gainsborough Dupont*, ca./v. 1770–5. Oil on canvas / Huile sur toile, 17.9 × 14.8 in. / 46 × 38 cm. Bequeathed by Lady d'Abernon / Légué par Dame d'Abernon, 1954. Photo © Tate

Established in 2015, Griffin Art Projects was founded by Brigitte and Henning Freybe, who began collecting art in the early 1970s. Griffin considers collecting practices as well as the methodologies, thematics and narratives that shape and direct both visual culture and creative work. Griffin also supports and develops solo and group projects and thematic exhibitions of works, collaborating with established cultural producers, guest curators, artists, writers and art educators, nationally and locally, to produce exhibitions, public programs and publications on contemporary art in the region.

Figure 1

Figure 1 Publishing Inc.
Vancouver BC Canada
www.figure1publishing.com

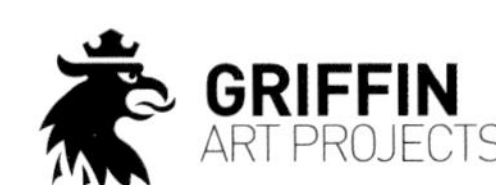

Griffin Art Projects
North Vancouver BC Canada
www.griffinartprojects.ca

Figure 1 Publishing and Griffin Art Projects are located within the traditional and unceded territory of the xʷməθkʷəy̓əm (Musqueam), Sḵwx̱wú7mesh (Squamish), səlilwətaɬ (Tsleil-Waututh) and S'ólh Téméxw (Stó:lō) peoples. / Figure 1 Publishing et Griffin Art Projects sont situés dans le territoire traditionnel et non cédé des peuples xʷməθkʷəy̓əm (Musqueam), Sḵwx̱wú7mesh (Squamish), səlilwətaɬ (Tsleil-Waututh) et S'ólh Téméxw (Stó:lō).